COLONIAL
METRoPOLIS

France Overseas:
*Studies in Empire
and Decolonization*

SERIES EDITORS:
A. J. B. Johnston
James D. Le Sueur
Tyler Stovall

COLONIAL METRoPOLIS

The Urban Grounds of Anti-Imperialism
and Feminism in Interwar Paris

JENNIFER ANNE BOITTIN

UNIVERSITY OF NEBRASKA PRESS | LINCOLN & LONDON

Portions of chapters 3 and 4 originally appeared as
"Black in France: The Language and Politics of Race
during the Late Third Republic" in *French Politics,
Culture, & Society* 27, no. 2 (Summer 2009): 23–46.
Portions of chapter 5 originally appeared as "In Black
and White: Gender, Race Relations, and the Nardal
Sisters in Interwar Paris" in *French Colonial History* 6
(2005): 119–35.

Library of Congress Cataloging-in-Publication Data
Boittin, Jennifer Anne.
Colonial metropolis : the urban grounds of anti-
imperialism and feminism in interwar Paris /
Jennifer Anne Boittin.
p. cm. — (France overseas)
Includes bibliographical references and index.
ISBN 978-0-8032-2545-9 (cloth : alk. paper)
ISBN 978-0-8032-7706-9 (paper : alk. paper)
1. Paris (France)—Race relations—History—20th
century. 2. Paris (France)—Intellectual life—20th
century. 3. City and town life—France—Paris—
History—20th century. 4. Anti-imperialist movements—France—Paris—History—20th century.
5. Feminism—France—Paris—History—20th century.
6. Africans—France—Paris—History—20th century.
7. Antilleans—France—Paris—History—20th
century. 8. Women, White—France—Paris—History—20th century. 9. France—Colonies—Africa—
History—20th century. 10. France—Colonies—
America—History—20th century. I. Title. II. Series.
DC717.B65 2010
305.42094436109042—dc22
2009051697

Set in Fournier MT by Kim Essman.
Designed by A. Shahan.

A ma famille,
to my family,
On several continents
but always near
And to Jens

CONTENTS

ILLUSTRATIONS

ACKNOWLEDGMENTS

Every twist and encounter in my journey through archives and libraries has shaped my work in significant ways. When I first arrived, Paris was in the grip of prolonged strikes. Not only was it far more difficult to navigate public transportation with two large bags, but the Archives Nationales, where I would have started my research, were closed. After the strikes they did not reopen: the asbestos plaguing their locales forced a temporary relocation and placed limits on document viewing. I thus spent far more time than expected at the Bibliothèque Nationale de France and elsewhere; the fortunate result was the juxtaposition between archives, literature, magazines, newspapers, and images that defines this book. Thank you to the archivists, librarians, and staffs at the many institutions I visited in my pursuit of such sources (AN, ANS, APP, BDIC, BHVP, BMD, BNF, CAF, and CAOM).

I could not afford a taxi from the airport when I arrived in Paris (even if I had been able to find one, a difficult endeavor during strikes) because when I started substantive research I had yet to land the necessary grants. My advisors did not allow my resolve to dampen, instead encouraging me to keep applying while researching. For their intellectual engagement, solidarity, and confidence in me, I cannot thank enough John Merriman, Christopher Miller, and Kevin Repp. Their creative research, critical thinking, and friendship have been truly inspirational.

They also made sure that I did not leave for France entirely without backing. Although I am a historian, Yale University's French Department found a spot for me in its exchange program with the Ecole Normale Supérieure. A room in Paris is not a small gift, especially when located only five minutes from the police archives. And after teaching my way through a few months of research, my luck with grants turned. I appreciate every single one of them all the more for the time I spent without any. Financial support came from a Bernadotte E. Schmitt grant from the American Historical Association; an Edouard Morot-Sir grant from the Institut Français de Washington; Smith Richardson grants from International Security Studies at Yale; a John Perry Miller grant from Yale; and last, but certainly not least, the Yale Center for International and Area Studies.

In France, days spent covered in the bits that crumble from aging acid paper (no matter how carefully one handles it) were made far less dry by evenings spent in good company. Sandrine Teixidor and Cybelle McFadden Wilkens are talented scholars whose companionship and work I marveled at over many a drink and meal. Déborah and Oscar Wollmann showed me their remarkable Paris. My aunt, Dominique Boittin, regularly invited me over for Sunday lunches and always had a *kir*, a devastating sense of humor, and selfless generosity on hand with which to warm my heart. Claire and Jean-Baptiste Danel shared their home and meals with me on numerous occasions and supported early research by handing me the keys to a *chambre de bonne*. Eliane and Maurice Lenoir created a home away from home in the 13ème for months at a time, and their cooking tips as well as Eliane's *coq au vin* and prodding to just finish the book are much appreciated. In Aix-en-Provence the famille Darbois shared a room with a poolside view, a quirky Renault 5, and endless supplies of *tapenade*.

Not only has writing given me far more respect for every work that graces my bibliography than I already had, but one of the most fascinating aspects of transforming this project from a dissertation into a book has been meeting many of the scholars who wrote these texts. In particular, the following ones read portions of the manuscript as commentators for conferences or helped me to work through theoretical or source-based quandaries in conversations: Naomi Andrews, Elisa Camiscioli, Julia Clancy-Smith, Alice Conklin, Brent Hayes Edwards, Laura Frader, Félix Germain, Herman (Gene) Lebovics, Patricia Lorcin, Gregory Mann, Dominic Thomas, Owen White, and Gary

Wilder. There is nothing small about such gestures, especially since you had no way of knowing how I would incorporate them into my work, and I thank you for your time. Richard Fogarty, Karen Offen, Mary Louise Roberts, and Tyler Stovall all read substantial portions or the entire manuscript at various stages: the depth and nuances of your readings are far more generous than I could have imagined.

I spent my time at Yale with a cohort of dreadfully accomplished people who somehow always found time to keep me smiling. Denise Bossy, Kate Cambor, Kat Charron, Catherine Dunlop, Michelle Herder, Faith Hillis, Maya Jasanoff, Edward Kehler, Charles Keith, Charles Lansing, Adriane Lentz-Smith, Ken Loiselle, Kieko Matteson, John Monroe (who first walked me through the Archives Nationales), Sara Norwick, and George Trumbull have shaped my work with everything from suggested readings to surprisingly relevant offhand remarks. Many still find the time to lend a thought or a shoulder when I need one, or simply to let me know how they are doing, which is most cherished of all. Christopher Bishop, Lien-Hang Nguyen, and Michael Purdy went from being great roommates to better friends. Rachel Chrastil energizes me with her focus and optimism. Liz Foster brought Dakar and the art of negotiating with taxi drivers to life for me. Also in Dakar, the vibrant Emily Musil was thoughtful enough to introduce me to her research and later to the generous Christina Firpo. Moreover I was lucky to have mentors early in my academic life whose minds and work could not possibly leave me indifferent: Robert Darnton, Nicole Dombrowski-Ritter, Anthony Grafton, and Eileen Scully. Stephen Vella, we all miss you.

At Penn State, all the faculty and staffs of the Department of French and Francophone Studies and the Department of History have been incredibly supportive. My lively graduate students motivate me with thought-provoking questions. My colleagues, Lila Corwin Berman, Tom Hale, Tijana Krstic, Joan Landes, Jennifer Mittelstadt, Bénédicte Monicat, Willa Silverman, Mrinalini Sinha, and Monique Yaari, took the time to comment upon portions of the manuscript. Also precious has been the guidance and friendship of Erica Brindley, Mike Eracleous, Tolga Esmer, Derek Fox and Carrie Jackson. At the University of Nebraska Press I would like to thank my editor, Heather

Lundine, for her serene efficiency and support, as well as the project editor, Ann Baker, and copyeditor, Linda Wessels.

I wish to thank my family most especially. My parents, Jean-François and Sarah Leith Paulu Boittin, gave me two languages along with everything else. To my father I also attribute my delight with jazz. To my mother I extend particular thanks for imparting her gifts of time, editing, and translation upon this book. My sisters, Margaret, Nathalie, and Isabelle, humble and revive me with stories of their travels across continents and many unstinting passions in life. They also know how to make me laugh. My grandparents, Jean-Marie Boittin and Anne-Marie Boittin *née* Morot-Raquin and Burton and Frances B. Paulu, have had more to do with our far-flung adventures than they realize. Finally I wish to thank my dearest friend and partner, Jens-Uwe Güttel. We met just before I started researching, which means that he has been with me every step of the way and has taken time away from his own work to read every chapter in this book. Even as I type these words he is announcing that another dinner is ready. I "owe" you months of clean dishes and far, far more. *Danke. Merci.*

INTRODUCTION

On May 6, 1931, a black man walked up the steps of a brand new metro station in Paris.[1] The Métro Dorée station was built as part of the French government's bid to lure what would eventually be 8 million visitors to the event known as the Colonial Exposition. Analogous to a world's fair, the Colonial Exposition was a project to showcase France's colonial empire both to its own citizens and to other nations. The policemen who were staking out the métro exit immediately noticed the man as he emerged from underground. After all, very few people of African descent were attempting to enter the exposition. Most Africans and Antilleans (people from the French West Indies, or Caribbean) were already inside its gates, in attendance not to visit but to perform aspects of colonial life for visiting dignitaries and other spectators.

Agent Joé, as he was known, was at the Colonial Exposition on its opening day not only to take in the sights. He was also an informer, there to report on what he heard and saw in the African, Caribbean, and other colonial milieus of Paris to the French authorities. If he had made it through the exposition's gates, his task would have been to locate other politically militant black men present at the event and take note of what they said and to whom they said it. Were they speaking to the performers, who had been sailed in for the exposition and were to be sent back overseas once it was over, hopefully without the baggage of Parisian anticolonial politics? Were they approaching white French men and women? However, with only a few hundred meters to go Joé was waylaid himself and arrested by the police inspectors, who discreetly took him to a police station nearby. Convinced that he was militantly opposed to France's presence in the colonies, they detained him until 6:00 p.m., perhaps in the hope that he would not cross paths with the visiting notables arriving that afternoon. None of the superiors to whom he usually reported came to his rescue, perhaps because they were at the Colonial Exposition.

A mere three weeks later, on May 28, Joé was once again confronted by the police. He was on his way to a meeting organized by the Federal Union of Students and the League Against Imperialism (LAI). A few meters from the door of the auditorium to which he was headed, he recognized one of the inspectors who had detained him on the day of the exposition's inauguration. The man eyed him suspiciously. Joé's words best describe what happened next:

> Seeing, once again, that stupid and idiotic gesture of policemen who seek only to aggravate everyone, and after my wife had told me that there was no one at the auditorium of the Sociétés Savantes . . . I made the decision to leave—and departed by the Rue des Grands-Augustins where we sat down at the terrace of a small café near the Seine. Still, during more than an hour that we stayed there, we were watched and hounded all the time by two men who seemed to us to be two policemen.[2]

This outburst has been preserved at the Overseas Archives in Aix-en-Provence, a hand-written document amidst the many typed sheets that make up the Service de Liaison avec les Originaires des Territoires Français d'Outre-Mer archival series (Service for Liaising with People Originating in the French Overseas Territories, SLOTFOM).[3] Even the thick, dark pencil marks that were intended to censor his irritation before it was typed into a report remain. Among the censored items was his criticism of the police as incapable of acting with dignity or intelligence.

This book argues that interwar Paris was a colonial space, meaning a space in which the specter of "empire" guided the self-identification of its residents as well as their social and political interactions. Joé's experiences illustrate the complexity of living in such an environment. He and his wife were two of the many black and white men and women who expressed their politics and culture though the prisms of race and gender. In the process they shaped Paris into a colonial metropolis.[4] Within this city, men and women learned to rearticulate their desires and dissents after deliberately or inadvertently introducing one another to their particular manipulations of identity politics. Thus here the term colonial, as opposed to imperial, reveals the agency, or autonomy, embedded in the act of occupying and utilizing city spaces—white women and colonial migrants all found their own ways to "colonize" Paris.

As these men and women exchanged culture and politics, they transformed this cosmopolitan setting into their locus of power. The possibilities for these men and women to challenge the political and cultural status quo were multiplied in Paris by their proximity to core administrative and political institutions and by constant encounters with empire. Like the port cities of Marseille, Toulon, Le Havre, and Bordeaux, Paris was a point of transit for colonial populations. Paris was also the hub of imperial government and a base for many artists and intellectuals. Black anti-imperial organizations—with their litany of exigencies ranging from equal civil liberties in the colonies to nationhood and independence from France—had their headquarters in the city. So did feminists, in a reflection of the centralization that has often characterized France. In Paris, empire took shape in the colonial migrants present on its streets, in the white men and women who had traveled to the colonies but were based in the city, and in the many images and representations of empire. Those without the vote and other civil rights discovered that the grounds for their struggles, and justifications they advanced in demanding their rights, were limited neither to the colonies nor to the metropole. Indeed, the two spaces were inherently connected and thus colonial and metropolitan men and women could play urban and overseas connections off of one another as they searched for effective arguments and unified fronts.

This book started with a two-part question: Were there any links between the French fascination with jazz and other forms of black culture during the 1920s and 1930s and the men and women of African descent who lived in France during that time? Was the cultural phenomenon known as, among other things, the *tumulte noir* (black tumult) in any way tied to the politics (including anti-imperialism) and social lives of those it supposedly represented? Answering this question called for learning about the African, African American, and Antillean men and women in France. Two ways of tracing the existences of black men and women soon presented themselves: through their artistic and literary productions and through their daily lives as recorded by the French state, notably in police records.[5] Combined, these approaches were not only fascinating but in turn structured the book's main premise: that Paris during the 1920s and 1930s can be considered a colonial metropolis. Why? In part because of what these sources do not explain. For example, what did it mean that African American actress, dancer, and singer Josephine Baker was mentioned in a report about the anti-imperialist from the French Sudan (today Mali) Tiémoko Garan Kouyaté? Why were most African and Caribbean intellectuals of the 1930s, such as the future Senegalese president Léopold Sédar Senghor, largely absent from police records? Why were their (until recently) less well-known female counterparts, the Martinican Nardal sisters, referenced comparatively often? Clearly certain organizations and names constituted focal points of black communities, but others only touched upon in the reports were also palpable parts of these networks. Moreover, not all those cryptically alluded to were black. Some were white women whose elusive lives, activities, and literary productions were relegated to references even more fleeting than those accorded black colonial men.

So how and why were white women, including a number of feminists, in contact with politically active, working-class black men? And who else was a part of these networks? My initial question had evolved so that I could no longer study only colonial migrants. With so many other people a part of the migrants' communities and horizons, this book explores what their interactions teach us about interwar Paris, the relationship between colonies and their metropole, and the manner in which class, gender, and race intersected among groups legally consigned to the outskirts of citizenship between the wars. The four overarching groups most often mentioned both in the texts written by black colonial migrants and feminists and in the police reports about them—black men, black women, white men, and white women—were not just talking about race, or class, or gender. Rather, through such categories they were also dissecting and coming to terms with France's relationship to its colonies, the colonies' relationship to France, and their place within that association.

Colonial Migrants and Feminists

Africans and Antilleans were intriguing members of France's pre–World War I past, interwar present, and for that matter twentieth- and twenty-first-century future. They had been integrated into the empire in two waves. During the early colonialism of the seventeenth and eighteenth centuries, France acquired parts of present-day Senegal in West Africa, as well as overseas territories in or near the West Indies including Guadeloupe, Martinique, French Guiana in South America, and, most famously, St. Domingue (today Haiti), which gained independence in 1804. Still France amassed most of its overseas territory throughout the nineteenth century during what is sometimes termed a period of new imperialism. North Africa (including Algeria), West and Equatorial (or central) Africa, the island of Madagascar (off the East coast of Africa), and Indochina (Vietnam and surrounding territories) all became colonies during this century.

Until World War I colonized citizens and subjects remained largely out of sight, far from metropolitan France, and thus were more representation than person to most French people. However during the war approximately 134,000 West African and Malagasy soldiers and several thousand workers, as well as numerous North African, Chinese, and Indochinese soldiers and workers, fought or labored in France.[6] In all, some half million colonial soldiers were deployed in Europe and in addition, 20,000 made their way to Europe from the older colonies such as Guadeloupe and Martinique.[7] Some found ways to stay on in France after the war and were joined by more colonial migrants. A definitive count of black colonial migrants during the interwar years is difficult to establish, in part because the numbers the police provided at the time often did not take into account Antilleans (who were French citizens); these figures conflicted with the police's own estimates that several hundred black men regularly attended political rallies in Paris alone; and records probably took into account only those Africans whose immigration status was regularized. Authorities calculated the presence in France of 379 French West and Equatorial Africans along with 462 Malagasies in September 1924 (out of 9,496 colonial migrants of every origin); of 2,015 Africans and 665 Malagasies in November 1926; and of 894 Africans and 559 Malagasies in June 1932 (out of 3,745 colonial migrants of every origin).[8] Approximately a third of what has been conservatively estimated as 3,000 to 5,000 African men in the country were believed to be in the Paris region (in all likelihood only 2 percent of the total African population, including North Africans, was female).[9] However, still according to the police, in 1926 there were as many as 10,000 to 15,000 black men in Paris alone.[10] The latter numbers probably include those from the French West Indies, although they still seem high and may very well take into account North Africans who were often simply termed African. Whatever the exact numbers, although some black colonies had been a part of France for far longer than areas such as Algeria or French Indochina, the latter populations were a more formidable presence in France by the 1920s and 1930s.

Why, then, focus upon black colonial migrants? They had enduring ties to France and to each other—in particular with respect to parts of Senegal and the West Indies. In order to capitalize upon the goods provided by the West Indies, France not only had to establish trading posts and ports, but (more problematically) to find manpower—slavepower—to produce these goods. Starting with France's first colonial empire, then, Senegal was linked to the Caribbean because France's ports in Africa functioned as the points of exit for slaves crossing the Atlantic. The history of slavery in both regions shaped how these men and women thought about colonialism and race in the twentieth century. Moreover, some colonized people in these territories were French citizens, but others were not. This contrast in civil and suffrage rights, often perceived as arbitrarily imposed by the French authorities, influenced considerations of what it meant to belong to a French republic legitimized in part by its claim to be founded on universal rights. The very fact that there were fewer black than other colonial migrants means that their strategies for coping with metropolitan life and building communities in the metropole are both less well understood and well worth exploring. For example, black colonial migrants in Paris were not only defined by authorities, but also defined themselves, through a manipulation of the language of race, thereby claiming transatlantic ties to Africa, North America, and South America. Finally, the *tumulte noir* as a phenomenon was distinctive. There were, of course, cultural manifestations of exoticism showcasing other colonial groups. However they did not contribute to the production of a superstar quite as ubiquitous as Josephine Baker, or a phenomenon such as jazz, both of which remain important parts of France's culture to this day. Nor did they rely upon a blending of cultures that stemmed from three continents and their islands.

Paris was transformed by the arrival of black colonial migrants after World War I, but it was also marked by a second major development: the growing presence of women, including outspoken feminists, in the public sphere.[11] Like colonial migrants, these women saw representations of themselves abound in popular culture. Following the war, women and black men renewed similar demands. Both groups wished to become full-fledged citizens with access to civil rights and perhaps even suffrage, either of France or of lands they hoped would soon be decolonized and transformed into independent nations. Several governments of France's Third Republic (1870–1940) found various excuses for evading these requests. Indeed women did not obtain the vote, and colonized men and women did not win independence or negotiate assimilation, until after the next world war. In the meantime colonized men and feminist women were in a strategic location for making themselves heard by both fellow migrants and other disabused metropolitans, since they had converged in Paris and other urban centers for their wartime jobs and often stayed there following World War I. The migration intended to fulfill the nation's need for a wartime workforce soon gave rise to an intellectual and political evolution that called into question a number of the tenets of Third Republic France, including the place of empire and of women in modern life.

What do the stories of black colonial migrants and feminists help us to understand? As a colonial space Paris was significant both to the colonized and to the colonizers. The city fostered and was nurtured by incredibly vibrant communities intent upon confronting various aspects of France's empire. Their stories reveal the many ways in which colonialism became a part of daily lives. This is not to say that empire was a system taken for granted. Instead, people seeking to assert themselves, or resist what they interpreted as the inflexible components of the imperial nation-state to which they all belonged, recognized the presence of colonialism. They tweaked their readings of it and found ways to integrate it into their struggles. The groups explored in this book demonstrate some of the ways in which a transnational system and local struggles for identity collided. Feminism, nationalism, and other forms of political militancy are sometimes assumed to be about difference, the construction of one identity in opposition to another. The story told here suggests that dialogue, openmindedness, and the construction of networks across disparate groups were also an important part of these identity politics.

Colonialism mattered, to put it bluntly, to a lot of people in a lot of different ways. This book focuses upon voices that murmured in response, those that spun intricate webs of political and social commentary, and those that roared. Some words have since been garbled or misplaced and others have simply not been considered, or not been contemplated in this particular manner. The focus upon black colonial migrants is not intended to exclude other colonial migrants or anyone else from the colonial metropolis. To the contrary, this book is also about North African and Indochinese migrants: not with respect to the vast majority of its examples, footnotes, or stories, but with respect to its understanding that multiple singular, local experiences— whether those of groups or of individuals—when contrasted to one another reveal connections, interactions, and patterns that taken together can help us to better comprehend the many facets of what made France an imperial nation-state.

Frameworks: Empire, Immigration, Diaspora, Race, Gender, and Locality

This book explores empire as it coincides with metropole, immigration as it overlaps with black and African diaspora, race as it intersects with gender and class, and the effects of specific locations upon all these frameworks. Let us then consider these contexts for a moment.

Ever since the French Revolution of 1789 first pronounced France to be a republic and a democracy based both on universal and on national rights, one question has lingered: how can an individual's rights be guaranteed by his or her humanity while being restricted by legal definitions of French citizenship and civil rights as put forth by the nation? Humanity should trump citizenship, and yet has not consistently done so within France's history. Otherwise, suffrage and civil rights would have been ubiquitous in every one of its republics, rather than being limited by gender, income, or geography.

Noting the ongoing tension between universal rights and how particular groups or individuals have been treated throughout modern French history, historian Gary Wilder proposes that we read France between the wars as an imperial nation-state. Understanding colonialism as merely some kind of blight on France, in need of condemnation or arduous justification, threatens to limit our reading of its history. As an intricate, albeit muddled part of France from the moment the country first became a republic, colonialism needs to be understood as part of what defines the nation, not something accidental, exceptional, or external to it. Once the nation-state is understood to be imperial, then our focus can turn to the many ways in which its people dealt with the paradoxes they daily experienced or witnessed. Or as historian Frederick Cooper suggests, we can consider how both the leaders of empire-states and those involved in political insubordination from within those systems were "thinking like an empire."[12]

Although France's imperial nature had more distant roots, it was after World War I that the French truly shifted from considering only "individual autonomy or national identity" to considering race and empire, a fact that helps to explain why the daily struggles of city dwellers in Paris commingled with empire during the interwar years.[13] The idea of a colonial metropolis based in mainland France makes sense from this perspective.[14] But how does recognizing Paris as a colonial metropolis help us to understand France as an imperial nation-state? Ever since scholars first started putting more emphasis on the central role of immigration in France, many studies have focused on migrants' relationships to the state and French perceptions of migrants (including xenophobia and racism).[15] These immigration studies intersect in intriguing ways with the rich and growing body of literature on how Africans, Antilleans, and African Americans in France were part of a diaspora with roots in Africa and slavery.[16] In approaching these fields I focus on migrants' agency, meaning how they functioned as a community that also defined itself internally, rather than solely in relationship to the republic. Moreover, I do not consider primarily the relationships that migrants entered into with colonial administrators and settlers. Instead, I delve into exchanges between men and women who although not its official representatives, were also not unconscious inhabitants of an empire.[17] There is still much to be learned about such personal, cultural, and social interactions in France by careful readings of sources such as the SLOTFOM series. They invite us to explore not just how black workers and intellectuals differed amongst themselves in their Parisian politics and lives, but also and just as intriguingly how black and white men and women interacted within the capital of an imperial nation-state.[18] Studying the interplay among empire-minded Parisians contributes to our awareness of how anti-imperialists and feminists were affected by one another, police informants, and the city itself.

Thus, this book further adds to existing literature with a systematic gendered analysis of intellectual, political, and social relations among the colonizers and colonized evolving in an urban setting. The importance of gender as a category of analysis for probing metropolitan-colonial dynamics has been well established, as has the importance of evaluating gender with race.[19] That being said, masculinity in particular remains underexplored within the francophone context, even though it was a crucial component of how early black, anti-imperial, working-class circles, as well as intellectual ones, functioned.[20] Likewise, the links among feminism, colonialism, race, and anti-imperialism are still far less well understood in the francophone setting than they are in the anglophone one.[21] Albeit not always in agreement with respect to what constituted feminism or its goals, many women in interwar France were conscious that both Paris and the imperial context could help them to elaborate their politics.

The last major theme upon which this book focuses is the importance of locality in our understanding of transnational imperial history. This study of the intricate links between metropole and colony substantiates the claim that social changes are reflections of both worldwide patterns and local contestations and therefore that scholars should consider "metropole and colony in a single analytic field."[22] Within this premise, I also consider the places in which struggles developed. Colonial histories warrant local analysis because this approach sheds light on the particularities of specific social and political systems.[23] Paris lends itself well to such local analysis because in this city the center and peripheries of empire coincided.[24]

The Jazz Age, Colonial Politics, and Parisian Spaces

The cultural phenomenon known variously as the jazz age, negrophilia, the *tumulte noir*, and the *vogue nègre* affected those considering colonialism.[25] Such people included African and Antillean students, workers, and intellectuals who created black nationalistic movements that permanently transformed the relationship between French colonies and the metropole. They not only generated the *vogue nègre*, in the case of performers, but also had their perspectives fundamentally altered through negrophilia's often explicit focus on exoticism and sexuality, an intersection that brought gender to the fore of race relations. In "Paris, Capital of the Nineteenth Century," the German philosopher, essayist, and critic Walter Benjamin argues that during world exhibitions the entertainment industry elevated "people to the level of commodities."[26] His analysis relates to the interwar years. In the twentieth century, Parisians flocked to the Colonial Exposition because they felt as though the world was coming to them, and black performers became a commodity, partially enthroned as "merchandise."[27]

Yet not only black migrants who rejoiced in the limelight but also those who were just walking down the street to buy their groceries risked being viewed as specimens in a Paris that sought out the museums, ethnography, and collections to which exotic memorabilia were imported.[28] The tension between everyday life, politics, and the cultural production of blackness is explored from several angles in this book. Josephine Baker, for example, chose the role of performer; the black, Martinican Nardal sisters had it forced upon them; African and Antillean anti-imperialists used their status as permanent spectacle to gain a foothold in the political and social circles of Paris, effectively reversing the exoticism imposed upon them; white men and women, in reaction to the *vogue nègre*, felt challenged to expand their circle of consciousness to include the outer reaches of the empire. Some white women formulated astute readings of the links between their own representations within popular culture and those of colonial individuals.

While the dissection of representations of blackness has previously led to some fascinating studies, this book steps away from the realm of the French social imaginary ("the cultural elements from which we construct our understanding of the social world") and into an analysis of how representations overlapped with, and influenced, interactions.[29] Superficial contacts, whether physical or intellectual, were often initiated in settings such as the Colonial Exposition or nightclubs. These were rather obvious places for Parisian constructions of colonial otherness. At times, exchanges were subsequently pursued into more complex and enduring relationships that were political, emotional, intellectual, physical, or social and moved through other Parisian spaces.[30] The mediums in which these interactions emerged comprised novels, newspapers, streets, political organizations, police reports, spies' minutes, films, graphic art, and more. Some spaces were tangible urban constructions such as streets or rooms sheltering political meetings. Others, such as newspapers, novels, and films, were elusive forums of a creative or intellectual type. Each chapter of this work is structured around such modes of expression, or sources, available to and favored by its urban characters. The chapters thus approach the same events, time period, and themes from different perspectives, thereby creating a series of snapshots of the many ways in which men and women fashioned Paris into a colonial metropolis.

Agent Joé in the Colonial Metropolis

Agent Joé was one such person. We met him at the beginning of this chapter, complaining to his superiors about being trailed and arrested. Joé's case illustrates how informants can be considered "participant observers."[31] They were heavily implicated in the revolutionary milieus upon which they spied. Reports such as those Joé wrote are repositories of details that illuminate otherwise obscure exchanges among Parisians. Their authors' identities were veiled by pseudonyms and their real names reserved for oral communication.[32] Yet much, including many Indochinese informants' identities, has been uncovered about their choices and lives that illuminates the significance of this source group as a whole.[33] Joé and other agents bring to light how unambiguous distinctions rapidly dissolved within the colonial metropolis.

In 1923 the Ministry of Colonies centralized surveillance of colonial migrants within the Centre des Affaires Indigènes (Center for Native Affairs, CAI). It later became the SLOTFOM, which is why the archival series has this acronym. Helping colonial migrants in the metropole was part of the justification for its existence, but the CAI's focus was spying upon and regulating urban associations.[34] The CAI worked closely with the Ministry of the Interior, and in particular with the French Sûreté Générale, or secret police, to recruit spies, translators, and so forth. The CAI also coordinated locally with the Prefecture of Police, another division of the Ministry of the Interior, and in particular with the prefecture's political branch (Renseignements Généraux), which had a section devoted to watching over migrants and detecting revolutionary colonial propaganda. In addition, the CAI exchanged information with the Ministry of Foreign Affairs and, overseas, with the Governors General of various French colonies and their local sûretés.[35]

Distinctions such as skin color and language made African, Caribbean, and Malagasy men stand out on the streets of Paris, but behind closed doors these attributes instilled a protective barrier. Informants could only be easily integrated when they originated from within the ranks of those upon whom they reported. Once recruited, their existence was normalized; for example they held routine jobs as cover for their role as informant. But why did they become agents? Pro-French sentiment may have persuaded some. Money was certainly a motivation, and so was coercion—perhaps release from prison in exchange for cooperation.[36] Neither of the latter factors was reliably effectual; in July 1927 Marseille-based agents, incensed by their near poverty, slurred the CAI and threatened to reserve bullets for each of their bosses.[37] However, authorities held two motivational trumps in hand: at any moment, they could force spies to return to the empire's periphery or they could blow their cover.[38] In November 1937 Agent Coco, knowing that he had been privy to details to which very few people had access, begged readers, "Please keep secret, for now, this information."[39]

Angry as it made him, being arrested and later shadowed in May 1931 protected Agent Joé. On that same day other members of the anti-imperialist organization known as the Ligue de Défense de la Race Nègre (League for the Defense of the *Nègre* Race, LDRN) were followed by policemen. One, the anti-imperialist leader Tiémoko Garan Kouyaté, confronted his tail only to hear "we have orders to follow you, don't complain or we'll arrest you pronto—plus when we leave around 6 p.m., two others will relieve us."[40] Later that day another black member of the LDRN slipped into the exposition. Rather than viewing his freedom of movement as a success, members of the LDRN became wary. If this man had not been detained, did that mean he was an informant?

At the next LDRN meeting, all those who had been trailed recounted their frustration. Agent Joé was present—he wrote one of the reports about the meeting—and he grumbled about his arrest to fellow members.[41] He was, in fact, the only person detained on the opening day of the exposition. The others were merely warned away. The details Agent Joé consigned in his note to superiors explaining why he never made it into the Colonial Exposition were exactly the same as those given in three other reports—but in the latter three documents his true name was used.[42] Overlap, in particular with respect to elements such as the police station to which he was taken, makes it reasonable to conclude that Agent Joé was Edmond Thomas Ramananjato.

Ramananjato was an extremely outspoken, intelligent and incisive member of the black community. He came to France from Madagascar in order to fight in World War I and then worked under exploitative conditions for a horticulturalist named Carriat. He was naturalized French in 1924. After arriving in Paris, Ramananjato became an accountant and lived in an apartment near the Moulin Rouge, which was at the heart of the heated Montmartre nightlife in which blacks were so exoticized. He was first noticed as being connected with the anti-imperial community in 1929, just as Agent Joé started signing his notes on the black community.[43] His central role in militant organizations was reflected in his multiple elections as treasurer and secretary of the LDRN and other anti-imperial organizations. He was also politically engaged in the Malagasy community. And as an informant with the proper linguistic skills, he wrote prolifically about Malagasy performers at the Colonial Exposition.

Joé certainly had a stake in the CAI's game of cat and mouse. Even his arrest may not have been straightforward. Occasionally arrests were planned by the CAI to bolster the credibility of its informants, and his May 6, 1931, arrest may have been one such set-up.[44] Yet this possibility is hard to determine in Joé's case because while he explained in a quick postscript to superiors that the two policemen "m'ont fait passer" for a known militant, the phrase has two contradictory meanings: they "passed me off as" a political militant or they "made me out to be" a political militant.[45] On one hand, soon thereafter Ramananjato was listed as one of only two people whom the leading anti-imperialist of the moment, Kouyaté, trusted.[46] On the other hand, so much of the CAI's system depended upon no one knowing who the informants actually were, that if this was a set-up it seems most likely the policemen were tipped off to the presence of an anti-imperialist by Joé's handler. In other words, the policemen never learned that he was an informant.

While the arrest may have been routine, there was nothing feigned about Joé's privately expressed outrage when he was tailed just a few weeks later. Agents' handlers were often highly suspicious of productive informants like Joé, prolific ones who were at the center of revolutionary milieus.[47] His spying did not preclude genuine anti-imperialist sentiment or that he would invest in maintaining a black colony in interwar Paris. After all, Ramananjato was convincing enough in his politics for several other informants to write reports about him. And he certainly openly rejected limits being placed on his freedom. When Agent Joé seethed, "*I* made the *decision* to leave," (emphasis mine) after noticing his tails, he attempted to regain control over the situation by asserting his authority. This language gains added meaning when one considers that his wife had just witnessed the humiliation of his second encounter with the police. Although political activists knew that they were being watched, they rarely meekly accepted this challenge from the authorities.

This book explores many examples similar to Joé's of how black men colonized and moved through Parisian spaces, at times aggressively. They, and others, constructed their identity in part through the conception of autonomous spaces. The multiplication of such spaces and manipulation of their environment, then, allowed black and white, men and women, to figure out how to define themselves, their politics, their communities, and their identities. While investing themselves in the shaping of traditional as well as nontraditional urban localities, black and white Parisians used their relationship to colonialism as both a way of coming to terms with their own identity, and an active process by which to ground themselves in, or even to "colonize," Paris.

A Brief Note on Terminology

Racial terms such as *noir* (black), *nègre* (loosely Negro), *métis* (mixed race), and *mulâtre* (mulatto), as well as their feminine equivalents *négresse*, *mulâtresse*, and *métisse*, cannot be translated precisely into English, and indeed in the French language have a very rich linguistic and historical background that will be explored throughout this work. Malagasies, West Africans, Antilleans, and the French constructed communities for themselves or were perceived in Paris in part through such language, but the categories of race, gender, and class are neither binary nor immutable. (For more on the problem of translating these terms see Brent Hayes Edwards, *Practice of Diaspora*.) Hence they will be left in French throughout, as well as the terms *indigène*, which here refers to a native of the French colonies, and *tirailleurs* (infantry troops made up of *indigènes*). "Colonial migrants" refers to colonized men and women living either permanently or temporarily in France (see MacMaster, *Colonial Migrants and Racism*). All translations are my own unless otherwise noted.

ABBREVIATIONS

The three most cited organizations in this book are the CDRN, LDRN, and UTN, three tightly linked anti-imperial organizations. To help distinguish among them, note that the chronological order in which they appeared in Paris mirrors the alphabetical progression of the first letter of their abbreviation: first the CDRN, then the LDRN, and last, the UTN.

AN	Archives Nationales, Paris, France
ANS	Archives Nationales, Dakar, Senegal
APP	Archives de la Préfecture de Police de Paris
CAI	Centre des Affaires Indigènes
CDRN	Comité de Défense de la Race Nègre (1926–27)
CDIRN	Comité de Défense des Intérêts de la Race Noire
CGTU	Confédération Générale du Travail Unitaire
CMFGF	Comité Mondial des Femmes contre la Guerre et le Fascisme
CNFF	Conseil National des Femmes Françaises
CP	Communist Party
LAI	Ligue Anti-Impérialiste
LDRN	Ligue de Défense de la Race Nègre (1927–3?)
PCF	Parti Communiste Français
PROM	Notes Sur la Propagande Révolutionnaire Intéressant les Pays d'Outre-Mer
SASFRD	Société pour l'Amélioration du Sort de la Femme et la Revendication de ses Droits
SLOTFOM	Service de Liaison avec les Originaires des Territoires Français d'Outre-Mer
UFSF	Union Française pour le Suffrage des Femmes
UTN	Union des Travailleurs Nègres (1932–?)

1 JOSEPHINE BAKER

Colonial Woman

Is this a man? a woman? . . . Is she frightful, is she ravishing, is she
black, is she white, does she have hair or is her skull painted black? No
one knows . . . this is not a woman, not a dancer; it is as extravagant
and ephemeral as music, the ectoplasm, you could say, of all the sounds
one hears.—PIERRE DE RÉGNIER, "La revue nègre"

When Josephine Baker finished her first performance in Paris in the
1925 show *La Revue Nègre*, critics and audiences did not know what
to make of her. The confusion they felt was perhaps best summarized by the series of questions the theater critic and author Pierre de
Régnier asked in the epigraph above. The show was conceived of in
the United States for a European audience and featured an all-black
cast of musicians and performers. At the beginning of the spectacle,
Baker played a comic role with bent knees, awkward movements,
rolling eyes, and a puckered up mouth. In contrast her grand finale,
known as the "danse sauvage" or "savage's dance," was unabashedly sexual and not in the least humorous. In it she portrayed the dead
prey of a hunter, played by the powerful Antillean dancer Joe Alex.
Naked, like Baker, except for the requisite feathers and beads, he arrived on stage with her slung over his shoulders.[1] Responding to the
drum beat, Josephine came to life and slipped off his back. The ver-
bose de Régnier attempted to capture this moment in writing: "This
dance, with its rare unseemliness, is the triumph of lewdness, a return to the mores of the first ages: the declaration of love made in si-
lence and with arms over the head, through a simple gesture forward,

from the belly, and a trembling of the entire hindquarters."[2] The orgasmic culmination created quite a sensation in postwar Paris.

Baker arrived in Paris just in time to capitalize upon the frenzy for which the very labels (*vogue nègre* and so forth) hint at the powerful impact blackness had upon the cultural transformation of the capital. Why and how Paris became steeped in a black vogue will be traced in this chapter through Baker's transformation into a colonial woman. From the mid-1920s to the mid-1930s Baker, with the help of existing media and those in her entourage, oriented her performances and imagery in such a way as to both reflect and influence existing attitudes regarding colonialism and race in interwar Paris. Although gossamer on stage, her roles as a colonial woman were very much grounded in her off-stage understanding of the colonial metropolis. Colonial migrants, feminists, writers in the mainstream press, and other Parisians all reacted to Baker. Even colonial migrants who eschewed her style as provocative and detrimental to their standing understood the power of her performances and responded to her as a colonial representative, although Baker was neither French nor colonial. Reactions to the *vogue nègre* she embodied are thus a good starting point for understanding the links that Parisians—colonial or other—established between the cultural production of images of blacks and the politics of race and gender consciousness in the imperial nation-state.

Increasingly scholars have moved away from biography and toward subtle analysis of Baker's cultural status as a discerning performer of race.[3] Still, more work needs to be done to ground Baker and refrain from studying her "as a sort of inconsequential stage alien, untethered to the world around her."[4] Baker wove a network of threads connecting various aspects of Parisian intellectual and cultural life. As a cultural symbol, she swayed not only the critics and avant-garde artists upon whom many scholars have rightly focused, but also white women writers and black colonial men and women in the Parisian capital. Reactions to performances of colonialism such as Baker's demonstrate how Paris was reacting to empire—not just unconsciously, but also explicitly.

This point is worth making because studies of colonialism's cultural impact have tended to bypass the conscious embrace of the colonial and its blending of political and cultural intent, and to focus instead upon representations, often veiled, of colonialism. Scholar Elizabeth Ezra's term "colonial unconscious," for example, underscores the all-pervasive yet largely unacknowledged infusion of colonialism into France's culture. It describes a desire on the part of some French to ostensibly seek contact with other cultures through a celebration of exoticism even while conserving their detachment from them.[5] The extent to which this ambivalent appropriation of colonial societies' traditions was internalized to the point of becoming unconscious, however, remains unclear, given the number of French critics and colonial migrants who referenced Baker while explicitly grappling with the impact of colonialism and race on the metropole. More likely, texts in which the tensions between welcoming exoticism and keeping it at bay were openly discussed coexisted with those in which the will to dominate other cultures went unquestioned (remained unconscious).[6] Although Baker generated layers of potentially ephemeral representations of colonialism, she was connected to Paris. The reactions she elicited often had as a second goal, alongside a straightforward review of her image and her performances, a desire to come to terms with the city as a locale for colonial interactions, and with the implications of colonialism more generally.

In 1925 Baker's tropical warmth was praised as a moment of rejuvenation for a grey and melancholy Paris, and for modern France as a whole. The critic de Régnier, in noting audience members' complex reactions, pinpointed one of several paradoxes surrounding her: while some spectators saw in her dance proof of the degenerate nature of the primitive, others marveled that it was a pure form of modern art and were drawn by its ability to express human emotions and instincts in an unadulterated manner. In part as a result of this dual interpretation, Baker has been read as a woman who managed to mold her image around the (African) primitive and the (American) modern.[7] She was a safe version of the other, a term that reflects a tendency of colonizers to construct their own selves and civilizations as the norm in opposition to those of the colonized. While influential, such readings downplay the importance of Baker's Frenchness and how over time, as a colonial woman, she reflected an effective civilizing mission (a dominant colonial doctrine during the Third Republic), to which critics directly referred. Indeed, the initial buzz might have fizzled out had Baker not capitalized upon the situation of Paris at the center of an empire. Certain technologies of cultural production—or the conception, dissemination, and consumption of Baker as a cultural product—contributed to her success. They also explain why, amongst many others, black African and Antillean students who were on their way to becoming fervent nationalists found it necessary to come to terms with Baker.

Civilizing Baker through Colorful Language

Although Baker had worked during her early teens in vaudeville shows, she was not a celebrity when she was invited by the first-time producer Caroline Dudley to join the *Revue Nègre* for the staggering sum of one thousand dollars per month. The *Revue Nègre* opened at the Théâtre des Champs Elysées and immediately attracted attention because of its entirely black cast—a novel idea in France at the time. However, a black cast was not enough to sell the show, and before it opened French producers decided the show was not sufficiently representative of (French perceptions of) black culture.[8] They revamped it, making Baker the star with the striking "danse sauvage." The show itself was not very popular but Baker's controversial performance prompted much debate.

Race was an undeniable component in responses to this performance. Jacques Patin, writing for the center-right newspaper *Le Figaro*, was fascinated by musicians whose "thick-lipped faces" had "large black hole-like eyes."[9] Bizarrely arranged geometric shapes provided a modernist backdrop for drums and tam-tams. The narrative began in a modern, American setting, complete with skyscrapers, and then as various tableaux were presented left "civilization" for an African jungle. Josephine played an urban, sophisticated African American, before "degenerating" into a wild, African woman. The revue's music paralleled her transformation as it progressed from soothing to, in the words of Patin, "shrieks, a shrill siren's whistle, hoarse gratings interrupting the bizarre melody until a horrifying din could be heard."[10] Although not comprehending the African American music, Patin admired its ability to capture sounds of the jungle, from the moaning of the wind to falling rain, from the rustling of leaves to the lion's roar. In a similar vein René Bizet, who published several books on film and music, suggested that "these blacks . . . quiver from their heels to the roots of their hair, singing with confident harmony and making us believe that they remember their native forests."[11] Baker and her fellow African American artists had not in fact traveled from colonial jungles or forests to Paris. Yet their music, dance, and singing could not be disassociated in these performances from the colonial backdrop their skin color and sets evoked.

The French used gendered images including the modern woman, the mother, and the single woman to confront change in postwar France.[12] As Baker's case suggests, the image of the colonial woman fulfilled a similar function as another such gendered image. Through it the highly visible black presence during and immediately after World War I was explored. Articles featuring Baker in the 1920s and 1930s uphold the contention that images entering the public domain did not necessarily reflect the reality of women's experiences.[13] The colonial situation in which both metropolitans and colonial subjects and citizens felt they had a stake had little to do with Baker's performance of the colonial woman. Yet Parisians used their readings of her to explore their fears, desires, politics, and basic perceptions of African and Caribbean colonies. In turn Baker learned, based on reviews that celebrated her darkness, how to classify and promote herself as a representation not only of what made Parisians shudder and shiver when thinking of the colonies (the dark jungles, the inscrutable *indigènes*), but also as a representation of the potential for civilization that colonialism could hope to accomplish.[14]

By 1895 the *mission civilisatrice*, or civilizing mission, was an official doctrine of the French colonial administration overseas.[15] While this mission's implementation changed over time, it nonetheless consistently rested upon the notion that France's tradition of universal rights, dating back to the 1789 Revolution, empowered the country's representatives to uplift "primitive" cultures that did not yet benefit from such rights. In particular, France's success at taming nature and social behavior, and thus at resisting tyranny on the part of the climate, geography, and other natural elements, as well as on the part of nondemocratic institutions, meant that several of the nation's colonial administrators felt an imperative to share such civilized progress with others. Descriptions of Baker reflect how this colonial doctrine was reiterated by those dwelling in Paris. Following World War I, colonial administrators revised their understanding of the civilizing mission in order to move away from their previously liberal interpretation of the doctrine. As an (unintended) result, they became increasingly less respectful of human rights. They were now wary of their previous strategy to form a new colonial elite of educated Africans and focused more on preserving the French race while simultaneously racializing France's colonial subjects. Baker's portrayal of colonial women referenced this new racialization. At the same time, her performance showcased an earlier, idealized application of the civilizing mission from before it was threatened by Africans who, according to some administrators, were inopportunely starting to use against colonialism the very language of universalism that had previously helped justify their "civilizing." Now the colonized were using these ideas in order to demand basic rights before the French administration deemed them to be ready for those rights.

The best examples of how Baker's performances allowed critics to process colonial preconceptions through their discussion of her blackness surfaced in 1930, during reviews of the music-hall variety show *Paris Qui Remue*, which was staged at the Casino de Paris. Baker had been away on tour in Europe and South America for three years. During her absence the male critics had had time to develop a gendered and racialist prose that far surpassed in their sophistication the frantic scribbles of their initial surprise-filled moments in 1925. The 1930 texts located both the primitive and the civilized in her persona and her performances.

Articles were replete with animal metaphors for Baker's body. She was seen as a surprising animal with long legs and shining teeth, a tropical bird of paradise who was free, supple, and vigorous, and beautiful as a panther. Animal images were not restricted to the elegant, however. She was also called a monkey, whose long legs and arms made it seem quite likely that she spent her time jumping and swinging from branch to branch in some tropical forest.[16] Rather than allow such images to be imposed upon her, Baker took her cue from them, generating publicity and reinforcing colonial references by keeping exotic birds and monkeys in her home and sometimes parading along the streets of Paris with a cheetah given to her by the publicity-savvy producer of *Paris Qui Remue.*

Zoomorphism was not the most surprising aspect of the 1930 writing style, although critics had brought it to the fore of their panoply of African references since the original 1925 performance. More telling of just how completely she had been drawn into colonial imagery was that critics now depicted Baker, an American, as a French colonial subject. They did so using phrases that referenced the rhetoric of the civilizing mission. Furthermore, they explored how her colonial representations challenged what they identified as traditional French culture. They appeared to agree with colonial administrators both with respect to the utopic possibilities for the civilizing mission, and to the potential dangers of an unmediated absorption of colonial cultures. They frequently ignored the three years she had just spent in other parts of Europe and in South America, and attributed her successes to France's colonizing efforts and Paris's civilizing effects. Critics declared Josephine "is the finest possible example of perfection in the intellectual molding of the black race by European civilization"[17] and Paris, specifically, was the city that had transformed and refined Baker.[18]

Few described Baker without dwelling upon the color of her skin. She was undeniably the other, whose dark skin fascinated men around her. Some viewed her as undergoing an eternal sun-bathing session. Others realized, as critic Gérard Bauer did, that "black, under Josephine Baker, is becoming fashionable again."[19] She was described as black or as an ebony Venus, *nègre*, dark perfection, Creole, bronze, rum- and cinnamon-colored. The adjectives tended to lighten as she developed the elegance, and poise, of any Parisian belle. While she was still identified with all the trimmings of primitive stereotypes in her performances, civilization had created an elegant young woman whose very skin seemed lighter and lighter at every glance.[20]

In reality, as recent scholarship on Baker confirms, she had taken a much more active role than critics acknowledged in developing an image of increased sophistication and in particular lightened skin color.[21] This characteristic, used by critics in part as a metaphor for her transformation into a French icon, was a metamorphosis she undertook for both personal and professional reasons. Changing political times, and especially her experiences in Central Europe during her travels from 1928 to 1930, were recorded in a work written by Maurice Sauvage, a journalist for the politically right-leaning, high-circulation evening Parisian newspaper *l'Intransigeant* and a poet who had previously ghostwritten a 1927 autobiography for Baker. While he was listed as the author of Baker's second autobiography, published in 1931 as *Voyages et aventures de Joséphine Baker* (Voyages and Adventures of Josephine Baker), most of the text is written in the first person, as though he was simply recording an interview in which his lines, as the journalist, had been erased. Baker's "voyages and adventures" referred to her almost continuous tours of Europe and South America between 1928 and 1930, when she began to downplay her role as the sexually uninhibited female.[22] Black women were generally sexualized in images including advertisements and colonial photographs, for example, that stereotyped black, Antillean women as erotic.[23] Baker broke such boundaries with performances and commercialization that gave male critics material that invited them not only to eroticize her but also, paradoxically, to both esteem and stereotype her comedic talents. However, during her European travels Baker, while maintaining the sensuality, started to set herself apart from caricatures of both the erotic and the burlesque in her performances. Instead, she emphasized a sophistication not usually associated with black women in interwar France.

In *Voyages et aventures* Sauvage used his lyrical and humorous style to tell stories such as that of Vienna, Austria, where church bells rang to signal the arrival of Baker as the Devil in person—a demon of immorality. Although his phrases blew events out of proportion, they allowed Sauvage's readers, Baker's audience, to understand that she had found a home in Paris, and that she started seeing herself as French after she visited other European nations. Her travels transformed Baker from a transient Parisian into a permanent one: "From country to country, in Europe, I learned to better know, and better understand France, by reaction."[24] Hence, her performances in Germany, dismissed by French critics as irrelevant to her "civilizing" process, were probably crucial to her changing self-image, instigating her decision to downplay her sexual, black image.

In response to her transformation Parisian journalists focused upon her whiter skin when she returned, as though responding to her personal sense of growing Frenchness. Why did these men focus upon her lightening, if they were still so fascinated by her blackness? Fundamentally, Baker was not marketable merely as a dark other, an image which by the early 1930s hinted a little too much at the growing unrest among black colonial intellectuals and workers seeking equality with white Frenchmen. Baker took such discomfort into account when playing several colonial women in the October 1930 revue *Paris Qui Remue*, in which she starred for a year and a day. The conversation surrounding the 1930 *Paris Qui Remue* continued to refer to her fearsome beauty. Her body and powerful hips, it was said, had splashes of a black color so fiery in nature, they gave meaning to the expression "Beauté du Diable," a phrase translated into English as "the bloom of youth," although the word devil, in Baker's case, was not innocent.[25] Critics, however, also believed that the French had managed to tame her dark nature. In *Paris Qui Remue*, Baker performed roles of Martinican, Indochinese, and African women, and even the Empress of Jazz.[26] As a colonized woman, Baker was transformed. Not only was her skin lighter, but critics also remarked upon her acquisition of the linguistic tools and poise that epitomized the ideal of a civilizing, colonial process.

Thus they wrote about how she had become paler since 1925, styling herself as a great lady who, through her composure, elegance, and hard work, and with the help of France's colonizing power, rivaled some of the most famous white French singers including Mistinguett, a singer and actress beloved in part because she had worked her way from poverty to stardom. Gérard d'Houville wrote for the mainstream newspaper *Le Figaro*, "[Baker] returns, no longer simply an anthropophagous beauty, with a fetish-like face traversed by three lightning bolts of rolling eyes and magnificent, devouring teeth: she is now an artist, a real one, whose savage talent and barbarous vitality have become her most original and most intense dramatic strengths."[27] Baker, like Mistinguett, worked hard to transform herself.[28] So even while they praised civilization's effects on her, critics recognized Baker's role in the transformation.[29]

Not all critics viewed Baker's alteration, or the growing popularity of dark skin, in a positive light. Some thought Latin culture was in danger of being subsumed by black culture, while others focused upon the critics' description of her whitening, and deemed such an idea as unnatural as that of Frenchwomen wishing to darken. The politically left-leaning newspaper *Le Quotidien* wondered: "Will she soon be a white *négresse?*"[30] Writing for the high-circulation and anticommunist newspaper *Le Journal*, the prolific author and playwright Clément Vautel suggested that "Josephine Baker is café-au-lait but if this campaign continues, Mistinguett will be chocolate," and then concluded "it is perhaps unfortunate that Mistinguett's truly French glory risks being eclipsed in this fashion by an exotic derriere."[31] Writing for *Le Soir* the author and pacifist Georges Pioch saw Baker's lightening as oddly contrasting with the veritable trend she had started by first appearing in France as a strikingly beautiful black woman. Speaking of white Frenchwomen, he concluded: "The more they were scorched and blackened, the prouder they were, the happier they were. How many will have despaired at not being able to transform into opaque darkness the whiteness so naturally a part of their charm!"[32] However, even negative criticism focused upon the overwhelming popularity of not only Baker's performances, but her entire image, and most seemed convinced that Baker had indeed become a French symbol of colonialism, even if colonialism's repercussions upon France were still up for debate.

As a colonial woman, however, even a lighter Baker depended upon her performance of race. Writing about Baker as a controlled colonial reflected these critics' desire to see modernity, technology, and civilization take what they considered to be the fundamentally positive characteristics of the primitive, such as authenticity, passion, and even sexuality, and use them to infuse new life into a modern world that many felt had had its values destroyed by World War I. Baker's wildly flailing arms and her overtly sexual moves generated hope. The *Revue Nègre* of 1925 had been marked by its degression from modernity to debauched exoticism. In contrast, the 1930 *Paris Qui Remue* kept the primitive and the modern tightly linked during the entire spectacle. Critics recognized the undeniably modernist aspects of the performance, and, in contrast with their reviews of the savage dance that had concluded Baker's first Parisian success, they appreciated the ultra-modern finale of the 1930 review: "Grand finale: super-modern, electric: one hundred electric dresses . . . Debauchery of electricity."[33] Baker had managed to make herself appear modern and French after only five years, while still capitalizing upon the exotic possibilities of her skin color. Baker's 1930 revue was certainly in the words of the critic G. de Pawlowski, who also wrote portions of the program notes, "a huge commercial undertaking but is also, at the Casino de Paris, a lesson in good Parisian taste," and one for which Baker was getting as much credit as the director Henri Varna, and sometimes more.[34]

Marketing Josephine: Technologies of Cultural Production

Baker had a hand in the product—herself—that hit the markets. Her independent role in this transformation benefited from a colonial backdrop that moved increasingly to the fore during the 1930s. Baker did not have to create a space for herself as a black woman, but rather had to differentiate herself not only from other African Americans (by playing the colonial woman) but also from black colonial subjects and citizens. She used various devices to help market herself, surrounding herself with men who also helped to create her. Inevitably, her success was grounded in the negrophilia that flooded Paris in the 1920s and 1930s. In fact, her commercial success contributed to the transformation of negrophilia from an avant-garde fixation to a popular *vogue nègre* attractive to a broader swathe of consumers. In both cases, her image was a political challenge, transforming the racial and gendered discourses of the 1920s.[35]

During the 1920s Paris succumbed, in the evocative words of scholar James Clifford, to "things *nègre*, an expansive category that included North American jazz, syncretic Brazilian rhythms, African, Oceanian, and Alaskan carvings, ritual 'poetry' from south of the Sahara and from the Australian outback, the literature of the Harlem Renaissance, and René Maran's *Batouala*."[36] The attraction of black culture was its primitive, wild, elemental, and often erotic characteristics, which lent themselves well to the avant-garde's interests. The term avant-garde is used here to describe a self-conscious group of artists, such as the dadaists and the surrealists,who sought both artistically and politically to shock and disturb bourgeois sensibilities and high culture.[37] The military origins of the term avant-garde (or vanguard) certainly referenced this engagement with politics and revolutionary ideals (including communism). These avant-garde groups sought to bridge the divide between high art and popular culture. Baker's arrival in Paris was timely, because she was an ideal conduit for this component of the avant-garde project.

Ethnographers and avant-garde artists not only amassed objects around which negrophilia crystallized, but then used it to further their studies of "primitive" cultures. For example the Mission Ethnographique et Linguistique Dakar-Djibouti, an ethnographic expedition launched by several major anthropologists in order to amass African artifacts, used the negrophilia sweeping avant-garde music, literature, and art to raise funds. The information and artifacts with which they returned from their mission in turn reinforced France's absorption with blackness. Three months after the expedition's return from Africa, in a further attempt by both Baker and the ethnographers to utilize negrophilia for their own purposes, she visited the museum of ethnography. She was photographed amidst primitive masks and other objects. Anthropologists and surrealists did not hesitate to place a black woman on display near the jumble they had collected, latching onto her while processing these newly acquired African objects and thereby transmitting them to a more popular audience.[38] Ultimately, the avant-garde sought to infuse the primitive with positive connotations such as freedom, and thus went against the grain of how "primitive" culture was traditionally scorned in bourgeois circles.[39]

The passion for all things black had its artistic roots in the period "nègre" of 1907–9 when the cubist movement, led by painters such as

Henri Matisse and Pablo Picasso, were drawn to African art for the first time as *"objets d'art*, rather than as curious *objets* [curios]."[40] The Zurich-based dadaists, who explored the irrational, amongst other subjects, were also drawn to Africa. For example on July 14, 1916, the founding members and central dadaist figures Hugo Ball and Tristan Tzara led an evening of drum-beating and invented chants, supposedly typical of black cultures.[41] This alternative celebration of Bastille Day, a French national holiday marking the Third Republic's roots in the 1789 Revolution, was particularly provocative at the height of a war that depended upon such holidays to bolster pride and unity.

While the passion for black culture, whether African, Antillean, or African American, originated with the prewar artistic movements, it was reinforced by the postwar avant-garde, especially by the surrealists, who are known for their fascination with the unconscious, fantastic imagery, and juxtaposition of seemingly incongruous subject matter. The vision this group held of a lush, naïve, sensuous, and spiritual black culture contrasted with the perceived cold rationalism—and sheer terror—of the Great War. Thus often the language emphasizing the primitive in black culture reflected fears of modernity and technology even though black culture spread through new technologies such as cinema, radio, and phonographs. Léopold Sédar Senghor, one of the interwar leaders of the cultural and political negritude movement that amongst other things sought to reclaim the celebration of black cultures from the French, later wrote of art in black Africa as a "sensual participation in the reality that underlies the universe, in surreality, more precisely in the vital forces that animate the universe."[42] His words point to the possibility for exploring universal qualities that drew French artists to black culture. Black artists existed in a strange space in which the civilized and the primitive intersected and combined to strike at the inhibitions of French society.

Surrounded by this disruption, Baker performed her role as a colonized, black, and female body to perfection, thus reaching the status of fetish for the avant-garde. She managed to avoid becoming replaceable and subject to conformity, a "fungible, mere specimen."[43] In order to maintain this image for a broader audience, especially in the early

1930s, Baker avoided associating with black colonial intellectuals and workers who were becoming increasingly virulent in their political demands for equality with white Frenchmen. She understood her potential as an object for consumption, needing only the proper modern packaging. Baker's relationship to the modernity both troubling and fascinating to the avant-garde, and integral to her ideal fulfillment of France's civilizing mission, was clear in the modes of distribution used for her image.

Baker lent herself to a French search for escapism through media that included print, posters, and film. The diffusion and creation of women's images through media and advertisement were controlled by a small group of men.[44] Baker had some control over the fashioning and distribution of her image, but it was filtered not only through the men associated with her venture, but through all who chose to comment upon her, from theater critics to journalists to novelists. Through this process, civilization mitigated the primitive in a manner recalling the social theorists Max Horkheimer and Theodor Adorno's assertion that within what they termed the culture industry, "individuals are tolerated only as far as their wholehearted identity with the universal is beyond question."[45] This toleration, in Baker's case, depended upon the mitigation of her performance through the universal setting of the imperial nation-state. Her marketing also revealed the talents of men who used various techniques to produce images of blackness and colonialism through Baker's controlled exoticization.

Early on, Baker created several memoirs, all of which she coauthored with Parisian-based writers. Sauvage was one example of just such a writer. In the 1920s he was known as a pacifist writer and won a prestigious literary prize, the Prix Gringoire, for his work *Le premier homme que j'ai tué* (The First Man I Killed). During the 1930s Sauvage wrote several works on Africa, including *l'Afrique Noire* (Black Africa), in which he detailed the horrors of colonialism while emphasizing the powerful and poetic beauty of the colonies. He and Baker knew each other well, as for a while Sauvage had been her unofficial secretary, answering fan letters and proposals of marriage.[46] They collaborated on two autobiographies including the 1931 *Voyages et aventures* and her first memoirs, *Les mémoires de Joséphine Baker*, published in

1927 when Baker was only twenty and had been in Paris for merely two years. Sauvage interviewed Baker extensively when collecting the material for both works, and indeed, Baker can be considered an author of all the books upon which she collaborated.[47] Still, she was not given much of a voice in her 1927 pseudo-autobiography. In the midst of a generally good-natured and tender (although highly creative and improvised, as many of her memoirs were) account of her days in Paris, Sauvage reminded readers what made her so attractive. He pictured her as a "comic nudity of bronze" whose "golden body and breasts were racked, passionately, by the spasms of desire and the pleasures of love."[48] His focus upon her sensuality was not surprising. However, he also emphasized how Baker unbalanced the French, returning them to a refreshing, primitive order.[49] The work was presented with a maximum amount of publicity about who Baker was and what she did, including several highly stereotypical sketches done by Paul Colin, an artist who became famous through his partly comical, partly erotic renditions of Baker's image. The preface was a selection of reviews by critics such as Pierre de Régnier that recalled her notoriety in the Parisian press. Finally, several appendixes indicated how popular Josephine was with fans. Included was a rather ghastly poem (the same rhyme was used to end every single line), written by Pierre K., which as an "Ode to the Black Dancer" focused upon her eccentric dancing, antique bronze skin, and her presence as an ethereal perfume of the tropics.[50]

Sauvage's memoirs of Baker's life were followed by André Rivollet's 1935 rendition. Rivollet's style closely matched Sauvage's, with an even greater and more open focus on Baker's ability to provide the French with a diversion from their humdrum lives. Rivollet stated that Baker represented an escape similar to that provided by boxing matches and the artistic projects of the dadaists and surrealists. He told readers how she transformed her suburban garden into a colonial forest and described all the animals she had adopted.[51] Furthermore, Baker was unabashedly presented by both Sauvage and Rivollet as an embodiment of the supposed sensuality of the black world. Referring to her affairs, lovers, and ultimately her sexuality reinforced her primitive aura as the dominant black Venus, a trope that followed

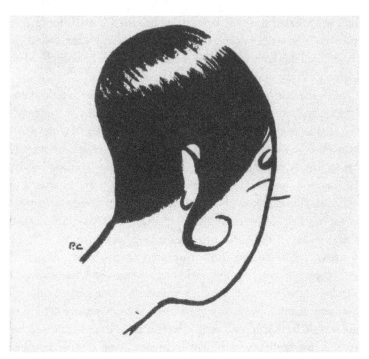

1. Paul Colin (1892–1985). *Profile of Josephine Baker.* From the cover of Baker and Sauvage, *Les mémoires de Joséphine Baker* (Paris: Kra, 1927). © 2009 Artists Rights Society (ARS), New York/ADAGP, Paris. Beinecke Rare Book and Manuscript Library, Yale University.

black women all through nineteenth-century French history.[52] She was undeniably being marketed to a melanomanic French audience. The memoirs were a tool furthering her colonial reputation, a method allowing the French to enter a supposedly savage fantasy world. She further sold herself by placing reviews of her dancing and fan letters in the book. Baker catered to Parisian audiences in search of the exotic in part through the printed words of white authors.

One man who helped to shape the cultural production of Josephine's image in the print media, phonograph records, and film by making use of her flair for publicity was her manager Pépito Abatino. A known hustler, and her sometime lover, Abatino helped her stage career by becoming her full-time publicist, putting her financial affairs in order, negotiating a film contract for her, and encouraging Sauvage to write her memoirs.[53] He showed a knack for disseminating and shaping her image, for example setting up a deal for a hair product known as Bakerfix to popularize Josephine's method of wearing her hair slicked to her head (see fig. 1). With Abatino's help Baker formed her own company to market this product.[54] He also arranged an endorsement for the liquor Pernod.[55]

These publicity arrangements illustrate the degree to which Baker pervaded and influenced French culture, becoming unavoidable as a symbol for colonialism. Pernod was and is the basis for a French drink, the anise-based *pastis*, especially popular as an aperitif in the South of France. Enlisting her image to market a product typically drunk by male workers as they relaxed over a game of *pétanque* demonstrated the extent to which she permeated mainstream culture and, more importantly, her image's ability to cross race, gender, and class boundaries.

Baker also found a willing market in the area of women's interwar fashions. Bakerfix and the slick hair associated with it played into the short-hair frenzy so popular with the *garçonne* of the interwar years. Furthermore, while Baker may not have launched the fascination with tanning noted and critiqued by so many journalists, she certainly arrived at the right time to capitalize upon the movement. A survey of the monthly Frenchwomen's magazine *Fémina* between 1919 and 1938 reveals that as Baker started to arrive in the pages of this magazine in the mid-1920s, the merits of tanning were increasingly debated. In the late 1920s *Fémina* advertised products and methods aimed at helping women obtain "healthy" tan skin. The magazine also featured columns and pictures analyzing tanning's impact upon women and society. *Fémina*, much like women's magazines today, always included a spread of the latest fashions modeled by elegant young women. Baker's presence on these pages alongside society women and chic Parisians confirmed that while being successfully marketed as a product, she had also become a valuable endorser of other products as a result of her fashionableness. Her natural darkness, combined with her growing sense of Parisian elegance, in every way reinforced growing trends favoring dark skin and short hair amongst this generation of French women.

Whenever possible Abatino and Baker also profited from developing technologies and modes of communication. Marketing her through the printed word was continued by a 1931 collection of reviews of Baker's 1930 performances at the Casino de Paris. Rather than allow these to yellow and fade from mind, Abatino presented them for publication in a collection entitled *Joséphine Baker vue par la presse française* (Josephine Baker Seen by the French Press). The newspaper clippings reviewed her work as a dancer and singer. Indeed the second part of the work focused entirely upon her singing, which was not previously marketable in part because recording technologies were still evolving when Baker first arrived in Paris.[56] Radio was first broadcast from the Eiffel Tower in 1921 and live radio performances by jazz musicians, alongside recordings, were important media.

The collection of reviews indeed happily coincided with the release of a compilation of Baker's songs by Columbia Records. Alongside explicit advertisements, many of the excerpts from articles focused upon her records as the reason behind Columbia's success at the time. Baker's voice, like her body and dancing, was treated by critics as an exotic instrument: "capturing here the sound of a saxophone numb with emotion, there the plucking with vibrato of a Hawaiian guitar, later the manner of an insistent ukulele."[57] Critics compared her rhythmic voice to those of singers Sophie Tucker and Vaughn de Leath, and praised her American accent—unlike these fellow Americans, Baker was singing in French—as an added dose of charm. In a further example of how one marketing technique blended into another for Baker, the collection of press reviews also included excerpts from another autobiography she planned to write.

Shortly thereafter the same publishing house, Editions ISIS, listed de la Camara and Pépito Abatino as authors for a "roman d'après une idée de Joséphine Baker," titled *Mon sang dans tes veines* (1931). While Abatino's only other work was the collection of press reviews, de la Camara had over twenty romantic novels, several of which were set in the colonies, to his name. Baker wrote a preface in which she immediately identified herself with the protagonist Joan. In fact the subtitle "d'après une idée" could mean both inspired by and suggested by, and Baker's preface suggests both interpretations were intended. She remembered as a child watching "dockers, blackened with soot and tattoos, who became white again when they emerged from the river's water."[58] Hence immediately broaching the topic of racial mixing, Baker went on to address her own mixed blood and her desire, from a young age, to escape the racial injustices of St. Louis, Missouri, for more exotic countries and stages: "We would dance, we would sing, covered in diamonds, pearls, and feathers, under lights brighter than the African suns."[59] In the brief preface, Baker guaranteed the sympathy of a francophone reader who would react indignantly to the illustration of racial injustice in the United States. The reader was made to understand why Baker had stylized herself as a colonial Frenchwoman in order to escape the indignities of being an African American. Finally, Baker emphasized her affinity with exoticism, or a metropolitan manifestation of colonialism, by clearly equating her dancing with freedom and the colonies, and in this manner underlining the purity and elegance of her new, stylized appearance, without upsetting its famous, exotic appeal.

The novel tells the story of the beautiful and innocent Joan, a black child who grows up in Massachusetts on the white-owned Barclay estate. She befriends and slowly grows to love the only son, Fred. The first description of Joan is clearly one of Baker, up to the slick haircut Baker marketed with her Bakerfix hair product. Although Joan is American, the emphasis upon exotic charm and the Nile reminds the reader of Baker's links to colonialism.

> A simple dress drapes her in its folds, emphasizing the perfect lines of a slender body and revealing feet wearing shoes without heels. The features of her face have an exotic charm. Black hair cut short and slicked down frames a charming head, the masterpiece of a master sculptor. It's youth personified, a bronze statue come to life! In the eyes filled with virginal grace a sadness lurks, obscure and languishing. Does Joan dream, unconsciously, of the cradle of her race on the black continent, to the south of the sacred waters of the Nile?[60]

In her innocence, Joan never declares, or even truly understands, her love for Fred, which she interprets as simple devotion. So she works on the estate and watches as he flirts with and then decides to marry a wealthy and beautiful Southern woman, Clarence Clifton. Clarence realizes that Joan has what Clarence considers an unnatural affection for Fred, who in return does not treat Joan as a mere servant. The situation climaxes after Joan saves Clarence from a runaway horse, seriously injuring herself in the process. With flowers, Fred thanks Joan for saving his fiancée, but Clarence views his gesture as a betrayal. In a dramatic scene, Clarence rides off on her horse while Fred chases her in his car until he crashes. He needs an immediate blood transfusion, and only Joan is in the immediate vicinity with the right blood type. After an agonizing few pages during which Dr. Anderson tries to justify his decision to mix "white" and "black" blood, Fred is saved. Joan leaves town, content with the knowledge that she has selflessly saved his life, and begging the doctor not to disclose her identity as the blood donor. Fred, however, slowly discovers the truth, and must tell Clarence that he can no longer marry her. In shock, Clarence pronounces the last words of the novel: "Poor Mr. Barclay, thus, having *her* blood in your veins, you have become a *white nègre*."[61]

Throughout the text, Europe is the arena where races can intersect. Joan learns about the existence of a black Madonna, to whom the Polish pray, and decides that she feels an affinity with these progressive Europeans. Dr. Anderson notes that on the battlefields of World War I the blood of all the races ran red. Finally, Joan senses that in Europe she and Fred might share the life of which she can only dream in the United States. These points prompt the reader to understand why Baker chose a home in France. The work packaged Baker's image with a naïve questioning of racial inequality and an emphasis upon Europe's enlightened stance. The audience could envision Joan as yet another character portrayed by Baker. Although Baker was not listed as the novel's author, she infused the venture with her image and patronage. Indeed at a time when Baker was becoming a white *négresse* in the eyes of many critics, Fred's transformation into her white male counterpart was an extraordinary development, suggesting possibilities for exoticism in every white man.

Abatino was not the only man to play an important role in establishing Baker's image. In 1925, the then unknown graphic artist Paul Colin was asked to produce a poster for the *Revue Nègre* overnight. Colin was born in Nancy in 1892, the son of a government worker. At fifteen, against his father's wishes, he became a printer's apprentice and three years later enrolled in the Ecole des Beaux-Arts (School of Fine Arts).[62] However, it was only after fighting in World War I—an experience that profoundly reoriented his approach and subject matter—that Colin started to work in Paris. After he chose Baker to be the centerpiece for his *Revue Nègre* poster, she quickly became one of his greatest inspirations, lending glamour to his depictions of blacks when they might otherwise have remained caricatures. Colin proved particularly adept at using Baker's body to capture the *vogue nègre* engulfing Paris and at depicting the manner in which she linked discourses of the primitive and the modern, the colonial and the Parisian, with her ever-moving body.

Throughout the *vogue nègre*, Colin decorated many of the black nightclubs in Paris, including the Plantation, La Boule blanche, and Le Nègre blanc. As a graphic artist, he was interested in getting art to penetrate the world, knowing that it would have to survive on its own once it was in the streets. He would later write that his style "originated in all the artistic schools, but especially in the futurism that defined the modern movement."[63] His three-color posters infused inanimate objects with life and movement. Colin differed from other graphic artists of the interwar years such as Jean Carlu, Cassandre, and Charles Laupot because his work was dominated by spectacle and dance rather than industry and commerce.[64] He emphasized the link between avant-garde art and graphic arts, arguing that graphic expressions always had to be at the forefront of artistic movements.[65] In describing Baker he agreed with other artists' evaluations of her potential to revive French civilization: "I can still see her frenetic, undulating, transformed by the exacerbated sounds of the saxophones. Did her dances from South Carolina announce the era of a new civilization rid, finally, of thousand-year-old constraints?"[66] His work was stylized, relying upon the artist and trained architect Fernand Léger's mechanism and pure colors as well as the cubist movement's use of angular drawings and geometric forms. In 1930 he became intricately linked with the modernist group of designers and architects known as l'Union des Artistes Modernes (The Union of Modern Artists), which included the artists and designers Carlu, Cassandre, and Loupot, and later the architect Le Corbusier and painters Sonia Delaunay and Léger. He was always aware, however, of the link between his own success and Baker's.

In 1927 he published a portfolio called *Le Tumulte noir* (The Black Tumult). This work was a compilation of satirical renditions of dancers and Parisian celebrities, whom Colin often drew as black even if they were white. His work focused upon movement, revealing the ticks, steps, and attitudes of celebrities dancing the Charleston. The vigorous strokes, similar to those he used to depict Josephine, conveyed the incredible sense of movement in modern dance. The forty-four lithographs depicted many of the iconic figures of the day, including Baker's white rival Mistinguett; the dancers known as the Dolly sisters; the French actor known as Max Dearly; the white actress Maud Loty (as an insolent, bare-bottomed black girl); the ballet dancer and patron Ida Rubinstein (under a palm tree); the white actors Maurice Chevalier and Parysis (as black men); the actress Spinelly (as a ridiculous, fat white woman dancing the Charleston naked in front of her mirror); and so forth.[67] Often, he portrayed black men dancing with white women, stressing the Parisian fascination with black, American, and colonial dances by depicting nightclubs. While he stereotyped, Colin's art was as incisive a portrayal of white celebrities as of black ones.

Baker was unquestionably the star of this collection. Colin drew her nearly nude dancing on a piano; wearing a banana skirt; dancing in the rain; and dancing topless behind prison bars. He revealed his admiration for her in his refusal after his initial sketches to denigrate her, unlike Sem, another caricaturist from the same period who drew Baker with a monkey tail (and whom Colin depicted with his own monkey tail in retribution). Certainly Baker understood Colin's importance in the cultural production of her image—in time he contrib-

2. Paul Colin (1892–1985). Poster, *Gala au profit des sinistrés de la Guadeloupe*, 1929. Imprimerie H. Chachoin. © 2009 Artists Rights Society (ARS), New York/ADAGP, Paris. Original at Bibliothèque Nationale de France, Paris.

uted sketches to both Sauvage's works and *Vue par la presse française*—
and hence she lent her support to Colin's 1927 work, thereby ensuring
the marketing of her image, when she wrote a brief introduction in
which she summarized the reason behind the collection: "I'll say it's
getting darker and darker in Paris. In a little while it shall be so dark
until one shall light a match, then light another to see if the first is lit
or not."[68]

Colin's contribution to identifying Baker with the imperial setting
was distinctive in part because whereas his early work was known for
its vivid evocation of black Paris and its nightclubs, in the 1930s it became increasingly politically engaged.[69] Several of Colin's posters reflected the surrealist interest in ethnography, and he designed a poster
for the Musée Ethnographique. Moreover, he showed his compassion
for the colonized through posters such as *Gala au profit des sinistrés
de la Guadeloupe*, designed to promote a 1929 gala organized by *La
Dépêche Africaine* to raise money for Guadeloupeans whose homes
had been destroyed by a recent tornado (see fig. 2).

His interest extended from such not-for-profit pieces to the décor
of a ballet entitled "L'Effort de l'homme" (Man's Effort), which celebrated Antilleans' courage in rebuilding the city of Saint-Pierre after its destruction by the volcano Mount Pelée in 1902. Colin was one
of many Parisians who after an initial encounter with Baker showed
increasing awareness of the imperial nation-state at large.

Printed materials, musical recordings, and graphic art were joined
by another medium through which colonial images of Baker were
disseminated: cinema. Abatino found lead roles for Baker in *Zouzou*
(1934) and *Princesse Tam Tam* (1935) just as sound films were becoming popular. She had tried her hand at the silent genre with *La Sirène
des Tropiques* (The Mermaid of the Tropics, 1927) but really came into
her own with sound films, a medium where she fit perfectly into the
colonial subgenre of cinema in which France appeared as the civilizing force.[70] In these films, which were yet another method of marketing Josephine, her characters were often placed in contexts that
allowed viewers to delve into issues of French identity, nationalism,
and escapism. The French appeared as the dominant force and their

discourses of power and hierarchy allowed very little room for subversion on the part of black women such as Baker.

In *Zouzou* Baker played opposite the heartthrob Jean Gabin. The film tackled issues of race and class, glamorizing the young Martinican singer Zouzou (played by Baker) as she soared from laundress to music-hall star. Her depiction as a wild, exotic, and beautiful young star in love with her inaccessible pseudo-brother (they were brought up by the same adoptive father) rendered in images a colonial discourse and eroticized race relations. Zouzou is a fantasy who will not actually attain her own desires, but rather embody the desires of the white French males who give her standing ovations. Thus she watches, powerless, as her true love goes off with a white woman while remaining oblivious to the little girl with whom he grew up and who has become a beautiful and passionate woman.

Princesse Tam Tam, while not nearly as replete with heartache, nonetheless reproduced schemes of metropolitan domination over the colonized. In it Baker plays the lovely Aouina, a young nomad possibly from the Berber population of Tunisia. The credits at the beginning of the film appear against the backdrop of a black drummer beating his tam tam, one of several examples of how Africans manifest themselves in what might otherwise simply be an Orientalist film.[71] The story appears to be a thinly veiled attempt to recreate Bernard Shaw's play *Pygmalion*, which is itself an interpretation of a Greek myth in which the sculptor Pygmalion falls in love with the statue he has created. A white writer, Max, and his secretary take off for Tunisia in order to escape the vicissitudes of Parisian life, and especially of Max's demanding wife, Lucie. While there, he meets the primitive and childlike Aouina, whose mischievous nature amuses him. In a dreamlike plot, Aouina returns to Paris with Max and his secretary, where they decide to pass her off as an Indian princess. As Max notes early on, "You know, these interracial stories. They're very fashionable." She passes until she is tricked through alcohol and African music into revealing her true nature as a colonized, erotic woman. Then, she strips at a society event, dancing to the wild beat of a tam tam. Instead of shocking her entourage, however, her performance makes Parisians love her all the more.

The dialogue and exchanges in this film reflect the racial discourse of the 1930s. When Max makes up his mind to escape from civilized Paris, he shouts: "Let's go visit the savages! To the real savages!" Max's comment was provoked by his wife's unruly behavior, effectively signifying that if he must be subjected to savage mores, at least he wants them to be in an authentic, overseas setting. As in much colonialist discourse of these years, primitivism had any number of positive connotations, especially in contrast to the Parisian setting. Max's many references to civilization are filled with contempt when his interlocutor is European, for he marvels at Aouina's nature, and yet are often defensive of civilization when he speaks to Aouina. One prolonged Aouina-as-rose metaphor has Max exclaiming at her natural beauty, his secretary commenting that nature also comprises manure, and their Tunisian manservant stating: "African flowers aren't made for living rooms." Aouina, tellingly, is given no voice in this exchange. When trying to find a way to teach Aouina about civilization, Max's secretary exclaims: "Teach her to lie!" After being shown the trappings of civilization (which include shoes, dresses, eating when a bell rings, and sleeping in beds), she travels to Paris. There, the first thing Aouina notices is a lack of authenticity: her room is filled with fake fish, fake gilded birds in a cage, fake sparkling flowers, and so forth. The audience understands that this lack of authenticity extends to Parisians, and especially the upper-class, catty women who are jealous of Aouina's success and use words such as "savage" and "cannibal" to describe her. Her depraved dance at the end of the film, as high society cheers her on, marks the triumph of the colonial "savage" in a modern world. She breaks apart the urban chorus-girls' constructions with her unbridled moves. However her success also signals the moment when she must leave, for her values cannot survive beyond an initial fleeting success in the metropole.

What these films captured is telling. *Zouzou* is dark for all its cheerful singing and dancing, and the star is tormented by her race as well as her talent; like Baker in her life or Joan in *Mon sang dans tes veines*, she is unable to find lasting love with a white man. Aouina, likewise, is not allowed to find true love with the seductive Max. Some films of this era were redolent with suppressed sexual power.[72] In Baker's case, the sexual was linked with the colonial interplay between race and power. Both films marketed Baker as a powerfully erotic, racial, and colonial woman, but at the same time they pointed to the underbelly of black life in Paris at the time. The fame and fortune black men and women entertainers won was a far cry from integration into French society.

Evasion and Rebellion: Baker and Black Paris

Baker's marketing as a colonial woman can be traced through the techniques of cultural production used to showcase her place in the imperial nation-state, but the success of these techniques can only be determined by how Parisians, colonial or otherwise, responded to her. Influenced by Baker's presence as a cultural symbol of colonialism, white female writers and journalists and black men and women implicated in French colonialism challenged the prevailing images of the black colonial woman spread by white French men, including critics and advertisers.

While the best-known reactions to Baker as a colonial woman were largely fielded by white male journalists, white Parisian women also reacted to her status. In 1929 Clotilde Chivas-Baron, the author of books on the French colonies based largely upon her personal experiences, wrote a manual for women preparing to travel to the French colonies. In *La Femme française aux colonies* (The Frenchwoman in the Colonies), Chivas-Baron thanked Baker for her impact as a cultural symbol, and specifically for her invention and marketing of the Bakerfix product. Writing about the difficulties of life in the colonies for Frenchwomen, Chivas-Baron discussed fashion challenges: "Some artifices are impossible in the bush, such as many a becoming hair style. Not much is soft and fluffy, no curls except nature's own; hair drenched in sweat does not hold waves. Josephine Baker has rendered a great service to straight-haired colonial women."[73] Chivas-Baron, while describing life in the jungle, nonetheless referred to a chic and Parisian Baker, whose fashion spread throughout the French empire. Another Frenchwoman, Marthe Oulié, used the vocabulary of a Parisian journalist in describing Martinican women: "Here are ten or twelve Josephine Bakers, with fine, crimped hair and bewitching smiles."[74] Baker's image managed to project itself onto descriptions of the very women she imitated in her performances. A third writer, Odette Arnaud, used Baker to render the scene of a typical French Caribbean dancehall for her French readers. Arnaud writes of a male dancer who cannot find a partner and so "imitates Josephine Baker's style, with her ostrich-shaped backside and her eyes rolling invitingly; he writhes around the couples like a contortionist and points his exaggeratedly long index finger at the sign warning the dancers not to bother the ladies."[75] These examples are representative of the degree to which white women also accepted Baker as a cultural symbol of colonialism. Using Baker, these writers titillated the metropolitan reader with the exotic while at the same time stopping short of projecting any sort of eroticism upon her, for reasons that we shall see included their own struggle with the exotic label projected on all women associated with colonialism.

Initial reactions on the part of African and Antillean Parisians were generally sympathetic and lighthearted, much like those of women writers. A largely Antillean-run Paris newspaper, *La Dépêche Africaine* (The African Dispatch), which employed both Antillean and French journalists, referred several times to a Baker whose cultural status was growing through marketing: "confectioners are also launching chocolate specialties imitating the shape and face of the star."[76] The sympathetic male writers believed that as Baker's symbolic value grew, she needed solidarity from blacks in Paris. Hence, journalists defended her when she was wronged in the white French press. After the critic Maurice Hamel wrote an "Irreverent letter to Joséphine Baker" in the publication *Cambronne*, Pierre Baye-Salzmann published a response in *La Dépêche Africaine*. He was shocked by Hamel's letter, which "expresses more than dislike of Josephine Baker, more than resentment; it expresses a hatred so deep-rooted it is black."[77] In his article Hamel explained that he had received a slew of letters warning against the black peril (or as Baye-Salzmann suggests in Baker's case, the coffee-colored peril). Hamel used these letters to fuel a personal diatribe against Baker. Quoting excerpts from Hamel's article such as: "This woman has no artistic value, no beauty; she is cynical, filthy, repugnant, etc.," Baye-Salzmann affirmed his community's support for Baker, explaining that "We always feel the strongest attraction for Josephine. We always value her gracefulness, like that of a spring flower, and her talent, which lies in some ineffable, deliciously childlike quality." The decision to defend Baker in this instance was a direct reaction to the links between Baker and the black peril occasionally suggested by right-wing journalists. In defending Baker, Baye-Salzmann was defending all blacks. In 1930 *La Dépêche Africaine* once more stood up for Baker, this time responding to an article written by Clément Vautel in his regular column for *Le Journal*. Vautel, whom we saw above lamenting Baker's challenge to Mistinguett's talent, seemed convinced that Baker's success in Paris was "a theme for very serious meditation." In response, *La Dépêche Africaine*'s contributor Charles Denys ironically posited a more widespread peril: "we are threatened by a black invasion."[78] Oscillating between scathing irony and serious defense, he reminded readers that when the French educated *indigènes*, they also taught them to compete. In a postwar era, Denys argued, the French were reevaluating their values and reconstructing the country:

> Nothing is more natural to poetic emotion than the expression of the primitive soul scattered through the virgin forest, the expression of pain or joy of a race long oppressed and that wishes to rid itself of its sorrow through spontaneous outbursts. We were introduced to a similar sensation when the *Ballets Russes* were revealed in France. The scandal was on the same magnitude.[79]

Linking the scandal surrounding Baker with the immediate prewar scandal generated by *The Rite of Spring* not only positioned her as a symbol of the reinvigoration of French culture, but also suggested that her shock value was a component of that rejuvenation. Igor Stravinsky's 1913 *Rite of Spring* was performed by the Russian ballet company known as the *Ballets Russes* and choreographed by renowned dancer Vaslav Nijinski. It stunned and divided the audience with its departure from conventional music (considered discordant), storyline (appearing immoral), and choreography (viewed as awkward jumping and clomping) in ways that seemed intended to bring the very idea of civilization into question.[80] For some colonial men and women, Baker was a symbol of all that black culture could hope to accomplish for France. Her presence in *La Dépêche Africaine* as a colonial woman worth defending exemplifies the solidarity found within this newspaper, which welcomed contributions from French, African, and Antillean men and women of both races. The black Martinican woman Andrée Nardal, for example, recognized the impact Baker's colonial image had upon Parisian culture when she noted in a study of the Antillean dance known as the beguine that, "launched in Paris with the *bals nègre* and sketched last winter by Josephine Baker in 'Paris-qui-remue,' the beguine is now all the rage."[81] However, unlike their male counterparts, Antillean women were wary and critical of Baker's role as a black colonial woman, and eventually came to express doubt and criticism of the enthronement of black bodies, as we shall see in chapter 5.

In contrast to *La Dépêche Africaine*, *Le Cri des Nègres* (The *Nègre*'s Yell) was a newspaper staffed by radical anti-imperialists who were very intolerant of the French presence in the colonies. These men, who belonged to organizations such as the Union des Travailleurs Nègres (Union of *Nègre* Workers, UTN), were equally aware of Baker's cultural status. In 1933 one of the most virulent leaders of this organization, Tiémoko Garan Kouyaté, contacted Baker directly. Several police informants corroborated that Kouyaté wanted Baker to participate in a black fête scheduled for April 1.[82] After getting the permission of fellow members, Kouyaté sought out Baker at the Casino de Paris, where they both worked at the time, Kouyaté in the supporting cast, and Baker as the star. One can only imagine the encounter between the anti-imperialist, impoverished, colonized part-time worker and the colonial embodiment. Kouyaté went to beg a favor of Baker, and left insulted by her refusal. A prior engagement, Baker explained, would keep her from attending the fête, but she promised to collaborate on a future event. Kouyaté might have taken her word seriously had she not already refused an invitation to an event in which he had participated in 1930. She had been asked, along with Kouyaté and several others, to speak at a conference organized by the Club du Faubourg, an organization founded in 1918 that met throughout the interwar period, often three times per week.[83] Specialists spoke on topics chosen for their diversity, and then participated in lively discussions with the audience. The conference was entitled "The French Colonial Policies" and asked questions such as: "Is there hatred between the races in the colonies? Who is guilty? Are women of color more alluring than white women?"[84] The desire to link Baker with such questions reflects how closely associated with the colonies Baker's image had become in five short years, even by those originating from the colonies. Her refusal to participate in such events contributed to the rift between her and other figures of black Paris.

By 1936, a year before she finally attained French citizenship, she found herself maligned rather than admired or supported in the black press. Journalists no longer viewed Baker as a woman in need of defense. Writers criticized her largely because she had come out in support of Benito Mussolini as he waged war against Ethiopia. In 1932, when she first performed in Italy, she met Mussolini and reacted positively to his personality and authority. In 1935, during a brief stopover in Rome, Baker heard a bellicose speech in which Mussolini defended his imminent invasion of Ethiopia in what became known as the Italo-Ethiopian (and sometimes also the Italo-Abyssinian) war. She told reporters that Haile Selassie, the Emperor of Ethiopia who fought Mussolini, was an enemy of the black race. In the eyes of her critics, her passage from dark skin to light was paralleled by a political one so that she now held the views of white men. In February 1936 the anti-imperialist and by then decidedly communist *Le Cri des Nègres* published an article by the elusive author Merlin in which he responded to an article in the mainstream newspaper *Paris-Soir* about a trip Baker made to New York City. Merlin had also recently been to Harlem and was shocked to see how negatively Baker interpreted her experience in the city. He declared that she could not hope to be made welcome by blacks, for "Josephine Baker, a black woman supporting Mussolini, could never receive a warm welcome, especially from *nègre* nationalists who feel the war in Ethiopia is a war to destroy the *nègre* race."[85] Merlin then wrote that "in all of Josephine Baker's written work we see the extent of her contempt for her race." He concluded that blacks had definitively unmasked poseurs and "whores" who for the sake of publicity disowned their race and supported bombers of hospitals and assassins such as Mussolini. He was careful to avoid accusations of libel by omitting to name Baker in this concluding sentence, although she was clearly mentioned in every other paragraph.

By the mid-1930s Baker was viewed by some in militant, black Paris as fascist by default and a traitor to her race because of her naïve and ill-advised political stance (one she later recanted). A decade after her arrival in Paris, Baker, whose success had been aided in large part by the *vogue nègre*, was perceived as a negrophobe. Kouyaté, who had already been given two reasons to mistrust Baker's reliability, agreed with Merlin's analysis, adding his perspective in a newspaper he started in 1936, *Africa*, which published an article on the life of blacks in Paris and Baker's venality. Kouyaté agreed with Merlin that Baker's trip to the United States was a profascist propaganda trip. He was truly outraged, however, less by her political blunders than by her alleged refusal to sign a contract for a new show at the Folies-Bergère music-hall solely because thirty other black artists were to share the stage with her. In a vehement diatribe Kouyaté, who perhaps felt personally offended since he had performed as supporting cast for her before, voiced his discontent:[86]

Thus, the notorious negrophobia of Miss Josephine Baker, herself a black woman, would keep 30 unemployed black artists from working. The latter would continue to burden the state as a result of the whims of a star embittered against her race, an agent of Mussolini. We must end this scandal. There are negrophobic Negroes just as there are anti-Semitic Israelites. Miss Josephine Baker is one of those, even though she started in 1925 in the company of humble black artists whom she now scorns.

The white artists of the "Folies-Bergère" must show solidarity with their black comrades under the direction of their union representative. They can stop Miss Josephine Baker from working in their music-hall. This star would do best to go display herself in Rome.[87]

Both Merlin and Kouyaté revealed in their harangues that the growing breach between Baker and Parisian blacks emerged as she became more French in her own mind. After all, during her visit to New York City, Baker found that she was not welcomed by Americans, black or white, although the French had always accepted her role as a civilized, colonized woman. Still, even members of the subversive racial counterculture of anti-imperialists supported Baker's position as a cultural symbol by developing their rhetoric around her actions, imagined or real, and stances.

In 1931 Baker was elected Queen of the Colonial Exposition.[88] Her coronation never took place, however, because she did not come from a French colony. Her performance in the 1930–31 Casino de Paris, during which her transformation from dark to light was consecrated, may have confused those who voted for her; France's colonial empire was the show's theme, and in it Baker portrayed many types of colonized women. Yet while she convincingly portrayed women from the Caribbean to the Far East, Baker was nonetheless an American. True representatives of the colonies were the Antillean and African men and women imported from the colonies for the sole purpose of embodying at the exposition a French conception of authentic Africanness. Like Baker these men and women represented an ideal of colonialism, muted in the metropole by an erasure of the violence and oppression that plagued the colonies.

Baker came to be seen as a representation of the colonies with the help of modern aesthetics and new or innovative uses of media such as film and graphic art. Her ability, using such technology, to diffuse continuously evolving images resulted in a paradoxical vision of her otherness. During a transformation mitigated by a multitude of gendered and racial discourses, she always retained a certain amount of control over an image that invited viewers to alternate primitive landscapes with modern ones, metropoles with colonies, and racial and gendered domination with subversion. The complexity and diversity of Baker's performances throughout the 1920s and 1930s reflected her skill and sensitivity as a performer, as well as the changing perceptions of colonialism within the metropole.

Baker and other black performers were active participants in a marketing of black culture that started largely with advertisement.[89] Although several men constructed and disseminated Baker's image, she was also active in its development. The artist Colin, the writer Sauvage, the manager Abatino, and Jean Lion, who married her in 1937 and thus enabled her to become French, largely helped her to cement her cultural status. Baker was recognized even by contemporaries as an independent and successful business entrepreneur (something it took scholars far longer to analyze in a sustained fashion) who shaped her transformation from dark to light skin.[90] As early as 1927, an article in *Jazz, A Flippant Magazine* noted Baker's skill at exploiting her own talent by playing the perfect hostess at a small cabaret in the northern district of Paris Montmartre, and later in her own Montmartre nightclub, *Chez Joséphine*, where she danced and sang for the pleasure of her guests, adding more profits to those already generated by her many performances.[91] As a performer, she pressed her image upon the musicians and spectators; she was a creator who ensured her endeavors' financial and artistic success. The critic Fernand Divoire noted in a forum for right-leaning intellectuals, the publication *Gringoire*, that "she grasps the orchestra, conducting it with all her body, inhaling the music."[92] Her presence in a revue was enough to impose its colonial theme.[93]

Baker's image as a colonial woman replicated Paris's transformation, on a cultural level, into a colonial metropolis. Marketing techniques contributed to her cultural production as a colonial woman and helped to sustain this image against the backdrop of the avant-garde's negrophilia, while strengthening its popular appeal by reinforcing the *vogue nègre*. Alongside avant-garde artists, theater critics initially responded to her performances and her image and were amongst the first to contribute to the print media that were so crucial to her marketing. This image was further diffused to ever more diverse audiences via advertisements and films.

Baker thus played an active role in inviting contemporaries to process France's investment in colonialism. For some she reinforced a thirst for exoticism. She enabled others to explicitly address the possible repercussions of having such representatives of black culture present in their capital. They explored aspects of the civilizing mission, including both its potential for the ultimate inclusion of outsiders into the French republic and the dangers of allowing exotic cultures and races to possibly pervert their own. Finally, Baker's emblematic presence even pushed some, such as Paul Colin, to grasp and scrutinize the ramifications of colonialism. Thus in many instances discussions of Baker included a conscious appraisal of colonialism's impact on the nation, even if only on a cultural level. More mainstream deliberations over Baker tended toward the unconscious in the sense that on the whole they avoided viewing colonialism as anything but a largely warranted, albeit problematic, enterprise. Yet alongside colonial migrants, some participants in the cultural production of Baker, such as Colin and the avant-garde, were far more interested in finding either nuanced or aggressive ways of attending to the underlying violence of the colonial enterprise and the fear and discomfort it generated. They headed in a critical direction, both vis-à-vis the colonial enterprise and thus, necessarily, vis-à-vis basic universal tenets of the republic.

Perhaps most intriguingly, the success of the colonial woman trope in firmly anchoring Baker to her Parisian home can be traced through the publications of all those who felt, for social or political reasons, that they had a stake in the imperial nation-state. These individuals, from French feminists to African and Caribbean anti-imperialists, wittingly or unwittingly validated her as a colonial woman through the way they absorbed Baker. Their own careers, as well as their political and social hopes and aspirations, were just as dependent as Baker's upon how strong a web of connections they could construct in Paris. The writings they left—complex, critical, and at times uninhibited discussions of France's colonial endeavor—invite us to peel back the many cultural, political, and social layers constituting a city that was a centerpiece in the metropolitan entanglement with empire.

2

DANCING DISSIDENTS & DISSIDENT DANCERS

The Urban Topography of Race

Jeanne Nardal, first arts graduate from the Antilles, amazed the boulevard with her elegant black silhouette, hat, pearl grey gloves, cane in hand like a heroine of "La Garçonne," activist for women's rights, accompanied by her younger sister Andrée Nardal, a true exotic beauty with a distinguished smile, voluptuous body, and of strict upbringing.

—VICTOR SABLÉ, *Mémoires d'un foyalais*

In the late 1920s Malagasy corporal Bernardin Rakoto, serving in the French army at Bastion 89 near Paris, was perceived by authorities as exerting a negative influence on his subordinates by politically proselytizing them. Just as vexing was the fact that he had a white French mistress who was the mother of his child. While recording the latter information, Agent Joé commented with disapproval: "Of course with grounds such as these, I've been told he's certain to get his discharge in France," thereby intimating that marriage to and conception with this Frenchwoman guaranteed Rakoto freedom to remain in France and spread his subversive politics.[1] Rakoto's story takes an ironic twist, however, for with his meager pay the sergeant had trouble supporting his mistress and child. As a result he was forced to forego actively propagandizing for Malagasy rights to French citizenship and instead turned to jazz, meeting his family's needs by playing the violin, piano, and even the mandolin in Parisian nightclubs. He was apparently a skillful jazz musician.

This story, one of many narratives recounted by police agents, raises the question of how black and white men and women interacted with each other in Paris. The transformation of the metropole into a colonial space in which the center and the periphery of empire coincided was topographical, tactile, political, and literary, amongst other things. There were places where exchanges that reshaped the city in these ways arose, whether imposed by the government, for example during the Colonial Exposition of 1931; open to the general public, as in dance clubs and the meeting rooms of black organizations; or chosen by individuals who embarked upon interracial relationships. The idea of a city constructed by the senses has been put forth in various ways by cultural historians.[2] These works have in common a desire to outline the intangible contours of spaces of human contact. Part of what made Paris into a colonial metropolis during the interwar years was the changing nature of its sensory topography, which induced contemporaries to partake in a form of urban spectatorship inspired by the impact of racial interaction.

Contact amongst black and white men and women developed organically in both public spaces and private ones. Such contacts changed the visual, acoustic, and affective topography of Paris and inspired witnesses and participants to record their perception of how interracial contact between metropolitans and colonials altered the city. Often, they found the injection of interracial exchange into Parisian spaces to be a useful starting point for framing critiques of social, cultural, and political Third Republic norms, including the place of colonial subjects or citizens, and of women, in the metropole.

As a colonial metropolis, then, Paris provided locales for interracial encounters that moved from public to private spaces, encounters that were not only intellectual and artistic but also personal, and that were not merely passing, but also enduring. Black colonial migrants established contacts on the streets of Paris; provoked other writers to explore—and themselves considered—the implications of the 1931 Colonial Exposition; incited surrealists and musicians to reassess contemporary culture through jazz; injected colonial culture into Parisian nightclubs; and, on a private level, befriended and fell in love with Parisians. Even as only one of the colonial groups present in Paris, black colonial migrants reveal the coalescence of the politics, society, and culture of colonialism within the empire's capital.

Connections between black and white men and women often took the shape of relationships, whether induced by friendship or desire, but just as likely were fleeting encounters on street corners or in cafés, apartment buildings, and the workplace. These, too, were part of the sensory transformation of colonial Paris. Antilleans and Africans did not simply dance and engage in politics in Paris, they also lived there, bringing Parisians into daily contact with the peripheries of their empire. The sudden influx of Africans and Antilleans during World War I was followed during the interwar years by a routine of work and relaxation. Victor Sablé, an Antillean who published his memoirs of the interwar years, was fond of noting the public displays unwittingly performed by blacks on the Parisian boulevards in and around the student district known as the Latin Quarter:

> On the boulevard Saint-Michel, Louis Achille, son of our respected professor and himself an *agrégé* in English, was very stylish with his Knickerbocker pants while Charles Saint-Cyr, student of medicine, and Roland Boisneuf, student of law, were strutting about in melon hats, with umbrellas, like real dandies. Bocle and Mezin paraded about in tails on the terrace of the café de la Source, while waiting for a taxi to take them to the engagement dinner for Deputy Delmont's son.[3]

Descriptions such as Sablé's, along with details on home addresses and meeting places supplied by police informants, suggest that race was a visually traceable movement through the metropolis. The gradual integration of race as a visual factor in everyday Parisian life inevitably placed some men and women on display as they went about their daily business, and shaped others into spectators, very much like the nineteenth-century *flâneur*.

Coming from the French verb *flâner*, or "to stroll," the term *flâneur* has a rich history of being used to represent someone who, by wandering the streets of a city in order to experience it, also probes among other things the spectacle and modernity of urban environments. The *flâneur* was in his earliest form a nineteenth-century man with both the wealth and the time to spend his days observing the city and who—in part as a result of his leisurely approach to the workday—remained on the margins of bourgeois respectability. He wandered in an urban context, drawing pleasure from the spectacle of the streets. Both the novelty of this approach to a city environment and the *flâneurs'* written musings describing the transformations of their cities into a modern metropolis led numerous intellectuals, including most famously the French poet Charles Baudelaire and the German philosopher, essayist, and critic Walter Benjamin, to theorize the implications of this type of relationship to the city.[4] One recent approach to the *flâneur* is put forth by historian Judith Walkowitz. She traced the mutation of the *flâneur* figure in London during the 1880s. There, the image of the bourgeois *flâneur* as urban spectator was directly challenged by a different sociological type of *flâneur*—working men and women who created their own form of urban spectatorship by forcing the boundaries between different sections of the city into increasing permeability.[5] Likewise, men and women walking the streets of Paris during the interwar years participated as observers and subjects in the spectacles of race and gender present in the streets of their city.[6]

Informants' notes allow us to draw some conclusions with regard to where French men and women might cross paths with their colonial counterparts. These trends are not meant to reflect those of the entire black population of Paris, let alone those of the entire colonial population, but do begin to indicate the types of contacts entered into by individuals whose politics made them worth watching. These encounters were ephemeral but reflected a changing metropolis in which colonialism was an ever-growing presence. Informants recorded home addresses of individuals suspected by the authorities of being dissidents. Overwhelmingly these were members of anti-colonial organizations such as the Ligue de Défense de la Race Nègre (LDRN) or members of an even larger organization, the Union Intercoloniale—an organization placed under the protection of a young French Communist Party (Parti communiste français, PCF), which grouped individuals from all French colonies and had a substantial black membership in the early 1920s (see table 1).

TABLE I. Distribution of Addresses for 86 LDRN and Other Black Colonial Migrants

Arrondissement	1	2	3	4	5*	6*	7*	8*	9	10	11*	12*	13	14*	15*	16	17*	18*	19	20
Total	0	1	3	2	26	8	4	2	1	5	3	2	2	6	4	0	6	7	2	2

*Arrondissements in which interracial couples lived.

Source: All SLOTFOM dossiers relating to Africans and Antilleans in Paris were surveyed for this data. See in particular SLOTFOM II/21, SLOTFOM III/3, SLOTFOM III/24, SLOTFOM III/36, SLOTFOM III/37, SLOTFOM III/71, and SLOTFOM III/73.

Recorded addresses suggest that subversive black men were overwhelmingly located in the Latin Quarter in the fifth arrondissement. More surprising is the fact that only two of the twenty Paris arrondissements, or municipal subdivisions of the city, housed no seditious colonial subjects, the first and the sixteenth (which does not mean that no other Antilleans or Africans lived there), and that so few of these leaders in dissidence lived on the industrial outskirts of Paris that were becoming known as the *banlieue rouge*, or red belt, in reference to the communist and socialist leanings of these largely blue-collar neighborhoods. Of course, some black colonial workers, although overshadowed numerically in the industrial sector by North Africans (Algerians, Moroccans, Tunisians), did live in the *banlieues* of Saint Denis, Bobigny, and Boulogne-Billancourt, which circled Paris to the north, northeast, and south.[7] Overall, these numbers suggest that Parisians in every arrondissement had the opportunity to cross paths with representatives of distant colonies. Furthermore, half of the arrondissements were home to interracial couples, allowing neighbors to witness firsthand love across the color line.

Equally important with regard to understanding the movements of black Parisians and interracial couples were the spaces occupied by black associations in their official and unofficial monthly gatherings (see table 2). Forty black associations, including prominent ones such as the Comité de Défense de la Race Nègre (Committee for the Defense of the *Nègre* Race, CDRN), the aforementioned LDRN, and the Union des Travailleurs Nègres (UTN), held their meetings in every arrondissement but the seventh, twelfth, seventeenth, and nineteenth. The Latin

TABLE 2. Distribution of Addresses for Meeting Places of 40 Black Associations

Arrondissement	1	2	3	4	5	6	7	8	9	10	11	12	13	14	15	16	17	18	19	20
Total	1	2	4	2	15	4	0	1	4	2	2	0	6	3	3	1	0	3	0	3

Source: All SLOTFOM dossiers relating to Africans and Antilleans in Paris were surveyed for this data. See in particular SLOTFOM II/21, SLOTFOM III/3, SLOTFOM III/24, SLOTFOM III/36, SLOTFOM III/37, SLOTFOM III/71, and SLOTFOM III/73.

Quarter was a popular meeting space, especially for socializing after official gatherings, signifying that to a certain extent organizations met near the homes of their core membership. However the distribution of meetings suggests that organizations made an effort to reach members and candidates for membership in every part of Paris, and that as a result Parisians in almost all these spaces witnessed race not only as the occasional passage of a black neighbor, but also as the arrival of thirty to forty black men (and some women) on a monthly basis at meeting halls and cafés. Meetings of the cross-colonial Union Intercoloniale at times gathered over one hundred black colonial migrants, as well as several hundred other colonial men and women. The LDRN's headquarters were in the eighteenth, but their meetings spread to the third, fifth, and twentieth arrondissements. Likewise, the UTN's headquarters were in the third but their official meeting places and favored socializing spaces radiated to the first, third, fourth, fifth, and tenth arrondissements. The Montmartre area on the west side of the eighteenth arrondissement, favored by African Americans and those seeking to experience jazz, was not favored by any of these associations. The LDRN's headquarters were in the eighteenth but remained safely away from exoticism through their location on the east side near the Simplon metro station.

A final element in this racial topography of Paris was the workplace (see table 3). When they were not moving from homes to gatherings, colonial migrants were traveling to and from their workplaces, adding a third dimension to their triangle of weekly traffic. Informants rarely noted specific addresses for workplaces, but the diversity of occupations suggests that whether or not they were moving a great

TABLE 3. Jobs for Antilleans and Africans in Paris

Job sector	Service Industry	Law	Finance	University Studies	Other
	– Shopowners, 3 – Cooks, 2 – Barmen, 2 – Taxi Drivers, 2 – Chauffeurs, 2 – Window Cleaner – Servant – Bottle Washer – Bon Marché Employee – Nurse – Store Employee – Café Worker – Dishwasher – Bouncer	Lawyers, 5	– Accountants, 5 – Insurance, 2 – Banking	Students, 7	– Factory Workers, 2 – Office Workers, 2 – Employee (Gare de Lyon) – Journalist – Retired Sea Captain – Postman – Typographer – Mechanic – Professor – Film Industry
Total=52	20	5	8	7	12

Source: All SLOTFOM dossiers relating to Africans and Antilleans in Paris were surveyed for this data. See in particular SLOTFOM II/21, SLOTFOM III/3, SLOTFOM III/24, SLOTFOM III/36, SLOTFOM III/37, SLOTFOM III/71, and SLOTFOM III/73.

distance in space, these individuals moved in class and were often placed in contact with French men and women through their jobs. Men considered to be dissidents rarely worked in the industrial sector, although they were more likely to be manual laborers than members of the liberal professions. A few were accountants or held desk jobs that would have limited visual contact to their fellow workers. Similarly dishwashers remained out of the public eye in restaurants and hotels, although they encountered the other kitchen staff. However, most of the professions were, in contrast, rather public. Lawyers worked with clients and in court. Chauffeurs and taxi drivers inevitably exchanged words and gazes with their fares. Shop owners or shop employees, for example at Paris's famous Bon Marché department store, were public figures, as was the window cleaner for the luxurious leather shop Lancel. Students came into contact with Parisians and others in their courses, and those who were working to obtain medical degrees as nurses or dentists also had patients. Finally, those who worked as barmen, bouncers, or performers played a highly visible role in Parisian nightlife.

Public Spaces, Private Connections: The Colonial Exposition of 1931

This infusion of colonialism into everyday exchanges was often discussed in conjunction with the highly visible, public, and government-funded Colonial Exposition of 1931. The Colonial Exposition was a recurrent theme in interwar accounts of the changes overtaking Paris, and has provided fascinating material for scholars interested in understanding the links between colony and metropole because the event was an example of colonial myth-making.[8] Like the colonial representations developed by Josephine Baker and others, the exposition was created wholesale—in this case by the French government—for the purpose of consumption by the metropolitan audience. Eighteen different ministries worked on the exposition between 1912 and 1931, and their efforts paid off when, between May 1931 and January 1932, eight million visitors (four million Parisians, three million provincials, and one million foreigners) attended the event.[9]

The 1931 Colonial Exposition was a space ripe in encounters, and many were not officially sanctioned by the government. A number of witnesses attempted to record the broad spectrum of interracial exchanges that radiated beyond the grounds of the exposition; commentators were particularly intrigued by what they believed constituted authentic, artless exchange between the colonies and the metropole. They were fascinated by what happened between those who crossed paths on the streets or in the workplaces of Paris. In 1937 Ousmane Socé published *Mirages de Paris* (Mirages of Paris) with the Nouvelles Editions Latines, a press that boasted authors such as the novelist and dramatist Henri de Montherlant and the prolific novelist Pierre Mac Orlan.[10] Socé was a veterinary student who joined the negritude thinkers Léopold Sédar Senghor, Léon Damas, and Aimé Césaire in founding their most well-known interwar publication, *L'Etudiant Noir* (The Black Student). Socé was engaged in French politics and became a representative of Senegal in the French parliament in 1937, just as his second novel was published. In it he tells the story of Fara, a Senegalese man who from a young age has dreamed of traveling. Armed with a French education obtained in Senegal, Fara gets a chance to travel to the metropole during the Colonial Exposition. Along with twenty other Senegalese men he takes a ship to France to work in Vincennes, where the exposition was constructed. There he meets Jacqueline, a young white *bourgeoise* who falls in love with him. Her family disapproves of Fara's skin color after they discover that he is more than a mere friend. Faced with a terrifying decision, Jacqueline chooses Fara over her family, although no mention is ever made of marriage. She becomes pregnant and gives birth to a *métis* boy before dying from complications of childbirth. Disoriented, Fara hands the child over to Jacqueline's parents and decides to return to Africa.

The tragic storyline conveys a complex critique of the exoticism nourished by such events as the Colonial Exposition and of interracial relationships. The narrator notes that after being seduced by European literature and heroes such as D'Artagnan in Alexandre Dumas' *Three Musketeers*, "a dangerous love of exoticism was taking shape in his child's soul, which was prone to golden illusions."[11] This use of the term exoticism, rather than implying a metropolitan manifestation of colonialism such as that embodied by Baker, suggested a reversal of the usual dynamic in which colonies imposed their seduction upon the metropole. Here the Senegalese child is enticed by visions of France, which he follows upon adulthood into the arms of a white woman. Upon first arriving in Paris, Fara is overwhelmed by the immense number of white men, and for the first time has a strong sense that his identity is determined by his skin color. In contrast, Parisian women emerge as powerfully sensual and yet approachable creatures:

> The dresses and coats shaped them into identical, impeccable Venuses whose very walk was a work of art. They knew how to walk with a spring in their step that let their bust and their head stay immobile with a grace reminiscent of a painting: this one was called "dreamy"; that one "scornful"; that other one "tearful." . . . Brunettes with pale complexions, blonds, autumn-colored; limitless eyes like a dream lost in the skies; black princesses with ginger lips; bodies tall, flexible, and smooth like bamboo!"[12]

Already entranced by the allure of Parisian women, Fara meets Jacqueline during the Expo when he approaches three young women and offers to be their guide. His elegant suit and command of the French language win the confidence of the young women.

Their courtship brings them to exotic venues where races interact daily, including the *bal nègre* at the Cabane Cubaine. The term *bal*, or dance, followed by a descriptive such as *nègre*, *antillais* (Antillean), or *colonial* (colonial) was used to describe a number of popular venues, including clubs such as the Cabane Cubaine, in interwar Paris. This one the narrator describes as "a black ethnographic museum to which every people had sent a specimen" that was an extremely popular nightclub where one could listen to jazz, Antillean music, and so forth.[13] Fara amuses Jacqueline with verbal sketches of the various specimens at this dance hall. After several weeks of separation, he kisses Jacqueline in a moment that hovers amidst violence, theft, and passion. His victory over Jacqueline becomes a momentary one over Paris, a city with which Fara is obsessed and that he embodies in jazz. Not only does the courtship move from one jazz club to another, but Fara's grieving upon Jacqueline's death occurs at a concert by the African American jazz composer and performer Duke Ellington. Even the final sounds luring Fara toward the Seine river are those of a distant tam-tam and guitar. For all its seductive powers, however, Paris lacks authenticity and therefore destabilizes Fara. Indeed this white woman, jazz, and the resulting mirage of Parisian exoticism eventually seduce and undo Fara.

European education presents much fodder for debate in this novel. During Fara's passage from Africa to France, French men note that "you must not awaken [black men] because you would just be molding them into 'dangerous elements' and once they grasp the situation, they will tell us to go to h***!"[14] As the novel progresses, the dangers of education are also debated from the perspective of Africans. While in Paris Fara becomes deeply attached to a community of colonial men from all over Africa. One in particular, a philosopher named Sidia, engages Fara in a bitter debate over the dangers of *métissage*, or mixing. Their definitions of the concept diverge. Sidia with his physical interpretation of the term argues firmly against the idea of bearing a *métis* child who would inevitably return to the white race instead of preserving the strengths of the black one. Thus Sidia accentuates the fears and anxiety that often separated Africans from Antilleans— more likely to have lighter skin—in Paris.

Fara, in contrast, believes that, "if you think about it everything is *métis*; on this earth there exists no pure race, no civilization that is not *métis*. You who are so proud of being one hundred percent black, you are *métis* with your European culture! You had to *métis* yourself intellectually in order to develop your mind."[15] Not only does Fara define *métis* as a pure form of interracial contact that holds a promise of universal hybridity, but he also transforms the term into a verb that gains the active power to alter individuals. After a debate that tests the limits of their friendship both men return to neutral territory, agreeing that African women need more education in order to sustain the interest of their male counterparts. They agree that education thus holds the potential both for an unhealthy seduction by French culture, and for the preservation of the black race against physical *métissage*. The conclusion of the book mirrors this tension. Fara's championing of a universalist *métissage* via interracial interactions appears to be condemned by an author who sacrifices the protagonist to his own philosophy. While Fara's death is not certain, it is a strong possibility since the reader learns on the last page of the novel that "Fara, delirious with joy, plunged into the Seine's cold water, warmed and enchanted by the visions he held in his arms."[16] Adding to this ambivalence is the fact that Fara's *métis* child, named after his friend Sidia, is almost completely absent from the narrative. Whether or not his life in a white home will be a happy one, he appears lost to black culture as Sidia feared. Although obscure in its message, this novel nonetheless provides the reader with a striking description of Paris as a colonial space. Moreover, Fara and Jacqueline's movements amidst white bourgeois households, black salons, jazz clubs, and the exposition expose the obstacles hindering interracial interactions.

The *métissage* tentatively defined by Fara in this novel was expressed from different perspectives by other Parisians who also picked up on how their city was being changed by a merging of cultures and ethnicities in and around the exposition. Géo Baysse's *En dansant la Biguine: souvenir de l'Exposition coloniale* (Dancing the Beguine: Memories of the Colonial Exposition) focused mostly upon the *bals*, or dances, that attracted crowds in several Parisian nightclubs during the exposition. In fact written in 1929, but timed to be published during the exposition, Baysse's work focuses largely upon the Guadeloupean, Martinican, and other women of color who moved with ease around Parisian dance floors. He traces his escapades with Antillean women named Flore and Fernande, who entice him through a number of dance spaces and especially two of the most well-known colonial locales, the Bal Nègre of rue Blomet and the Boule Blanche, which were both hosted and frequented by black migrants. Emphasizing, like Ousmane Socé, the international and interracial atmosphere of these *bals*, Baysse senses the same transformation in Paris that undoes Fara: "I feel as though I were obsessed by this image of a modern Paris. I feel as if our capital is changing from day to day. It makes me wonder."[17]

Baysse closely associates exotic women with jazz in a lighthearted narrative that flirtatiously presents, and does not condemn, a changing and often illusory Paris. His fascination with color reflects that of male journalists pondering Baker, and Baysse both acknowledges the humor of the Parisian fascination with exoticism and replicates it in his descriptions. He caricatures the ineptitude of some white dancers in the jazz age, much as Paul Colin did with his sketches, and seems especially fascinated by the American women who dance with Antillean men, noting: "One has so much fun in Paris that it would be unfortunate to return to the land of prohibition without having tasted all its freedoms."[18] Such portrayals of white women dancing with black men were a consistent theme for writers and caricaturists. Colin repeatedly sketched black men and white women dancing together and the photographer Brassaï, a Hungarian photographer born Gyula Halász who documented Paris at night, took pictures of mixed crowds at the Bal Nègre and the Cabane Cubaine. Although not critical of this nighttime *métissage*, Baysse does challenge what he considers to be artificial behavior, thus replicating themes that carry over both from Socé's novel and from Baker's experiences of Paris. For example, Baysse ridicules Antillean men who dressed in a European style, disapproves of women who powdered their skin in order to lighten it, and pokes fun at a friend who is obsessed with tanning until she can pass for a woman of mixed race while dancing at the *bal colonial*.[19] No one escapes his amused scrutiny, which provides an interesting commentary on contemporary social mores. The exotic decors that have overwhelmed Paris are a direct result, Baysse concludes, of the fact that "all the prejudices you [the reader] had concerning the black element have slowly disappeared."[20] Dubious as such a statement appears, it accurately reflects one strand of the contemporaneous debate by putting forth both one argument for, and one repercussion of, the dissemination of black culture in and around the Colonial Exposition.

Baysse's text was not alone in detailing the fascination with colonial *bals* and the emergent contrast of various shades of black and white in Paris. The prolific academic and writer Jean Camp and his coauthor André Corbier were glib in their portrayal of colonial men who defied Parisian expectations in *A Lyauteyville, Promenade humoristique et sentimentale à travers l'Exposition Coloniale* (In Lyauteyville, a Sentimental and Humorous Stroll through the Colonial Exposition). In front of the Greenland exhibit, one of the authors asks a black man in *petit nègre* (a bastardized French commonly taught to *tirailleurs* with the understanding that they were unable to learn standard French): "Ti vouloir connaître neige, brrr . . . hiver li dents qui font ta, ta, ta . . . ?" which roughly translates as "You want meet snow, brrr . . . winter teeth go ta, ta, ta, ta . . . ?" To his great embarrassment, the supposed savage is a *licencié ès lettres* (arts graduate) who speaks perfect French, has been hired to work in the exposition, and who while not overjoyed by the idea of cold weather making his teeth chatter, is far less pleased with fitting the author's preconceptions of the *nègre* as savage.[21] After presenting a number of such pastiches the narrator concludes that Parisians should be careful: "the Colonies will want to take their revenge. Soon you will see each of them announce, with posters, an INTERNATIONAL PARISIAN EXPOSITION."[22] Like Ousmane Socé's presentation of a protagonist who falls under Paris's spell, Camp and Corbier's text is—occasionally—a perceptive commentary on interwar disruptions of the boundaries traditionally maintained between colonies and metropole. Exchanges between the races not only created but also broke down stereotypes that distance from the colonies might otherwise have maintained.

"It's with one's hair, after all, that one plays music"

Baysse, Camp, and Corbier were joined in their comments on how race changed Parisian spaces and attitudes by an impressive array of intellectuals, both black and white, who often debated and discussed exoticism through an analysis of the artistic merits of jazz and Antillean music such as the beguine—a rumba-like dance for couples. By the late 1920s possibly the most high-profile arenas for contact between Europeans and colonials were jazz clubs and nightclubs. They were interpreted as just such a space as early as 1921 when one of the first Parisian jazz clubs, *Le Boeuf sur le toit*, drew the postwar avant-garde surrealists through its doors. From then on, these intellectuals and artists were especially avid participants in the racial exchanges made possible by jazz. They were particularly intrigued by how the music created venues, and more generally set the tone, for the widespread and popular injection of non-European artifacts, images, and cultures into Paris. Musicians, too, were naturally drawn into conversations about the place of race and jazz in interwar Paris. Both the avant-garde and musicians recognized the manner in which jazz, like Baker in some ways, could set the tone for a more general dialogue about the impact of the growing black presence in the metropolis. Opinions and analyses were freely offered, often inconsistent (even on an individual level), and inconclusive, but then, that very lack of definition was what first attracted many surrealists and musicians to these colonial and African American art forms.

In the words of the art collector Paul Guillaume, the avant-garde viewed black culture as "the most satisfying indicator of the great contemporary anxiety."[23] Exploring remedies for the great economic and political malaise of the early 1930s, and in reaction to the devastating and inhumane technological modernism precipitated by World War I, the surrealists had a more complex encounter with black artistic movements than many other sections of white French society. They expressed their interests in part through collecting, an inclination shared by many surrealists.[24] This practice both responded and contributed to the presence of black culture in Paris. Surrealists perceived that Paris was being changed by the authenticity of black culture and hoped to foster this transformation. They were drawn visually and acoustically to jazz clubs and more generally to all things African and Caribbean. Even though surrealists were a far from uniform group, they maintained a consistent interest in black cultures.

Of course some surrealists were fascinated by jazz and Josephine Baker only in rapidly passing, fetishistic phases. Yet a fair number were far more systematic in their investigations of African art. Nancy Cunard, an English editor and writer who published a number of texts about black culture and by black writers in her Paris-based My Hours Press, wrote in her memoirs of the links between the surrealist penchant for collecting and ethnography: "Ethnography, the study of sculpture, carving, and other handmade objects once thought of as the work of mere 'savages' from ancient Africa, Oceania, and of the Indians of both the Americas, were greatly admired and prized, and several of the surrealists eventually became expert ethnographers from their sheer love of such things."[25]

Cunard accurately reflects how some surrealists, including the ethnographers Marcel Griaule, Michel Leiris, and André Schaeffner (who was also a musicologist), maintained their interest in black culture through scientific means. They were amongst those who organized the Mission Dakar-Djibouti, which traveled from Senegal in West Africa all the way to Ethiopia in the east, collecting objects, taking photographs, and filming those they encountered. Griaule argued that, "because of the increasingly close contacts being established between Europeans and *indigènes*, ethnographic studies and collecting are becoming more and more pressing."[26] Even for a two-year expedition across Africa, Paris's fascination with black culture turned out to be relevant. On April 15, 1931, a boxing gala to raise money for the expedition showcased the black boxer Al Brown confronting the white Roger Simendé. It was organized by museologist Georges-Henri Rivière and attended by the likes of ethnographer Paul Rivet (who founded the Musée de l'Homme), writer Jean Cocteau, arts patron Viscount de Noailles, sociologist Marcel Mauss, and, of course, Griaule and Leiris themselves. The event underscored how important original items, including men and women such as Baker, the boxers, and the musicians, were to surrealists who saw reproductions (whether recorded, filmed, or otherwise fabricated) as lacking the authenticity and dreams of evasion that black culture and artists evoked.

The organizers of the Mission Dakar-Djibouti identified jazz clubs as one of the locales for genuine contact in the metropole. For example Leiris, who was also a writer, in his 1939 autobiographical narrative translated into English in 1963 as *Manhood* evoked jazz as:

a rallying sign, an orgiastic banner, currently fashionable. It had a magical influence, which can be likened to a possession. It was the best element to give true meaning to these *fêtes*, a religious meaning, with communion through dance, latent or manifest eroticism and drink—the most effective means to bridge the gap which separates one individual from another in any type of gathering. Brewed in violent, warm gusts of wind from the tropics, jazz tasted enough like a doomed civilization, like humanity subjugated by the machine, to express as completely as is ever possible the state of mind of at least some of us . . . First revelation of the *nègres*, of a colored myth of Eden which would draw me to Africa, and beyond Africa, to ethnography.[27]

Leiris's jazz was an exotic vision of the tropics, a cocktail inebriating the senses with the taste of jungles and deserts, but one which led him to the pursuit of ethnography much as Baker led Colin in a critical direction. His appreciation of jazz on both an exotic and an intellectual level was typical of the surrealists, who sought to challenge others by collecting provocative objects even while pursuing a clinical, scientific attitude that manifested itself in academic treatises of jazz as both a music and a culture.

One place that surrealists added jazz to their collections was in *Documents*, a publication edited by writer and intellectual Georges Bataille and including contributions by Leiris, which was filled with ethnographic and archaeological features as well as art and music criticism. *Documents* presented music as an item alongside objects such as African artifacts. Haphazardly, in true surrealist form, these arts were freely associated to constitute representations of a multidimensional black civilization. There was no one theme to the surrealist discussion of jazz; it was part of an eclectic hodgepodge on display. Like Leiris, the contributor André Schaeffner had a true passion for jazz. An ethnographer and a musicologist who worked at the Musée de l'Homme, an ethnographic museum where many African artifacts were displayed once it opened in 1937, he co-wrote with André Cœuroy what was possibly the first ethnographic study of jazz, very simply entitled *Le Jazz*. With chapters such as "Rhythm among the *nègres*," Schaeffner and Cœuroy traced the music from Africa to the United States and into the work of French contemporaries such as composer and teacher Darius Milhaud and composer and pianist Maurice Ravel.[28] Schaeffner's acknowledgement of jazz's impact on contemporary French composers was significant. His recognition of jazz's roots led to a widespread acceptance of its origins as early as the 1930s. For example, writing for the bilingual (French-English), Paris-based African and Antillean publication *La Revue du Monde Noir* (The Review of the Black World) in 1932, Gisèle Dubouillé echoed Schaeffner's analysis on jazz. Indeed she addressed its implications for the dance halls of Paris when she stated: "The music of modern dance—from tango to rag-time, and without forgetting the beguine and the blues—is indisputably of African inspiration."[29] Schaeffner's ideas in retrospect may appear self-evident, but they were incisive and provocative in his day. Not surprisingly, Schaeffner wrote a number of articles on jazz for *Documents*.

Writings such as Schaeffner's allowed surrealists to complicate the usual exotic refrain. They were interested in jazz from both artistic and scientific perspectives. Surrealists, more explicitly than any other interwar group, unearthed elements of modernism within the so-called primitivism of jazz and hoped that such art forms would regenerate the artistic, cultural, and political scene. The point is that as contemporaries they shared Socé's character Fara's understanding of the term *métis*, for they revealed jazz in Paris as a racial hybrid of African American music and Caribbean and African cultures, and thus as a vehicle not only for the fetishism of the French, but more importantly for counterpolitics of various origins.

The daily disarray that they believed embodied jazz inspired surrealists to place ethnographic commentary and anecdotes side by side in venues such as *Documents*. The power of jazz lay in its ability, somewhat like Baker herself, to penetrate high and low culture and spread quickly, thanks to the technology of phonographs and film. In this manner, it landed simultaneously in the consciousness of the general public and the intellectual musings of surrealists, both of whom had difficulty defining the term. Before writing their work *Le Jazz*, Schaeffner and Cœuroy submitted a questionnaire to contemporary musicians, artists, and writers, many of whom were not surrealists, with questions such as: what is jazz music; does it have an influence upon modern concepts of aesthetics; and will an original and independent form of jazz come into existence? In June 1925, they published the results in the newspaper *Paris-Midi*, which interested stockholders and racegoers but also included gossip items and information about shows. Most who answered the questionnaire reacted positively, accepting jazz as an independent form of music, but when pressed, they had trouble defining it.[30] That lack of definition was one reason the surrealists latched onto jazz in their critique of contemporary society. This vagueness also reflected, however, the multiple roles played by jazz and the spaces in which jazz was performed.

Indubitably, contacts with another race were an essential component of the surrealist vision for transforming Paris in the post–World War I era. Cultural exchanges among the public and the performers in jazz clubs suggest that one determining factor of French identity during the interwar years was racial interaction in a specifically urban and gendered context. Scholars have noted, just as contemporaries did in the 1920s, the extreme difficulty of finding any precise definition of the term jazz, especially since both in their musical and cultural forms the meanings of the word constantly shifted.[31] Jazz came to represent a number of themes of modern Parisian life, including the influence of foreigners, mobility, and continuing change in an urban setting.[32] All these occurrences were essential to the French understanding of their identity past, but especially future, in the twentieth century. The Parisian equation of jazz with black culture was one aspect of this redefinition of French identity.

In 1934 the jazz critic and aficionado Hughes Panassié wrote *Le Jazz hot* (Hot Jazz), a work that echoed Schaeffner's in pursuing scholarly precision in its definitions of jazz. Race played an important role in this work, creeping into his discussion of leading musicians. Panassié subdivided chapters on these skilled performers of various instruments into sections on white and sections on black musicians. He felt that the styles of these musicians differed according to race, and concluded that the black brass musicians playing in America or visiting France were unsurpassed.[33] As a result of such comments, even prominent white French musicians such as trombonist Léo Vauchant and violinist Stéphane Grappelli felt relegated to the back of a jazz scene that was dominated by expatriate African Americans.

Aware that they were being dominated visually, and thus acoustically, some French musicians explained the phenomenon with racialist or racist comments that occasionally took the form of labor disputes. The publication *Revue Jazz-Tango* (for a while also called the *Revue Jazz-Tango-Dancing*), first presented itself in October 1930 as a "monthly review of dance music and orchestras." With articles by critics such as Panassié, the publication lasted through 1936 promoting—as its editors announced in the first number—young French talent and a specifically French jazz. The endorsement was a cultural one reinforced by two laws that regulated the presence of foreigners in Parisian nightlife. The laws of August 11, 1926, and August 10, 1932—intended to protect French workers—stated that only ten percent of the musicians hired by hotels, cafés, restaurants, and *bals* or dance halls in the Paris region could be foreigners.[34] Unfortunately for French musicians, audiences disagreed with lawmakers, as the writers of *Jazz-Tango* continually noted. In November 1930, one article sarcastically stated: "One needs above all one thing, to be successful in Jazz: lovely, black and frizzy hair . . . I maintain that it's with one's hair, after all, that one plays music."[35] The pianist Stéphane Mougin agreed with these statements in his own diatribe, writing: "Under the aegis of this quadroon, approximately a hundred picaninnies without any precise mother tongue are taking all the best spots, which talented musicians would have at their disposal if they did not have the misfortune of being white."[36] Driven by monetary concerns and pride both nationalistic and musical, but largely steering away from personal animosity toward black jazz musicians (possibly because they needed to work with them), these Frenchmen seemed skeptical of the interracial connections and cultural rejuvenation celebrated by surrealists.[37]

Intriguingly, even black musicians agreed with the gist of their detractors' statements. The black African American boxer Gene Bullard, for example, decided to take up the drums between fights in order to make a little more money. "I think I was rotten," he later wrote, "but it seemed every dancing place wanted a colored jazz drummer, and they had auditioned me before hiring me, so what could I lose?"[38] Such examples of blacks—whether American, African, or Antillean— turning to jazz or working in venues that presented the music in order to earn a living were not unusual. Consider Corporal Rakoto working as a jazz musician when he realized that his politics could not feed his family.[39] The situation was unsettling for white musicians, who in the paradoxical extreme were forced to "black up" in order to fit in with the musical scene. Such was the case for pianist Alain Romans, the only white musician to play under the American drummer Benny Peyton at the Casino de la Forêt in the early 1920s.[40] Only if he painted his face was the owner willing to give Romans the opportunity to showcase his talent. Such stories reflect the complex implications of cross-cultural contacts. So does the fact that even while some musicians critiqued the ramifications of the visual grip in which blacks held many Parisians, both black and white musicians contributed to creating the very atmosphere—in clubs, on the radio, and via phonograph records—that invited interracial contacts.

Dancing the Beguine

Commentaries on Parisian nightlife, and on how jazz or beguine transformed sensory experiences in these settings, were not limited to white men, be they journalists, authors, surrealists, or jazz musicians. Antilleans, for example, also responded to the growing popularity of black music in Paris, remarking first upon its impact and then upon its implications both in and beyond the dance halls. The beguine musician Ernest Léardée came from Martinique to France just as the jazz craze hit, and profited from the extent to which jazz was, for many nonspecialists, an ill-defined musical form, but one that thereby benefited numerous members of the black community. He owed his initial success in Paris to a *bal antillais* (Antillean dance hall) located at la Glacière, an industrial and working class neighborhood of the thirteenth arrondissement. Parisians' desire to participate in this cultural demonstration was frustrated by the requirement to present a colonial passport at the door before being allowed to enter. By choosing to exclude those who were not guests of colonial men and women, this *bal* was atypical, creating a space that was unique through its removal from the general fervor for black culture.

The Antillean intellectual Paulette Nardal provided a tantalizing description of this *bal nègre* in the Franco-Antillean newspaper *La Dépêche Africaine*. Visitors crossed a large courtyard with several chestnut trees. After buying tickets, they entered a long room that doubled as a coatroom and a buffet area where drinks and sandwiches were sold. Nardal was impressed by the authenticity projected by the décor of the dance hall: "In this setting, *noirs* feel at home. No shocking contrast, as in other dance halls, between them and a violently European setting. Nothing in this room reminded them of France, with the exception of a few Parisians, lost in the crowd of peoples of color."[41] In her account Nardal included, much like Ousmane Socé in *Mirages de Paris*, a type-specific description of various shades of black, complete with the racial terminology of the day: "in this room the artist might detect the entire palette that makes the black complexion so difficult to reproduce. It runs from the carnation white of the *mulâtresse* with flat hair; to the matte black of the *négresse* with the abundant and perfectly curled hair; without omitting the harsh blond of the *chabine*; the cinnamon-colored brunette; all the rich nuances of precious woods and the *capresse* color of sapodilla." Nardal compared the conductor to a jazz-band leader, but focused upon harmony and fluidity to differentiate the dancers from their jazz counterparts—a defense of her national music's particularities, which was a theme in both her and her sisters' writings. Nardal concluded that by the time the lights started flashing at 12:30 a.m. to signify closing time, all classes had been united in their search for authenticity.

This protected enclosure did not last, for Léardée became so popular that within two years he bought his own nightclub: the Bal Nègre at 33 rue Blomet. Here Nardal's tones of black were abruptly lightened as all of Paris came to dance at a *bal colonial* in which musicians played to a full house four times a week. The *bal nègre* became a pole of attraction, Léardée would later write, for "it had become fashionable to go dance *chez les Noirs* . . . in this unusual space where all races and all nationalities mixed."[42] One of Brassaï's photographs, taken at the Cabane Cubaine, reveals the sociopolitical ramifications of such colonial settings (see fig. 3). It illustrates the potential for conversations, dancing, friendship, or love but it also calls attention to one woman who—staring unsmiling at the photographer—appears both taken aback by and cognizant of the spectacle implicit in such a popular venue.

Léardée's dancing arena became especially popular around the time of the Colonial Exposition of 1931, when "you will find there every race, black, yellow, white."[43] Léardée suggested that the black element dominated in his club, but Ousmane Socé's descriptions of such

3. Brassaï (Gyula Halász, 1899–1984). "At the Cabane Cubaine, Montmartre." Circa 1932. Photo Michèle Bellot. Private Collection. © Estate Brassaï-RMN. Réunion des Musées Nationaux/Art Resource, New York.

dance halls depicted them as swamped by the white element.[44] The *bal colonial* was in Léardée's words a "ritualistic ceremony in which all peoples are united in the same passion for rhythm of dance."[45] Socé agreed: "Frenchmen, Americans, Germans, and Englishmen were all subjected to the tyranny of rhythm; the orchestra kneaded them as it pleased, in turn quivering, bitter, or drunk with happiness!"[46] Léardée attributed the popularity of his *bal* not only to the Colonial Exposition but also to its discovery by the surrealists and artists including author André Gide, writer and diplomat Paul Morand, Bulgarian painter Jules Pascin, American photographer Man Ray, and Polish painter Moise Kisling.

Yet Léardée was a bit worried about the press's willingness to associate his club with imaginary and exalted descriptions of the beauty and sensuality of Antillean women much like those of Baysse. Even Paulette Nardal was caught up in such descriptions before she realized the full impact Paris would have upon women of color. While she would later lament the exoticism forced upon them, in her description of the *bal nègre* at la Glacière Nardal provided lavish portrayals of female dancers including one "with red-brown tones that you sensed must be soft to the touch like silk."[47] Perhaps the extent to which the beguine would be distorted and eroticized by the French press was not yet clear in 1929, but merely two years later another Nardal sister, Andrée, contended in an "Etude sur la Biguine Créole" (Notes on the Biguine créole) for the French-English bilingual literary and cultural publication *La Revue du Monde Noir* that, "in the true beguine the dancers do not embrace. They mime the eternal pursuit of woman by man."[48] Andrée and her sisters felt themselves forced to defend the beguine as a respectable dance, and they had good reason to do so. A 1932 article in *Jazz-Tango* stated that the beguine had become "an excuse for the rubbing of genitalia and swaying that one would do well to leave to the talent of Josephine Baker and that would never be respectably exhibited in a . . . respectable establishment."[49] Even the feminist newspaper *La Française* entered the fray, mentioning a *bal nègre* at the Théâtre des Champs-Elysées where white women appeared to be objects of ridicule on the dance floor next to the graceful performances of their black counterparts.[50]

Technical definitions and differentiations offered by Paulette and Andrée Nardal were intended to educate a Parisian audience that was largely unaware of the general *métissage* of overseas music. Léardée remarked that all forms of exotic music including Caribbean, Cuban, South-American, and jazz were recklessly mixed in havens for black culture.[51] For many Parisians the American Charleston and the Antillean beguine were just two facets of the same jazz. Moreover the multicultural arena of *bals* suffered from being portrayed with a dark side. In *Mirages de Paris* Socé's descriptions made Paulette Nardal's seem tame. One dancer, Ketty, created "the cyclonal universe in which the voluptuousness of her honey skin spun and in which— by dint of wishing to follow the rhythm—the galloping desire of men was lost."[52] Some surrealists aimed to provoke with their explorations of fetishes and sexuality in their magazine *Documents*. In some ways they were not necessarily more inflammatory than mainstream print matter. The danger of the *bals* lay, several of the latter texts suggested, in their interracial nature. In such a highly charged milieu, scandal was expected and sought after.

A number of incidents noted in police informants' reports seemed to indicate that relationships pursued from the *bal* to the private sphere or vice versa were doomed to spectacular failure. The African store assistant Diallo B. met a Frenchwoman named Eugènie C. at the Bal Nègre of the rue Blomet in March 1931.[53] They rapidly became lovers, and seemed quite happy even after Diallo started requesting money from his mistress. The affair ended dramatically when Eugènie turned up to visit her lover after one of his prolonged absences, only to find him in bed with another woman.[54] In another incident Gottfried C. from Cameroon caused some scandal at Léardée's *bal* when he arrived with a woman who decided she would rather dance with someone else. Gottfried objected and fought violently with his date. Eventually he slapped her, to the consternation of witnesses.[55]

Gottfried's outbreak was tame, however, compared to one that propelled Léardée's *bal* onto the cover of an issue of *Détective*, a magazine that emphasized the dark underworld of urban life via detectivelike investigations.[56] *Détective* underlined the *bal*'s seedy reputation with the headline "From the *bal nègre* to court," which went on to tell the lurid details of a fight that ended in violence and centered around interracial competition for one dance partner.[57] The event occurred on December 16, 1928, when a Frenchwoman, Jane Weiler, shot her (French and white) husband, Robert. Whatever Jane Weiler's motivation, *Détective* in its scandal-driven recounting focused on an Antillean woman referred to as "la Martiniquaise" who allegedly seduced Robert with her dancing, and perhaps turned her charms upon Jane as well.[58]

All Antillean women were easily endowed with Josephine Baker's swinging hips and an anonymous Martinican woman's deadly seduction. As a result, a third Nardal sister's critique of "Exotic Puppets" in *La Dépêche Africaine* was a necessary indictment of the excessive exoticization of women simply based on their color. Jane Nardal's 1928 diatribe designated Baker's arrival as the turning point for black women: "Here it is that a woman of color leaps onto the stage, with lacquered hair and a sparkling smile; she may still be wearing plumes or banana leaves, but she introduces Parisians to the latest Broadway goods (Charleston, jazz, etc.). The transition from past to present, the welding of virgin forest and modernism, is what black Americans have accomplished and rendered tangible."[59] Avant-garde artists drank up such images, tantalized by the modernity in which black women were packaged by concert halls, music halls, and phonographs recordings. Jane Nardal showed vivid insight into the colonialism of spectatorship in Paris, emphasizing the tension that existed between modern and primitive and the dangers, for the exoticized one, implicit in negrophilia. She identified an aesthetic categorization imposed upon some blacks, one in which the visual impact of their skin, while granting them easy success in Paris, distracted onlookers from the incisiveness of their minds. Her article was legitimate self-defense against the onslaught of exoticism and the notoriety of the black woman in the context of jazz, beguine, and dancing. Indeed, even black contemporaries had a tendency to overemphasize the seductive beauty of Antillean women. When in his memoirs Sablé wrote of Jane that she "amazed the boulevard" and was like "a heroine of 'La Garçonne,'" and of Andrée that she was an "exotic beauty" with a "voluptuous body," he was certainly contributing to their exoticization. Even if Paulette's description as being of "medium build, knows how to carry herself, black, fine face radiating intelligence, holds a literary salon" was far tamer, the overall implications of such descriptions were that these women were on display in Paris.[60]

As a contemporary and herself an object of exoticism, Jane Nardal shrewdly perceived a mechanization of black women within the *bal*'s context. Metropolitans did not, however, merely attend Léardée's *bal* in order to observe colonial men and women on display.[61] Although fictional, Ousmane Socé's storyline suggests that these *bals* were also places where interracial relationships such as that of Fara and Jacqueline developed. Diallo B. and Eugènie C. pursued their affair from the *bal* to the bed. The *bals* were one of the most prominent arenas in which both contemporaries and historians could and can witness and record occasionally spectacular displays of love that ignored the color line. There are indications, however, that interracial exchanges were unavoidable in more tame Parisian spaces as well, and that alongside dramatic examples of failure such as those cited above, relationships often succeeded.

Bringing Colonialism Home

When they were not at nightclubs in and around Montmartre and when they were not involved in political work, how much, and to what extent, did black and white Parisians come into contact, and what impact did the black colonial presence have upon the metropolis? With the passing of time the tracing of interracial contacts and relationships is a difficult task. However, references in police documents and novels help fill a void in our reading of this period. Antilleans and Africans deemed worthy of surveillance worked, relaxed, and entered into private relationships with partners. Thus, they can be followed not only through the streets and nightclubs of Paris, but into a far more personal range of encounters with Parisians.

Recently scholars have developed a growing interest in exploring sexual and/or marital relations between blacks and whites in France.[62] World War I, with its massive importation of colonial soldiers and workers, allowed a sudden intensification of contacts between colonized men and Frenchwomen. These ran the gamut from glances exchanged on streets to intimate relationships.[63] The latter were controversial encounters, attacked by French men including colonial authorities, and help to explain why the nonwhite labor force was not renewed in the interwar era. Still, even taking such protest into account, relationships rendered difficult or impossible by the morals and habits in the colonies could occur in Paris. Thus in a 1936 article devoted to the question of love in the Caribbean, author and journalist Blanche Vogt noted that while nature occasionally triumphed over racism in matters of love, within the Antillean context "it is impossible for a black man, even rich, even cultivated, to become engaged to a young white girl. Of course, there are typically French unions in which the husband is black, and the wife is white; but these weddings

TABLE 4. Anti-Imperialist Men's Relationships

	Malagasies	West Africans & Antilleans	Totals
MEN'S MARITAL STATUS KNOWN	27	25	52
Married	11	18	29
Partnered (domestic)	12	1	13
Single	6	6	12
WOMEN'S ORIGIN			
White French	20	11	31
European, black, or unspecified	3	8	11
CHILDREN			
Métis	11	5	16
Unspecified	3	2	5

Note: Of the 27 Malagasies, 2 were involved in two relationships each. Thus there is information for 29 (11 marriages, 12 domestic arrangements, and 6 singles, equals 29, not 27).

Source: All SLOTFOM dossiers relating to Africans and Antilleans in Paris were surveyed for this data. See in particular SLOTFOM II/21, SLOTFOM III/3, SLOTFOM III/24, SLOTFOM III/36, SLOTFOM III/37, SLOTFOM III/71, and SLOTFOM III/73.

take place in the Metropole."[64] The ultimate fear was not the links between colonized men and Frenchwomen in France, but a reversal of the colonial order of things overseas if European women were allowed to become objects of desire for colonial men.[65]

Informants such as Agent Joé almost always noted the marital status of African and Antillean men, and the partner's race. They were also careful to write down any potentially immoral parameters of the relationships. As a result of such notes, we can trace trends during the 1920s and early 1930s amongst fifty-two men who were deemed politically subversive by Parisian informants. Twenty-five of the individuals traced were from the Antilles and French West Africa, including anti-imperialist leaders such as Lamine Senghor and Tiémoko Garan Kouyaté. Only eight were specifically designated as being of French nationality; six were war veterans. Of twenty-seven Malagasy men, only three were identified as French, although eighteen had fought in World War I.

Nineteen of the twenty-five Antilleans and Africans were recorded as being involved with women (see table 4). The others were single. Eleven were specifically designated as being involved with Frenchwomen and three with European women of undefined origin. In contrast only two partners were noted as being women of color; no information was given for the other partnerships and marriages. Finally, of seven children noted, five were *métis*, making Ousmane Socé's novel pertinent in the context of black Paris.

Numbers were slightly different for the Malagasy population. A total of twenty men out of the twenty-seven for whom we have information regarding their relationships with women were involved with French ones (in some cases more than one). Eleven relationships were marriages and twelve were relatively permanent domestic living arrangements described in French as *concubinage*. Once again an overwhelming number of the children listed were *métis*, in this case eleven of the fourteen children noted as being born of these relationships. While for the Antillean–West African population four of the six men who fought in the Great War were involved with white women, thirteen of the eighteen Malagasies who fought were involved with

Frenchwomen. The fact that twenty Malagasies were involved with Frenchwomen compared to only eleven Africans and Antilleans may be explained in part by age. Several Antilleans and West Africans listed were substantially younger than the Malagasy veterans (Kouyaté, for example, was only twenty-four at the time this information was noted); the difference in age might account for the difference in marital status. Unfortunately, the archives do not make it easy to consistently compare data over the span of the interwar years. The late 1930s might have shown very different data for the Antilleans and Africans, whose growing maturity and length of stay in France may have led them increasingly toward Frenchwomen.

Interracial relationships could be attractive for a number of reasons. In part, there simply were not many black women in Paris. Some of the veterans and political activists who felt France owed them a blood debt were undoubtedly intrigued by settling that debt through Frenchwomen, although such relationships were most likely sustainable only for the short term. To a certain extent, the attraction of Frenchwomen may have been practical; Corporal Rakoto's impregnation of a Frenchwoman could have been, as put forth by Agent Joé, purely a calculated strategy to help him remain in France once his military service ended.[66] Agents' comments nonetheless reveal that many of these relationships were solid ones: according to them only five relationships ended in separation. The higher level of education of Frenchwomen compared to African women may have been yet another factor, as suggested by Ousmane Socé in his novel. In his memoirs Victor Sablé also commented upon education, noting that "many young men, their studies over, returned to their homes after having married a blond-haired, blue-eyed girl. Then families felt frustrated: the sons married on the continent, while the [Antillean] girls, who had stayed behind, beautiful and well educated, were having trouble enduring the chastity imposed by celibacy."[67] In this case, in contrast to Ousmane Socé's Sidia and Fara in the African context, Sablé contends that Antillean women were educated but that they were simply too far away to distract their male counterparts from metropolitan trysts with Frenchwomen. Sablé nonetheless concluded that "in the island mentality, sexuality and patriotism were indissoluble" just as Sidia intimated that for anyone of the black race, sexuality and patriotism should be inseparable.[68] For the most part we still have much to learn about the reasons for these unions. Fittingly, the unpredictable and private nature of passion and love masks the full range of emotions and justifications motivating such interactions.

When police spies passed along details, they were not simply recording information. They also infused their perspectives into these reports, and at times even appeared intent on alleviating either their boredom or that of their readers with juicy tidbits and stories of relationship failures. One report stated that the Malagasy Clément R. lived with a twenty-three- or twenty-four-year-old Frenchwoman in all likelihood named Yvette D. Yvette was suspected of being a woman of rather loose morals who would go out alone to haunt the cafés of Montparnasse while her partner was at work.[69] Another agent explained that Maria H., born in Switzerland, was first engaged to the Cameroonian Henri P. and then promised an engagement by his friend Laurent K., also Cameroonian. She paid the debts of both men but married neither.[70] Probably Maria was lucky, or clear-sighted, for after Laurent begged over 1,800 francs from Maria in order to pay various debts, he married Marie L., a thirty-five-year-old employee of the renowned department store Galéries Lafayette. Marie L. was exploited financially by Laurent, who had no specific profession but instead drifted from waiter to chauffeur to barman. In another such *report*, the Malagasy Daniel R., who at one point worked for a shoe factory, married a Frenchwoman with whom he had two daughters before abruptly abandoning them in Toulon and decamping for Paris, where he took a Malagasy *métis* mistress. His French wife traveled all the way to Paris to see her husband only, in the illustrative words of Agent Joé, to be "kicked out like a dog."[71]

Those commenting upon interracial Paris outdid one another to tell such stories. Agent Désiré spoke with disgust of the Frenchman Jean R. and in particular his wife Madame R., also white, who was openly prostituting not only herself but their eighteen-year-old daughter as well. Most of their customers were black men from French West Africa.[72] Agent Joé related an even more sensational story in which a Malagasy junior officer caused substantial drama. He became the lover of the white wife of a wounded French war veteran and "kidnapped" the woman (apparently with her consent) for three days.[73] The musician Ernest Léardée recounted in his biography an invitation to a peculiar soirée that turned out to be a high society gathering of nudists where his dark body was the star attraction for the Frenchwomen (and apparently for a number of the men as well).[74] Finally, Agent Joé noted that bad blood reigned amidst Malagasy artists at the Colonial Exposition because Frenchwomen kept company with some but not all of the fifty-four men who worked there (they were accompanied by only eight Malagasy women).[75]

Stories such as these stand apart from the household squabbles and partner swapping generally delineated by agents, for they symbolized the postwar reversal of the colonial order of things. Whether or not the Jean R. women were engaged in systematic procuring and prostitution, as opposed to occasional flirtation and duplicity, the possibility of white women prostituting themselves to black men placed both groups outside the usual power dynamics. West Africans could envision both mother and daughter R. purely as objects of desire, without the respect expected within a marriage or civil union. Likewise the kidnapping of the Frenchwoman by the Malagasy, even if it was not a kidnapping but rather a consensual tryst, embodied the fears of emasculation that haunted metropolitan soldiers returning from the front. Such extreme representations of both racial and sexual societal destabilization during the interwar years did not necessarily reflect the norm of interracial sexual and emotional relationships, just as the exoticism prevailing in nightclubs was not necessarily the dominant or sole characteristic of interracial contacts. However, serene relationships were less likely to be recorded or commented upon than unstable ones. Agents rarely reflected upon the consequences of balanced and healthy interactions, nor would there have been much reason for their superiors to call upon them to do so.

Thus one type of interracial contact that was rarely mentioned by contemporaries was friendship. Their lack of potential for disruption of sexual norms meant that friendships were unlikely to make it into police spies' reports. Instead, newspapers and novels mentioned such contacts. For instance, the French author and journalist Louise Faure-

Favier earned much praise in the black press for one such portrayal of a budding interracial friendship. She wrote a novel that stands apart from those of most of her contemporaries because it depicts a refined and educated black man. While the novel has one essential premise of a sexual relationship between a Frenchwoman and an African man, it can also be viewed as a commentary from a uniquely feminine perspective not on love across the color line, but upon friendship between two races.

Louise Faure-Favier was known in the French press as a woman of extraordinary talent. As a journalist and aviator she broke a number of barriers professionally. She also endeared herself to an exceptionally diverse crowd: from feminists to surrealists to black men. Not much is known about Faure-Favier's life. She was born Jeanne Lucie Augustine Claudia Faure-Favier in 1870, but wrote under the name Louise Faure-Favier until her death in 1961. She was considered by some the first Frenchwoman to become a professional journalist.[76] Her primary focus in journalism and her passion in life was aviation. She traveled on the first civil airplane during its first flight and inaugurated several other civil airlines. She wrote the first official French guides on aerial tourism, as well as the first French novel on civil aviation. Her articles likewise detailed her adventures in flight. In June 1922 she published an article in the high-circulation, internationally respected magazine L'Illustration about the first commercial night flight from Paris to London and back, which she flew along with eight men. Her fascination with this technology prompted Faure-Favier to participate in the first live radio report from an airplane flying over Paris. Speaking to an interviewer sitting in the Eiffel Tower, she described the joys of aerial tourism and the beauties of an illuminated capital by night. Eventually she flew to Africa, an adventure recorded by the pilot and politician Lucien Bossoutrot in La Belle aventure du Goliath de Paris à Dakar (The Goliath's Lovely Adventure from Paris to Dakar) and prefaced by Faure-Favier.[77]

Faure-Favier's fascination with the technology of aviation was not unique. The avant-garde also repeatedly demonstrated a grudging admiration for modern innovations, fearing on the one hand their abuse in warfare, and admiring on the other their impact upon society. In

1945 Faure-Favier published her memories of Guillaume Apollinaire, the soldier-poet killed by influenza in 1919 after he survived several World War I injuries, including one that left him with a star-shaped wound on his forehead.[78] Amongst numerous other intellectual and artistic accomplishments, Apollinaire coined the term "surrealism," thereby crystallizing with his terminology the postwar avant-garde artists' movement. He used to visit Faure-Favier in her Parisian apartment, and was joined there by artists such as the writers André Billy and René Dalize and the painter and printmaker Marie Laurencin.[79] Faure-Favier's interest in interracial relationships stemmed from both her contact with the avant-garde and her travels to Africa. Thus the two topics that shaped Faure-Favier's 1928 novel, *Blanche et Noir* (White and Black)—race relations and woman's aptitude for reaching across racial lines—were not merely prompted by the exoticism of the 1920s.[80] As an epigraph for her novel, after all, Faure-Favier used a line from Apollinaire's "The Sighs of the Gunner from Dakar" in the collection of poems entitled *Calligrammes* that wondered, "Why ever is it better to be white than to be black?" Likewise, her feminist vantage point materialized before the late 1920s. As early as 1910 she wrote the preface to a work on "feminists before feminism." Hers was a lifelong respect for the struggle to obtain women's rights.[81]

Louise Faure-Favier's *Blanche et Noir* recounted from the perspective of a white girl an interracial love affair that resulted in the birth of the girl's *métis* uncle. At age five the protagonist, Faure-Favier's namesake, Jeanne, discovers the existence of a grandmother, Malvina Lortac-Rieux, whom no one in her family ever mentions because the grandmother had a child the exact same age as Jeanne, an uncle conceived with the grandmother's African lover, Samba-Laobé. The reader follows Jeanne's remarkably open-minded discovery of another race while noting that she is surrounded by prejudice and discomfort on the part of family members who are ashamed of this black relative. At first acquiring knowledge of Africans through children's books, she creates scenarios of cannibalism and imagines black husbands for herself. She is inevitably reprimanded for her imaginative playing. Meanwhile, she discovers the circumstances of her grandmother Malvina's shame. Malvina was happily married for some time. Her husband Jean Lortac died in 1885 and instead of remarrying Malvina became completely focused upon their son, Henri. Once Henri finished his studies and married, however, Malvina began to feel unwelcome in her own home. She decided to leave and took advantage of the 1889 Exposition Universelle, the world's fair for which the Eiffel Tower was built, to travel to Paris. There, while dining on the first floor of the Eiffel Tower, she met the first black man she had ever seen: "In the middle of her life, she was discovering Paris, pleasure, and the black race. This *nègre* was dressed in the European fashion, wearing a grey suit."[82] Seduced, she left Paris for Senegal, where she remained until her death.

Titillated by such images, Jeanne begins to privately envisage interracial sexual encounters, while publicly defending the black race whenever she overhears racist or ignorant comments. Jeanne prepares her *licence ès lettres* (arts degree) at the Sorbonne University in Paris and there meets an American woman whom she asks—certain of her moral superiority as a Frenchwoman—why there is antagonism between blacks and whites in America. The woman sardonically comments: "Yes, it is with such sentiments that you have decided to give the *nègres* in your colonies the right to vote, the right to inheritance; you have made them citizens."[83] Shocked, Jeanne begins to wonder whether her black uncle (whose existence preoccupies her constantly) has been denied certain basic rights for purely racial reasons. In 1914 World War I breaks out and Jeanne, like many French people, lives a lifetime in one tumultuous year as she rapidly becomes a fiancé, wife, and then widow. In order to make ends meet Jeanne starts working in journalism as a secretary and works her way up. For one assignment she travels to Brittany in order to write about wounded Senegalese soldiers and finds them closely followed by Breton women: "And I was not a little surprised to see these blond damsels hanging from the necks of these tall black men, tenderly hugging and kissing."[84] Having spent much of her life surrounded by prejudice, she notes this new form of racial relations with joy.

After the war Jeanne becomes an aerial journalist and decides to travel to French West Africa in order to write a guidebook and meet her African uncle. In preparation for her departure, she travels one last time to her home in Rieux and there finds her African uncle, François Laobé-Rieux. "His black eyes, very beautiful, looked straight at you and revealed intelligence and self-control."[85] He speaks perfect French, having studied at French universities, traveled throughout Europe, and married a Frenchwoman. He fought first as a *tirailleur* and then as a pilot during World War I. During a long conversation—which for many critics made up the crux of the novel—Jeanne and François agree upon the existence of racial injustice and the importance of fraternity between the races. As François wonders who can ever truly befriend another race, Jeanne passionately states that "women, with their open minds and their better hearts, are the true civilizers," a term that here expresses that women can enlighten and unify the men of all races.[86] Although earlier in the novel she trusts French civilization to spread justice, Jeanne changes her mind in a conclusion that has women spreading harmony amongst the races. As she flies toward Africa Jeanne proclaims: "Fraternity of races, I am flying toward you."[87]

Faure-Favier's novel incorporated a number of biographical details. She had Jeanne mimic her growth and development as a professional and an intellectual. Journalism, flying, writing aerial guidebooks, and traveling to Africa were all biographical elements. Faure-Favier later asserted: "I did not invent anything with respect to the black intellectual elite of Paris and Senegal. I am honored to have as my friends a few very cultured black men and it is through frequent contact with them and their white wives that I was able to come up with the driving idea behind this book: the fraternity of races."[88] Hence Faure-Favier's work drew from personal observation of successful relationships anchored in the colonial metropolis. She used her friendships with men of color and the white women married to them to build her text around the basic tenets of French republicanism, which were first pronounced during the 1789 Revolution but only officially adopted during the Third Republic: *Liberty, Equality, Fraternity.*

The protagonist Jeanne alludes once (and positively) to intercourse as an aspect of love across the color line. The narrator notes that others were not as open as Jeanne when imagining such contacts and might consider them "black fornication."[89] However, these sexual references were in no way shockingly explicit, especially when compared with such novels as Victor Margueritte's *La Garçonne*, a novel that was banned, censored, and a bestseller because of its detailed portrayal of a liberated woman's sexual mores (which were not interracial).[90] Faure-Favier's work in no way provoked such distaste amidst critics, for it focused overwhelmingly upon the fraternal aspect of interracial contacts.

Writing for the right-wing newspaper *l'Ami du Peuple*, Maxime Revon devoted most of his article to Faure-Favier's biography. He then summarized her intentions in *Blanche et Noir*: "Mme Faure-Favier proves once again that a good-looking *nègre*, elegant and well-groomed, and especially one who has a well-kept plane, is more seductive than a little white runt, neglected and dirty, who moreover forgets to clean his cow."[91] Revon was evidently not swayed by her literary techniques, noting that the final conversation between Jeanne and her uncle was obviously contrived and directed toward the reader since they actually agree about everything they are saying. However, since Faure-Favier seemed so convinced that the time for a connection between black and white was at hand, and since Revon suspected that Jeanne was modeled after Faure-Favier's own image and experiences, he gave her work, and in particular its intentions, the benefit of the doubt.

Critics in the Franco-Antillean newspaper *La Dépêche Africaine* thoroughly enjoyed Faure-Favier's attempt to present a successful interracial relationship. Noting a boom in postwar colonial literature, the critic Pierre Baye-Salzmann ranked her novel alongside those of André Gide, the writer of Guyanese origin and winner of the prestigious literary Goncourt Prize René Maran, and the writer and painter Lucie Cousturier. Baye-Salzmann, who also wrote about Josephine Baker, welcomed Faure-Favier's work with pleasure: "The very fact that a Frenchwoman of pedigree willingly contemplates the union of a white woman and a black man gives us great hope for the future."[92] However what he truly appreciated was the book's ability to go beyond negrophilia and depict nuanced Franco-colonial interactions. Dissatisfied with simply satirizing the European mentality, Faure-Favier also produced "a subtle cross-section of the modern French spirit." Touched by his praise, and *La Dépêche*'s reproduction of quotes from her novel, Faure-Favier responded with a letter to the editors. She expanded upon her specifically feminist interests with words that suggest that some women recognized a similarity between their search for suffrage to remedy their inferior status as partial citizens, and the black desire for political freedom. "Have the Fathers of the Church," Faure-Favier concluded, "not decreed that women had no soul . . . The fathers of literary critique in 1928 decreed that blacks could not have genius. The two decrees are equal."[93] Thus Faure-Favier appealed to her black readership and established that she and other women wished to befriend another race because they were victims of similar cultural and political oppression. With her novel, Faure-Favier demonstrated that individuals with education and cultural refinement (regardless of which culture) could find friendship and, one day, equality.

As they moved from work to home and political meetings, colonial migrants wove their way through Paris while creating a web of flickering encounters, some of which went on to burn more steadily. Although hardest to document, these contacts may have marked Parisians even more than the exoticism both forced upon and freely portrayed by Baker, jazz musicians, and others who were not performers by their trades. Once multiplied to encompass the estimated ten to fifteen thousand Antilleans and Africans living in Paris and daily establishing contacts, the impact race and colonialism had upon Paris during the 1920s and 1930s becomes clear. Moreover, some components of their stories undoubtedly echoed those of the numerically dominant colonial groups in Paris—North Africans and Vietnamese. These migrants also contributed to the transformation of Paris into a colonial metropolis. They too lived nearby other Parisians; engaged in performances of race (voluntarily and not); introduced aspects of their cultures' arts and music to Paris; and, as expected, slept with, married, and befriended the French.

Black colonial migrants were conceivably somewhat unusual in their—at times imposed—transnationalism. When it came to music and nightclubs, for example, surrealists, performers and audiences often blended genres in fascinating ways that reflected the extent to which cultures from three continents were considered as one. Still, a fair number of Parisians were interested in distinction rather than mere amalgamation. Whether the reasons were scientific, political, or personal, they wished to see beyond a generalized colonialism. Many encounters did not end in friendship, love affairs, or marriage. However even brief concurrences permitted an embodiment of colonialism more familiar and enduring than Baker. They made colonialism unavoidable in the metropolitan context. Colonies, long peripheral to their metropole or considered as an extraordinary and compartmentalized presence—for example during times of war—were no longer consigned to being represented by performers of exoticism, advertisements, and other media. They were integrated into daily life and found down the street or even in the apartment next door.

3 A BLACK COLONY?

Race and the Origins of Anti-Imperialism

We use it as a watchword for rallying: a torch! It is with great honor that we revel in the glory of calling ourselves Nègres, with a capital N. It is our nègre race that we wish to guide on its path to total liberation from the yoke of slavery to which it is subjected. We want to impose the respect due to our race as well as its equality with all the other races of the world, as is its right and our duty, and we proclaim ourselves Nègres!

—LE COMITÉ, *La Voix des Nègres*

Black workers sought unity in race. The problem was that they did not all agree upon what it meant to be black. One of the most persistent underlying tensions within black, anti-imperial organizations was the question of who, truly, was a fully committed member. On the surface, differences of opinion often had to do with perceptions of race. Thus, in a December 1932 meeting Félix Denis could address the question of a growing *métissage*, or race mixing, in the Antilles and argue that "elements of mixed blood were the most fervent partisans of reducing blacks to servitude."[1] Therein lay the puzzle: could the color of one's skin (at times also discussed in terms of blood) determine one's politics of anti-imperialism?

Black colonial organizations functioned at the grassroots level, and in the process their members became a "black colony" in Paris. As a place, then, Paris enabled connections among members of the African diaspora to flourish.[2] Its spaces of interaction were constantly moving, contested, and redefined by both the populations of African descent, and the other Parisians around them. In part, the spaces through which this black colony moved continually evolved because Africans and Antilleans were far from uniform in their politics. But the black colony also used unceasing contact with others to define itself. The black colony thus further shaped itself through exchanges with Parisians, including the police and its spies. All these encounters forced a continuous reevaluation of their status as both racialized and colonized men.

The metropolitan story of black anti-imperialism in its nationalist, independence-seeking form was shaped in significant ways by World War I. For colonial soldiers, participation in a war that was not theirs marked a sea change, not only because of the experience itself—horrifying as it was—but also because it produced new reasons, and a new language, with which to challenge their relationship to France. Specifically, a phrase repeatedly uttered by veterans and other colonial migrants in postwar years (and still to some extent today) was "blood debt."[3] Blood shed in the trenches, some argued, should be compensated by France with certain rights. The exact nature of the rights to be extended depended on the speaker, and hence the definition of this debt—much like that of anti-imperialism itself in these early years—fluctuated. But both legal rights such as citizenship, and monetary rights such as increased pensions, were among the many demands the debt inspired during the interwar years. While in West Africa the language of the "blood debt" appears to have been mastered mostly by veterans from within a military culture, and only uneasily digested by civilian anti-imperialists, generations of black men who came to Paris after the war were drawn by and referred to this sense of debt.[4] Whether or not they understood fully what veterans sought when invoking a "blood debt," civilian migrants in Paris nonetheless responded to veterans' war stories or found ways to make the war their own by invoking a shared experience of French exploitation, and thus a certain connectivity among all colonial migrants. Thus not only did veterans define early anti-imperialism through their language of the "blood debt" and membership in anti-imperial organizations, but their stories also helped to shape civilian anti-imperialists' ideas and thus became the fodder for anti-imperial demands. Whoever the speaker, the acrimony generated by the war shaped interwar politics by gendering them (male) the blood debt was owed to men, and subsequent racial and colonial debates were framed with debates and gestures that referenced manhood.

Many immigrants, colonial or other, were habitually recorded as names and numbers in police registries; nevertheless, understanding the shift in colonized men's perspectives that took place during the war, the police placed those who sought nationalist independence from France under heavy surveillance.[5] That surveillance did not deter black men (students, navigators, shopkeepers, artisans, laborers, domestic employees, and more) from creating political spaces in which to hash out their anti-imperialism, and police archives allow us to unearth these men's agency in Paris.[6] Records show that black men challenged the imperial nation-state in which they lived; the same records also demonstrate why and how these men were able to come into their own as distinct political and social entities defined by blackness, masculinity, and colonialism, even while under surveillance. The role that race played within working-class communities that included both veterans and civilians explains in part how anti-imperial, black migrants related not only to one another, but also to the rest of Paris.

Agent Joé's arrest during the 1931 Colonial Exposition interrupted a flow of information that started with spies and ended in a monthly report produced by the Ministry of Colonies: "Notes on Revolutionary Propaganda Related to Overseas Lands." One subsection of the report was always entitled "The Black Colony." Those words underscored the workers' budding understanding of race as a marker under which to gather. They pinpointed the authorities' sense that black men were defined by their race, as well as by their colonial status. And they emphasized that racial visibility, even in an everyday occurrence such as a black man's movement through the streets of Paris, was both a device that facilitated tracking anti-imperialism and a reason for elaborating it. More than anything, however, the words "black colony" reflected the manner in which black workers were carving out a space for themselves in the metropolis. There was nothing simple about gathering under a black marker—especially since what it meant to be black was hotly contested. Thus the choice to make race an integral part of metropolitan, anti-imperial politics reflected both the burden of racial consciousness generated by the *vogue nègre*, and an uneasy search for a symbol that could hover, however falteringly, above all the other factors that influenced and defined black men in Paris. Thus African, Caribbean, and Malagasy working-class anti-imperialism mirrored these men's relationships to race, and to the metropolis.

Anti-Imperial Organizations and Their Leaders

Many of the tensions within these communities were funneled through discussions and encounters that took place under the aegis of official anti-imperial organizations. In July of 1919 the first Pan-African Congress was held in Paris so that African nations could present a unified front when protecting their interests at the Versailles Peace Conference, which gathered world leaders seeking to tie up the many loose ends left by World War I. The Congress spurred black men in the city to articulate their aspirations. A number of black organizations sprang up during the early 1920s, including the Fraternité Africaine (African Fraternity), l'Association Panafricaine (Pan-African Association), l'Amitié Franco-Dahoméenne (Franco-Dahomean Friendship) and the Ligue Pour l'Accession aux Droits de Citoyen des Indigènes de Madagascar (Malagasy *Indigènes'* League for Access to the Rights of Citizen), but the first association to group large numbers of black men was the Union Intercoloniale (Intercolonial Union) in 1921. The Union Intercoloniale grouped members from all the French colonies. In 1921 and 1922 it was controlled by its Indochinese, Malagasy, Reunionese, Guadeloupean, and Martinican membership, but by 1923 North Africans had started to dominate it. Black African questions remained consistently on the periphery of the group's meetings and its newspaper *Le Paria*, which helps to explain why black men created their own organizations. This detachment was further exacerbated by the 1925 Rif War pitting Spain and France against Berbers from the Moroccan Rif region.[7] The Union Intercoloniale and the French Communist Party organized protests that demanded the evacuation of European forces and supported independence of the Rif, and indeed the North African membership of both organizations was momentarily bolstered by these requests. However, black men were ambivalent about protesting the war, largely because they worried that communists were losing sight of their exigencies. Thus the Rif War instilled a cleavage amongst politically active colonial migrants in Paris, threatening to separate the North African from the Indochinese and black migrants.[8]

The first majority-black organization to decisively shape anti-imperial sentiment in Paris was the Ligue Universelle pour la Défense de la Race Noire (Universal League for the Defense of the Black Race). It was founded in May 1924 by the enigmatic Marc (Quénum) Kojo Tovalou Houénou, who was portrayed in police reports as a playboy born in Cotonou, Dahomey, in April 1877. More precisely, he was the son of a wealthy merchant and studied law at the University of Bordeaux before moving to Paris to practice law. During World War I he enlisted in the French army. While the war shook him, only in 1924, after white Americans refused to sit next to him at a Montmartre café, did race consciousness become an explicit part of his politics.[9] Although apparently not an active communist, he was associated with the French Communist Party. He was also linked to the Jamaican Marcus Garvey's Universal Negro Improvement Association, which promoted black nationalism, transnational unity, and the possibility of a return to Africa for all those of African ancestry. Houénou's own organization set goals that included "to develop solidarity amongst individuals of the black race; to group them for the rebuilding of their native land; to protect them from acts of violence, physical cruelty, or abuse; to combat the dogma of the inferiority of races of color; to assist its members morally and materially."[10] In its early forms, anti-imperialism primarily expressed racial solidarity and challenged racial discrimination. Demanding that colonialism be abolished was not yet the dominant strain.

The vice president of the Ligue Universelle, René Maran, was a black French West Indian novelist whose controversial work *Batouala* condemned the premises of the civilizing mission in Africa but nevertheless received the prestigious literary Goncourt Prize in 1921. Maran was one of the reasons the Ligue Universelle was eventually dismantled. Most radical groups in Paris were outspoken in their contempt for Blaise Diagne, the first African to be elected to the French legislature. Although an astute politician, Diagne was censured by black critics as a traitor to his race. Diagne and black activists differed over his role in the recruitment of black colonial troops during World War I, communism, and nationalism. On October 15, 1924, the Ligue Universelle's newspaper *Les Continents* published an article by Maran accusing Diagne of being an agent of French colonialism and of receiving a commission for the forced enrollment of *indigène* soldiers during the war. Diagne successfully sued Maran and editor in chief Jean Fangeat for libel. The court sentenced Fangeat to six months in prison, a fine of 1,500 francs, and 2,000 francs in damages. As a result, the newspaper, and soon thereafter the Ligue Universelle, ceased to exist.[11]

Almost immediately after members of the first political organization were forced underground, another appeared with a different leader but similar goals. The black community's perception that the first group had been persecuted by government officials facilitated the constitution of a second. The Comité de Défense de la Race Nègre (CDRN) was founded in March 1926. From the start, the CDRN was more radical than the Ligue Universelle, in part because of one of its leaders, Lamine Senghor.[12] Born in Senegal in 1889, Lamine Senghor arrived in France as a *tirailleur* during World War I. After being wounded and gassed in battle, he was discharged from the army in Dakar in 1919. He moved to Paris, turning to politics after witnessing the inequitable treatment of veterans who were not French citizens.[13] In Paris he married a Frenchwoman, worked as a postman, and took evening classes at the Sorbonne. An unapologetic member of the Communist Party for much of his militant career, Senghor exploited Blaise Diagne's prosecution of the Ligue Universelle in order to enroll about a dozen young, politically inexperienced, and radical black men in his organization. Quite logically, he became president of the CDRN, which by late 1926 had attracted three hundred members.

The CDRN, like its political successors, split as a result of personal and political differences among leaders and members. Members such as Maran complained that "blacks were stupid to tear each other apart and would do better to defend their race rather than to speak of politics with the communists, which just causes them trouble."[14] Not heeding Maran's warnings, and embittered after losing the organization's elections and seeing new officers take over in what they perceived as mutiny, the communist splinter group led by Senghor christened itself the Ligue de Défense de la Race Nègre (LDRN) in 1927, eventually founding *La Race Nègre* (The *Nègre* Race) as their newspaper.

By March 1927 Lamine Senghor was increasingly weakened by tuberculosis, which was aggravated by the poison gas he had inhaled during the war, and needed to rest more and more often. A new individual moved to the fore of racial politics in Paris: Tiémoko Garan Kouyaté. Kouyaté gradually replaced Senghor at the head of the LDRN, taking advantage of the time Senghor spent convalescing and traveling to recruit members outside of Paris.[15] Senghor's split from the LDRN was not solely a matter of travel and illness. He had also mishandled or perhaps embezzled (he died before anyone discovered exactly what had happened) a substantial portion of the LDRN's rather pitiful funds. In November 1927 he tendered a resignation that was rejected by the new Secretary General Kouyaté, who declared that the LDRN could accept it only once all accounts had been settled. Senghor tried to defend himself—he had recently separated from his wife, but more dramatically, paralysis was taking over his body—but to no avail.[16]

On December 3, 1927, the LDRN's leaders learned of Senghor's death while reading the Communist newspaper *L'Humanité*. Although Senghor's final interactions with blacks in Paris were sour, the LDRN displayed solidarity by paying to transport Senghor's body to Paris, buying flowers for the funeral, and financing his daughter's return to family in Senegal. It refrained from besmirching his name, in part because ties with potential donors to the organization needed to be maintained, and publicly slurring Senghor's name could slow the already difficult task of fundraising.[17] Privately, however, members of the LDRN complained bitterly about the financial situation in which they felt he had left the organization.

Kouyaté headed the LDRN from 1927 to 1931. He was born April 27, 1902, in Segu in the French Sudan (now Mali). He studied at the renowned Ecole William Ponty on the Ile de Gorée in Senegal before working as a schoolteacher in the Ivory Coast from 1921 to 1923. He then made his way to the Ecole Normale in Aix-en-Provence, France. Kouyaté was amongst the first six Africans invited to the teacher-training school for three years of upper-level studies with an annual stipend of 2,800 francs. By October 1924 he had been expelled, probably because he had been circulating communist propaganda amongst students. He seized the opportunity to move to Paris where, like Lamine Senghor, he audited courses at the Sorbonne.

While he led the LDRN, the organization was plagued by police harassment, acrimonious debates about whether it should be involved with the French Communist Party, and indecision about whether Kouyaté was the ideal leader. Debates raged, in particular, over whether the LDRN should attempt to create a revolutionary nest of black, colonial agitators within the metropole.[18] By March 29, 1932, agents for the police wrote that the organization had been dismantled.[19] In everything but name, however, the organization continued to exist. Kouyaté and key members retained their leadership roles and were the founding members of the Union des Travailleurs Nègres (UTN) and its paper, *Le Cri des Nègres*.

The communist Stéphane Rosso and Agent Joé/Edmond Thomas Ramananjato helped Kouyaté with the June 1932 founding of the UTN—one of several examples of how engaged the informant was in the communities upon which he reported. Arriving in France in 1918 as a volunteer, Ramananjato was discharged from the army in 1923 in order to "benefit from" a postwar job with a horticulturalist, Monsieur Carriat. Carriat's firm was one of two that hired Indochinese and Malagasies to work for them during the war. Enjoying the supposedly docile workmanship provided by these men, at the war's end Carriat requested that the Ministry of War send *tirailleurs* whose tours of duty were almost or completely up in exchange for offering to teach them the craft of horticulture in preparation for their return overseas. After being released from the army, many Malagasies signed contracts with the horticulturalists, who promised they would receive an extra 75 centimes per day of work as a bonus when they had fulfilled their contracts and left France (a step toward encouraging their subsequent departure from the metropole).

However, the appalling conditions and egregious paternalism of the bosses led a number of Malagasy workers to leave without their due. Indeed, like the spaces of war these workplaces put a particular burden of shame, especially in their paternalism, upon black men, contributing to their decision to demarcate postwar political spaces as male ones. The Ministry of Colonies acknowledged a bit late that none of the *indigènes* had learned anything about horticulture, although the teaching of a trade was stipulated in their contract. The food was terrible and prepared in unsanitary conditions (bread was left unprotected and was covered with flies), while beds were filthy.[20] Ramananjato was not the only man to leave such exploitative conditions ready to participate in the anti-imperialist organizations of the 1920s and 1930s. He, Kouyaté, and Rosso made a passionate trio for the regeneration of a radical group.

Kouyaté proposed that the new society group all blacks in the metropole. But first, he summarized the creation of its direct predecessors, the CDRN and the LDRN:

> In all of this intrigue, one must see the hand of the police; terrified by the Ligue's progress, it has put everything in motion to torpedo it. But we must not let ourselves be demoralized; since the government is hounding our combat organizations, let us constitute a *nègre* association that, under the guise of a charitable organization, will politically educate its members and continue the struggle for the independence of the *nègre* race currently exploited by European imperialism.[21]

Kouyaté's acknowledgement that police harassment contributed directly to an elaboration of race politics is particularly informative, suggesting that while surveillance may not have initiated discontent amongst colonial workers, it certainly reinforced it. The organization was founded on a politics of oppression and fittingly it was the ex-*tirailleur* Ramananjato (Agent Joé) who suggested a new name, Union des Travailleurs Nègres, so that workers exploited like he was would not confuse it with the LDRN.[22] The UTN's official purpose was "to ensure the emancipation, the cultural development, and the material and moral mutual aid of *nègres*."[23] However Kouyaté soon found himself at odds with the organization. By October 1933 he had been not only abandoned by the UTN, which continued to be active until 1939, but also excluded from the French Communist Party.[24]

The CDRN, LDRN, and UTN, in their more radical forms, constituted a tripartite core of black anti-imperial thought in France. There were similar tensions in each organization revolving around the extent to which communism should be a component of anti-imperialism, whether black men from different parts of the colonial world were really part of the same struggle and race, and how they should communicate their politics to other Parisians and colonized men. There were also similar goals in these organizations: emancipation from colonialism, political viability, and social equality. These men's anti-imperialism made itself known alternatively and inconsistently by requests for independence from France; demands for the rights associated with French citizenship—often expressed in eloquent, republican language; and requests for the righting of the wrongs implicit in colonialism, whether cultural, social, political, economic, or physical.

The language of nationalism, or independence, was the most extreme of this litany, and was reported on a regular basis by informants. Calls for independence started with the first black leagues in Paris, in the early 1920s, but became increasingly strident after the first of the explicitly anti-imperialist organizations, the CDRN, was created in 1926.[25] At an anti-imperial congress in Brussels, Belgium, in 1927, CDRN members Lamine Senghor and the Antillean Max Bloncourt respectively demanded "the complete independence of the African colonies" and "the complete independence of the Antilles."[26] But such views were not held only by stalwart communists. After he was expelled from the Communist Party, Kouyaté created a group called Solidarité Coloniale (Colonial Solidarity) that in 1934 promised to work on the "liberation of peoples colonized by French imperialism."[27] Of course, Kouyaté had a history of communist affiliation, but consider also the Haitian Ludovic Lacombe who, during a 1932 meeting of the LDRN, announced his belief that anti-imperialist but noncommunist *nègres* were being scared off by communist members. He confirmed that he himself was a "nationalist, but anti-communist *nègre* who wanted no master, white or red."[28] Thus while anti-imperialists had in common their clamoring for national liberation, such ideas came from men with diverse political and personal backgrounds. This range clarifies in part why liberation was never the sole goal of any of these organizations. Instead, hope for national independence or a unified African state alternated with the formulation of more specific short- and long-term measures to better the status and daily lives of blacks both in the metropole and overseas.

While strong leaders were instrumental in creating the organizations and their fearlessness was a motivator in the intricate game of cat and mouse these groups played with the authorities, the membership and second-tier officers were consistently the same through the interwar period. They weathered the storms that led to repeated ousting and juggling of leaders. Indeed, while leaders were crucial in their ability to rally support, make their cause known, and draw the authorities' ire, members lent continuity to the politics of anti-imperialism.

Passion and conviction were requirements for black anti-imperialists. Just before the CDRN splintered, Senghor was repeatedly punched by another member who did not approve of him.[29] This violent politicking reinforced the sense that these men were building a space in which they not only negotiated and constructed their critique of imperialism, but also elaborated their understanding of manhood, shame, and honor. Both Kouyaté and Senghor wore as badges of honor the arrests that occurred when they went on missions to unify colonial workers in other parts of France. Senghor, for example, was arrested during a trip to Marseille in March 1927 when he refused to show his papers to the police. In part because he was freed in short order, the incident was interpreted as a symbol for the power of unity by blacks in Paris who had immediately organized protests of his arrest.[30] Members needed the same dedication as leaders since they, too, were not immune to police scrutiny far less discreet than spying. Just before the LDRN was dismantled, Kouyaté was accused of embezzling funds, like Senghor before him, including donations made by one of few financially solvent members, Emile Faure, a *métis* who had grown up in France and had an engineering degree.[31] Police seized the opportunity afforded by the ongoing investigation that Faure had initiated with them to search the LDRN's headquarter, removing all copies of the most recent issue of *La Race Nègre*. They also searched outraged members' private homes and copied a ledger that contained the names and addresses of all LDRN members, valuable both because it was the mailing list for its newspaper and because it permitted French authorities to identify all those who were drawn to anti-imperialism.[32] Workers were uncompromising when defending their property, privacy, and beliefs, and they believed Kouyaté and Faure had suffered from a lapse in judgment in allowing the French justice system to poke its nose into their affairs. Members did not feel the need for any more exposure than they already had as black men in Paris. In retribution, they purged Kouyaté as well as his opponent Faure.[33]

These dismissals exemplify the extent to which workers maintained control over the daily affairs of their groups. They understood themselves to be defenders of the black colony. Whether they chose to protect or overthrow their leaders, or alternated between the two reactions, they resisted government intervention and ensured the continuity of their politics at a grassroots level, thus preserving the integrity of the political space they had carved out for themselves on metropolitan soil. The ongoing metamorphosis of these organizations and rapid rotation of leaders throughout the interwar years in fact contributed to protecting members. Organizations such as the LDRN were quick to disavow ties with communism once more radical members such as Kouyaté were purged. If a leader marked as suspicious or dangerous by French authorities, or involved in a lawsuit like Kouyaté, managed through his actions to shine too much light on the other members, his ties with that association were often severed, at least momentarily. More temperate members then took control, constituting more moderate or completely different groups that, for a brief time, remained independent of political obligations to institutions such as the Communist Party.

Yet the authorities' omnipotent presence, although a hindrance to the daily operations of the CDRN, LDRN, and UTN, and a potential reason for divesting organizations of their leaders, did not always have the desired inhibitory effect. No matter how uneasy entente appeared amongst various elements of the black presence in Paris, perceived injustices committed by the imperial nation-state—including surveillance—inexorably led to a sense of community, and at times may have been the only thing black men had in common. Which is why despite mounting anger in the face of vigilant prying by the Ministry of Colonies, members of radical organizations were proud of the authorities' interest. Government prying unified. Kouyaté and others also believed the growing number of harassing policemen and informants reflected the associations' strength. The spying only proved that they had become contenders, as a black colony, on the French political scene. In Kouyaté's words, "a political society truly deserving of the name, such as the League, should be proud of this [scrutiny]."[34]

Nègre versus Noir, African versus Antillean

In some ways early anti-imperialists were motivated by the French government's opposition and spying—but their elaboration of politics reflected far more than pride and the rejection of a meddling government. There was a shifting and dialectic relationship between race and other factors that determined anti-imperialism, including citizenship, geographic origin, politics, and social standing. Much of the tension amongst black men was expressed through the categories of race used by members of the organizations, and picked up on by the police. The most common terms were *blanc* (white), *noir* (black), *nègre* (loosely Negro), and *métis* (mixed), although the terms *négresse* (Negro woman) and *mulâtre* (mulatto) also peppered reports. The terms had made their way into the French language toward the beginning of European colonialism, between the middle of the sixteenth and early seventeenth centuries. *Métis* was used to describe the children of parents who fell into different racial categories. Throughout the nineteenth and early twentieth centuries, *métis* was a category fiercely debated with respect to how it might affect an individual's biological as well as social status.[35] While *nègre* and *noir* both signified blackness, *nègre* was perceived as derogatory.[36] In the 1920s, however, the term was repossessed by black workers who wanted their race to be-

when
did this
translate
- how

speak political engagement. So by the 1920s *nègre* versus *noir* denoted a commitment to politics, not color. *Métis* and *mulâtre* were slightly more complex terms.

?.

Spies noted as early as 1927, when the CDRN split into two organizations, the CDRN more moderate and the LDRN more radical, that in addition to political ideology, another great divide existed within the black community: the geographic origins of its members. Indeed, one of many factors determining the 1927 split was the discord between a Guadeloupean activist named Joseph Gothon-Lunion and the Antilleans on the one hand, and Lamine Senghor and the Africans on the other. In one of several debates that took place before the CDRN's division was born out in March 1927, a man named Dionson made the antagonism explicit:

> The Antilleans, Martinicans, and Guadeloupeans who believe themselves to be of a superior essence consider *nègres* from Africa and the Indies to be inferior beings and forget their own origins; yet they know well that their own ancestors are African blacks sold as slaves and transported to the Antilles. The black race must make such divisions disappear and we must place ourselves on the grounds of true fraternity; I, said Dionson, am a *mulâtre* born of a white father and a black mother, but I am proud of being a *nègre*. We are all *nègres* exploited by a common enemy that we must fight; whether we are Antillean, African or Indian, we are brothers, and we must reach out to one another fraternally in order to fight for our emancipation.[37]

Dionson believed that he had crossed the *métis-nègre* line by understanding the origins of the African diaspora, but he also clues us in to the links between race, geography, and class. Dionson analyzed the problem as follows: Antilleans—who were products of the slave trade, since after the French claimed their Caribbean colonies they had imported slaves as their labor force—had been around Caucasian and other races long enough to be more mixed than many Africans. As a result of their "mixedness," Antilleans did not feel as passionate about anti-imperialism, or independence. CDRN members would often challenge one another simply for being *mulâtre*, African, or Antillean, a reflection of this difference in passion.[38]

Within the Caribbean, as the psychiatrist, philosopher, and revolutionary Frantz Fanon explained in *Black Skin, White Masks* (1952), hierarchy based upon race had a rich tradition of its own, with established differences between the "almost-white," the *mulâtre*, and the *nègre*, and between Antilleans and Africans. The Antillean distaste for being misconstrued as Senegalese, and the concomitant sense of superiority with which Antillean men had traditionally snubbed other black men from across the empire, was absorbed into metropolitan understandings of race. While Fanon went on to explain that Antilleans who imbibed hierarchies of race were generally not men of the working class who always "knew they were black," the metropolitan black man's mistrust of those who proclaimed themselves *noirs* was, for all these reasons, to be expected.[39] Yet in proclaiming himself *nègre*, the interwar activist Dionson appeared to contradict what Fanon would later add to his discussion of race in *Toward the African Revolution* (1955). In his chapter on "West Indians and Africans" Fanon explained why "the enemy of the Negro is often not the white man but a man of his own color" and furthermore that "in 1939 no West Indian in the West Indies proclaimed himself to be a Negro, claimed to be a Negro. When he did, it was always in his relations with a white man."[40] Following Fanon, Dionson's rhetorical gesture would have been unheard of in the interwar Caribbean. In contrast, the existence of a black colony within Paris made Dionson's racial awareness, which he expressed in linguistic terms, possible in the metropole.

Dionson's assessment reveals that degrees of blackness reflected a complex and subtle blend of cultural and political divisions. In noting that the Antillean-African division was more geographic than racial, Dionson exposed part of what race meant to early anti-imperialists, and why organizations appeared to divide so easily. By October 1928 the division within the black community was a political and classist one, which manifested itself along geographic lines but was often reduced to platitudes such as the idea that *métis* might betray the black race. Antilleans in Paris were more likely to have arrived as students and remain as white-collar workers and intellectuals. Africans who came as soldiers, workers, or students felt that the Antillean intellectuals looked down on them. Even at the beginning of its existence, the third prominent anti-imperial organization, the UTN, felt challenged by its Antillean component. For example, in November 1932 Pierre Kodo-Kossoul, a black naturalized French hospital worker originally from Dahomey who was one of several members to transfer his allegiance from the LDRN to the UTN, "apologized to the two women present, noting that *nègres* are asses if they cannot even explain themselves and get along. He criticized the assembly for raising an Antillean question given that all *nègres* are of the same race and defend the same cause."[41] Kodo-Kossoul subtly shamed the overwhelmingly male audience with his apology to the female witnesses of their political discord.

Within all three organizations the debate regarding geographic and class origin often translated into a semantic battle over whether the name of the group should contain the term *noir* or the term *nègre*. Using *nègre* was considered a powerful statement about the desire to take control of a pejorative descriptive previously employed by Europeans in an attempt to affirm white superiority. *Noir*, in contrast, while certainly not devoid of politics was less charged with a radical, aggressive form of anti-French politics. From the outset, some members of the CDRN argued that *nègre* should be replaced by *noire* so as to attract and retain moderate members. Only a few months after it was set up, in July 1926, the title was in fact officially changed to *noire*, only to be surreptitiously switched back to *nègre* by January 1927, just as more radical elements, led by Lamine Senghor, were attempting to regain control of an organization that they feared had become moderate.[42] This battle of the names saw yet another reversal a few months after the CDRN's radical members created the LDRN. The moderate members who were left behind reserved their allegiance for the Antillean Maurice Satineau. Satineau kept the CDRN's title, but changed the word *nègre* back to the less politically charged *noire*, thereby positioning both himself and his organization as a more moderate alternative to the budding LDRN.

Early debates thus foreshadowed the appropriation of the term *nègre*, which culminated during the mid-1930s in the political and literary movement known as negritude. In choosing the word *nègre*, even in an underhanded manner, black men were exploring a reaffirmation of their race. In the first issue of *La Voix des Nègres* (The Voice of the *Nègres*), a newspaper associated with Lamine Senghor and the CDRN that appeared only twice, in January and March 1927, an article appeared on the front page entitled "The Word *nègre*" and signed by "the Committee." In this extraordinary piece, *nègre* was explicitly placed in opposition to words less charged with race and class, such as *men of color* or *blacks*. These classifications were created by those in power (Europeans) to divide blacks amongst themselves, allowing some (the unspoken adjectives here were Antillean or mixed race) groups to believe that they were superior to others. Appropriating *nègre*, however, encouraged all those oppressed by their pigmentation to unite.[43] Repeated references to the divide between *noir* and *nègre* by the black colony in newspapers, and by the spies in police notes, made it clear that debates over terminology reflected ideological divisions.

There was another dimension to the tension in Paris's black colony—a silent one. Antilleans had been French citizens since the abolition of slavery in 1848 and were distinctive in their long-standing guarantee of citizenship. West Africans from the Four Communes of Senegal (Dakar, Saint Louis, Rufisque, and Gorée) had also considered themselves citizens since that date. And indeed, ever since they had first elected a deputy to the National Assembly in Paris in 1848, the latter were distinguished from all other Africans. But their status as citizens was repeatedly questioned and openly challenged by various French courts, ministers, and governors until World War I. In 1915 and 1916 the West African deputy Blaise Diagne negotiated the right of Senegalese from the Four Communes, known locally as *originaires*, first to be eligible for standard military service—which most importantly meant being conscripted in the same manner as French troops and not being segregated from metropolitan French troops in separate colonial, *tirailleurs* units—and subsequently to be considered full French citizens.[44] Thereafter, *originaires* who were now officially full citizens cohabited with Africans who were merely subjects. Some interpreted Diagne's negotiation of rights for *originaires* as signifying that acquisition of citizenship was somehow a consequence of wartime service, a particularly natural conclusion given that as early as 1914 Africans even outside of the Four Communes had tried requesting citizenship in exchange for their wartime service.[45] This belief explains in part why in the postwar years the notion of a "blood debt" gained in import. Why, some wondered, should the *tirailleurs* from the rest of West Africa not also be granted citizenship after fighting for France?

Why, then, with such a long-standing tradition of debate, politics, and contradictions surrounding it, was citizenship not more openly deliberated amongst black workers in Paris? Why was the focus race? Because race was subjective and was considered even by those of mixed race, such as Dionson, to be a question of self-perception. One could choose to be *nègre*. One could choose to be an anti-imperialist and believe that race unified colonial men. One did not simply choose to be a citizen, and citizens were sometimes strong allies in the anti-imperial struggle. Citizenship had the potential to divide black men in Paris when, for example, being born ten meters outside the Four Communes was enough to demarcate citizens from subjects. Worse, perhaps, in these very male circles one must remember that Frenchwomen also did not have an essential privilege of citizenship: suffrage.[46] Was a focus upon lack of citizenship perhaps too obviously a form of emasculation for those black men who—not from the Antilles nor residents of the Four Communes—could also not vote?

Informants necessarily absorbed fellow workers' perceptions of race, and thus listed alongside the politics, addresses, workplaces, marriages, lovers, and children of anti-imperialists their race in the recognizable terms of *noir*, *nègre*, or *métis*. Using that terminology reflected the informants' understanding of the manner in which the tensions generated by repeated clashes and counter clashes in politics, origin, citizenship, and race informed relationships among workers, as well as the black colony's relationship to the metropolis at large. In particular, those who considered themselves to be *nègre* were worth spying upon, since they were colonial workers who believed race was a method of unifying men as a black colony, and of goading them on in their anti-imperialism.

Early anti-imperialism was born in anger, drawing on the personal motivations of its charismatic leaders and the desire of all its members to find ways to dissent with authorities. Grievances could be on a small scale—a member of an organization inappropriately trailed through the streets of Paris—or a much larger scale—rights not extended following World War I, or massacres in the colonial setting. Indeed, at times the leaders seemed to grasp at straws of injustice, and at first glance, their ire appears unfocused. However, although several black organizations came and went in interwar Paris, anti-imperialists were remarkably consistent in their convictions as well as in their techniques for communicating those beliefs. The black colony constituted itself in meeting rooms and on the streets of Paris, pushing and prodding these spaces to meet their political needs, and using them to forge alliances from Paris to the colonies.

Communism

Agents and colonial workers were not alone in understanding that race and self-identification with race informed politics. Communists also concluded that the metropolitan contingent of black men, at least those who were blue-collar workers, bitter ex-soldiers, or otherwise living precariously in the metropole, might feel isolated in their visibility. In return, certain black leaders and members—either out of conviction or self-interest—decided that communism could help to define anti-imperialism financially, politically, or both. Their decision was not without its repercussions. If some members accepted ties with the French Communist Party, others refused them, and some contested the very idea that European politics had any place in the racial struggle of the African diaspora.

The Communist Party's interest in French black organizations became unequivocal in 1927, when the second of the anti-imperial triumvirate, the LDRN, was created. At this time the French Communist Party was partially funding the organization.[47] Certain members, including Kouyaté, were drawn to communism's promises of a worldwide anti-imperialist policy. They sought support because they feared that political and social isolation—as minorities within France and as geographic outliers overseas—might prevent them from dismantling the French colonial system. Even though black organizations had two or three hundred members in each of several major cities of the metropole and supporters in the colonies, the speed with which organizations were disassembled and reassembled meant that they needed a foundation of strong support, both moral and financial. By January 1929 the LDRN was accepting monthly payments from the French Communist Party ranging between 800 and 2,000 francs.[48] These sums were devoted to propaganda and the printing of the monthly paper *La Race Nègre*.

Far from freely accepting this windfall, members questioned it. In a December 1928 meeting, the Martinican vice president Camille Sainte Rose, an employee of the French postal service, took Kouyaté aside and asked him to explain how the LDRN was paying its rent. Kouyaté responded that they were sharing the 100-franc monthly fee with the Ligue des Femmes pour la Paix et la Liberté (Women's League for Peace and Liberty), a pacifist women's organization. Sainte Rose made him out to be a liar, and the conversation ended with Kouyaté's hands pressed firmly around Sainte Rose's throat.[49] Once again an insult was being defended with a brawling violence that seemed codified as a method of defending one's honor in these black circles. Still, Kouyaté knew that he could not strangle all his opponents, and so with the help of the ever-militant treasurer, Stéphane Rosso, he kept the inner workings of the funding secret from members.[50]

As late as 1935 the communist Rosso declared "not all our *nègre* comrades know that we are under the supervision of the Party."[51] These oblivious members may simply have hoped to avoid being noticed by the government, perhaps convinced that being black and colonial had sufficiently marked them. Certainly, as early as 1925, authorities had pinpointed what they considered potentially dangerous links between the Communist Party and colonial men both in the metropole and overseas. One note on revolutionary propaganda warned: "In France, the Communist Party endeavors to act simultaneously on the colonial workers and certain intellectuals coming from our overseas establishments and destined, in the spirit of the Party, to shape the leaders of the sections to be created in the colonies."[52] Another more racially explicit note explored the race's supposed predilection for mysticism, arguing: "the black man is all the more apt to let himself be dragged along under this influence because he believes that he will thereby more easily escape from his intellectual childhood."[53] In ornate language, the analyst elaborated upon the specific dangers of bolshevism:

Today, as Slavic nihilism has torn itself from hazy reveries in order to crystallize around unnatural Marxism, bolshevism attracts the denigrators of the established order of things. Sovietism perfectly discerns its potential for expansion; it knows that by yielding to the modalities of different places and races, by concealing for a while, if necessary, its ideology, it can find support everywhere against the "capitalist" states that it wishes to ruin in order to ensure its own existence.[54]

The Antilles and West Africa were amongst the regions identified as most likely to be influenced by communism—threatened regions in which communists might join pan-black movements in asking for the total liberation of French colonies.

The danger, according to the authorities, lay not overseas but in colonized men who had been to the metropole. Injustice, and hence the motivation for rebellion, originated in the paternalism and violence of colonialism. Discrimination germinated into theories and beliefs, such as nationalism or communism, in a metropole that allowed workers and intellectuals of different origins and conditions to mix. Then, ideas spread back to the colonies via newspapers and individuals, traveling on ships manned by sailors whose conditions were miserable enough that they could often be persuaded to smuggle revolutionary documents. The final leg of the journey, from metropole to colony, was what the government most sought to prevent with its surveillance of black migrants. Officials in the metropole and the colonies agreed that cooperation was vital, especially since communism was intensifying: "it would seem necessary to exert a discreet and meticulous surveillance in this milieu since it is not possible given the current state of legislation to force the cessation, in the metropole, of this dangerous propaganda."[55]

Naturally, the Communist Party did not see itself merely as a financial backer for anti-imperialism. It believed that anti-imperialists could be useful for disrupting noncommunist states. Leaflets geared toward wooing black men were published by the Red International of Labor Unions, more often known as the Profintern. Created to assemble labor unions of various origins, the Profintern attracted the radical union known as the Confédération Général de Travail Unitaire (CGTU) and formed in France in July 1921 as a communist-leaning offshoot of a French union created in 1895 known as the Confédération Général du Travail (CGT).[56] The Profintern circulated brochures with titles such as "Under the Imperial Yoke: Imperialist Orgies in Africa," in which provocative language challenged imperialism and manhood:

> Not only have imperialists succeeded in annexing all of Africa and subjugating African working populations through the use of armed forces, dupery, deception, the corruption of chiefs, and by resorting to alcohol and the Bible; but each night the European "civilizers" also organize drinking bouts and orgies, kidnapping young *négresses* and seducing married women,—this is their principal occupation.[57]

The focus upon orgies and the seduction of black women challenged black men by suggesting their emasculation by white invaders—a visceral appeal to their instinctive outrage.

If such crude tactics were necessary, it was because communist influence over black anti-imperialist organizations was convoluted. The communist-leaning CGTU seldom lived up to its anti-imperialist rhetoric, and rewarded anti-imperialist organizations such as the LDRN with stock propagandistic phrases but little direct action. The Comintern—the common name given to the Communist International or Third International, founded in Moscow in 1919 when the break between bourgeois socialism and communism was pronounced—as well as the Profintern were also relatively weak in their organization of black nationalistic movements. As early as 1922, a Black Bureau was formed as part of the Executive Committee that organized the

Comintern from Moscow. However, only after the 6th Congress in 1928, which gathered communist parties from around the world, did the Black Bureau become an international black secretariat responsible for transmitting communist directives to national parties, while ensuring a liaison between the Comintern and Profintern. Soon thereafter, in July 1928, the Comintern created a Black International, with headquarters in Hamburg. Its location resulted in some problems for meetings even before Hitler came to power in 1933. While the French had trouble controlling blacks within Paris, because they could rarely come up with legal grounds for forbidding meetings, they could refuse to grant passports for international travel. A 1930 International Conference of Black Workers in Hamburg was poorly attended because several delegates from Paris and West Africa were unable to obtain passports.[58]

One concern of the Black International was how to use metropolitan syndicalism to unite all anti-imperialist associations.[59] Thus by November 1932 nine black members of the French Communist Party's colonial section in Paris met regularly. Their discussions covered everything from how to convert other black men to communism to which causes to support to how to deal with rogue members. Yet even at the height of their involvement with communism, black men knew that patriotism colored the colonial politics of the French Communist Party.[60] If, communists increasingly argued, the colonies were to gain freedom, they would become easy prey for Hitler and Mussolini.[61] Moscow may have wished to groom black men as anti-imperial leaders, but colonial migrants in Paris suspected that the French Communist Party, and fellow French workers, did not truly value their colonial interests.

Many black men, like North Africans and Vietnamese, moved away from communism after suspecting that their nationalist dreams could only at best be partially fulfilled by an increasingly centralized Comintern. However, Africans and Antilleans had reason to feel particularly isolated. The French Communist Party's newspaper *L'Humanité* published several substantial surveys of immigrant life in France designed to convince French workers not to give in to xenophobia when faced with foreigners they suspected of stealing jobs and breaking strikes.[62] For the most part, each series focused upon European im-migrants. One exception was a 1926 series that included articles on the Chinese and North African presence in the working-class suburbs of Billancourt and Gennevilliers.[63] Still, very few articles mentioned black Africans or Antilleans, a logical enough tactical decision on the part of the French Communist Party given their small numbers com-pared to other migrants, but not a choice likely to elicit wholehearted collaboration from the black migrant population.

Apprehensive though they might be about the benefits of com-munism, members who remained supporters of the French Commu-nist Party transformed black politics by bringing with them its "bol-shevization." This push for the theoretical homogeneity and structural reorganization of communism started in 1924. By 1929 the Party was implementing Moscow's call to aggressively pit class against class during a period when the Comintern foretold the imminent collapse of capitalism.[64] The resulting structural changes within the French Communist Party, among them the transfer of previously local or-ganizational cells to the workplace, contributed to its alienation of many dedicated anti-imperialists, both French and colonial. Other ongoing practices added to some anti-imperialists' estrangement from the Party, including the increasing intransigence of its political posi-tions as well as the evictions—or at times the resolute departures—of Free Masons, members of the Ligue des Droits de l'Homme (Human Rights' League, a nongovernmental organization founded in 1898 and still around today), and revolutionary syndicalists (in a nutshell, radical trade unionists). As for the call to pit class against class, while conflicts inspired by perceived differences in status predated this di-rective, after 1929 workers more unequivocally articulated their mis-trust of educated colonial men. Thus through black communists, the French Communist Party and Moscow played their part in drawing the lines within black anti-imperialist circles. Kouyaté was just one ex-ample of how communist and black politics intersected. He was slated to attend Stalin University in Moscow before his fall from grace, the same school attended by Ho Chi Minh (the future prime minister and president of the Democratic Republic of Vietnam) and a number of Africans and African Americans, many of whom complained about the living conditions in Moscow and Soviet racism.[65] Kouyaté's break with communism was emblematic of how easily the delicate search for balance between political autonomy and financial backing could leave the Party without strong leaders, and strong leaders without their organizations.

Causes Célèbres *and Connected Communities*

Direct links with communism, even while they were challenged, guaranteed financing and the hope for access to the pages of well-established newspapers such as the organ of the French Communist Party, *L'Humanité*. These links, in turn, allowed black men to construct spaces in which to connect with white workers in Paris, and through them with a broad community of anti-imperialist, antifascist, and pacifist organizations. By the time the UTN advanced to the forefront of black anti-imperialist politics in Paris in 1932, its members had found a common fear and enemy other than the colonizing power of France: the rise of fascism across Europe. Such political developments naturally reinforced ties with communism, but they also allowed the radical UTN to explore causes that were of interest to more moderate Parisians. With each new crisis, from the trials of nine African American boys in Paint Rock, Alabama, to Hitler's accession to power in 1933, radical black organizations gained increasing recognition and acceptance amongst French and international activists.

Francophone black workers were not self-absorbed when it came to the African diaspora. They were particularly mindful of the lynchings and other oppression to which African Americans were subjected. The Scottsboro affair, for example, was a powder keg for outraged francophone blacks and further reinforced their links to other Parisians. The Ligue anti-impérialiste (League Against Imperialism) was one of many organizations that championed the cause of the nine African American boys sentenced to death. Founded in Brussels, Belgium, in February 1927 with the blessing of the Comintern, the League was immediately placed under the honorary presidency of people such as Albert Einstein, the French pacifist Henri Barbusse, and the American author Upton Sinclair. With its headquarters in Berlin, Germany, the organization more or less developed as a front for the Communist Party at first, but not all its members were dedicated communists and by the mid-1930s Moscow showed dwindling interest in the association.

From the time of its founding the League Against Imperialism was closely affiliated with French anti-imperialists, antifascists, and pacifists; the early anti-imperialist leader Lamine Senghor was chosen as its first vice president. Senghor delivered a violent anticolonial speech at the 1927 inaugural conference in Brussels.[66] Agent Joé/Ramananjato, the Malagasy *tirailleur* who was forced out of horticulture and into accounting after his disastrous apprenticeship with Carriat, was another example of a black anti-imperialist who decided to support the global goals of the League Against Imperialism. In 1934 he became a paid organizer for the League and, although remaining a member of the UTN, he eventually left the upper ranks of the latter. The League used humanitarian and liberal discourse to promote a unified, transnational front of antifascism and anti-imperialism. Although language presented a barrier, the need for unity amongst races was a significant goal.[67] While the League officially discouraged any revolutionary movements (other than communism), particularly those with nationalistic characteristics such as Garveyism (black nationalism as defined by Marcus Garvey), Zionism, and so forth, members were diverse in their politics.

The Scottsboro affair, which quickly became infamous in Paris and worldwide, represented just the sort of case that would strike a chord with the League Against Imperialism's mottled membership and magnetize a far broader audience as well. On March 25, 1931, in Paint Rock, Alabama, nine black youths on a freight train were arrested for rape after two white prostitutes dressed as men were found on the same train and lied to the police.[68] After four different trials were conducted over four days, all before all-white juries, eight of the defendants were found guilty and sentenced to death. Outraged by an egregious abuse of human rights, people around the world responded. Indeed, the internationalism of the case and its ability to provoke a powerful reaction worldwide was one of its distinctive features.[69] The Comintern spearheaded an international campaign that took Ada Wright, a widow and domestic servant who was the mother of two of the boys on trial, across Europe in an effort to gather support for the accused and seek a reprieve. Very quickly, however, the Scottsboro case transcended political or class divides among the people it moved. Outrage over the case logically made its way into the League Against Imperialism's forums and the UTN's newspaper *Le Cri des Nègres*, but the case's outcome was also challenged by Socialists and liberal intellectuals in France.[70] At a time when fascism endangered racial relations, and countries promoted nationalism, Scottsboro moved beyond a traditional vision of blacks as other and dangerous and inspired a politically unified front that in many ways sought to challenge and overturn the existing Europe. Black colonial migrants in Paris, and organizations such as the UTN, momentarily basked in widespread antiracist sentiment.

Another *cause célèbre* helped cement the recognition of a black colony in Paris and reinforce its ties to Parisians: the 1931 Colonial Exposition during which government-sanctioned exhibits of black men and women made those who unofficially wandered the alleys and streets of Paris appear all the more spectacular and exotic. Those alleyways were an important space in which to recruit new members into black anti-imperial organizations. As early as 1929, when the exposition was still being planned, the Dahomean hospital worker and militant Pierre Kodo-Kossoul suggested that the LDRN should attempt to protect and support the blacks who would arrive in Paris (ironically, precisely what the government's Centre des Affaires Indigènes said it was doing). Moreover, the LDRN should ensure that these performers were not abandoned to their fates by the French government after the Colonial Exposition was over, something that he argued had happened to soldiers and workers in the aftermath of the Great War.[71] In November 1929 a section of the LDRN gathered under Kouyaté's presidency to debate the exposition. Members viewed it as yet another manifestation of French imperialism: "They will rip from their homes *indigènes* who will then be exhibited as attractions; once the exposition ends, they will be thrown out on the street without being cared for and many will die of cold without ever seeing their families again."[72] Along with the potential repercussions for participants, however, LDRN members viewed the Colonial Exposition as an exciting opportunity to encounter compatriots from their home colonies.[73] Rather than admire recreated African villages like the Europeans, Africans and Antilleans were thrilled by the opportunity provided by this event to contact fellow colonial men and women and reminisce about their homes in the colonies.

By March 1931 the League Against Imperialism, along with several other associations, picked up on the LDRN's concerns. A call to boycott the exposition emanated from the League Against Imperialism's headquarters in Berlin, and the decision was also made to organize an anti–Colonial Exposition that would contest the official exposition. The anti–Colonial Exposition relied heavily upon collecting and displaying disturbing images of violence in a colonial setting, and Parisian LDRN members were active in gathering documents for the exhibit.[74] Given their penchant for collecting, as well as their interest in the colonial setting and counter-politics of various kinds, it is not surprising that surrealists were also strong supporters of the anti-exposition. The writers and surrealists André Breton, Georges Sadoul, René Crevel, and Louis Aragon were among the more famous signatories of a tract entitled "Ne Visitez pas l'Exposition Coloniale," (Don't Visit the Colonial Exposition, May 1931). They begged readers "to respond to speeches and executions by demanding the immediate evacuation of the colonies and the indictment of the generals and the civil servants responsible for massacres in Annam, Lebanon, Morocco, and central Africa."[75]

With such strong support, the anti-expo opened its doors on September 19, 1931, several months later than the organizers had hoped. It was open to the public on Thursdays and Saturdays from 3:00 p.m. to 11:00 p.m. and Sundays from 10:00 a.m. to 6:00 p.m. Admission was set at 2 francs. Located in three rooms of the Soviet Pavilion, which had been built for the 1925 Art Deco Exposition, the first floor displayed twenty panels of photographs, illustrated newspapers, posters, and maps. Photos showed the daily lives of colonial subjects and citizens as well as high-ranking colonial administrators such as the Resident-General of Morocco Marshall Lyautey. Several pictures depicted the *indigènes* being tortured or killed. A second room exhibited colonial art, including wooden sculpted statuettes, masks, musical instruments, and leopard and snake skins. A third room displayed the life of peasants and workers in the USSR in an unsubtle attempt to showcase the good life under communist rule.[76] The LDRN estimated that over five thousand visitors visited the Pavilion; all were indignant when presented with the violence perpetrated in the colonies, and some joined the organization. Since Kouyaté, Ramananjato, and other black migrants were on the anti-exposition committee, the success was complete for the LDRN.

Opposition to the Colonial Exposition was not limited to calls for a boycott: workers also tried to engage Parisians and colonized men and women within the gates of the event. Authorities quickly came to the conclusion that LDRN members might taint the spectators and the performers with anti-imperialist, nationalist, or communist politics. That was why agents such as Joé were asked to infiltrate the pavilions, especially after hours, in an attempt to trace any contacts between colonized men and women visiting Paris for the exposition and those who were permanent residents of the metropole.

Nonetheless, the most international of the interwar *causes célèbres* transcended these race- and colonialism-centered affairs. Cases such as the Scottsboro one, and protests such as the anti-exposition, were just two examples of how anti-imperialists were joining the League Against Imperialism and other groups and individuals in rejecting what they viewed as an increasingly dangerous Europe defined by colonialism, nationalism, oppression, and the most worrisome "ism" of all: fascism. Instead, they called for an international focus upon humanitarianism, pacifism, and unity. Antifascism, then, was a third *cause célèbre* in interwar Paris. Black anti-imperial groups, which had previously been limited to promoting their causes with few resources and inadequate access to far-reaching social and political networks, were able to mine the international frenzy of debate over fascism for both financial and moral support. Ramananjato and other members of the UTN tapped into the growing cohesion among anti-imperialist and antifascist idealists in order to multiply the spaces in which they could conduct their politics.

In the 1930s turmoil in Africa, Europe, and the United States (often expressed through the lens of race) reinforced unity between those committed to anti-imperialism and other Parisian groups. As historian Richard Cobb recalled, "France was living through a moral and mental civil war . . . one had to choose between fascism and fellow traveling."[77] Certainly the UTN tried to use antifascism as a standard under which to gather black organizations. For example, in June 1933 in the basement of the Café de la Samaritaine on the rue de Rivoli on the Seine's Right Bank, Kouyaté assembled members of eight black organizations. One representative was a young Léopold Sédar Senghor, future first president of independent Senegal, who was just starting to emerge as a student activist. Kouyaté emphasized the material and moral aid the UTN aimed to provide, and its desire to support blacks in Paris.[78] Léopold Sédar Senghor promised to try to persuade his Senegalese student group to join. It never did, and Senghor subsequently was ambivalent about recognizing ties between 1920s radical groups, and 1930s student movements.[79]

A more sweeping example of how this "mental civil war" played out in France was the Stavisky Affair. Alexandre Stavisky, a corrupt businessman of Russian origin, was linked in a fraudulent scheme with high-level left-wing government officials, thereby providing the perfect opportunity for extreme right-wing groups to express their discontent with any form of left-wing politics. In order to escape arrest, Stavisky fled to Chamonix in the French Alps. There, he shot himself as the French police closed in upon his room. Extremely suspicious of a suicide that it was convinced was murder, the right-wing saw in this event a left-wing cover-up.[80] In an escalating drama, paramilitary and protofascist groups such as the Croix de Feu poured into the streets of Paris on February 6, 1934, hoping to provoke a coup d'état through these riots. In response leftist and labor groups also took to the streets in a bid to try to stop the protofascist groups as they fought their way to the Chamber of Deputies, the French legislature during the Third Republic. Black radicals joined the ranks of other workers and left-wing intellectuals. An anticommunist from Senegal named Adolphe Mathurin, who had been a member of the LDRN, later recalled that "the parties of the Left had appealed to us to come out on the streets . . . On Feb. 6th and afterwards we were there, along with Communists, Socialists, and Radicals against the supporters of Coty and the Croix de Feu, who carried poles set with razor blades, and used to single us out."[81] The implications of the links between blackness and spectacle carried fresh significance when right-wing rioters were armed with sharp edges.

Indeed, if the Colonial Exposition in 1931 marked a watershed year in terms of kindling anti-imperialist awareness, then February 1934 was a turning point for linking radical black groups to the rest of leftwing and actively antifascist France, motivating them to take to the streets of Paris as protestors and activists. Their politics spread from meeting rooms and the confines of expositions to public demonstrations. Radical blacks were not only concerned by right-wing rampaging, but also by the powerful seduction protofascist groups exercised on disaffected and disabused World War I soldiers, including colonial ones. At a July 1934 meeting of the UTN, the communist Stéphane Rosso

warns his comrades against the propaganda of certain political leagues that are trying to attract to their ranks natives of the colonies. We have nothing to gain from the establishment of a fascist regime in France. Wherever fascist dictatorships have implanted themselves in Europe, the result has been, for our race, new vexations and a reduction of our political and social rights. Remember that Hitler, as soon as he came to power, dissolved all existing *nègre* organizations in Germany. We must thus make every effort to keep our comrades from allowing themselves to be led toward fascist organizations.[82]

This growing sense of insecurity focused not only upon the dangers posed by fascism to *indigènes*, but also upon the possibility that some of them would be led to support fascism as a result of dissatisfaction with the French administration.

Rosso's fear was not groundless. Some right-wing parties in France did recruit colonial migrants, in particular North Africans, for their paramilitary organizations. The attempt to turn North Africans into political soldiers deeply disturbed many colonial migrants. Organizations such as the League Against Imperialism tried to reason with potential targets by denouncing "the maneuver of national elements who do not fear, today, to appeal to the patriotism of those whose fathers they had massacred on the battlefields."[83] The communist newspaper *L'Humanité* also weighed in, explaining in an article published on May 1, 1934, what might have motivated a few Algerians: "In order to convince Algerians—who are almost always unemployed and in dire straits—to participate, fascists offered them blue shirts, boots, cigarettes, and even money. They have them do physical education while riling them up against Jews and foreigners. Recruiting takes place in the Algerian cafés with the help of promises of miracles."[84]

Perhaps in part to offer an alternative path to colonial migrants, between 1933 and 1935 the French branch of the League Against Imperialism organized campaigns that drew attention to colonial abuses in Morocco, Syria, and Indochina. The organization sought to critique the colonial œuvre in all its abusive forms.[85] Although antifascism ultimately failed to join Kouyaté and Léopold Sédar Senghor, it nonetheless made for a compelling argument in persuading individuals to leave their chosen militant path and join with others, even if only momentarily, to share a drink.

With political links to communism, pacifism, and antifascism, and geographic connections as far afield as Moscow and the United States, anti-imperialism was more than a mere blip in the French colonial project, especially since metropolitan anti-imperialists were so dedicated to creating even the most tenuous of footholds on overseas terrain. Colonial administrators had no doubts that anti-imperialism threatened to undermine their authority. They believed that its seed was usually planted in the metropole, for it was those who had "evolved" the most in their civilization, through education and proximity to Europeans, who were also the most likely to develop hatred of the white race and upper classes. According to colonial administrators in French West Africa, dressing in European garb, listening to jazz, or singing the French national anthem, "La Marseillaise," were all hallucinations of civilization that drifted away once Africans returned to their deserts.[86] But anti-imperialism stuck. A 1927 political report for French West Africa argued that "the propaganda that targets and uses them takes hold precisely when these auxiliaries' minds, having received the germ of a good education, have not yet had the time to learn how to filter for themselves, and eliminate, noxious ideas, but instead such minds constitute the ideal terrain for receiving and nourishing bad seeds."[87] This sort of paternalism, whether stemming from the Communist Party or the French administration, was one reason anti-imperialists were determined to stand on their own two political feet, even as French officials stubbornly maintained that nationalism made no political sense in French West Africa.[88]

The anti-imperialism that germinated in the metropole was, ultimately, also destined for a colonial context. Organizations worked very hard to get their newspapers and tracts across the waterways. They requisitioned sailors who ensured the liaison with the colonies. The colonial administration tried everything to block them. French West African and Malagasy colonial administrations partially funded the Centre des Affaires Indigènes in order to keep track of their colonial subjects and citizens. They created regulations to prevent distribution, display, and sales of extremist newspapers and tracts within the colonies, even when these items were permitted to circulate in the metropole; spied upon sailors once they reached African ports; produced long lists of banned newspapers (which included *La Race Nègre*, *Le Cri des Nègres*, *La Dépêche Africaine*, and many others); and distributed lists of metropolitan anti-imperialists that included all the usual suspects. They claimed, often, that bolshevism did not have a foot upon which to stand in the colonies. But anti-imperialism was clearly a persistent threat, for no matter what they did, newspapers and tracts kept coming. Shipments and mailings arrived in French West Africa on a regular basis; Kouyaté's name and politics were known in Senegal; and it was certainly the intent of malcontented *tirailleurs*, sailors, workers, and ex-students to use their Parisian experiences to firmly plant anti-imperialism's roots in the colonies. Spreading anti-imperialist (or, as the authorities also called it, anti-French) sentiment had its dangers. Citizenship was withheld from those who displayed anti-French ideas.[89] Yet anti-imperialists were not easily deterred, and their commitment was bolstered by the knowledge that spreading anti-imperialism to the colonial context was a necessity if severance from France was to become truly possible.

Of course, envisioning links with West Africa, Madagascar, and the Caribbean and actually succeeding in establishing them were two very different things. The story here has been that of Parisian anti-imperialists. There are many tangible traces of their success in sending their politics back home, but how and even whether these were incorporated into politics at the grassroots level overseas is another story.[90] The nuances and range of metropolitan anti-imperialism indicates that anti-imperial struggles in any space—metropolitan or colonial—were far more complex than a blanket rejection of French colonialism. Colonial migrants needed to be creative and flexible, relying upon the community-forming notion of belonging to a "black colony" in the metropole, while also understanding that they were inextricably linked to their overseas homes and thus that theirs was a transnational audience.

In the end, the "bad seeds" of communism, pacifism, antifascism, and anti-imperialism, nourished by stubborn men and some women and by intricate organizing, found ideal terrain in Paris and the tantalizing suggestion of a promising environment in the rest of France's empire. No wonder police reports termed these men a "black colony." After all, they were actively colonizing Parisian space—at the center of the French empire—intellectually, politically, and culturally. And much like the imperial nation-state with which they struggled, their metropolitan colony had obstinate links to overseas territories.

4 REVERSE EXOTICISM & MASCULINITY

The Cultural Politics of Race Relations

*Nightclub. Montparnasse. It's filthy rich. There the cream of society
and the swells meet up. Orchestra* nègre. *Mewing of the saxophones
... Women "of the world" and their companions "out on the town."
One of these women, little, dry like an unemployed man's bread,
simpers: "Aren't they sweet, those* Noirs,*" like she might say, "Isn't
he cute, that little dog." Oh yes! You only know us as the* nègre
*who laughs, the entertainer for men and women of leisure! But behind
our radiant lips, there are teeth. Teeth that gnash at times!*

—"DE MON COIN," *Le Cri des Nègres*

In November 1932 the communist cell of the newly formed Union
des Travailleurs Nègres (UTN) met and discussed how to sell the
organization to black men in Paris. The politics of race and anti-
imperialism had created a core, political black colony, but there was
an entire sociocultural dimension to colonial Paris that still needed
to be affected. Hence, one member argued that above all they should
not "immediately impose communist politics upon members. They
should augment their membership by attracting *indigènes* with fêtes
and lectures."[1] The UTN could attract workers as they exited their fac-
tories, in the cafés they frequented, and by inviting them to parties.
Perhaps unbeknownst to these black men, Ho Chi Minh (known to
the French at the time as Nguyên-Aï-Quôc) employed a similar technique, stopping Asians on the streets of Paris and thereby using racial
visibility to his political advantage.[2]

Henriette Carlier, the secretary of the French Communist Party's colonial section, tried to lead meetings such as this one with an iron fist. She demanded that communist UTN members of her black colonial section attend classes on propaganda and insisted that all correspondence from Africa be divulged to the Communist Party.[3] A German woman whose real name was Eva Neumann, Carlier was sent to France in the 1920s by the Comintern. She married a French communist, Aimé Carlier, so as to avoid problems with the French police. As a white woman amongst black men who had very little room for any women within their organizations, her influence may have been tenuous, but she chose to ignore this fact. In June 1933, during another meeting of the communist cell, the hospital worker Pierre Kodo-Kossoul pursued the theme of cultural politics by reasoning that the UTN consisted of several factions, some of which were not interested in the communist doctrine, and that encounters with apolitical members needed to be handled with care. Carlier would have none of such reasoning and preferred to bulldoze Kodo-Kossoul, explaining that communists simply could not accept sugarcoating political objectives.[4] Black men, she stated firmly, would only receive independence if they obeyed the orders and directives of the French Communist Party's colonial section.

Carlier's audience, comprised of African and Caribbean men, listened. However, these men had already discovered that their capacity for independent thought and action depended in part upon preserving certain intellectual, social, political, and cultural spaces for themselves while in France. This they did in part by using masculinity and race to their advantage. So in the end they ignored her and responded, amongst other things, that their newspaper *Le Cri des Nègres* had to remain autonomous lest it stop "reflecting the ideas emanating from the *nègre* milieu."[5]

The black colony was sculpted from the elements of racial and political solidarity, but Paris was still dominated in their eyes by white men. In consequence, strategies for sociocultural independence could not follow straightforward political lines, in particular with respect to the phenomenon of negrophilia. Neither Agent Joé nor the anti-imperialists were immune from the *vogue nègre* so well embodied by Josephine Baker. They understood that blackness not only made them more visible on the streets of Paris, but also shaped their own milieus. How did black men respond to their categorization as exotic others when faced with a *vogue nègre* that threatened to leave them voiceless? How did they reinforce their control not just over the political milieu they had forged in part through racial bonds, but also within the broader cultural sphere of the capital?

Two strategies helped them to navigate this elusive space. Implicitly they gendered their political world male, defining it through masculinity and sidelining, although not excluding, the women who accompanied them. Masculinity defined how people related to one another, whether in unity or division, within black groups—a phenomenon that remains understudied in the metropolitan, French context.[6] The denial of rights that in the eyes of these Africans and Antilleans had been earned in the mud of the trenches contributed to the at times violent need to defend honor and manhood within black political circles, for example vis-à-vis French colonial policies, one's opinions, and one's family. Explicitly black men reversed exoticism by seemingly embracing the *vogue nègre* only to then use it to spread the politics of anti-imperialism. The two gestures—spreading black politics via culture, and creating a masculine political setting—were not unrelated. Going out in Paris meant meeting white women, and such encounters often became more than casual, social interactions. The politics of anti-imperialism opened up an array of possibilities for affiliation and interaction with predominantly European political groupings. Masculinity and what is here termed reverse exoticism were, in contrast, very much products of black men's agency in the sociocultural spaces of Paris they chose to invest with political meaning: dance halls, nightclubs, and cafés.

The Communist Party's choice of Henriette Carlier as the head of their black colonial section was ingenious. Less threatening than her male equivalents, she was one of several women who crossed a racial boundary closed to French men who were too strongly identified with colonizers. Members were wary of Comrade Henriette's authoritarian, outside intervention, but they were used to the presence of white women—their wives and associates' wives—at meetings.[7] Indeed, these women were common enough participants in black politics that they did not always need to be heeded. Thus, during Carlier's tenure as head of black communist Paris, leaders decided that the special handling of reluctant members proposed by Kodo-Kossoul and others should not be just an occasional device, but should instead become a full-blown strategy for wooing Parisians into consciousness about the colonial metropolis in which they lived.

Reverse Exoticism

During the interwar years, with more and more of the men and women exoticized by the *vogue nègre* present on metropolitan territory, the initial objectification associated with negrophilia became a multiplicity of interactions that were no longer confined to the artistic realm but had translated into everyday encounters.[8] The response of those who were not professional performers and nonetheless found their bodies and cultures placed on display was twofold. The straightforward although far from effortless reaction was rejection of this objectification. A more convoluted alternative was to recognize the objectification as a potential communication device, a method of translating politics via the allure of exoticism in order to disseminate anticolonial ideas. By reversing the exoticism imposed upon them, colonial subjects could reclaim their own culture while exploiting the French fascination with it. Reverse exoticism used the urban fascination with race to break away from the constraints of metropolitan politics.[9] In linking a culture of exoticism with political goals, militant organizations related to a broader Parisian community. Reverse exoticism forced the colonial metropolis to come to terms with the very objects of its cultural fascination. Dances were even more difficult to censor than newspapers.[10]

The reverse exoticism strategy was particularly innovative when considering that across Europe there was often what might appear to be a counterintuitive disconnect between left-wing party politics and popular culture. In Soviet Russia, for example, the Communist Party was wary of flapper fashions and popular movies, while in Berlin the youth involved in agitational theater troupes distressed their communist organizers with their unfettered interpretations of revolutionary politics.[11] Reverse exoticism was an example of the Left working through popular culture. However just as importantly it was an example of how black migrants—several of whom were not the youth habitually studied with respect to the Left and popular trends—set themselves apart from the Communist Party through an innovative use of the potentially constraining theme of negrophilia that was traversing local popular culture. Thus with reverse exoticism they were finding methods of bypassing not only government tactics and structures, but also of wrestling hegemony away from the Communist Party.

Brushing Carlier's objections aside, the UTN organized a first exotic fête in the northern, working-class suburb of St. Denis in December 1932 under the chairmanship of the deputy mayor of St. Denis.[12] An eclectic assembly of individuals attended, including a number of European and North African workers lured by the moderate entry fees and an invitation that promised a performance of dances such as the rumba and the beguine.[13] In an interesting twist, accompanied by three musicians described vaguely as Arab, it was a white (not colonial) woman who supplied part of the exotic allure of the event by belly dancing.[14] Approximately 520 people came to the concert, and 190 men and women stayed to dance; many were European and North African workers living and working in the very industrial St. Denis. During the intermission, the anti-imperialist Tiémoko Garan Kouyaté made a speech in which he argued that the event reflected a unity of working classes that transcended race.

Four months later the UTN organized another event, this time in the student-dominated area of Paris known as the Latin Quarter, near the metro stop Maubert Mutualité. A large poster advertised a grand exotic fête with a concert, several boxing matches, and a "bal de nuit" for the nighttime dancers in the audience. The orchestra would perform music specifically described as black jazz, as well as beguine and other Creole and modern dances. Performers included an African dance troop and an Antillean dancer named Ira, who though not ethnically described, promised to perform savage dances for the audience. Three of the ninety posters were strategically placed near the Duroc metro stop, on the border between the seventh and the sixth arrondissements, to attract those coming and going from the Ministry of Colonies. Others were placed near the buildings of the senate and the national assembly. This event was manifestly meant to appeal to and educate all those with an interest in colonialism and exoticism, including administrators and other officials.[15]

The event wooed its audience by announcing female performers of a sensuality with colonial characteristics, and male performers of power. The most famous female performer in the genre was Josephine Baker. The UTN was thus elated at the idea of seeing Baker on stage as the most recognized embodiment of the *vogue nègre*, even if ultimately Kouyaté failed to persuade her to join their ranks. The ease with which anti-imperialist men latched onto Baker as the perfect vehicle for their undertaking—both as a representative of colonialism and as a celebrity bound to attract an audience—shows how reverse exoticism allowed them to manipulate existing representations of otherness to their own political ends. In their desire to attract Parisians, organizers modeled their fête on the colonial venues of Parisian nightlife, for example setting the price of drinks at five francs because that was precisely what people paid if they went to popular nightclubs such as the Bal Nègre of the rue Blomet. They openly discussed nighttime outings during meetings, using their social forays into Paris to come up with a blueprint for these events.[16]

The strategizing paid off. With 400 in attendance, Kouyaté did not even wait until the intermission before making a brief but fiery political speech. As he explained that the UTN sought to unite blacks in the metropole with those in the colonies, he was greeted with effusive cries of "Down with war! Down with Hitler!" and perhaps in part as a reaction to the 1931 Scottsboro Affair and U.S. racism more generally, "Down with America!"[17] Especially in this age when Hitler was expelling the Jews from Germany, Kouyaté argued, racial divisions sprang neither from workers nor intellectuals but from the colonizing powers. Prejudice needed to be suppressed at every level of the population, from children who were taught that black men were savages to imperialist administrations.[18]

Thereafter, black groups regularly organized social events during which speeches such as these were made. Dances were attended by hundreds of people, and were organized in different parts of Paris so as to attract crowds representing diverse classes and backgrounds. At each of the events, the white majority of dancers crossed paths with a core group of seventy Africans and Antilleans. That same nucleus was instructed to dance at nightclubs and go out to cafés where they might be able to reach those who would be sympathetic to their anti-imperialist cause. Reverse exoticism was used in both formally arranged and preexisting settings as a method of establishing autonomy from the French state, the PCF, and the cultural and social influences of negrophilia. Still, not everyone favored the idea of exploiting the Parisian fascination with race for a political cause. As early as 1927 one member of the Ligue de Défense de la Race Nègre (LDRN), who later went on to be a member of the UTN, argued that "we must not . . . make a pleasure society out of this organization created to support struggle and emancipation"—a sentiment that takes on a particular meaning when placed within the context of the wooing of Frenchwomen that accompanied reverse exoticism.[19] Other members complained that the events always cost the associations more than they collected from entrance fees. Before the St. Denis event, the communist Stéphane Rosso grumbled that the UTN's money might be better spent on printing *Le Cri des Nègres.*[20]

Since the St. Denis and Maubert-Mutualité fêtes resulted in deficits, why did the UTN continue its program of outreach? While evidently UTN members were keen dancers and socializers, they also always considered the political factor. In one evening, they could reach hundreds of people by juxtaposing political ideals and culture. Choosing strategic locations such as a student and an industrial area of Paris further secured them a diverse audience. And indeed, they did move outside their usual circles as they prepared for both the Maubert-Mutualité and the St. Denis fêtes, making both themselves and their newspapers known to others. Nancy Cunard, the English patron of black culture and editor who published *Negro: An Anthology*, wrote to the UTN shortly before the fête asking for a subscription to *Le Cri des Nègres* and suggesting that she might be able to put organizers in touch with four African American jazz musicians willing to play for free. According to organizers she proceeded to attend, as did Etienne Léro, the editor of the communist and surrealist manifesto *Légitime*

Défense, who along with several other members of the audience also subscribed to *Le Cri* on the spot.[21] Both remained in contact with the UTN and its members after this initial encounter, and Cunard was still an advocate for the organization in 1938.[22] Likewise, the Maubert-Mutualité event drew a diverse crowd that included George Padmore —the Trinidadian communist and leading Pan-Africanist—and two of the Martinican Nardal sisters.[23] Soon thereafter informants noted that newly minted members, including a lone, unidentified, white man, were swelling the ranks of UTN meetings.[24]

Kouyaté, who spoke at both fêtes, showed remarkable persistence in his cultural politics. He suggested in 1926, just after the Comité de Défense de la Race Nègre (CDRN) was first organized, that he would initiate dances and form jazz bands that together would render the organization attractive.[25] He understood that the rationalization for large social events was to try to stay in touch with colonial migrants and white men and women all over Paris.[26] Others also understood. In a March 1935 meeting of the UTN, after Kouyaté had been forced out of the organization, the question of how to recruit was again broached. With expenses covered by the Communist Party, members decided to explore cafés and bars in all the arrondissements, and also attended *bals* and other pleasure arenas where black and white men and women gathered.[27] They chose to invest the black, Parisian topography of nightlife with political meaning.

Coordinating black events within a negrophilic Paris was a strategy, but also a matter of self-respect in a city that had usurped the black man's control over his own culture. In 1928 the organization known as l'Union Interraciale organized an evening of performances by artists of many origins, including American, Chinese, Hindi, Japanese, Palestinian, Sudanese, Syrian, and Vietnamese. The organizer, a young Chinese man named Cheng Tcheng, stated that for the first time Paris had witnessed an interracial evening. When one of the participants dissented, he argued:

> You are evoking the exotic milieus of the Left Bank, the studios and cafés of Montparnasse. That's true. Amongst these groups created by professional ties, interests, or just luck, one can ask

for a beer in all the languages of the world. But I doubt you can find there a friendship as complete, as warm, or as profound, as that found here, tonight.[28]

In a capital already heavily laden with exotic venues, only an event organized not only for but also by all races could truly be considered interracial; and a truly interracial event was by its very nature political.

Masculinity and the White Women of Black Paris

In their anti-imperial organizations black men created a space, however precarious, in which to develop their ideas amongst peers. Whether faced with opposition from within their organizations, or from more moderate groups, debates remained vigorous and opinions were freely exchanged. That their politics were informed by their gender and race was reflected both in their demands and in their way of making their demands known. The vehemence with which they defended their honor, and the parameters of war and suffrage (both male domains in the early twentieth century), defined their politics and left women an ambiguous place in the anti-imperialism of the interwar years. After all, when the Profintern played up an emasculation of the colonized by referencing orgies forced upon African women by white colonizers, its goal was to provoke black men into becoming members of the Communist Party. The gesture was intended to inflame African men, even if it probably had an effect upon Frenchwomen as well.

One way of underscoring the extent to which the anti-imperial arena was a male one is to understand the responsibilities women had within the radical black organizations of the 1920s and 1930s. How anti-imperial men positioned themselves vis-à-vis the women in their ranks was a component of their elaboration of a masculine milieu: their gestures became masculine in part because they were in contrast to, and witnessed by, Frenchwomen. Masculinity, also termed manhood, is a constantly fluctuating means through which men define their spheres of influence and power.[29] In interwar Paris the process was demarcated in part by these men's status within the colonial framework but also by both their self-perceived and outwardly imposed understanding of race as a category defining and defined by their bodies and politics. Against the metropolitan backdrop, black men clung ferociously to expressing their authority through masculinity. Yet many men of African descent lacked the full citizenship, and in particular suffrage, that was a significant feature of masculinity among white European men, effectively sexing them male.[30] The presence of Frenchwomen in their ranks lies in stark contrast to the masculinity that dominated these associations, but shaped black men's understanding of their relationships to political rights, women, honor, and violence.[31] The situation of women in these racial politics, and in particular of Frenchwomen, was a tricky one. They found a place in the oral clashes of anti-imperial organizations, but their marginalization demanded continuous repositioning. Informants who infiltrated these organizations were not particularly intrigued by the social or political status of the women present. Yet women still crept into police reports and colonial newspapers in three specific ways. First, they were a generally anonymous but quantifiable presence at meetings. Second, they materialized as the wives of active members. Third, they slowly surfaced as independent political thinkers whose ideas shaped the nature of these organizations.

Agents usually quantified women by specifying the exact number present at each gathering, and their skin color with qualifications ranging, as for men, from white to black, and included variations such as *métisse* and *négresse*. A typical entry read: "July 6, 1926: General Assembly of the Comité DRN: sixty or so people including 17 black women, 4 Indians, and 3 Annamites [Vietnamese]."[32] At times the small number of women allowed agents to give specific names, removing them somewhat from the anonymity of the "female" category, and usually placing them instead into the "wife" category. Hence a Vietnamese agent with the pseudonym Désiré noted in 1927: "21 *nègres* out of 150 convoked, and 3 Europeans including Madame Max Bloncourt."[33] During this same meeting Lamine Senghor, assisted by Kouyaté and Sainte-Rose, established a Seine section for the LDRN, thereby marking the first official split between the radical and moderate black organizations of the late 1920s. Two white Frenchwomen were chosen to help run the newly formed radical section: Madame Kodo-Kossoul, who became secretary general, and Madame Max Bloncourt, who became treasurer general after her husband was named president.[34] Neither woman was given an identity separate from that of her husband (in most reports, not even a first name was mentioned). Nor were women mentioned on a regular basis in accounts of meetings, other than in the recording of their presence. Yet wives of active members were repeatedly voted into positions of relative power, albeit roles that relegated them to bookkeeping and note-taking, and opened them up to disparagement.

Jeanne Kodo-Kossoul, for example, attended almost every meeting as the secretary for the LDRN, and was not shy about speaking up. She was married to Pierre Kodo-Kossoul, who in 1929 was the vice president, had been naturalized French two years earlier, and was a nurse at the Beaujon hospital in Paris.[35] As the secretary, Jeanne Kodo-Kossoul was asked to summarize a financial situation that was generally far from stable. In consequence, she occasionally played the role of public verbal punching bag. When she berated members for not paying dues, they countered by suggesting that she or other leaders had embezzled their money.[36] Her position was further complicated by her race. In 1929 Madame Kodo-Kossoul was appointed to represent the LDRN at a congress in Frankfurt. However, her selection induced criticism. An African working for the Paris waterworks named Sangara Sabia, supported by his friend the Haitian engineer Camille Saint-Jacques, spread rumors about the woman who "being of the white race was not qualified to represent them in Frankfurt."[37]

Jeanne Kodo-Kossoul met a number of conditions that might have led to her eventual exclusion, as a white woman and political activist, from a male-dominated, black organization. The situation came to a head in December 1930 while she was giving an account of the financial situation of the Seine *département*'s section of the LDRN. Tempers swiftly flared as she accused the current president, Faure, and the adjunct secretary, Koïté, of being too quick to blame others for financial mishaps that were entirely their responsibility.[38] In the heat of the quarrel that followed, Koïté defended Faure and in so doing attacked Madame Kodo-Kossoul, alleging that she was in league with the radical opposition leader Kouyaté (this was shortly before the

LDRN split and the UTN was created). Koïté charged that her actions were inimical to the interests of the LDRN. As soon as he realized that his wife's—and therefore his—honor was at stake, Pierre Kodo-Kossoul physically threw himself upon Koïté. President Faure eventually managed to soothe everyone's nerves, and Madame Kodo-Kossoul showed pluck as she coolly finished her report.[39] Still, like most women who attended meetings on a regular basis, she could not escape the status of wife and Frenchwoman, which obscured her role as independent political thinker.

Although violence was infrequent, over time fisticuff duels that linked honor and masculinity surfaced as a regular alternative to verbal invective. Honor, a distinct feature of masculinity for French and European men in particular from the nineteenth century onward, helped to regulate the patriarchal social arena.[40] However it was a tricky attribute of manhood. Not only was its definition in constant flux, but moreover men had to continuously reassert it. Duelling was one of the highest forms for expressing one's honor in bourgeois, pre–World War I France, exemplifying the strength and moral fortitude of those invested in this very dangerous and martial sport. One reason given to explain its popularity at the time was that it fulfilled the function of reestablishing the honor of Frenchmen who as a group had lost the 1870 war to the Germans and were thus feeling, consciously or unconsciously, emasculated.[41]

The duels of interwar colonial Paris were clearly not those of pre–World War I France, with their codes and traditions. Instead, they were shaped by the ethics and practices of the working class, with boxing replacing arms. They were very much a product of their times, but they fulfilled a function similar to the traditional duel with respect to linking honor and masculinity. These practices regulated a male segment of society reminded by a war that was not its own of how it had succumbed to European dominance without gaining much in return. By demanding constant awareness of one's self, politics, and family—and the ways in which such components of one's identity could be slighted—these violent recesses from political discussions became a method for defining manhood. Their masculinity was importantly not established only vis-à-vis the socially dominant white men of interwar France, but within the circles of black Paris. The burden of physical violence that followed assaults upon a member's honor was not always placed as directly upon a woman's shoulders as in Kodo-Kossoul's case. Yet even when women did not trigger it, physical violence between adversaries bolstered the patriarchal nature of anti-imperial communities while relegating women to their sidelines. As a result of such contentious situations, an August 1932 general assembly of the UTN raised an interesting question. Pierre Kodo-Kossoul spoke up at this meeting to ask that the wives of black men be allowed to take part in the Union's administration, clearly keeping his wife and the LDRN's precedent in mind as he demanded this right. Several men challenged his proposal, arguing that only black men should lead the association. The ensuing debate ignored the absence of black women at the head, or at any other level, of the association. Men appeared unconcerned by colonized women's lack of representation, perhaps content that while potentially their skin color qualified them for office, the question was not truly pertinent with so few African and Antillean women present in Paris. In essence, the deliberation therefore concerned only the white wives of black leaders.[42] Overtly, African and Antillean men were not troubled by the color of these women's skin, or for that matter the potential for nepotism, but rather by their status as married women and "the serious drawbacks that would inevitably result if they were to leave their husbands."[43] Race and nationality were not an explicit part of the conversation, perhaps in part because Frenchwomen did not have many more claims to the rights associated with citizenship than black men and hence their race and nationality were not considered intimidating. The problem, instead, was that women in positions of power threatened to unbalance the ascendant masculinity of black Paris. Kodo-Kossoul's proposal was contentious because of what might happen if a white woman who assumed a political role became subsequently independent from her husband. The paternalistic tone of this debate was reinforced by the fact that in considering the importance of marital status as a necessary qualification for participation in anti-imperialist organizations, no one stated outright that married women might in fact already be showcasing their individualism by playing too great a role in them.

4. Brassaï (Gyula Halász, 1899–1984). "Couple at the Bal Nègre, rue Blomet." Circa 1932. Photo Michèle Bellot. Private Collection. © Estate Brassaï-RMN. Réunion des Musées Nationaux/Art Resource, New York.

This thought may, however, have been on the minds of all those who sought to challenge the right of married women to participate at all.

To what extent did gender color the politics of reverse exoticism? Black organizations were dominated numerically by men. Although gender dynamics were rarely openly discussed at anti-imperial meetings, the fact that white women were present at dances and other evening activities was an acknowledged part of the pleasure of organizing or infiltrating such venues. On Christmas Eve 1937 a dance co-ordinated by the Committee for the Defense of Cameroun's Interests was overwhelmingly attended by interracial couples—black men and white women—the same ones who most commonly frequented the *bals nègres* of Paris (see fig. 4). In the months leading up to the event, a major concern for organizers was that black men might attend other dances in Paris instead of this one because they preferred to spend time with "the French, and especially Frenchwomen."[44] Although not explicitly discussed at anti-imperial meetings, perhaps in deference to the few women present, the allure of the Frenchwoman who remained untouchable in the colonial setting seems to have played a part in attracting colonial subjects to the politics of reverse exoticism.

Frantz Fanon, the Martinican intellectual, devoted an entire chapter in his 1952 *Black Skin, White Masks* to understanding the question of why black men—in particular those educated or living in France—were attracted to white women. With so many interracial couples frequenting the black circles of interwar Paris, his thoughts on the matter are certainly worth exploring here. In very blunt terms, Fanon suggests first and foremost that in gaining the love (or lust) of a white woman, the black man finds a way to become white: "when my restless hands caress those white breasts, they grasp white civilization and dignity and make them mine."[45] His analysis rests heavily upon the Martinican-born French Guianese writer René Maran's novel *Un homme pareil aux autres* (A Man Like Any Other, 1947), which he presumes to be autobiographical.[46] It focuses upon the inner conflict caused by a black man's love for a white woman. Fanon quotes its main character, Jean Veneuse, as explaining that black men tend to marry "in Europe not so much out of love as for the satisfaction of being the master of a European woman; and a certain tang of proud revenge enters into this."[47] Domination and revenge, not love, motivate such marriages. Fanon reinforces this thought by quoting a 1949 speech by the Martinican writer and professor Louis Thomas Achille, in which he posits that interracial marriages might be merely a black man's attempt to exterminate the racism from which he has long suffered. Some, Achille explains, "marry persons of a class or a culture inferior to their own whom they would not have chosen as spouses in their own race and whose chief asset seems to be the assurance that the partner will achieve denaturalization and (to use a loathsome word) 'deracialization.'"[48] Achieving equality with the dominant white race is the underlying motivating factor behind these unions, especially significant because historically, Fanon adds, black men sleeping with white women were castrated. Thus, one of the first things a black man does upon arriving in the metropole is enter a brothel and sleep with a white woman. The second is to take the train and head to Paris, which thus also plays a role as fantasy. When he returns home to the colonies with a white woman on his arm, he is the envy of his fellow colonized men.

Subjugation, revenge, conquering racism—these methods of revealing one's power cannot be dismissed. But to what extent do Fanon's thoughts directly apply to the men and women of interwar Paris whose lives were perhaps the stuff of novels but were not, in the end, fiction? First, in his text both black and white women are largely relegated to the role of mere sexual beings, pawns in the manly struggle for power.[49] In this sense Fanon's text buttresses our understanding that women were an essential part of black men's construction of sovereignty and a sense of self, but it does so by reducing their wives and partners to a void within colonial Paris. Fanon renders white women largely voiceless or pathological, blames black women for desiring white men and whiteness, but in contrast appears to sympathize with Veneuse and other black men. In short, Fanon gives us a male perspective on interracial relationships. Second, women made up, as we have seen, only approximately two percent of the black colonial population of interwar France. All other motivations aside, most men who remained in France for a long time had direct access only to French-women. This may have had a psychological effect upon them, but not necessarily the one described by Fanon. Third, these women may or may not have been of an inferior class when they married these men, as suggested by Achille, Fanon, and Maran, but they were clearly outspoken within black organizations, and were educated enough to participate actively and cogently both in meetings and in publications. Theirs was, in other words, often a long-term and vocal partnership with their husbands.

Beyond the fact that Fanon's analysis seems skewed toward the male perspective, there are two others factor that can help us to understand what might otherwise appear to be a disconnect between his post–World War II analysis and these prewar relationships. Fanon included in his long quote of Achille a phrase that might seem rather out of place, in which Achille explains that his focus was upon "certain interracial marriages entered into outside the normal conditions of a happy household." Here, then, is the key to understanding Fanon and others' analyses of interracial marriages: the point was not to dwell upon the private, domestic moments that added up to functional relationships. After all, the examples Fanon uses to explore the place of white women in the male struggle for power center around white women's fantasies involving black men (with rape and sexuality being blended in perplexing ways as Fanon asks, for example, "does this *fear* of rape not itself cry out for rape?").[50] They include a girl who confides in Fanon her terror of going to bed with a black man; a prostitute who is brought to orgasm by the mere thought of going to bed with a black man; the same prostitute who is obsessed with discovering why a woman she knew went mad after spending one night with a black man, and how she might be able to recreate this scenario for herself; and the women who, when asked by black men doing their military service in Europe to dance, "made involuntary gestures of flight, of withdrawing, their faces filled with a fear that was not feigned" even though, as Fanon goes on to rationalize, in the public venue of a dance hall they were perfectly safe.[51] Instead, the point was first to explore the repercussions of these relationships' public display for worldwide social and cultural politics. And second, the point was to focus upon the moments of transition when black men first came into or out of contact with white men and women, for example when leaving their colonies for the first time, first arriving in France, or returning home again.[52] In the end, Fanon makes clear that whether or not all partnerships between black men and white women were motivated completely, in part, or not at all by such impulses as subconscious yearnings for equality achieved through sexual practices, or outright retribution via the constant humiliation of an intellectually and socially inferior white partner, they were most often analyzed and interpreted as such.

Not surprisingly, then, even before Fanon's time black colonial migrants and informants discussed the preference some had for social events at which Frenchwomen were present. Especially when leading anti-imperialists were involved, that predilection was at times contentious. In *A Long Way from Home* (1937), an autobiographical work, African American Harlem Renaissance writer Claude McKay recounts a fascinating conversation between Lamine Senghor, described as "a tall, lean intelligent Senegalese and his ideas were a mixture of nationalism and international Communism" and a Senegalese café owner in Marseille. The café owner argued that Senghor's marriage to a white woman detracted from his racial politics. Senghor "replied that he felt even more bitterly about the condition of Negroes because he was married to a white woman; and as Communism was international, it was an international gesture for him to be married to a white woman, especially since white chauvinists objected to intermarriage." Senghor then reminded the café owner that he was omitting one detail—his own partner was also a white woman. In response, the café owner objected that leaders had to be held to higher standards for two reasons. First, "colored women will not follow Negro leaders who are married to white women." And second, he took the example of Blaise Diagne, the first black man (as opposed to *mulâtre*) to be elected a deputy in Paris, where he promptly married a white woman:

> Now his mulatto children despise us black Senegalese. Now
> if Deputy Diagne had a colored wife for his hostess in Paris,
> wouldn't that be propaganda helping our women and our race?
> But I think the French preferred Diagne to have a white wife,
> rather than have a colored woman as a political hostess in Paris.
> Soon as we tried to do something for ourselves as a group, they
> did something else to make our action ineffective.[53]

Since "mulatto" was an insult, as we have already seen, because of its political connotations of pliancy, assimilation, and ultimately betrayal, this café owner's analysis is particularly insightful.[54] It adds another layer of meaning to the slur implicit in the terms *mulâtre* and *métis*, since the sons and daughters of many anti-imperialists who deemed themselves to be *nègres* would later have to choose whether to consider themselves *nègre* or *mulâtre*—and might always be considered *mulâtre* by those around them. In other words, *mulâtre* was not only a political insult, but one whose meaning depended entirely upon the very specific context of this first generation of Parisian anti-imperialists. To a certain extent Achille, Fanon, and McKay remind us that even marriage was a political act, a reverse exoticism in which women constantly reminded their husbands, those husbands' colleagues and friends, and any Parisians who happened to pass them on the street or in a nightclub, that bedrooms were also part of colonial Paris, spaces in which a colonial taboo could be broken. And however such relationships played out in the intimacy of apartment buildings, rather than settle into a metropolitan existence, men still tried to dominate the public, political arenas.

The language of race was thus another important means to preserve pride and honor. In his novel *Banjo*—an interesting fictitious juxtaposition to *A Long Way from Home*—McKay reflects upon the "race men" who lived in the popular quarters of Marseille during the late 1920s. Women were for the most part sidelined by them, with the exception of Latnah, whose vague, "Oriental" origins cause her character to condemn men of color who prefer white women (to her) as companions. As such, Latnah appears to embody a position more frequently found in the Harlem branch of the American Communist Party during the 1930s than in France.[55] In the United States, where black and white both men and women were present in much larger numbers within one organization, interracial dating and marriages occurred on a regular basis. However after black women rose in the ranks, they started to inveigh against relationships between black men and white women. In France, where there were so few black women, racial politics not only easily remained largely male, they were also a process through which to sustain masculinity, or self-respect, within colonial milieus. Indeed men often only considered women of color with respect to the bearing of their reproductive roles upon the politics and language of race. In *Banjo* McKay's character Ray is a writer who lives near the port of Marseille amidst those who were either forced into or chose a nomadic lifestyle, which, however precarious, nonetheless affords them much more autonomy than that available to them in predominantly white, French milieus. In this setting, Ray quickly becomes immersed in the language of race. He is warned by a Martinican student not to mix with the Senegalese (a blanket term referring to all Africans throughout the novel) because they are both the dregs of Marseille society and the reason that blacks in France are being treated increasingly poorly. Ray chastises the student for allowing education to overshadow race pride, but finds that these prejudices run both ways when shortly thereafter he is sitting in a crowded African bar and hears a student from the Ivory Coast analyze Antilleans in the following terms: "they got more advantages than we and they think they're the finest and most important Negroes in the world."[56] Inspired by this race talk, Ray gives one of the only sustained commentaries on women of color in the novel. He argues that if they were not "inhibited by race feeling" they would prefer white men to black because the former stood for power and property, before concluding—in terms very reminiscent of the café owner in *A Long Way from Home*—that activists such as Senghor should know better than to encourage such attitudes by consorting with white women.[57]

In the end, back in Paris the question of whether or not wives should be allowed to help lead the UTN was resolved in their favor, and the assembly voted to allow Frenchwomen (as long as they were married to black men) to participate in the organization's administration.[58] Many an anti-imperial leader must have returned to a more peaceful domestic setting as a result of the outcome. Jeanne Kodo-Kossoul, amongst others, certainly took advantage of the privilege and continued to attend meetings as late as 1938, after her husband was deceased.[59] While the organization had become more tolerant of women's presence in their ranks by then, the status of widow—as opposed to divorcée—perhaps also allowed her certain privileges. For the most part, however, black milieus had found a way to retain a modicum of control over these women. Their access to anti-imperialism was predicated upon family status—which interestingly enough meant that anti-imperial organizations had views similar to those of many Third Republic policy makers' views on marriage and women's roles.[60] Thus when women voiced opinions, their husbands' honors were at stake. Collectively, these men and women's devotion to anti-imperialism was made far more personal by family ties.

Jeanne Kodo-Kossoul was not the only woman whose ideas influenced the tenor and organization of the UTN. In July 1933 Madame Ramananjato, Agent Joé's wife, suggested that the organization open a room to the public at the Union headquarters.[61] This particular proposal was accepted, but more often police spies reported that she was accused of shirking or doing shoddy work, which included the thankless task often handed to women of collecting dues that members seemed resolutely unwilling to pay. While defending herself, she would become involved in heated discussions, during which she threatened to resign, and take her husband with her. One member concluded that she felt the need to "often generate discord during meetings."[62] Nonetheless, Madame Ramananjato demonstrated surprising endurance, just as Jeanne Kodo-Kossoul had, especially given that Monsieur Ramananjato worked as an informant for the government. Her threat to remove him from the organization was especially pernicious under those circumstances, and may even have given her husband added credibility. Either she was unaware of her husband's informant status or—and this seems more likely given their close association as UTN participants—she reinforces the notion that he was ambivalent in his political engagement and that his complex status and motivations elude simplistic categorization. One wonders whether Madame Ramananjato influenced and perhaps gendered her husband's vision, and in turn that of other agents. Agent Joé often ended his reports with the comment "please find enclosed the newspaper of La Ligue des Femmes pour la Paix" (League of Women for Peace), which he might well have received in his wife's name. Furthermore, information regarding Jeanne Kodo-Kossoul's presences, absences, and political commitment was often presented by Agent Joé, although he was not always as forthcoming with information about his own wife (for example, he appears to have omitted mention of her race or nationality in his reports). In the end, Madame Ramananjato seemed as devoted to the UTN's cause as her husband, and was committed enough to suggest changes and reform—through a feminine lens.

It was on Sunday, January 30, 1938, sometime between 4:00 p.m. and 7:45 p.m., that Madame Ramananjato became the first person on record—aptly chronicled by her husband—to challenge the black, female void in radical black organizations in Paris. She got to her feet at a general assembly and asked why "no *nègresse* woman [*sic*], or wife of a *nègre*, has ever wanted to join the UTN; do their husbands, *nègres* and members of the UTN, believe it would dishonor their women to bring them [to meetings]?"[63] The men ignored her challenge with respect to the absence of black women in their organization, focusing tellingly upon a manly confrontation between two of the members on an entirely different matter, but the question was a shrewd one. Not only did it address McKay's café owner's fear that black women would be disillusioned when confronted by black leaders who preferred the company of white women. The question also reflected the extent to which honor and masculinity shaped the membership of anti-imperial organizations, intimating that black men did not wish to share political ground with black women, and that honor was not just a construction of the French middle class. The rhythms of interwar anti-imperial circles were beaten out by men who found a measure of comfort in the solidarity of fellow black colonial men, even when that comfort was given virile expression. In part this explains why women—both French and colonial—chose to look elsewhere when they wished to make their voices heard.

5

IN BLACK & WHITE

Women, *La Dépêche Africaine*, and
the Print Culture of the Diaspora

*In this country, she will never be a woman like the others, with a right
to a woman's happiness, because she will never be able to blot out, for
the others, the absurdity of her soul fashioned by Occidental culture but
concealed by an objectionable skin.*—ROBERTE HORTH, "Histoire sans
importance/A Thing of No Importance"

Despoiled everywhere, enslaved everywhere, we are still queens.
—MARGUERITE MARTIN, "A Mes Soeurs"

In the fall of 1935 the black Martinican woman Paulette Nardal arrived
at the Union des Travailleurs Nègres (UTN) headquarters. She picked
up a pen, not, as was her habit by then, to craft an elegant, pithy, and
feminine depiction of the black woman's experience in Paris. Instead
she committed her ink to dozens of envelopes, helping the UTN mail
its newspaper, *Le Cri des Nègres*. That particular edition caught her
eye because it decried Mussolini's invasion of Ethiopia. Yet how did
Paulette Nardal, an educated woman from the French Caribbean, end
up working side by side with workers and Communists from Africa?
Her path to male-dominated, anti-imperial meeting places was a cir-
cuitous one that started its route in the 1920s, when she began writing
for a Paris-based Antillean newspaper titled *La Dépêche Africaine*.

One of the various metropolitan spaces black colonial subjects
carved out for themselves was their own print culture. As a medium,
newspapers revealed the defining interests of the many black organiza-

tions of interwar Paris, and the differences among them. While financial setbacks and censorship (including self-censorship) distorted the thoughts expressed in this manner, the printed word was a preferred vehicle for spreading ideas within Paris, throughout the metropole and, or so the black colony hoped, eventually to the colonies. For the historian, newspapers are especially interesting as counterpoints to police records because the latter might mislead us into overlooking the importance of women in the anti-imperialist movement.

Newspapers reveal the presence and participation of a number of female intellectuals and militants, both black and white, in the racialized colonial politics of the interwar years. Some of these women emerged as leading thinkers who considered race, gender, economics, politics, and society in interwar debates about colonialism. They were pioneers in the development of a racial and feminine consciousness that linked metropolitan and colonized individuals and groups. Via newspapers black women, led by Paulette and her sister Jeanne (more often known as Jane) Nardal, were able to successfully connect feminist middle- and upper-class women with negritude thinkers and anti-imperialist members of the working class.

As active participants in the black milieus of the mid-1920s to 1930s, women used their gender to create interstitial spaces in the Parisian press. These activities, in turn, helped them form an identity-defining community: a constellation of black and white women interested in conversing about colonialism and feminism. They then used their sociopolitical pliability to pop up in unexpected places, as Nardal did at a meeting of working-class, anti-imperial men. This distortion of boundaries redefined and expanded the spaces anti-imperialists had delimited in part through masculinity, and stemmed from the ability of some black and white women to cross the boundaries of race and gender. These women created alternative, metropolitan intervals in which they made their way amidst black and white intellectuals, workers, and revolutionaries, all male.[1]

Differentiating Women in La Race Nègre *and* Le Cri des Nègres

La Dépêche Africaine was the organ of a moderate black organization, the Comité de Défense des Intérêts de la Race Noire (CDIRN, not to be confused with the CDRN), and enjoyed popularity and continuity within the Parisian landscape between 1928 and 1932.[2] In 1929 circulation hovered between twelve and fifteen thousand copies, compared with an average of two to three thousand copies for the paper of the LDRN, *La Race Nègre*, or that of the UTN, *Le Cri des Nègres*.[3] In contrast to both papers, *La Dépêche Africaine* had an entirely different commitment to addressing social injustices in terms that were both racial and gendered. Women were not passive victims, but celebrated as instigators of peace, equality, and humanitarianism; they were not simply the objects of inquiry within these articles, but also their authors.

All three papers were viewed with distrust by authorities, but Maurice Satineau's *Dépêche* soon gained acceptance in the administrative milieu, prompting one report to state in August 1928 that after six issues its articles had become less virulent because "it is difficult at one and the same time to insult the authorities and appeal to their benevolence."[4] Monthly administrative reports claimed that for the first six months *La Dépêche Africaine* camouflaged anti-imperialism in the first few pages only to let it materialize on an inside page entitled "La Dépêche Humanitaire" (The Humanitarian Dispatch).[5] One police report went so far as to claim that "at first, this paper appeared as a truly two-faced one, outwardly respectable although engaging in anti-French propaganda."[6] However, such analyses seemed to ignore the fact that pages devoted to politics, economics, literature, and society were not as controversial by their nature as the one devoted to humanitarianism, which could scarcely avoid appearing contentious with its portrayal of the horrors alongside the benefits of French colonialism. Observers initially mistrusted Maurice Satineau and his paper essentially because of his connections with Marcus Garvey, a Jamaican citizen who was notorious within the French administration as an agitator for black independence worldwide. Garvey stayed in Paris for a few days in October 1928, and thereafter maintained contacts with Satineau. As a result, the police were suspicious of *La Dépêche Africaine*'s editors, suggesting that "although they feign a respectful attitude toward France, most of these *nègres* are anti-French."[7] One police report even suggested that they pretended sympathy for the French administration with the sole objective of currying favor to obtain lucrative situations within the colonies. If nothing else, such comments hint not so much at duplicity as at the self-censorship that necessarily constrained editors and writers.

Mostly *La Dépêche Africaine* avoided the controversy generated by *La Race Nègre* and *Le Cri des Nègres*, both of which focused almost exclusively upon racial injustices, often publishing sketches or photos of corpses with bylines identifying them as victims of colonialism in Africa or racism in the United States.[8] The goals of the latter newspapers included incitement, provocation, and an education of their readers that was often interpreted by authorities as propaganda. The papers were closely tied to their organizations, unlike *La Dépêche Africaine*, which eventually surpassed the renown of the CDIRN, which had instigated its creation.[9] The readers they sought to attract, not surprisingly, were also quite different, mirroring to a great extent the origins of the respective editors. *La Race Nègre* and *Le Cri des Nègres* attempted to reach a primarily working-class African public (even occasionally publishing articles in various African languages) while *La Dépêche Africaine* sought instead to reach an audience that included men and women of all races, including administrators, colonial subjects, and intellectuals.[10] While all three papers aspired to establish connections with the colonies, articles in *La Race Nègre* and *Le Cri des Nègres* focused almost exclusively upon events overseas, using the metropolitan setting as background, unless an especially brutal or racist event directly affected the black community in Paris. For example, the colonial migrant Joseph Vambat made it into *La Race Nègre* in June 1930 after the owner of a little bistro attacked him while he sat calmly in a Chinese restaurant favored by LDRN members on rue Sommerard near the Sorbonne University. The black man initially bested his Parisian aggressor, who then returned with five friends: "they hit him so much that he had two broken teeth, a scraped ear, and a wounded leg."[11] Vambat was arrested, unlike the white men who had beaten him.

With such accounts filling its pages, the paper was not surprisingly banned in a number of colonies including French West Africa, ostensibly because of its anti-French character.[12] The postal service and customs agents were warned to seize and destroy copies of the paper on sight.[13] Within France, censorship laws were not as rigorous. As a rule, papers and magazines were most likely to be censored if they were considered immoral, and in particular pornographic.[14] Occasionally political papers were also restricted, especially communist papers whose goals were ultimately to undermine the government's authority. Often, authorities could count upon libel, or items construed as libel, to surface in the pages of such political papers.[15] For similar reasons some North African and Vietnamese newspapers or issues were prohibited, usually because they demanded complete independence from France.[16] *La Race Nègre* made the list of banned colonial newspapers at least once. No explanations were given for the ban, which may very well have been a one-time sanction in which a particular issue was seized to prevent distribution.

La Race Nègre was believed by the police to have communist tendencies, and yet escaped censorship, if not harassment. Sold in kiosks around Paris, especially in the Latin Quarter and on the Avenue de Wagram, which extends off the Place de l'Etoile/Place Charles de Gaulle (which has the Arc de Triomphe at its center), the newspaper was deemed by the police to be hostile to the French colonial administration. Yet they did not establish that the paper was funded by a political party, and hence could not classify it as blatantly propagandistic. This loophole might be another reason leaders of the LDRN and UTN masked their affiliation to the French Communist Party. For all their extremism, the administrators of this newspaper were considered to be "in their private lives, the objects of good intelligence," much like their counterparts who published *La Dépêche Africaine*, the Guadeloupean Maurice Satineau and *femme de lettres* Marcelle Besson.[17]

In the LDRN's newspaper, women were even more underrepresented than in informants' reports about the organization's meetings. The often anonymous journalists, when they did in fact discuss women, sought to use them to accentuate injustices in the colonies by placing them in the habitually deemed subservient roles of mothers, wives, and victims, thereby further validating the need for a defense of the black race mounted by its men. This classification reflected the roles women were expected to play within the radical organizations that backed these papers. Women appeared as wives, for example, when mixed marriages were discussed. Thus one writer scrutinized a law that granted foreigners citizenship when they married Frenchwomen. They claimed it was designed in response to the supposed savagery of black men. White women were supposed to civilize black men by conferring citizenship upon their husbands, even while being protected by the French administration from tarnished reputations, since the women ended up married to French men, not colonial subjects.[18] As the Colonial Exposition dominated the racial landscape of 1931, another article satirically suggested that white women should be sent to the colonies and paraded around naked so that black men could study them, thereby reversing the situation of the many colonized women who performed their race and culture during the 1931 Colonial Exposition.[19] Such articles reinforced the links between masculinity and the defense of the black race, while suggesting that black women needed to be protected by black men from the white male gaze.

La Race Nègre was published on and off as an organ of the radical LDRN from June 1927 to February 1932, and then under different and more moderate leadership from November 1934 to February 1936. *Le Cri des Nègres* overlapped with *La Race Nègre*, publishing monthly issues from August 1931 to May 1936. *Le Cri des Nègres* encountered distribution problems that reflected those of *La Race Nègre*, and used similar strategies to overcome postal censorship. The newspaper was smuggled into the colonies in large picture frames or concealed within other newspapers such as *l'Excelsior* (a right-wing society paper printing 100,000 copies during the 1930s), *Le Petit Parisien* (a moderate paper printing approximately 1.5 million copies), *l'Echo de Paris* (a conservative paper that declined from 300,000 to 100,000 copies between 1919 and 1937), and so forth.[20] *Le Cri des Nègres* also focused upon colonial injustices, and was rarely interested in presenting an independent female voice: few articles were written by or for women. Women were often simply an example of an exploited group of victims. The UTN's more open contact with the Communist Party, and in particular with a female contact person (Henriette Carlier), may have accounted for the slightly greater awareness of women's issues and questions in *Le Cri des Nègres* than in its predecessor. Several calls to arms addressed themselves directly to women, suggesting that black women participate, for example, in a "Gathering of Women of all countries" in July 1934. The brief passage concluded: "Against all forms of oppression and especially colonial oppression, fascism, and imperialist wars, you, women who give life, stand up!"[21] A long letter followed up on the initial invitation to the 1934 gathering, in which women were identified as particularly marked by wartime horrors in overseas territories, including the bombing of villages in Indochina, India, Syria, or Morocco, the death of children, the destruction of harvests, and so forth.[22]

These two examples were initiated by women who were not members of the UTN. However, they seem to have elicited a response from the UTN since thereafter women were mentioned more frequently within the pages of *Le Cri des Nègres*. For example two articles, "Colonial Realities: The Black Woman in Africa" and "A Gift of Colonization: Prostitution," focused upon forms of exploitation that debilitated the indigenous woman.[23] The former detailed the heavy loads carried by African women over long distances, while the latter argued that prostitution was inexistent in French Equatorial Africa before colonization. However even these articles, signed by a man identified only as "l'Africain" (the African man), and thus penned with the male gaze in mind, differentiated women as subjugated and in need of defending rather than able to speak for themselves, and thereby doubly effaced them.[24]

La Dépêche Africaine: *Black Women and the Printed Word*

Paulette Nardal (1896–1985), along with her sister, Jane Nardal, is considered by a number of literary scholars to have been a founding thinker of the negritude movement. Negritude has traditionally been associated with Aimé Césaire, Léon Damas, and Léopold Sédar Senghor.[25] The term was coined sometime in 1936–37 by the poet (and later politician) Aimé Césaire, and first appeared in print in his seminal poetic work about returning to the colonial setting after years in the metropole and simultaneously coming to terms with race consciousness: *Cahier d'un retour au pays natal* (Notebook of a Return to My Native Land, 1939). Césaire, Damas, and Senghor sought to participate in a literary, cultural, and intellectual movement of black poetics within the francophone world. Negritude has attracted more attention than any other literary and political movement in the black circles of interwar Paris. Recently scholars have reevaluated the role of black women in the genesis of the negritude movement to include the Nardal sisters.[26] Paulette Nardal can be viewed as a "cultural intermediary" for her role in bringing various strands of black internationalism together.[27] She is a powerful example of how women carved an intellectual and political space for themselves, using gender to inhabit an otherwise patriarchal, metropolitan city by crossing boundaries of race, class, geography, and politics. Gender categories had the potential to constrain through their quite rigid distinctions, but women were able to define themselves in such a manner as to make their way into the interim spaces of interwar Paris, first via print, and then in person.

There has been some rather animated debate regarding whether and in what manner Paulette Nardal (or her sister Jane, for that matter) was a feminist.[28] The discussion is complicated by the many varieties of feminism at the local, French, and international levels, including theories of black feminism often generated from within the United States.[29] Certainly, time and place matter: the specificity of the Nardal sisters' situation in Paris and the fact that this context shaped their language should be accounted for in attempting to frame their ideas, as should the fact that whatever their feminism, it was still "nascent" during these years.[30] Some of the designations given Paulette in recent years include "black feminist internationalist" and "African feminist."[31] Such labels rest upon observations that she considered herself to be part of a transnational community of African descent, indeed depended upon this network, and that she empathized with and sought to protect its women. Paulette's focus over time seems to have skewed toward African and Antillean colonial women (although not ignoring African American women). This orientation extends from her education as a francophone intellectual who in the interwar years had lived only in France and Martinique, and who was writing from Paris.[32] With so few other colonial women in the metropole, she showed creativity in reaching out and working not only with the fraction of women of African descent around her but also the white women who shared her Catholic faith, and the African and Antillean men who dominated both intellectual and working-class colonial circles. In this sense, she was in a different situation in France than black feminists in the United States, who although a minority, usually did not have to look far to see a comparatively significant community of black women.[33] Nardal's gaze was sweeping when it came to finding allies and friends, but piercing when it came to identifying with both colonial and metropolitan (including some African American) black women.

Paulette Nardal was the eldest of seven sisters, all of whom were extremely accomplished. Unfortunately, her activities in interwar Paris must be reconstructed, since most of her correspondence, writings, and historical documents were destroyed a first time in 1939 when her ship was torpedoed by the Germans, and a second time in a 1956 fire at her family home in Martinique.[34] What remains are traces of the Nardal sisters in a series of publications and a salon, all of which culminated in the development of francophone race consciousness and negritude. With *La Dépêche Africaine* the Nardal sisters helped to establish contacts between black intellectuals and white Frenchwomen who would go on to become political allies during the antifascist movement of the mid-1930s. *La Dépêche Africaine* was a paper run by Antilleans who sought to improve upon French colonialism with egalitarian principles, thereby positioning themselves as a revisionist group of moderates. Paulette Nardal was introduced to the paper by her younger sister Jane, who joined the staff when the publication first appeared in February 1928.

From the paper's inception, Maurice Satineau felt the pressure of being associated with Parisian radical blacks, as well as that of agents who suspected him and his peers of espousing similar politics of alienation. As a result, he declared his independence in a letter published early on. In protest against opponents of colonial reform who tried to portray the CDIRN as communist he wrote, "Nothing could be more wrong. Perhaps they are confusing our Comité with the so-called Ligue de Défense de la Race Nègre, where a few of our lost compatriots have strayed, which is, in fact, affiliated with the Communist Party."[35] He continued by stating that his group sought to combat communism, which could only stunt the political, social, and cultural development of colonial populations and repress humanism.

The committee thus positions itself beyond any of the political ideologies (communism, socialism, radicalism, etc.) that perturb and divide the metropole. Its politics are purely humane. It strives to make racial prejudice disappear, to combat the injustices and errors committed in the colonies, and to help France's true face—made up of equity, justice, goodness, and love—shine forth in the colonies. It inspires, in a word, the immortal principles of the glorious French Revolution, which state 'men are born free and equal in rights;' the rights of man are sacred and must be respected and defended without distinction of race or color.[36]

By concluding with a direct reference to the French Revolution of 1789 and the "Declaration of the Rights of Man and Citizen" that embodied many of its principles, Satineau established the political leanings of his group as anticommunist and idealistically liberal, while illustrating the level of education that would typify those who wrote for his paper. On the first page of its first issue, the paper proclaimed as part of its goal the desire to reserve many of its columns for intellectual and artistic people of color.[37]

Satineau developed his paper without distinction of race or gender, allowing Jane and Paulette Nardal as well as white women such as Marcelle Besson to partake not only in writing but also administering the paper. In February 1928 *La Dépêche Africaine*'s list of forty-one collaborators included lawyers, high school and university teachers, *hommes de lettres*, politicians, journalists, artists, students, and five women. Its first issue demonstrated the extent to which women might transform an organization and a paper with their ideas while establishing lasting intellectual and political connections. Paulette and Jane Nardal represented black female voices within these pages, but they did so in the company of an articulate cast of feminist white Frenchwomen, whose presence Marguerite Martin represented in the first issue. If *La Dépêche Africaine* stands out as a unique space in interwar

Paris, it is because black and white women shared it when exploring, unfettered, how feminism and femininity shaped and were shaped by colonial conversations in the metropolis.

On the front page in February 1928 was an article by the pacifist Marguerite Martin. Her prior publications included pamphlets such as *Droits des Femmes* (Rights of Women) and *Rôle des Femmes dans la Paix* (Role of Women in Peace).[38] In her article, "To My Sisters," she proclaimed a sisterhood amongst all women: "For the same life lives within us and quivers in our entrails, springing forth from us through the same pains and bringing with it the same hopes."[39] The birthing process unites women, Martin maintained, just as their capacity for overcoming servitude will: "despoiled everywhere, enslaved everywhere, we are still queens." Her call to arms invited women not only to connect, but also to promote world unity in a search for equality beyond race or class. Martin was one of several educated white feminist women who first became interested in race and colonialism because of their involvement with *La Dépêche Africaine*. Their sustained interest in such questions was cemented by the political turmoil of the 1930s, which generated alliances between them and the more radical organizations of black Paris.

The same February 1928 edition also included an article by Jane Nardal, entitled "Black Internationalism." The political undertones of this essay laid the groundwork for negritude. Nardal discussed the schism produced by World War I in the francophone black's consciousness, as well as ideas of a global community in which she argued the francophone black could develop a race consciousness.[40] She noted with stark realism that "previously the most favored blacks watched their brothers of color with haughtiness, presumably believing themselves to be of a different essence." Possibly from her feminist perspective, this statement sums up the many divisions of colonial, masculine Paris but does so with a touch of irony in the face of the seemingly ineffective discord that was such a prominent part of anti-imperial communities.[41] She identified the emergence of a race consciousness that transcended class barriers, thereby arguing for a racial unity that Marguerite Martin had proclaimed in gendered terms. Moreover she analyzed the influences of the *vogue nègre* upon "Afro-Latins" who, as a result, would start thinking about the meaning of race more care-fully, and develop a political race consciousness. Avant-garde artists, whom she called "snobs," taught "many *noirs* who were themselves surprised that there existed in Africa an absolutely original *nègre* lit-erature and sculpture." With this article's considerations of how blacks reacted when they began to understand the value of their art, Jane Nardal introduced a nuanced perspective to the colonial community's understanding of negrophilia's impact upon interwar Paris. Negrophilia could force "assimilated" black men and women to reconsider their black origins and their acceptance of the basic inequalities implicit in exoticism and colonialism. Her article reflected the masculine overtones of the black community around her by addressing how World War I brought these (at the time, all male) migrants together in the metropole and by using only male designations (*brothers* rather than *brothers and sisters*). Al-though she and her sister would in coming months and years address the place of women in this international community, at this point she had perhaps not yet figured out how to explicitly address the role of women in Paris. Or if she was indeed the "Mlle Jeanne, Martinican" described as the adjunct secretary for the pan-colonial Union Inter-coloniale organization in 1926, she had had more experience with the masculine milieus of Paris when she wrote this article (she first ar-rived in Paris in 1923, so it is a plausible connection).[42]

Unlike her sister Jane's political articles, Paulette's were mainly to be found in the section of the paper entitled "La Dépêche Lit-téraire" (The Literary Dispatch). They were pastiches of insight-ful comments upon various black musicians and actors, and lyrical short stories about Martinique or Martinicans in the metropole. In "The *Nègre* and Dramatic Art" Nardal focused upon a Sudanese ac-tor, Monsieur Benglia, whose "cries of passion are cries of the flesh."[43] Nardal's biographical pieces exposed the Parisian black community's complex range of artistic abilities, and in particular how they could escape the pigeonholes of jazz and the African American dance of the Charleston. She continued this defiance with "A Black Woman Sculp-tor" about the African American sculptor Augusta Savage.[44] Paulette also wrote a number of articles focusing upon artists who were jazz or beguine performers. She detailed the athletic as well as aesthetic capacities of the beguine dancer Jeanne Longrais: "To the furious rhythm of the Negro orchestra's music, she executed, with swaying hips, those twists of the waist that show a suppleness and resistance to fatigue rarely found in other races."[45] As both her choice of topics and her comment upon the black race's endurance reflect, Paulette's early work used the performing arts to comment upon life in the black colonial metropolis.

In 1929 Paulette Nardal turned to fiction in order to communicate her understanding of the black woman's existence in Paris. Nardal's short story "Exile" told the story of Elisa, who works as a cleaning lady in a Paris that through her eyes materializes as sad, gray, and shining only under the cold rain. Paris mirrors what Elisa hates about life in France: the "appalling regularity of European life, that exactitude that is an enemy of the imagination."[46] On her crowded bus ride home from work, she dreams of her colonial island in terms that might have been those of Charles Baudelaire: "you lose yourself to the sweetness of living in languid air." Her daydream contrasts with the scene around her: "tense faces, hard eyes, the closed or indifferent physiognomies of white men and women." Eventually, Elisa's son Colomb saves enough money to pay for her trip home, but not before the reader discovers that even an exhausted cleaning lady is subjected to the fascinated gaze of Parisians on the prowl for the exotic.

Elisa's story shows Paris from the point of view of a black, working-class woman. Although Nardal speaks for and through her of a common black experience, Elisa's story serves as a valuable reminder that even with so few black women in Paris, there were some who were neither highly educated nor from established, colonial families. Unfortunately they are the most difficult to locate; no substantive traces of sub-Saharan African women in interwar Paris have been uncovered.[47] For the moment, the city's interwar history is dominated by Antillean women, many of whom were middle to upper class. With time, more stories of the African and working-class women of the colonial metropolis will hopefully emerge. But the fact that even during the 1930s the privileged and Antillean Nardal gained a reputation as someone who spoke for black women of every class and nationality indicates just how inscrutable her fellow travelers were at the time and hence still are today.

Paulette Nardal tried to make them less so, observing how Elisa and others were encumbered by Parisian gazes and felt a keen sense of exile that was not Nardal's alone. Her short story captured an opposition between metropole and colony that marked the pages of *La Dépêche Africaine*. Nardal's articles focused not only upon Paris but also upon Martinique with stories such as the humorous "Martinican Story (History)," about five women who try unsuccessfully to use witchcraft to keep their men faithful. In response to recent devastation caused by the volcano Mount Pelée, Nardal wrote "For the Martinican Disaster Victims" to find support and solutions for those who had lost their lands and homes.[48] In depicting an artistic and literary backdrop that was contextually Parisian, Nardal explored and elucidated Antillean ties to Paris.

Unlike some of the writings by women for *La Dépêche Africaine*, Paulette Nardal's pastiches were neither militantly feminist nor obviously political in nature, although they were uniquely feminine, as the subjects of her work were, for the most part, women. Her work contrasted with that of her sister, Jane Nardal, and also with that of the white journalists Marcelle Besson, Carly Boussard, Marguerite Martin, and Yvonne Netter. Each of these women sought to tie her own feminist struggles with the globally inclusive egalitarian goals of the newspaper, focusing upon exploitation and using backgrounds in law and political engagement to write sarcastic or seditious pieces about race and gender. But there were other articles that analyzed the Parisian setting and, like Paulette Nardal's, seemed to locate alienation in urban life. Carly Boussard, described by editors as a *femme de lettres*, augured Nardal's "Exile" piece with articles on modernism and the metropole. In her column "Aside" Boussard developed a commentary on modern life in the literary and philosophical traditions of Charles Baudelaire, Walter Benjamin, and German sociologist Georg Simmel. The bustling movement of modern urban life contrasted starkly with the colonies' timelessness. Fashion in Paris, Boussard wrote, was women's obsessions with seizing an impossibly fleeting moment.[49] In that moment, "the most pressing concern of our contemporaries is a frenetic search for the unknown, the novel. A need that has as its corollary speed: one must go quickly, quickly to see and experience as much as possible."[50] The desire to absorb as much as possible encompassed exoticism, which was safely consumed in cinemas and music halls. Boussard even addressed the fascination with the *garçonne*, midway between tomboy and flapper, who plagued moralists during the interwar years. She saw these young women as emblematic of the postwar years. They were not decadent even when they fraternized with men, for their intelligence and deep ties with society prevented their degeneration, she argued.[51] These articles reflected *La Dépêche Africaine*'s desire to address a complex audience that was very much an urban, Parisian one with concerns as diverse as feminism, immorality, and exoticism. Colonialism and its political, social, and cultural repercussions were indissoluble from the concerns of modern urban life that characterized the metropole in the interwar years.

Marguerite Martin's second article, "Sunday Promenade: Impressions of a *Nègre* Village," depicted the peculiarity of importing colonies to Paris. She wrote about an African village that had been imported to the Jardin d'Acclimatation, a zoo in the Bois de Boulogne on the western edge of Paris that was notorious for its exhibits of colonized people. With sarcasm she begins her 1928 account that might easily have been written about the Colonial Exposition of 1931: "For our pleasure," Martin wrote, "we have not only snatched big cats from the desert, we have also domesticated man."[52] The irony of these African villagers asked to reproduce their daily habits under a grey Parisian sky did not escape her attention, nor did the oddity of African women forced to dance as though spectators were not staring at them from beyond the partition. Martin found the dance somewhat ridiculous until she remembered a dancehall in which dolled-up Parisian women tried to move to the rhythms of a frenetic jazz music, a sight she found far more disturbing. In a moment oddly reminiscent of nineteenth-century novelist Emile Zola's juxtapositions of machine and modern life, Martin described a woman standing near her: "'How primitive!' exclaimed next to me a pale, thin young lady— some salesgirl from a department store who had escaped for a moment the horrors of unwholesome promiscuities; the artificial lights;

the harassing surveillance of a supervisor or foreman." Martin paralleled modern and primitive, white and black, until Africa eventually appeared filled with health and vitality, leading her to add scathing criticism of France: "Because in our country, of course, there are no vile dead end streets where the odor of urine catches in one's throat, where the banister and walls make one's hand sticky and ooze filth and misery." Although her tone was ironic, Martin's contact with colonialism inspired a heartfelt desire to address poverty and squalor in the metropole as well as racial injustices in France's empire. She discovered a utopian glimpse of hope in two children, one white and one black, who at that young age still have the potential to see mirrored in one another similar desires, hopes, and passions. Even if these two children did not connect, Martin predicted that others would so that eventually "LIFE triumphs." And of course life, as Martin had demonstrated on the front page of *La Dépêche*'s first issue, was imparted by women.

Other women wrote about suffrage and the economy, replacing the cultural metropole so well depicted by Paulette Nardal, Boussard, and Martin with a political one. Yet they still emphasized the role women played as go-betweens and skilled navigators of both private and public space. Marcelle Besson, a white Frenchwoman who cultivated connections with the Caribbean by writing for two Guadeloupean papers with socialist tendencies, was especially comfortable in the role of critic.[53] She wrote articles such as "Woman and Colonial Action" in which she addressed the role of women in the educational evolution of indigenous populations.[54] Approaching the colonial question as primarily a social one, Besson explored the role women might play in improving the indigenous existence by dissipating exploitation through their presence. In an article on the Franco-colonial economy, Besson envisioned a close collaboration between metropole and colonies in which *indigènes* might equal Europeans as financiers and ensure that money flowed into, and not just out of, the French colonies.[55] Besson seemed most comfortable discussing economics and politics rather than writing fiction, and her work was thematically linked by the ever-present social question that dominated her writing. She wrote several articles on the economic page of *La Dépêche*

Africaine addressing the shortage of housing for working families.[56] She believed housing laws needed to be broadened to include not only metropolitan workers, but also the Guadeloupeans whose homes had been destroyed in a recent tornado, which we saw depicted by Paul Colin in chapter 1. This eclectic collection of articles had in common both the desire to address the intricacies of connections between metropole and colonies and their female authorship. However, when contrasted with its radical counterparts *Le Cri des Nègres* and *La Race Nègre*, *La Dépêche Africaine*'s reliance upon female authorship gains in political significance. After all, these journalists' work was not always militant in the sense of being written by self-proclaimed feminists clamoring for suffrage. It reflected diversity in its ability to broach a range of topics, many of which would not have been viewed as traditionally "female." Women's articles appeared on the front page as often as they did in the political, economic, humanitarian, or literary sections. However, both Jane and Paulette Nardal, alongside their white female counterparts in *La Dépêche Africaine*, created a space that black and white women shared comfortably with men. Women found a venue in which to elaborate their sociocolonial critiques of the metropolis. Masculinity performed a certain function in anti-imperial organizations, allowing men to buttress their sense of community and political engagement. The women who colonized Paris came up with different strategies, using their gender to initiate interracial alliances that crossed the usual boundaries of race, class, and politics. As we shall see, they created connections between radical black organizations such as the UTN and white feminists whose primary concerns were suffrage and an international humanitarianism, which fit well with anti-imperialism. Paulette Nardal led the way in establishing such connections with a diverse portfolio of encounters that radiated from her initial work in *La Dépêche Africaine*.

Connecting Black Paris

La Dépêche Africaine was only the first of several papers that linked sexes and races in the search for an understanding of the colonial process. In it the Nardal sisters presented ideas that they later developed more fully in several other papers and a salon. The spaces for contention and political soul-searching created and organized by the sisters encouraged contacts amongst black intellectual women and their male counterparts, and eventually fostered negritude. Less well known are Paulette Nardal's encounters not only with the feminist writers of *La Dépêche Africaine* but also, if fleetingly, with the radical black organizers of the UTN. After their contact with *La Dépêche Africaine*, Paulette Nardal and her sisters took multiple paths through mid-1930s Paris. Paulette and Jane Nardal wrote for several newspapers, and their ideas underlie the negritude movement and the general development of a francophone black political consciousness. At the same time, Paulette interacted with the UTN and many other groups as she militantly opposed the Italo-Ethiopian war in 1935.

In the early 1930s the Nardal sisters gathered African American, African, Antillean, and other intellectuals in their home. The salon, perhaps more aptly described as a *cercle d'amis* (circle of friends), was held Sundays at 7 rue Hébert near the train station in the southwestern Paris suburb of Clamart.[57] Louis Achille, a cousin of the Nardal sisters, would later describe "a feminine dominance that determined the tone and the rites of these convivial afternoons quite unlike a corporate circle or a masculine club."[58] Once masculinity no longer cemented gatherings of black colonial subjects, tea with milk replaced alcohol, and the dinner hour was always respected, as was the train schedule back to Paris which, if disregarded, would have left participants stranded in Clamart for the night. Paulette, the eldest of the sisters, presided over the salon along with Jane, who had studied classical literature and French in Paris. Jane and Paulette were the first black women to study at the Sorbonne while Andrée, the youngest of the seven sisters and also present at the salon, was a gifted pianist and student.[59] Achille remembered the salon's ambitions almost sixty years later in these terms: "We touched on Parisian or world-wide current affairs, while avoiding potentially personal politics; we reflected on colonial and interracial problems; the growing influence of men and women of color in France; and we warned one another of any expressions of racism in order to fight against them elsewhere, through appropriate means."[60] This description hints at some intriguing connections, with respect to both subject matter and tone, between these gatherings and *La Dépêche Africaine*, although there was an important difference: the salon was remembered exclusively as a gathering of men and women of color. However, like *La Dépêche Africaine*, this salon, in part because it was protected from the *tumulte noir*, encouraged black colonial women to grapple with their gendered roles in Paris.[61]

In 1931 the salon inspired publication of *La Revue du Monde Noir*, thus expanding its literary, cultural, and humanist discussions into printed words that sought a similar racial and intellectual exchange. *La Revue du Monde Noire* was a bilingual French and English review whose six issues addressed themselves to a mixed audience. Its goals were tripartite: giving black intellectuals a chance to publish artistic works; educating its readers about black civilization; and creating a bond among blacks of all nationalities. With these goals "the Negro race will contribute, along with thinking minds of other races and with all those who have received the light of truth, beauty and goodness to the material, the moral, and the intellectual improvement of humanity."[62] By declaring a connection to humanism, the Enlightenment, and the 1789 Revolution, the editors used a strategy much like Satineau's in the early days of *La Dépêche Africaine*. The paper's directors declared their affinity for France and her cultural and political traditions with proclamations of *Liberty, Equality, and Fraternity*, thereby removing themselves from the suspicions surrounding even such moderate papers as *La Dépêche Africaine*. The purportedly apolitical articles included "The Negroes and Art," by Louis Achille; "Notes on the Biguine Créole," by Andrée Nardal; poems by the Harlem Renaissance writers Langston Hughes and Claude McKay; "Race Equality," by Louis-Jean Finot; and investigations such as "Is the Mentality of Negroes inferior to that of white men?" by E. Grégoire-Micheli, a member of the Institut International d'Anthropologie (International Institute of Anthropology).

The review's apolitical tone was inspired by a desire to escape the persecution reserved for militant papers, but also to obtain partial funding from the Ministry of Colonies.[63] The editors included the Nardal sisters, the Haitian scholar Léo Sajous, Louis-Jean Finot, and the black American educator Clara Shepard. Of these individuals, only white Finot made the police nervous. Reports noted that he was married to a black violinist with whom he had four children. His relatively temperate political opinions did not disturb the police as much as his marital relationship. Madame Finot played the violin in various Montmartre nightclubs and slept most nights in a room she rented in that neighborhood. The police were unnerved by Madame Finot's independence, and they concluded that while her husband might be socialist, more alarmingly he was driven by negrophilia to become the principal instigator behind *La Revue du Monde Noir*.[64] Thus while seemingly shifting their assessment from the political to the social, onlookers were in fact reflecting upon how a disturbance of the social fabric—through a somewhat nontraditional marriage that also happened to be interracial—was a sign of anti-French politics.

As the existence of such reports demonstrates, the paper was never truly apolitical, since the very act of founding a bilingual, international, and multiracial review in 1930s Paris was provocative. Furthermore, the presence of women editors at *La Revue du Monde Noir*, as at *La Dépêche Africaine*, gave women greater control over their writing and editorial discretion. Thus several articles addressed the intersections between gender and race. Authorities quickly modified their assessment of the challenges posed by both the social dynamics and politics of such a publication and as a result the Ministry of Colonies withdrew funding, leading to an abrupt termination of the review in April 1932.[65] Still, the conversation started by women of color was well under way by then, and women were at ease expressing their politics.[66]

Indeed, the politics of gender were a gateway to expressing racial politics, as Paulette Nardal demonstrated in *La Revue*'s last issue. In her 1932 piece "Eveil de la conscience de race/Awakening of Race Consciousness," while contrasting black francophones with African Americans she argued: "Quite different was the situation among the American Negroes. Though they are not of pure African origin either, the deliberate scorn with which they have always been treated by white Americans, incited them to seek for reasons for social and cultural pride in their African past."[67] The lack of such oppression on the French part, Nardal continued, explained why it took so long for Antilleans to awaken to race consciousness. She did not explicitly address how working-class colonial migrants in the metropolis had struggled with questions of race in a number of gatherings during the 1920s, and had even laid some of the foundations for negritude, either proudly proclaiming their blackness by appropriating the descriptive term *nègre*, or differentiating themselves by favoring the word *noir*. But, like Fanon in a sense, she did talk about how travel from the colonies to the metropole transformed Antilleans. For the most part educated and all French citizens, Antilleans were slow to become conscious of the oppression occasioned by their race. When that consciousness did emerge, it was in Paris and via newspapers and in particular *La Dépêche Africaine*, a venue that was shaped by black and white women as a flexible point of colonial contact. Nardal hoped this movement toward race consciousness would culminate in the newly minted space: *La Revue du Monde Noir.*[68]

When developing her concept of race consciousness, Nardal made two interesting distinctions. First, she saw the emergence of race consciousness as a specifically feminine ordeal. And second, she believed race consciousness to be a collective movement of young women. In 1963 Nardal would write: "We were but women, real pioneers—let's say we blazed the trail."[69] And what allowed a new path to be mapped out was the ongoing performance forced upon women of color in the colonial metropolis. She was introduced to the performativity imposed upon women by the conjunction of their sex and race by the October 1928 article her sister Jane wrote for *La Dépêche Africaine*, "Exotic Puppets," which used the key figure of Josephine Baker to link negrophilia to the development of black race consciousness. Black women appeared exotic no matter how they constructed their own identity, so they took the colonial project quite personally.

The belief that the forced performance of black sexuality in Paris was intimately linked to women's racial politicization was further reinforced, in Paulette's view, by Roberte Horth in the second issue of *La Revue du Monde Noir*. Horth wrote "Histoire sans importance/A thing of no importance" while she was preparing a prestigious French teaching exam, the *agrégation*, in philosophy. It was published in 1932, the same year she died in Paris, aged only 27.[70] Nardal later identified in this article a "feeling of uprooting" that was a specifically feminine alienation. Addressing the repercussions on a black woman's psyche of having the role of exotic object imposed, this article marked a turning point for Nardal. Horth, a woman from French Guiana, sketched the Parisian existence of Lea, a student much like the Nardal sisters whose studies led her to the metropole. Once there, she "entered a great university whose sole concern was to lead mind [*sic*] into the path of progress, regardless of class or race."[71] Content in this institution, Lea soon understood that outside its doors she was a mere fetish, welcome in her acquaintances' drawing rooms but not into their confidence. Lea concluded that not only were women's minds effaced by their bodies, but their bodies did not match their minds. Black men could rely upon masculinity to ground them in Parisian, colonial milieus, but black women saw their intellect and their femininity simultaneously denied—being a black woman, in Paris, was a marginalizing struggle.

Paulette and Jane had been building up to this realization but Horth made the gendered alienation within this racial way of life explicit. And indeed, a few months later Paulette Nardal located the turning point for francophone race consciousness in Horth's article and its articulation of how race linked with gender prevented anonymity and thus passivity in the metropole. In the 1932 "Awakening of Race Consciousness" Paulette Nardal affirmed not only the budding race consciousness that would develop into negritude, but also the essential role played by women in the awakening of the black race: "coloured women living alone in the metropolis, until the Colonial Exposition, have certainly been less favoured than coloured men—who are content with a certain easy success. Long before the latter, they have felt the need for a racial solidarity which would not be merely material. They were thus aroused to race consciousness."[72] This sentiment is powerfully illustrated by a photograph taken during the Colonial Exposition of white men staring at a black woman who gazes steadily at the photographer (and hence the viewer; see fig. 5).

5. In the foreground a Sudanese woman sits, surrounded by the curious crowd of visitors. International Colonial Exhibition of 1931 Series. Location: Exhibition Pavillion, section of French West Africa. 1931. Réunion des Musées Nationaux/Art Resource, New York. Original at Médiathèque de l'Architecture et du Patrimoine, Paris, France.

Racial solidarity was guided not merely by color. Instead, gender changed the parameters of race by giving black women the power to regroup away from early anti-imperialism, creating not so much a core as a tangle of connections that reflected their power. They constructed connections to black men, and white women, via the autonomous (and tellingly entirely cerebral) space of newspapers. When Nardal identified the emergence of an explicit race consciousness, she marked a turning point for the intellectual preoccupations of all blacks in interwar Paris away from the working-class, material solidarity that existed before the Colonial Exposition toward an intellectual and cultural one that soon became known as negritude. She further announced the possibility of a feminine connection that redefined the parameters of race consciousness and race relations.

L'Etudiant Noir

While first *La Dépêche Africaine* and then *La Revue du Monde Noir* allowed the Nardal sisters to explore their feminist race consciousness, neither they nor these newspapers have been nearly as celebrated by their contemporaries or scholars as *L'Etudiant Noir* and its contributors.[73] This newspaper has been singled out as the periodical that generated negritude. For years only the first issue of *L'Etudiant Noir* (1935) could be found, an issue that showed its African contributors were limited early on to Léopold Sédar Senghor, and that the paper was an outgrowth of *L'Etudiant Martiniquais*, a more pedestrian and geographically limited publication.[74] Like its predecessor, *L'Etudiant Noir* had material as well as philosophical concerns: its first three pages reported the overseas students' outrage at having their stipends withheld by the French government, and their partially successful attempts to reverse this situation. The articles written by Aimé Césaire, Léopold Sédar Senghor (who was Senegalese), the Martinican poet Gilbert Gratiant, and Paulette Nardal were of a very different nature. Their articles continued in the vein of *La Dépêche Africaine* and *La Revue du Monde Noir*, using culture to understand race, black life, and what it felt like to be other.[75] However, what happens if we consider *L'Etudiant Noir* not from the perspective of negritude and race consciousness alone, but also reflect on its position with respect to previous articulations of masculinity and feminism, in particular in contrast to *Le Cri des Nègres* and *La Dépêche Africaine?* The importance of Paulette Nardal's position within black colonial circles was confirmed by her participation in yet another cultural project that redefined race and the role of women in 1930s Paris. *L'Etudiant Noir* may have been a newspaper written by and for intellectuals as opposed to the working class; it nonetheless remained as masculine, in many ways, as the anti-imperial newspapers of the interwar years. Césaire and Senghor, both of whom attended the Nardals' salon, were inspired through their visits to analyze the complexity of the black presence in Paris and the repercussions of the problem of cultural assimilation already explored in 1928 by Jane Nardal in *La Dépêche Africaine*. But they were equally concerned with exploring their existence as black men.

Césaire's article "Nègreries: Jeunesse noire et Assimilation" (*Nègreries*: Black Youth and Assimilation) used sarcasm to approach the question of assimilation and warn of its dangers: "if assimilation is not madness, it is definitely foolishness, for wishing to be assimilated is forgetting that no one can change the fauna."[76] His words echoed those proclaimed in the very first *La Voix des Nègres* when he said: "Today's young *nègres* desire neither subservience, nor assimilation, they desire emancipation." And like the pages of *La Race Nègre* or *Le Cri des Nègres*, the article addressed men. Césaire analyzed European clothing such as ties and melon hats that allowed black men to mimic white ones. Indeed, the focus throughout is upon what makes a man with phrases such as: "men, we will say, for only man walks without a private tutor on the great paths of thought," or, "one must fight; first with lost brothers who fear themselves." While the French language certainly privileges the masculine, Césaire did not think to write brothers and sisters, or to address women's fashion as well as men's.

Senghor also favored the male voice in his article "L'Humanisme et nous: René Maran" (Humanism and Us: René Maran). In this contribution, he studied black identity within the French context via the author of *Batouala*, René Maran, in order to understand the two forces that he believed governed black man: reason and intuition. In a prefiguement of negritude, Senghor identified the need for "a cultural movement that has the black man as its aim, Occidental reason and the Negro spirit as its research tools; for one needs reason and intuition."[77] He, like Césaire, repeatedly focused upon the black man, explaining that "being *nègre* is . . . being human, for the black man remains a man." Even his insults were gendered. In seeking to denigrate "literary monkeys" who copycat black humanists through sensationalist novels, Senghor quipped that only "young girls in hothouses" still read them. The phrase suggested that only girls who were completely secluded from the world, as greenhouse plants subjected to artificial heat (a suggestive image), would be silly enough to become avid readers of such fraudulent novels.

Gratiant, like Césaire and Senghor, continued Jane Nardal's and Horth's attempts to come to terms with their identities as African and Antillean Europeans. Gratiant investigated the complexities of mixed blood in a European context in much the same manner as Horth, but with a Marxist twist. His article "Mulâtres . . . pour le bien et le mal" (*Mulâtres* . . . for Good and for Evil) invited readers to reflect upon how the *mulâtre* first came into existence. He placed the burden for this race mixing squarely upon the shoulders of the black slave woman who: "had her race, of course . . . but would lose it, if not within herself, then within her progeny; she no longer had her religion, but a new one imposed by force and guile; she no longer had her language, but a new one imposed by necessity, Creole; she no longer had her civilization, but a new one imposed by necessity, civilization of compromise between that of the master and an African civilization already vanquished and practically eliminated."[78] While Gratiant did not overtly blame these women, he nonetheless surmised that *mulâtres* were the result of a transformation of the race produced by women. A complete one, at that, for he then resumed his essay by speaking of the son born of this master-slave union, and considered that he himself (implicitly as one such son) was more attracted by the bodies of black or mixed race women, and by the faces of white or mixed race women. Even here colonized women were reduced to exotic bodies. Gratiant concluded his essay by a cry of revolt: "I bellow: I am *nègre!*" As a result, he allied himself with the newspaper *Le Cri des Nègres* and what he termed the "political struggle of the mass of exploited black men, wretched of the earth." The tools he acquired from a white civilization forced upon his foremothers could now further the alliance among struggling black men. Since in black milieus *mulâtre* was an insult signifying assimilationist politics, his proclamation, which rested upon a corporeal definition of women, reveals how firmly anchored he was in the colonial metropolis.

That almost every political contribution to *L'Etudiant Noir* focused upon black manhood, in some way or another, is not particularly surprising given the masculine context of working-class, anti-imperial circles. However, this male focus confirms that black women were equally sidelined in black intellectual circles, and makes Paulette Nardal's lone female voice all the more potent. In her contribution, Paulette Nardal built upon ideas she had previously developed for *La Revue du Monde Noir*. Her short piece "Guignol Ouolof" (The Wolof Puppet/Farce) takes place as a woman eats dinner in a small Latin Quarter café before attending the theatre. The initial description of this café, "illuminated by a barbarous riot of neon tubes," was reminiscent of Nardal and Martin's articles for *La Dépêche Africaine*, with its intimation of an overly mechanized, performance-oriented Paris.[79] A black man arrives, ridiculously garbed, selling peanuts. The black female character in this piece reacts: "Revolting? Perhaps from the perspective of an overly Occidentalized, black Antillean woman. But this black man is there to the great delight of the white customers." Not entirely certain how to respond as he approaches her table, she grows nervous, wondering whether she will be implicated in his spectacle or whether, to her shame, she will rebuff or ignore him. These were the uncomfortable choices, Nardal suggests, facing a black woman whose skin and sex automatically placed her within the realm of spectacle.

That spectacle was reinforced by the setting for the story: a pretheatre dinner. The woman wonders whether the black man's outlandish appearance only reinforces the white stereotype of a grotesque, comical black person. Ultimately and instinctively she realizes that the color of their skin links them and that she must respond, thereby verbalizing the race consciousness Paulette and Jane had previously identified. So the Antillean asks this black man whether his costume bothers him. He responds that he is an actor and if "white people want someone to make them laugh; I don't mind . . . at least, I can eat . . ." Nardal's exploration of a sense of exile and also of the need for racial unity beyond class came to the fore with this brief interlude, a short story poignant with the history of Nardal's thoughts upon the topic. Thus Nardal surfaced within this issue of *L'Etudiant Noir* as a connection to previous periodicals, demonstrating the extent to which her and her sister's early journalistic work shaped considerations of race and gender in interwar Paris. The feminist space created by *La Dépêche Africaine*'s association of black and white women writers allowed the black woman's voice to mature and gather strength in subsequent publications.

"How could they remain indifferent?"
Ethiopia and Race Consciousness

Of those who are remembered for their contributions to black periodicals, Paulette Nardal was one of few who truly breached class, and as a result she is cited several times in police reports.[80] During the mid-1930s Nardal continued her racial transformation of Paris by leading temporary alliances between moderate white feminist organizations and black radical militants. She also directly influenced women in black radical organizations by becoming the first woman to have her political opinions published in the UTN's organ, *Le Cri des Nègres*. Nardal, as we have seen, was a filigree to be traced throughout all of these black papers after *La Dépêche Africaine* was first published in 1928.

The female presence within the pages of the LDRN and the UTN's radical newspapers was limited until in 1934 several calls for gendered unity, generated from outside anti-imperial circles, were placed within those pages. By 1935 black women were the subjects of articles, but were granted no agency. In June 1935, a telegram sent by Paulette Nardal appeared on the first page of *Le Cri des Nègres*.[81] She wrote as the secretary of the pacifist and international Comité Mondial contre la Guerre et le Fascisme (World Committee Against War and Fascism, also known as the Amsterdam-Pleyel movement), which had as a primary concern in 1935 the Italo-Ethiopian conflict. Like the Scottsboro affair, Mussolini's aggression against Ethiopia (also known as Abyssinia) helped to rally militants, whether they were pacifist, antiimperialist, or antifascist, in mid-1930s France. The first meeting organized in Paris under the auspices of the Comité International pour la Défense du Peuple Ethiopien (International Committee for the Defense of the Ethiopian People) attracted eight hundred blacks, Arabs, and whites in one place.[82] By that first meeting on September 2, 1935, more than eighty organizations had joined the cause, including some from England, Spain, and Italy. Many of these groups were feminist, or led by women, such as the Comité Mondial des Femmes Contre la Guerre et le Fascisme (World Committee of Women Against War and Fascism, an outgrowth of the Committee Against War and Fascism), the Union Féministe Egyptienne (Egyptian Feminist Union, Cairo), the Ligue Internationale des Mères et Educatrices pour la Paix (International League of Women and Women Educators for Peace) and so forth. Hundreds of organizations were joined in this common cause by the time Mussolini sent four hundred thousand Italian troops to invade Ethiopia on October 3, 1935.

With this event in mind, for a brief while Paulette Nardal worked alongside members of the UTN to mail *Le Cri des Nègres*, which had started condemning the conflict in its April/May 1935 issue.[83] Nardal's ability to navigate along class and race lines was not a foregone conclusion, since she was more highly educated than many UTN members and, education aside, did not depend upon manual labor for her livelihood. The UTN was plagued by a variety of internal demarcations; lines were drawn in particular by the categories of class, race, and geographical origin. As an intellectual and an Antillean, Paulette Nardal's acceptance at UTN headquarters was unusual, and in terms of direct personal contact, sporadic, diminishing when faced with the usual Antillean/African and intellectual/worker divides.[84] In October 1935 a General Assembly of the UTN was marked by a critique of Tiémoko Garan Kouyaté and Paulette Nardal, who were accused of dividing blacks within Paris. Although informants did not give details, one reported that a student present at the meeting suggested there were simply too many divisions between workers and intellectuals.[85]

Although Nardal's background provoked tension, her ability to cross onto the pages of *Le Cri des Nègres* spoke to the manner in which women, like the anti-imperial men of the interwar years, eventually used their gender to their advantage. The intricately constructed web of relations established by black and white women had, finally, chipped away at the black organizations' masculine front. The oppressed woman was replaced with an activist woman. After £500,000 were raised in support of Ethiopia's cause in the British colonies of Gold Coast (today Ghana), Nigeria, and Sierra Leone, Paulette Nardal took charge to figure out how this sum could be routed, via the Comité International pour la Défense du Peuple Ethiopien, to the Negus of Ethiopia, Emperor Haile Selassie.[86]

She also wrote an intriguing article titled "Levée des races," which can be loosely translated as "Rise of the Races," although importantly the word "levée" also has military connotations (raising an army) and referenced the idea of a group's "outcry."[87] Nardal's article, which first appeared in *Métromer* and was reprinted in the Dakar-based newspaper *Le Périscope Africain*, had several goals. First, she was interested in putting to rest the paranoid assumption that because black men and women everywhere supported Ethiopia, and that nations such as Japan joined them in their stance, this international alliance somehow signified a coming war of the races. Second, she sought to explain why people of African descent felt so implicated in Ethiopia's war. And third, in a resounding conclusion she demonstrated why and how their investment signified not diasporic peoples' rebellion against Europe and the United States, but instead the innate humanism of all modern men and women.

She addressed the misbegotten concept of a war of the races by reminding the French public that ten thousand ethnic Somalis (one of the groups in Ethiopia) had volunteered to fight for them during World War I. In other words, this country was on France's side. She then argued at two different points in the article that the Italo-Ethiopian conflict had "drawn the attention of the entire world" and hence naturally that of black men and women. Yet she did not simply dismiss peoples of color as imitators. Instead she asked: "how could they remain indifferent, in spite of their loyalty, to the fate of the last truly free black empire?" Loyalty to the West could coexist, she pursued, with a "purely sentimental, irrational, truly racial reflex of like drawn to like." After all, a "common soul" united people of African descent: "In a state of brutal shock at events, black populations disseminated around the world—who still yesterday were so indifferent to one another—suddenly found a common soul again in the common defense of Ethiopia." Note that here the starting point for her transnational reading of a common black movement was Mussolini's invasion of Ethiopia.

Why did people of African descent have such a unified reaction? Nardal saw two sets of reasons, the first emotive and the second rational. On the emotive side she explained that although "so loyal, so assimilated, so conformist," colonized blacks were nonetheless mysteriously linked to their race: "around this empire entrenched in its high mountains, their passionate thoughts weave heroic dreams." She used words such as "sentimental," "sensitive to poetry," "irrational," and "reflex" to describe this response, words that were startlingly in line—given that they were written in 1935—with the poetic arguments and descriptions later presented by the male leaders of negritude to describe people of African descent. Nardal then addressed logic, writing: "the reasoned element of this awareness of racial solidarity is on one hand a reaction against the feeling of inferiority that one sought to inculcate in the *Noir*, and on the other hand his original sense of justice." With respect to the first component of reason she explained that for too long the *noir* had been deprived of his race pride and that the response to Ethiopia reflected his discontent. However she quickly added that such pride was unlikely to become arrogance because unlike fascists in Germany and Italy who wished to "*bouffer du nègre* (be violently anti-*nègre*)," "the races of color evolve and imbue themselves with the intellectual currents that traverse modern nations." Nationalism and the right to sovereignty—such as that of Ethiopia—were examples of such modern ideas. Likewise "the implacable laws of nations' economic expansion are happily compensated, in the modern conscience, by the evolution of the idea of colonialism toward more humane ends. This selfless emotion found in many men of the white race proves to us that the human family *is one*, in spite of ethnic differences." Having surreptitiously rendered white men fundamentally "emotion"al (just like black ones), and twice referred to international humanism, she concluded with a lone, explicit reference to women: "Is the pain of an Italian mother faced with her massacred son more poignant than that of an Ethiopian mother?"

This article, like many of those written by Paulette and her sister Jane, was a model of fine distinction and potential contradictions. She associated emotional, spontaneous racial outbursts with the fundamental humanism that marked the modern world. She melded emotion with reason in men of all races; African origins with a (welcome) European and American assimilation and education; and after addressing throughout much of her piece the black man (*le noir*), she closed with a reference to Italian mothers while nonetheless, in her construction of this last sentence, just slightly elevating the Ethiopian ones by making them the last group mentioned in the article. She managed to wrap into one piece multiple audiences (men; women; Africans including of course Ethiopians; African Americans; Antilleans; Italian mothers (but not fathers); and all non-fascist Europeans). And she managed to say something that might touch each of those audiences. She explained and justified a transnational black race consciousness, albeit by giving as its unified starting point the war itself. Perhaps the war was an easier turning point to explain than anti-imperialism, communism, or even the race consciousness generated by an alienated existence in Paris, but this event also likely marked a political turning point for Nardal. Thus this article reflects the core of Nardal's struggle to maintain an extraordinarily refined positioning even while foregrounding her beliefs in international humanism with a familial construction and a black woman at its center.

As a result of such persistent networking in several milieus, Nardal found a place for women in the newspapers of even the most radical organization. Shortly after Nardal started working with the UTN, other women followed in her footsteps. In December 1935 the success of a woman at an antiwar meeting in Brussels made it onto the front page. The woman remained nameless in *Le Cri des Nègres* but was identified in the pages of a pacifist, antifascist, and feminist newspaper, *Les Femmes dans l'Action Mondiale*, as Amita Very.[88] She was, like the Nardal sisters, Martinican and black. Very's speech, made in her capacity as a representative of the Comité Mondial des Femmes contre la Guerre et le Fascisme in front of fifteen hundred delegates, was liberally quoted by an anonymous author who spoke of this Antillean woman as a comrade. Her speech marked a break with most texts written by the Nardal sisters, gaining in militancy as she sought to challenge an imperialist war. Pacifism came second to demands for an internationalist, feminist unity. "We reach out," Very proclaimed, "to women from all over the world, without distinction of race or nationality, to defend an ideal that is common to us all."[89] Her race, as well as her sex, made the call more powerful in the confines of a newspaper such as *Le Cri des Nègres*, whose radical audience viewed outsiders with suspicion. Very, instead, was claimed as one of their own, inspiring the editors—perhaps bolstered by Nardal's presence—to repeat and accentuate her gendered call for unity: "We must send doctors, nurses, medicine, and sanitary material. All women must labor for this cause. Furthermore, they must demand that sanctions be applied against the fascist aggressor." With these words, *Le Cri des Nègres* started portraying women as active members of their community.

The growth of fascism and its bellicose potential at a time when many feminists were pacifist or communist led to a moment of harmony among Parisian feminists, black anti-imperialists, and pacifists when the Italo-Ethiopian war broke out. The many women present in *La Dépêche Africaine* initiated networks that allowed gender, race, and class to mingle comfortably for a common cause. Nardal's Comité d'Action Ethiopienne (Committee for Action on Ethiopia) was closely linked with the Comité International pour la Défense du Peuple Ethiopien, which united organizations including the UTN and suffragist groups to which women such as Marguerite Martin belonged. The result was a transformation of all these groups, with greater racial and sexual awareness not only among those who developed negritude, but also within more radical black organizations.

Nardal's active and prominent display of female-led political protest and humanitarian organization had a second effect as well, by legitimizing the previously disputed roles of Frenchwomen such as Madame Ramananjato or Jeanne Kodo-Kossoul. They were no longer simply wives of anti-imperialists whose honor could be impugned, but women who rallied to the common antifascist cause. A few months after Nardal responded to the struggle against fascism and Mussolini by establishing working contacts with the UTN, Jeanne Kodo-Kossoul and other women emerged from their silent status as marital other for the first time since the newspaper's founding in August 1931. In 1936 Jeanne Kodo-Kossoul was inspired in her writing by Nardal's Italo-Ethiopian cause. Previously women had only worked indirectly for the militant newspapers. For example, Jeanne Kodo-Kossoul had translated two letters from English for *La Race Nègre* in 1927 and 1929.[90] In the first article she authored, Kodo-Kossoul challenged the journalist Pierre Jacquier, who had written an article for the right-wing newspaper *Le Jour*, a newspaper known for favoring Mussolini that averaged 250,000 copies. Jacquier in fact wrote about the Ethiopian conflict and condemned the antiwar propaganda by organizations such as the Comité International pour la Défense du Peuple Ethiopien et de la Paix. Kodo-Kossoul's pithy reply argued that propaganda was not necessary to persuade blacks that solidarity with their race should not be equated with hatred of other races, but rather with revolt against all enemies of peace and unity.[91] In a second article Kodo-Kossoul challenged the League of Nations. She criticized its inability to condemn Italy and voiced her fear that its failures would set in motion unilateral action by Germany and other nations whose wars in the colonies might, eventually, destroy these occupied lands.[92] Perhaps Nardal and Kodo-Kossoul's vocal participation in political debate inspired Mme Ramananjato to demand in 1938 that the anti-imperialists explain to her why there were so few black women, and in particular black wives, in the UTN.

Between January 1927, when *La Race Nègre* was first published, and May 1936 when the last known *Le Cri des Nègres* appeared, women changed the printed word in black newspapers and periodicals. Initially portrayed as passive victims, they were later invited to join white feminist organizations. Building upon such connections, black and white women eventually found a new place within radical organizations as independent political thinkers rather than secretaries who were pettily challenged over financial matters. Within this time span, the years 1932 to 1935 marked a defining period in the literary and historical movement known as negritude, as students and intellectuals joined together to publish the best-known colonial papers of the interwar years and searched for a racial manifesto that might shape the future for francophone blacks. Some women, such as Paulette Nardal, participated at different levels in each of these movements, becoming sociopolitical chameleons able to unite, motivate, and inspire men and women of different races, classes, and persuasions. They did not erase the masculinity that made anti-imperialism a comfortable political space for black men. Rather, they created alternative spaces through a multitude of contacts and shaped those spaces by their use of gender and race. Black women in Paris argued that their race consciousness was made possible by their gender. Using the medium of print they geared their political messages toward all women, urging them to unite.

By entering the overwhelmingly male spaces of the UTN with a political message couched in gendered terms, the Nardal sisters also defined a place for women in the masculine circles of interwar Paris. The year 1935 was a turning point, then, for the women of colonial Paris, as well as a year of radicalization for Paulette Nardal with respect to her active participation in transnational movements. After 1935 she wrote of sisterhood and evoked the need for unity not only with other Antillean women, but also colonial women more generally. In February 1939 she wrote in *La Femme dans la Vie Sociale* (Woman in Social Life): "In the name of the women of black Africa, my sisters, I join my voice to those already raised to ask that the integrity of the French territory be preserved."[93] She continued, in terms echoing those of Marcelle Besson from *La Dépêche Africaine*, "Do the women of Africa, givers of life, not also have something to say while the future of their children finds itself so tragically threatened?" All in all, in a declaration asking France to protect its colonies from German expansionism that was published in a Catholic women's newspaper,

Nardal referenced either the women of black Africa, or black women more generally, four distinct times. The newspaper's white editors revealed that this was not new language for her, considering her to be someone "who has so often raised her voice on behalf of her sisters of color."[94] Both Paulette and Jane were members of the organization behind the newspaper, the Union Féminine Civique et Sociale (Civic and Social Feminine Union) and were active with its Commission for Understanding Among Races. Created in 1925 as a religious counterpoint to the predominantly secular feminist organizations of the interwar years (and still around today), the moderate organization sought to engage Catholic women in the defense of women's civil rights. When Paulette Nardal spoke of sisterhood, then, it reflected both her feminism and her social Catholicism. Here was yet another thread in the Nardal sisters' tapestry of contacts.

The Nardal sisters moved in an international community that had, at its core, other people of African descent. By 1939, as she prepared to return to Martinique, Paulette Nardal's world vision had drifted to a different side of the Atlantic—Africa—even while Jane continued to think and write about the United States, for example in a 1938 article on the history and creative fortitude of African American washerwomen.[95] After 1935 both sisters wrote about and participated in movements for women's rights, and in particular colonized women's rights. Their interest was not explicitly suffrage, but rather establishing cultural and social strategies for protecting, supporting, and recognizing women of various classes and origins in their daily struggles. Paulette Nardal eschewed classification between the wars, in fact using interstices to create a community for herself and her sisters within Paris. In resisting any one label, she showed a commitment to the at times paradoxical, and certainly nuanced, task of figuring out how to be black, Catholic, colonial, French, humanist, international, and woman, a dizzying undertaking that made her in some ways a typical French feminist trying to forge a place for herself within a system defined by its ambiguities.[96] Yet over time her writings and community involvement kept coming back to speaking about and for women of African descent. In many ways Paulette and Jane were gathering their thoughts in their 1928 to 1939 metropolitan writings. This period can, therefore, be considered a starting point for their political and social activism. They nonetheless managed to be consequent in the manner in which they kept coming back, in various ways, to the elucidation of what it meant to be black, colonial, and French; the meanings and implications of race consciousness; and the manner in which gender inflected colonial and metropolitan existences. By the late 1930s they had created an expansive and intricate community that blended people of various beliefs, origins, and social standings even while placing a transnational sisterhood of black, colonial women at its core.

On the eve of World War II, Paulette Nardal was still present at UTN meetings. On April 9, 1938, she took on fascism with a speech in which she emphasized the dangers of masking one's skin color with a European education and of allowing Hitler to acquire the French colonies.[97] She also announced her plans to travel to one such colony, Senegal.[98] Her sentiments and proposed action were reflections of the evolution of Nardal's political and racial engagement, including its physical continuation in rallies and travels. She had come to understand by 1932 that women were uniquely placed for developing race consciousness and encouraging solidarity in the face of injustice. In reaching such conclusions she influenced and was inspired by women who moved amidst black and white intellectuals, workers, and revolutionaries. Using newspapers to circulate ideas to wider audiences, she and other women were able to transform the multifaceted Parisian spaces in which class, colonialism, gender, and race were debated during the interwar years.

6

"THESE MEN'S MINOR TRANSGRESSIONS"

White Frenchwomen on
Colonialism and Feminism

*[Women] are the ones who will force the cessation of the terrible
antagonism between races and who will keep men—who have already
fought over territories, religions, and money—from killing each other for
colors . . . It will be enough for them to decree that the black race equals
the white race and that beauty resides there as well as it does here; that a
black brain is structured like a white man's brain; and that there is only
one humanity.*—LOUISE FAURE-FAVIER, *La Dépêche Africaine*

In 1930, in one of several articles she wrote for *La Dépêche Africaine*,
Marguerite Winter-Frappié de Montbenoît responded to the *métis*
question, an ongoing debate involving anthropologists, government
officials, and others regarding the legal, social, and "scientific" ramifications of being *métis*. As the president of la Française Créole—The
French Creole, a Paris-based organization that since at least 1909 had
been providing opportunities for social gatherings for French men
and women from the old colonies, including La Réunion, Martinique, Guadeloupe, and French Guiana—she saw in the illegitimacy
that marked the children of mixed race the seeds of sedition: "these
children of indefinite race stay on the margins of society and become a danger in their legitimate revolt."[1] She broadened her analysis of these concerns in another article in which she called *métis* the
"péchés de ces Messieurs," or "these men's minor transgressions."[2] More
of a gentle rebuke than a slap across the face, this carefully word-
ed phrase well reflects the delicate position in which Frenchwomen

found themselves when confronting colonialism. *Métis* was not the only topic that demanded such careful handling; French men repeatedly "transgressed" with various actions and inactions that women deftly understated as "minor."

The white Frenchwomen involved in *La Dépêche Africaine* also included the lawyer Yvonne Netter, the social activist Marguerite Martin, and the writer Lucie Cousturier. Their names, and those of the writers Marthe Oulié and Denise Moran, likewise surfaced in the pages of the feminist newspaper *La Française*, published in Paris. They were not the wives of anti-imperialists, struggling to reconcile their personal lives and their politics, but they had in common with these wives a desire to make their voices heard in an imperial nation. As a result, understanding how feminists absorbed colonialism invites us to explore not just their social and political backgrounds but also the extent to which the print matter they produced reflected changes in a public sphere shaped by negrophilia and reverse exoticism, amongst other colonial discourses. Because these women published in Paris and lived there at least occasionally, exploring why they came to write about colonialism and what they said reveals how the city became a colonial metropolis. It did so in part as a result of its centrality in the dissemination of the print matter of both the colonizers and the colonized. The content of publications emanating from Paris also discloses how women writers and their audiences absorbed or rejected, but in any case were introduced to, a range of stances on colonialism. As a colonial metropolis, Paris not only allowed white women to come into contact with black colonial citizens and subjects, but also placed women of very different persuasions, feminisms, and backgrounds in contact with one another—inviting them to exchange multiple perspectives on the impact of colonialism and the links between feminism and colonialism. Paris acted as a clearing house through which authors and journalists transferred their ideas via books, articles, and encounters.

"The multiple misdeeds of colonialism"? Why Women Started Thinking about Colonialism and Race

Like their predecessors who had focused upon slavery and abolitionism, Frenchwomen during the interwar years positioned themselves as mediators between France and her colonies.[3] These outspoken women were all the more remarkable because their expressions of dissent were disproportionate to the presence of women in the colonies acquired during the second wave of imperialism.[4] The first attempt to send women overseas was organized by the French Colonial Union, an organization designed to defend colonial commercial interests as well as the colonizers themselves. When the Society for the Emigration of Women to the Colonies was created by the French Colonial Union in 1897 to recruit fifty to sixty young women to work in the colonies, and it was hoped, marry French men, almost five hundred women applied to emigrate.[5] Still, only colonies such as Algeria and Tunisia in North Africa, parts of Tonkin in French Indochina, and the upper plateaus of Madagascar were considered appropriate for women. Within six years approximately one hundred women had left for these territories.[6] But only in the 1920s and 1930s did metropolitan concerns such as natalism and eugenics lead the government to encourage men to bring their wives with them overseas, in the hope that this would stem the tide of interracial relationships while allowing women to fulfill their natural role as civilizers, a role some feminists were all too happy to accept.[7]

What did Frenchwomen have to say about colonialism and race at this point in time? Like feminism—which for some was not about suffrage but about the acquisition of the other civil rights of men—colonialism and race elicited wide-ranging responses. Many feminists, even while critical, supported French colonialism. From their perspective women's roles overseas should have two main focal points: how to redress colonized women from their presumed inferior status and how to use the colonial space to further the feminist cause.[8] Since scholars are still working on disentangling the many links between French feminists and colonialism, a useful point of comparison is the British imperial feminists who discussed Indian women using a language of sisterhood at the turn of the century.[9] In interwar France this language was echoed with words such as order, civilization, and education, all of which were considered to be spheres of potential female influence. However Frenchwomen who actively engaged in the colonizing process often also argued that their duty was to the French civilizing mission broadly defined—not just to colonized women—

even while at times using indigenous women's strengths to denigrate the patriarchal system that framed their imperial nation-state. They were riveted by a balancing act between protecting their own rights and forging a place for themselves within the existing French state; protecting the rights of those they presumed to be in a far worse situation; and yet recognizing and even using as justification for their own struggle for rights that in some colonial spaces, colonized women were perhaps better off than colonizing ones.

That same series of internal contradictions applied when women thought about race. They considered the meaning of race during the interwar years by engaging with a cluster of topics including pronatalism, *métissage*, white slavery (the alleged sale of Frenchwomen in colonial spaces), and the question of whether upon marriage Frenchwomen should be allowed to keep their nationality independent from that of their husbands.[10] This last right was granted, but not until 1927, and the debates surrounding it were revealing. They reflected how much the term *race* encompassed at the time, still extending to demarcate various European nations from one another, but also that women who married colonized men and were thus forced to acquire their (supposedly uncivilized) husband's very ill-defined colonial status, were considered to be in an especially perilous and shameful position. In particular, observers feared that women who married Africans, Asians, and others might find themselves engaged in polygamy, but with French statutes and laws no longer protecting them. Interracial marriages were thus decried in some circles. Whether thinking about race or about colonialism, French feminists, who were faced with the irony of belonging to a republican nation with universal rights that did not extend to all its individuals, responded with an inconsistency that nonetheless had an internal logic given the framework within which they had been placed. At various times they either accepted and reproduced existing hierarchies, rejected them, or found ways to do both at once.

Two elements defined the French feminists of the interwar years with respect to their thoughts on the imperial dimension of their country. First, they were given a range of choices as a result of the postwar situation. While the imperial framework that guided their responses to colonialism was largely not of their making, they could align themselves either for or against its injustices and in either case found their stances strongly backed by political parties, national and international organizations, and other feminists. Whether or not they agreed with it, the rising language of anti-imperialism and pacifism influenced these women's perceptions of colonialism. Thus some of them were willing to critique imperialism as a system based on a hierarchy of race and gender, and not just to carve out a place for themselves within the colonial enterprise. Second, French feminists found themselves strangely demarcated in spite of all their transnational ties—few Western European women did not have the vote during the entire interwar period. As a result of being blocked from the vote, Frenchwomen expressed themselves through organizations, publications, and a focus on social causes both metropolitan and colonial that allowed them to become implicated in the many nuances of the politics of their day.[11]

The question remains of how and why Frenchwomen started engaging with the conundrums posed by colonialism and race. How and why did women speak of the black empire, their relationship to its representatives in Paris, and their understanding of how overseas spaces related to and shaped their capital? Frenchwomen's sense of Paris as a colonial space was augmented by the movement that characterized how those who published related to the margins of empire—many of these feminists came and went, or were placed in contact with women who traveled, much more easily than other Parisian groups that transformed the city into a colonial metropolis. Both their professions and their means allowed an interchange between center and periphery. Thus while their home and base for publishing and direct contact through personal or group meetings remained Paris, their ideas were shaped by the French, Africans, and Antilleans they met abroad, as well as by those in Paris. For many of the women writers discussed here the impetus for viewing feminism and social issues in a colonial context was the literary space imagined by the Nardal sisters and others in *La Dépêche Africaine*. Feminists transferred colonial interests not just to women's meetings and newspapers, but also to yet another medium that shaped Paris into a colonial metropolis: books, particularly travel literature. Travel added a dimension to relationships in the colonial metropolis: exoticism was mollified by the realism of overseas travel, in particular because several women considered their position in the metropolis when writing about black men and women.

The initial contact in Paris with colonial concepts and travelers was critical. Few of these women had a predisposition, as a result of their background, to taking an interest in colonialism and its repercussions within the metropole. Instead the colonial question often emerged as a logical continuation of the social one, which was the attempt by writers and politicians to respond to the moral and economic quandaries that the working class was presumed to face in a modern, urban setting. Women such as Marguerite Martin, motivated by contacts established in the colonial metropolis, explored the social and political ramifications of colonialism in *La Dépêche Africaine*. Martin was born Marguerite Jeanne Brunet in l'Aiguillon-sur-Mer, which borders the Atlantic in the Vendée region, on September 17, 1877. She was the daughter of an army officer and completed her high school studies before becoming a primary school teacher at the death of her father. After her marriage in 1912 she moved to Paris, soon joining the coordinating committee of the feminist organization known as the Union Française pour le Suffrage des Femmes (French Union for Women's Suffrage, UFSF) and becoming a member of the Groupe des Femmes Socialistes (Group of Socialist Women), which submerged feminists within the French Socialist party founded in 1905 and known as the Section Française de l'Internationale Ouvrière (French Section of the Worker's International). As a feminist she wrote propaganda, contributed to two socialist papers—*L'Action Socialiste* and *L'Equité*—and became active with the Ligue Nationale pour le Vote des Femmes (National League for the Women's Vote) in 1914.[12] After World War I, disillusioned with what she termed bourgeois feminism, she joined the Communist Party in 1921. However, she was evicted in December 1922 because she refused to abandon Freemasonry. In 1924 she wrote for the feminist newspaper *La Voix des Femmes* and in 1928 she was a columnist for *La Dépêche Africaine*, dealing primarily with social questions and criticizing the colonial project.[13]

In her early books, which were devoted to defining feminism and defending women's rights, Martin only occasionally referred to other cultures or races, preferring to focus upon suffrage. Martin viewed feminism as "the battlefield that women lacked: feminism is attacking ignorance, hypocrisy, and untruthfulness."[14] By 1926 she increasingly focused upon women's use of pacifism to fight ignorance. As a result she started thinking about colonialism, for example when she gave a talk in the thirteenth arrondissement on the Left Bank of Paris for the Ordre Maçonnique Mixte International le Droit Humain (International Order of Mixed Freemasonry) and identified the need to undo "the multiple misdeeds of colonialism."[15] Martin claimed that only if both sexes worked together would peaceful unity emerge worldwide. It was a logical step for her to call for the intermingling of races as well as sexes in her articles in *La Dépêche Africaine*.

Yvonne Netter proceeded along similar lines from a fascination with the defense of women and their rights to the defense of races. Netter was born in Paris on April 8, 1889. In 1911 she married Pierre-Isaac Gompel, and when he divorced her in 1918 she resumed her studies as a lawyer. When she was admitted to the Paris bar in 1920 as a doctor of law, she was one of approximately two hundred female members.[16] Netter preferred to support social causes and as a young and unabashedly feminist as well as female lawyer, Netter created a stir. Her books were praised by fellow intellectuals such as writer André Billy and the white French, colonial writer Denise Moran, who believed Netter gave modern women the tools necessary for understanding their condition.[17] Netter was, like Martin, a member of the UFSF and from 1934 to 1939 directed the Société pour l'Amélioration du Sort de la Femme et la Revendication de ses Droits (Society for Bettering the Lot of Woman and Claiming Her Rights). Finally, again like Martin, she was an associate of the only mixed Freemason group, Le Droit Humain. Given the connections they shared, Netter's argument in 1936 that "it's up to women to organize world peace" was almost self-evident.[18] While Netter did not write for *La Dépêche Africaine*, she was named as a supporter (her picture appeared in the first issue) and allowed her fame to buttress the newspaper's launch. Perhaps her interest in the paper had been sparked by the 1924 trial in which Blaise Diagne sued René Maran's newspaper *Les Continents*. Yvonne Netter was listed as the assistant lawyer for the defense and would have come into direct contact with Maran, who was a star defense witness.[19] By the time *La Dépêche* was founded a few years later, Netter was known in black Paris, establishing one of many links between feminism and colonialism.

In some ways the connections between white women and black men and women during the interwar years might seem logical. Both groups were intimately scarred by World War I. They had lost husbands, brothers, and fathers or had themselves worked or fought for the French nation and empire. As a result they emerged from the war believing that in compensation for their sacrifices, the white, male French citizens should grant them equality for the debt of blood they had paid.[20] And just as French-speaking Africans were considered too irrational and uncivilized to make suitable citizens, and thus were refused the vote, so too were Frenchwomen in 1922.[21] Such parallels aside, links between women and colonial migrants were nevertheless far from uncomplicated. While some women supported and identified with black citizens and subjects, the majority responded to colonialism in a convoluted manner that reflected their hopes and aspirations for women's rights. The postwar conditions were such that few women remained absolutely fixed in their colonial position or feminism, even though most insisted upon the unique perspective the feminine gaze provided on colonialism. So if their politics differed, at times dramatically, these women agreed that they had the indispensable touch for bettering colonialism as a social configuration—for redressing "these men's minor transgressions" and for isolating the wrongs they believed were implicit in a structure created by men to depend upon an uneven relationship amongst races and, they added, sexes.

La Française, *the* CNFF, *and the* UFSF

While by the 1890s the suffrage movement was well established in France, throughout the Third Republic feminism remained a dynamic and diverse and far from cohesive movement.[22] As suffragists fought to gain equality—beyond the penal code and tax law, which did not exempt women—two especially large associations emerged that grouped those women who tended toward republican, secular, radical, or socialist feminism, and those who actively campaigned for the vote.[23] The first was the Conseil National des Femmes Françaises (National Council of Frenchwomen, CNFF), affiliated with the International Council of Women, which promoted women's rights worldwide. Founded in 1900–1901, the council was an umbrella group with an initial membership (calculated through the membership of its subgroups) of twenty-one thousand women. Numbers reached seventy-three thousand in 1906–7, by which time the CNFF was advocating a feminism predicated upon political rights for women.[24] In 1906 the general-circulation feminist newspaper *La Française* was established by feminist Jane Misme, who founded it by organizing a discussion circle drawn from the literary and artistic worlds and consisting of women able to help finance the paper. The paper devoted considerable space to the issues of alcoholism, depopulation, prostitution, and pornography and became the official organ of the CNFF in 1921. The organization itself ballooned to one hundred fifty thousand members by 1929, and two hundred thousand members before World War II.[25]

The UFSF was from its inception closely linked with the CNFF, and many women joined both groups. Founded in 1908 in order to provide a link with the International Woman Suffrage Alliance, an organization that explicitly advocated suffrage for women, the UFSF grouped suffragists, many of whom were already members of the CNFF, and garnered the support of women such as Cécile Brunschvicg. She led the UFSF until in 1936 she became a member of the Popular Front government, which brought together a coalition of left-wing parties, including Radicals, Socialists, and even, in a response to rising fascism across Europe, some Communists. By March 1914 the UFSF's membership numbered twelve thousand women and seventy-five *départements* had sections. The UFSF increased rapidly to one hundred thousand members by 1928.[26] Throughout this period the group eschewed violence in favor of consistent activism.[27] Still, the inability of Frenchwomen to obtain suffrage in the interwar years (they would vote for the first time in 1945) seemed unfair as they watched integral suffrage laws pass in the United States and Canada in 1920. They found it harder still to watch the British implant suffrage for women in East Africa and South Asia. Mustafa Kemal Atatürk, founder and first president of the Republic of Turkey, in 1930 and 1934 made the woman's vote a component of his westernization of Turkey. During the interwar years women voted in Palestine, parts of China, several Latin American republics, Estonia, Azerbaijan, Trans-Jordan, Kenya, and other places.[28]

French feminists published a number of articles outlining their opinions in *La Française*. This paper deserves attention because, as the organ for the CNFF and a supporter of the UFSF, articles were intended to reach as large a readership as possible. The CNFF grouped organizations that ranged from Catholic to secular to pacifist and hence *La Française* reflected an exceptionally broad and diverse group of women. Still, the newspaper primarily addressed the reformist feminists who belonged to both organizations. The reformists tried to instigate change through legislative or electoral reform within the existing political system, as opposed to moderate feminists who were on the right of the political spectrum—Catholic and supporting traditional definitions of femininity—or radical feminists who denounced all facets of masculinity, in particular with respect to sexuality and family, and tended toward anti-capitalism.[29] How the editors of this paper chose to present colonialism, especially since one of them—Brunschvicg—was preparing a successful political career, provides considerable insight into how feminists were introduced to race and gender within the metropole.

Between 1921, when *La Française* first became an organ of the CNFF, and 1939, colonialism occupied an expanding space within the columns of the paper. All French colonies were presented and debated, with greatest attention paid to North Africa and the influence of Islam upon female colonial subjects. Women also expressed a grudging interest in the colonial subjects and citizens of French West Africa, the Caribbean, and Madagascar. Articles focused upon the treatment of indigenous women, the role of Frenchwomen, the rise of feminism, exoticism, and, at times, criticism of the colonial system.

Many writers for *La Française* assumed that black women were mistreated in Africa. White women could therefore take on the role of savior, since male-dominated France was sacrificing its beliefs in natural rights and the principles of French civilization in order to placate indigenous men and respect local customs. Even while making such generalizations, writers complicated their own stories by introducing another aspect of black, gendered civilization: the strength and freedom of women within these so-called primitive societies, and the possibilities open to them for self-liberation. The French reader was introduced to a complex vision of race and gender by colonial connoisseurs such as Winter-Frappié.

From the island of Paul et Virginie in the Indian Ocean's l'Ile-de-la-Réunion, Winter-Frappié arrived in Paris in 1885, a very different sort of colonial migrant, and quickly became implicated in the empire's capital city. She was an enthusiastic feminist and did not shy from political involvement: she became a press representative at the French Chamber of Deputies in 1906 and in 1912 was sent to Madagascar (it is unclear by whom) because of her sustained interest in the colonies. *La Dépêche Africaine* claimed in 1930 that she was "the only French woman to have understood that there can be no evolution in the colonies without the moral improvement of the indigenous woman."[30] In her articles for *La Dépêche*, Winter-Frappié argued that complete assimilation would be a mistake, since it discounted the laws and habits of the colonized peoples.[31] Moreover she believed that women, both colonized and French, were the key to establishing civilization in the colonies.[32] Her arguments were all the more progressive because individuals with origins such as hers, known as *Békés*, formed a highly specific and exclusive class in the old colonies.[33]

Winter-Frappié's contributions to *La Française* were similar to those in *La Dépêche* and became more frequent after January 1927, when she started supplying information on Malagasy marriage laws. She informed readers that Madagascar had progressive mores: polygamy was not tolerated, marriage could not be forced, men were fined for taking a young woman as a lover without marrying her, women passed their names on to their children, and if parents died, children became the wards of the maternal grandparents.[34] While the first three examples simply showed Madagascar as relatively "civilized" in contrast to other colonial cultures, the last two in fact described a revolutionary, matriarchal society that far surpassed the French colonizer's vision of gender relations.

Winter-Frappié's presentations at the Musée Social, the Parisian republican think tank created in 1894, reflected the roots she had grown in the metropolis but also seemed to categorize her as a republican reformer and colonial sympathizer.[35] In fact, she was breaking down the careful boundaries that elevated metropolitan women above their colonized counterparts. In a March 1927 article for *La Française*, which by this date had a column "La Femme dans les Colonies" (Woman in the Colonies), Winter-Frappié further expanded her progressive approach to black women. She first repeated the widely-held belief that the black race had remained primitive thus far because of its isolation in Africa, and that "when it comes to women's status, one notes that the force-based system employed by males has made her, in Asia as well as in Africa, a serf, a slave, useful for repopulation, sexual pleasure, and after for the most tiresome of labors."[36] However, Winter-Frappié then departed from convention when she argued that the answer to the black woman's problems did not lie only in the white woman's civilizing capacity, a popular argument with some feminists, for she explained: "there exists and has always existed an insurmountable antagonism to the white woman. She . . . believed herself to be superior to indigenous women and considered herself to be above teaching little *négresses*." While attenuating these assertions with a suggestion that women no longer held these racist prejudices, she nonetheless believed that the answer to the African or Caribbean woman's predicament lay in her education by other women of African descent. The only negative reaction she foresaw should such an education take place (and she argued the scenario had already been successfully implanted in the Antilles) was one that also plagued young feminists who had conquered the man's world for the first time: "There does remain a sort of pride, of slightly naïve vanity, always tainted by a spirit of antagonism that I could compare, to a certain extent, to the feelings of feminists tackling the careers previously reserved to men, and that can be translated with the words: 'Well! We too were able to gain those degrees, those promotions and that education!'" Winter-Frappié likened the education and search for racial equality by African and diasporic women to a search for gender equality. In so doing she did not entirely break with fellow writers for *La Fran-çaise* (more inclined to showcase the Frenchwoman as savior) for she also emphasized the exceptional role that European women with their maternal instincts could have in transforming the world. Although lightly reprimanding white women for presuming superiority, as the article progresses and although the other sex is never overtly mentioned, men begin to appear as the true failed designers of empire and civilization: they are the transgressors.

The convoluted nature of Winter-Frappié's analysis of gender in the colonies was in fact typical of how Parisian and other metropolitan women were exposed to colonial issues. An emphasis upon the spread of feminism in the colonies was contrasted with the rights the indigenous women already had (rights at times denied Frenchwomen). In Paris, methods for expressing such nuanced analyses of the colonial situation sprouted far more easily than in many overseas urban spaces, where the French settlers often displayed a unified front. Thus Sister Marie-André du Sacré-Cœur, who often corresponded with *La Française* and had devoted her life as a missionary to West African women, published her work on black women with a major Paris press.[37] She agreed with Winter-Frappié that indigenous women were primary agents of social change without whose support no French influence would last.[38] In April 1937 another author used the metropolitan venue of *La Française* to explore the strengths and privileges of African women such as those in the small village of Kibiro, who were hereditary property owners in charge of the salt, which was the village's only source of revenue.[39] With such stories Winter-Frappié and others repeated the ideas of their reformist male counterparts who during the interwar years also noted that women could have a positive influence upon social situations in the colonies.[40] Women departed from this view, however, when they contemplated why and how gender was a defining category for understanding colonialism both from within the metropole, and from its colonial outskirts. Some women also started to articulate race as a defining category, one that in many ways intersected with gender. This juxtaposition prompted them to question current hierarchies even as they began to construe civilization not only as a French mission, but also as a series of interracial connections between women and, in the longer term, men. Winter-Frappié and others believed that the solution to black women's situations did not lie in blithely imposing French civilization upon them.

Exposition Coloniale—The Feminist Perspective

In 1931 a number of feminists involved with the CNFF, the UFSF and the Musée Social organized the third Estates General of Feminism in Paris. They chose as a theme and space for the gathering the Colonial Exposition, thereby acknowledging the important role that both this event, and Paris in general, played in mediating the metropolitan engagement with colonialism. Their choice might also suggest that these women played unambiguously into the colonial project and the binaries of exoticism (white rational French/fantastic other). Yet the Colonial Exposition was a space of contestation of the colonial order of things as well as a moment of governmental propaganda. Not only were African and Caribbean men (and other colonial subjects and citizens) spreading anti-imperialist propaganda, but now women were also occupied with claiming suffrage and equality in the colonial context. Their methods were less confrontational but their convoluted distaste for the fantasies projected on black and white women in the overseas territories, and their struggle for a strong civilizing mission, were apparent during the Estates General. Feminists also worked very hard during this congress to present themselves as deserving of suffrage, going out of their way to emphasize their usefulness in the colonies and their dedication to the civilizing mission. *La Française* accelerated its coverage of the event and of the colonies in general to reflect the mood of this gathering of feminine minds and their colonial focus.

A few weeks after the expo opened its doors, women traveled to the colonial metropolis with the help of negotiated reductions in train fares and free return trips at fixed dates immediately before and after the gathering.[41] The official endorsement and promises of participation were overwhelming and included those of the governors general of Algeria, Indochina, French West Africa, French Equatorial Africa, Madagascar, and so forth.[42] A committee of women with a proven record of interest in the colonies prepared the gathering and a preliminary questionnaire that was sent throughout the metropole and the colonies. It included questions on the organization of health care, social work, the legal and moral situation of women and children, legitimate and illegitimate unions between *indigènes* and the French overseas (metropolitan unions were not mentioned), the moral situation of *métis* children, education of colonized children, and the impact of Frenchwomen overseas.[43] These themes were summarized during panels in which women designated as specialists analyzed each colonial region while addressing the importance of a female presence in the colonies.

Women represented themselves during the Estates General and in the pages of *La Française* as spreading feminism while defending the civilizing mission. Amidst reports on the financial or hygienic misery of colonial women of color, individuals such as Rachel Dogimont, a missionary in Togo, noted that educating African women, for example, would help them become "intelligent women and mothers, no longer allowing themselves to be squashed by man because, educated and developed, these women know that they have become equals. By preparing them in this manner, we are conscious of doing good feminism."[44] Instituting equality enabled women to plant the seeds of feminism in the colonies. In her presentation on the legal and moral situation of African women Mme Marius Leblond commented upon the black race, which was ripe for feminism in the old colonies. There "the woman of color, even more than the majority of society, white women, has a sense of her independence and her personality. Without leadership, that sense often evolves into quasi-anarchist insolence. No population is more suitably qualified to successfully progress under the influence of a prudently progressive feminism."[45] She identified with her presentation one of the goals inspiring feminists in the colonial context: spreading (moderate and therefore nonthreatening) feminism.

The generally self-congratulatory note was not often marred by debate or discussion, but there was some divergence within the ranks. In her talk on missionaries Rachel Dogimont (herself a missionary) commented upon the negative repercussions of French civilization:

We're not all that proud of admitting that wherever civilization has penetrated immorality has developed for, alas, Europeans who penetrate the Colonies do not always bring the best of themselves. And that is why young black girls are debauched by the white men who momentarily grant them an idle and easy life, giving them pretty clothes and jewels, before abandoning them with *métis* children who become true pariahs. As a result, prostitution is rapidly spreading through African coastal towns and seems to be almost legal.[46]

Dogimont's comment was one of the least subtle indictments of the colonial project. Yet she focused her discontent upon men. In her vision the white man corrupted the black girl and encouraged prostitution. However women, she insinuated, could still accomplish the civilizing mission so badly botched by men. Mme Letellier, speaking about medical and social careers overseas, identified the obstacles faced by nurses, social workers, and doctors in French Equatorial and West Africa as language and more importantly "the difference between races—incomprehension. Different conceptions of life, death, honor, decency—the *indigènes* shock us, we shock them too."[47] Her provocative statement was both pessimistic and oddly progressive in its recognition of mutual cultural incomprehension. The Europeans were not presented here as any less ridiculous than their colonized counterparts in the racial exchange.

There was, however, only one instance of pointed critique of the uneven power structures implicit in colonial-French relations. On May 31 Mme Georges Hardy, who was the wife of the director of the Ecole Coloniale, which trained future colonial administrators, spoke on the "adaptation of educational methods to the traditions and needs of the colonies." Covering questions of language (should children be taught in French or in their mother tongue?) and of the uneven rate of education that led girls to lag behind boys, she seemed somewhat unnerved by a commentary from the audience. Writer Marthe Oulié suggested that in Tunisia, where French and indigenous children were taught separately, this situation instigated resentment and anger amongst the colonial subjects.[48] Oulié thus turned a debate about education into one about racial equality by arguing that a reevaluation of interracial socializing had to begin during childhood, just as Marguerite Martin's 1928 article for *La Dépêche Africaine* had proposed that interracial entente would be naturally initiated by children.

Femmes de Lettres

Oulié was one of several Paris-based white colonial travelers presenting a complex spectrum of colonial visions. They both supported and challenged the meeker indictments of an overwhelmingly male colonialism presented in the colonial metropolis's spaces such as the pages of *La Française* and the 1931 Estates General.[49] The genre of the colonial woman writer was even less established than that of woman writer during these years. Little information exists on those who approached a topic that required either facing a still-taboo interracial sexuality or extensive and often independent travel in regions considered dangerous and reserved for the male sphere of influence. Women of the upper classes tended to infuse traditional feminine genres such as the romance novel with personal experiences and a sense of the exotic.[50] Indeed one of the genres that women truly mastered both as readers and writers was the real-life adventure. As a result scholars have shown a growing interest in the literature of the other produced by women during the interwar years.[51] Women writers engaging with the colonial project tended to write fictionalized travelogues, which either proselytized the colonial project for the metropolitan woman or expressed disapproval of the European colonial lifestyle. The gendered vision presented by women such as Oulié, Cousturier, or Moran often explicitly attenuated the exoticism so favored by male journalists discussing Josephine Baker. In so doing these women found their own ways to reverse exoticism. They did not use the same methods or have the same goals as anti-imperialists. After all, women writers did not use face-to-face interaction, but instead used books published and read in Paris to advocate links between colonizers and colonized. Still, Oulié and Cousturier in particular occasionally had both literary and sociopolitical ends in mind when they used exoticism as a device in their works. Of course, they also played into the exotic trend in literature. Nonetheless those who were concerned with translating the colonial venture into a vision for metropolitan eyes often avoided the sensuality that was such an essential component of exoticism, or used that same sensuality to advocate interracial contact.

Marthe Oulié's dissent during the 1931 Estates General in Paris was based upon extensive knowledge of the colonial order of things and was not that of an outsider, since she was a member of the UFSF (founding the Sceaux section) and the CNFF. An archaeologist and a sailor, she became a *docteur ès lettres* (PhD) at the age of twenty-five after studying at the Sorbonne.[52] Many of her works were celebrated not because of their colonial subject matter, but because she was unusually adventurous in her travels. For example, she wrote *Bidon 5* after participating in a motor rally across the Sahara desert (her car placed sixth) and was awarded the literary prize of the Touring Club of France for the best book of the year "celebrating the beauties of metropolitan and overseas France."[53] Oulié reported her findings on overseas locations using different types of media. She filmed two documentaries in the Levant: "Au pied des cèdres du Liban" (At the Foot of Lebanon's Cedars), and "La Syrie aux cent visages" (Syria of the Hundred Faces). Not only did she write travel novels but she also worked as a reporter.[54] With her propensity for difficult modes of transport in distant locations and her ability to work in mixed media, Oulié racked up literary prizes and other distinctions including the Czech *Lion Blanc*, the French *Mérite Maritime*, the Tunisian *Nicham*, and, from the Haitian Government, the *Honneur et Mérite*.[55]

The award from the government of a black country that had won independence from France in 1804 was particularly appropriate for a woman who contrasted exoticism with realism. Oulié devoted several articles and works to undoing preconceived metropolitan ideas of "whoever thinks Creole, thinks nonchalance."[56] Mindful of her Parisian audience, like the Nardal sisters she denounced such presumptions regarding black and also white colonial women: "But when you visit them, you retain of these islands [Guadeloupe, Haiti, Martinique] an industrious impression. One works, despite the oppressive heat, in offices, in schools. The factory worker is at his post late at night, and the farmer in his sugar cane field."[57]

Her emphasis upon the extraordinary performance of colonial

workers of color was reinforced when she published *Les Antilles filles de France* (The Antilles, Daughters of France) in 1935. Oulié's book made it into a collection titled *voyageuses de lettres* (literary women travelers) just in time for the tercentennial celebration of the Antilles' occupation by France. The existence in her prominent, Paris-based publishing house, Fasquelle, of an entire collection devoted to women travelers reflects the extent of feminine travel literature's popularity. Indeed Oulié's choice of topic in 1935 reflected not only her interests but also a canny ability to read the intellectual and cultural trends of her time, an alignment with exotic themes that reflected her understanding of the metropolis that was at the center of her colonial travels.

Oulié's text was in some ways a very traditional travelogue, but at the same time it harbored some perceptive commentary. For example, she offered a somewhat contrarian vision of Antillean workers as hard workers (rather than the more dominant image of indolence) even while incorporating in her text elements that in the Parisian context of the *vogue nègre* immediately resonated with her metropolitan readers.[58] However, Oulié did not merely play into the exotic discourse. For example, she presented Martinican women as myriad Josephine Bakers. Later, however, she commented that Martinicans no longer wished to be a colony and instead that they proclaimed "death to exoticism" in rebellion against the sensual and ultimately divisive vision metropolitans had of colonial subjects.[59] Indeed, her reading of cultural and political trends was perhaps the most inconsistent aspect of this book, almost as though she was not quite sure how to reconcile what she had seen and heard overseas and in the metropole with what she thought the mainstream audience to which her witty travel book was marketed wanted to hear. She was clearly aware of the potential for race-driven as well as class-driven struggles overseas.[60] And she appeared to dismiss them, suggesting that the only problem in Martinique and Guadeloupe was a lack of education in some areas and a resulting resentful sense of inferiority.[61] Yet earlier in the work, while talking about a new dance club near Martinique's capital, Fort-de-France, she quipped as though speaking about one of Paris's colonial nightclubs that it was "an innovation that would most likely invite more wide-ranging contact with the class of color."[62] She presented interracial dancing as a solution to the social demarcation that remained between these classes/races. So while dismissing the possibility that truly anti-French and communist sentiments had found their ways to the Antilles, Oulié also managed to mention, without apparent critique, that some Antilleans challenged Martinique's status as a colony and sought to refute dominant cultural trends of exoticism, and that contact between the races still left much to be desired. At such moments, she seemed aware of the leading intellectual and political trends that circulated among Antilleans in Paris.

Throughout, Oulié waffled between her criticism of a metropole peopled by morose white women who dreamed of exotic locales and a replication of the language of exoticism, which she used so that it might help metropolitans to feel familiar with the colonial setting. Oulié's use of symbols associated with the empire reflects how the definition of exoticism shifted when applied to white women writers. Parisians projected sensuality upon colonial symbols such as Baker, and the Nardal sisters recognized that this sexualized exoticism was then forced upon them. Black women rebelled by establishing a feminine political race consciousness. Writers such as Oulié realized that colonized men and women were vexed by the metropolitan search for exoticism, and avoided merely sensationalizing the colonial setting and its subjects, instead presenting symbols that were more often eroticized in Paris as anodyne and asexual. She, Cousturier, Moran, and women who published in *La Française* often avoided the fantasy of the sexualized colonial being and concentrated instead upon using recognized colonial symbols, such as Baker, in order to translate what they witnessed into terms that could be understood by metropolitan readers. Furthermore, while exploring her discomfort with the racial ordering of power, Oulié recognized the negative repercussions of ignoring the colonial subjects who desired assimilation. In some of her other work she speculated, as though echoing Winter-Frappié's ideas, that women would be crucial in establishing lasting links, especially "with the races of color's middle classes, who, when displeased, are the first to cause revolt."[63] She acknowledged the need for a policy of equality between races and between metropole and colonies while recognizing the potential for revolt should such prejudices not be righted soon. In the meantime she admired feminist activity in the black diaspora, such as Haitian women who had the spirit to organize a suffragist paper.[64] As for Haiti's revolt against France more than a hundred years earlier, she branded it "heroic."[65]

The interest in interracial politics, women's hard work, and the spread of feminism was a necessary alternative to more traditional descriptions of marvelous overseas territories because some white colonial women felt the need to join black women in challenging exotic tropes such as those projected onto Baker and the Nardal sisters. Several feminist texts suggested a prevailing assumption in metropolitan France that white colonial women were considered exotic. In the colonial setting, exotic traits celebrated with regard to black women such as Baker were transferred to white women, an aura that pursued them back to Paris. As a result, white women needed to defend white as well as black colonial women, and emphasize above all that these were not hedonistic beings corrupted into sexuality by the overseas climate. Aware of being potential objects of the exotic discourse, writers and travelers such as Oulié trod gingerly around the *vogue nègre*. The Creole woman, or white woman born and raised in the old colonies, was especially tormented by stereotypes underscored by an excerpt from a Frenchwoman's diary printed in the Franco-American review *L'Evolution Féminine*:

> A Creole is an extremely pretty woman with large doe eyes; a Mongolian woman's feet; and a waist that undulates like vines waving in a breeze. Creoles are unthinkably seductive and graceful but they also have the indolence of a vegetable, and the laziness of a paralytic caterpillar. They spend their days softly swaying in hammocks suspended from banana trees.[66]

The colonies were powerful enough in the French imaginary to project exoticism upon not only those who originated there but also those who had lived or worked there even temporarily, for after returning to Paris the aura of the colonial still swathed these travelers. While women were not always subjected to quite so much fantasy, they had a sense that they were not often enough portrayed as "brave, tenacious, compassionate, unaffected, and good."[67] Oulié was joined in her defense of Creoles and other white colonial women by writers for *La Française* such as Henriette d'Alexis who in a 1931 "Letter from Africa" written in Niamey, Nigeria, insisted that being a white colonial wife or woman was a difficult task.[68] What was most often interpreted by metropolitans as a languorous life—because children were often sent back to France and the women were assumed to be having a ball without them in the tropics—was in fact a life of sacrifice. The steady contributor to *La Française* Huguette Champy elaborated upon d'Alexis's words when she explained that white colonial women often had to choose between their husbands and their children, who were too sickly or in danger when living outside urban areas.[69] The emphasis upon hard work and sacrifice stemmed from two principal fears. The first was the perception so pithily expressed by Ida Sée: "it has been said and said again that our colonial empire does not interest women, that their settled way of life pins them to the capital city."[70] Women battled in the colonies the same charge of political and social apathy which men used to refuse suffrage in the metropole. The second fear that guided these women's self-defense was that many colonialists were antifeminist.[71] Emphasizing the importance of Frenchwomen's roles in the colonies responded to both concerns.

Oulié defied traditional assumptions about race or gender with well-informed travel narratives. The image of the stereotypical white Creole woman or the lazy *indigène* was undermined by Oulié's admiration for an independent black nation (Haiti), her challenges to typical hierarchies (white over black, man over woman), and her admiration for feminist women, white or black. Her independence as a traveler and thinker was a more irrefutable argument for subversion of tradition than was her membership in feminist organizations or occasional references to feminism. At times Oulié was criticized for her mordant humor and reevaluation of the metropolitan-colonial relationships.[72] Yet editors of *La Française*, and her readership, regarded her as an authority. A range of Parisian-based newspapers hired her to return to the Antilles during France's celebration of three hundred years of colonialism there. They included *Le Journal*, known for its literary pages but also for its anticommunist, right-leaning yet anti-Hitler stance; the literary *Revue de Paris*; and the *Journal de la Femme*, created in 1932 as a feminist weekly with a circulation of one hundred fourteen thousand. Her ability to add complexity to colonialism (no matter how imperfectly—after all, she kept in mind her mainstream audience and presses) through her wry portrayal of the barriers to mixed marriages and her inclusion of *métis* and overseas feminists in her writings, gave her work a uniquely feminine exoticism defined by the realism of a traveler.[73] For her the colonial project, and especially the civilizing mission, was imperfect because white men dominated it.

From Cousturier's Vogue Nègre *to Moran's Popular Front: The Cultural Politics of Class, Race, and Sex*

Some women far surpassed Oulié in their revolt against the racial inequalities they believed were integral parts of French colonialism. Lucie Cousturier and Denise Moran's works resonated with indignation and insubordination after they recognized that race was used as a tool for refusing certain rights.[74] Both discovered the colonial application of race as a category for denying equality after spending time with *indigènes* within the metropole and overseas. Cousturier and Moran shared a common background: they were both charged by the Ministry of Colonies with writing reports about living conditions in French West Africa. Neither stopped at submitting their reports; both also published colorful and at times outraged accounts of the colonial setting, including glimpses of discrimination and violence in Africa and in France.

In contrast to their male counterpart André Gide, whose portrayal of colonial wrongs has been abundantly commented upon both by his contemporaries and scholars today, little has been written about Cousturier and Moran.[75] Cousturier (1870–1925) started her career as a painter. Her landscape, floral, and portrait works were frequently exhibited at the Salon des Artistes Indépendants (Salon of Independent Artists) and she was a pupil and friend of the pointillists Paul Signac and Georges Seurat.[76] Her first direct contact with colonial migrants was during World War I, when she and her family lived in the south of France near Fréjus, where Senegalese *tirailleurs* were stationed. Soon thereafter, in late August 1921, she was invited to write a report for the Minister of the Colonies Albert Sarrault that was a "Study of indigenous family life and more specifically of the role of the indigenous woman and in particular the influence she has in the moral shaping of children."[77] While working on the report, she traveled through portions of French West Africa between September 1921 and July 1923. Yet Cousturier was also a part of the colonial metropolis since not only she, but also her novels, paintings, and official reports traveled through it often enough that she referred to herself as a Parisian. Indeed her entire corpus of work, rather than merely her artistic œuvre, contributed to her contact with the colonial metropolis's African and Antillean community. For example René Maran, who admired Cousturier, published lengthy excerpts from her official report in *Les Continents*. In particular he focused upon her incisive analysis of why wealth, education, and the creation of a local elite were essential elements of successful colonialism. This report provided the background for several of her books.

Cousturier's first book, *Des inconnus chez moi* (Strangers at My Home) was published in Paris in 1920 and focused upon *tirailleurs* during World War I. In an account based largely upon her work as a French teacher, Cousturier quickly established the unique perspective she believed her sex offered upon matters of race. She vividly illustrated the Senegalese soldiers as refined and intelligent using both her artwork (see fig. 6) and her words, and in so doing criticized the colonialist mentality of racial subservience albeit while avoiding any appraisal of colonialism itself.

In her book she explained, for example, how the Senegalese were "recruited" by force, using the story of a young *tirailleur* named Ghibi who joined the army after his mother was threatened with imprisonment. Cousturier accentuated the common experience of the war by reproducing the heart-wrenching war correspondence she maintained with her students once they left for the front. Against the backdrop of France's accumulating blood debt to the colonies, Cousturier recorded the ungrateful metropolitans' disregard for these colonial men's

6. Lucie Cousturier (1870–1925). Nègre *writing*. Watercolor. 63 x 47 cm. Photo Gérard Blot. Réunion des Musées Nationaux/Art Resource, New York. Original at Musée de l'Annonciade, St. Tropez, France.

conditions, speaking directly to the French skeptics around her. She did so by focusing upon the soldiers' individuality, using names and details to counteract her observation that whites did not wish to distinguish one African man from another. Her criticism extended to the French army, which taught its *tirailleurs* a version of French known as *petit nègre* that reduced the language, for example by leaving verbs in the infinitive, eliminating some verbs entirely (such as, according to Cousturier, to be, to want, to love, and to know) and using personal pronouns in their objective form (i.e., me seeing cat).[78] Cousturier reproduced this reduced form of French even while noting that her students knew they were being ridiculed for the stunted language they had been taught: "'It's French only for *tirailleurs*' they acknowledged sadly. One of my more spiteful students insists that 'these are words found by Europeans to take the piss out of the Senegalese.'"[79] Perhaps in response to her students' dismay, in her later books Cousturier no longer consistently reproduced the *petit nègre* that marked her first work.

Cousturier asserted that women responded differently to race and colonialism both within the metropole and overseas. She noted that French "women—even the most ignorant ones in the world being more clever than the colonial army's subalterns—abandoned after the first *bonjour* exchanged with the strangers the idea of saying: '[black men] are monkeys' in order to affirm: 'they are children.'"[80] Her skepticism of the French Army extended to how lower-ranked French officers in the colonial army treated African soldiers. In critiquing French soldiers she relied on describing Africans with the prevalent stereotype of the *grand enfant* (big kid). A variation on the good savage, her use of this trope implies that she had ingested the labels of her day. However like Oulié she had a precise use for referencing the *vogue nègre*. She used exotic trends to stave off the criticism that she was facing for her humanistic presentation of intelligent Africans and to soften her accounts of French ignorance. She gradually moved away from such tropes (although never entirely putting them aside) after drawing her reader into the text, focusing more and more often on Africans' insights into how the French perceived them. Later in her text, then, Cousturier could ask a *tirailleur*:

You say Europeans do not regard the Senegalese as they do other men? True, they say that the black man's head is not made in
the same way as theirs.

Maybe it's true said Damba Dia with gloom.

But maybe it's not true, because they also say that women
are less intelligent than men . . .

What? said a startled Damba, here women are not regarded
as well as men? But I have always seen women in France do the
same things as men.[81]

By the end of this conversation Cousturier presented herself and all
women as equal to colonial men in their mistreatment by white men.
Damba Dia's incredulous response evoked the idea that the search for
rights united white women and black men.

In her 1925 book, *Mes inconnus chez eux: Mon amie Fatou, Citadine*
(My Strangers at Their Home: My Friend Fatou, Urbanite), published
by a different Parisian press, she returned to this theme. Writing this
time about Guinea, in French West Africa, she noted that there she
became an asexual being, a "Monsieur-Madame" who admired "these
followers of a misogynist religion [who] seek advice from a woman.
They know how to disregard gender."[82] Africans repaid Cousturier's
deference with esteem for white women's evenhandedness (they con-
sulted her as a judge) and with empathy for women's unfair situation
in France much like that shown by the *tirailleur* Damba Dia who saw
men and women doing the same work in the metropole and therefore
presumed equality. Gender was thus an important theme for Cousturier, and was part of the reason she gave for why and how she started
to see West Africans as more than mere exotic images. How, though,
did she propose that others might come to share her understanding
both of Africans' humanity and of their sentiment that they were being treated as inferior? The response for Cousturier lay in exoticism
not merely as a way for her to establish common ground by conjuring
popular images for her audience, but also as a means of establishing
direct contact between metropolitans and colonial migrants. Recon-
ciling the *vogue nègre* and colonialism with humanism and equality
was a consistent theme in her work.

Cousturier's reflexivity—she remained consistently self-critical and self-aware in part through a biting humor she applied to herself along with everyone else—extended to an understanding of the dangers inherent in allowing exotic perceptions of Africans to mask their humanity and thus the colonial system's imbalance. In her first book, Cousturier recounted how in 1919 she accompanied Damba Dia, the accidental feminist, to Paris. As she showed him around the metropolis, some people they encountered believed that she was initiating a "savage" to civilization, others that she was showing a soldier on leave the metropolis, and her friends that she was satisfying the querying mind of a student and foreigner. That she and Damba Dia ended up in Paris in a text largely based in the South of France reveals the pull of this space to colonial migrants and metropolitan writers considering the links between overseas territories and mainland France. However her reaction to showing Dia Paris was more significantly an early glimpse of how she believed the *vogue nègre* might play a key role in enabling metropolitans to comprehend colonialism in human terms. When showing Dia around Paris, she argued that at her side he was neither a savage nor a burden to her, but rather a new pair of eyes inviting her to reconsider familiar objects. "His presence amplified me" so that "I walked alone, as usual, but as though wearing a pretty new dress, and with new strokes and gazes for all the objects."[83] In this rather odd passage she tried to capture the sensation that accompanied gaining a new and different appreciation for old sights. Dia had inspired her to newly interpret the world, her painterly eye gaining in perspective and depth as a result of his presence. In contrast, Cousturier explained that most French men and women allowed their perceptions of Africans to be manipulated by scientists or government officials. For example in her 1923 *La Forêt du Haut-Niger* (The Forest of Haut-Niger) Cousturier wrote that "colonial ethnographers show us circumcision rites and all the rites of *nègre* societies while telling us: here are the *nègres*, see and touch and acknowledge that these are not men!"[84] In other words the ethnography that fed into the exoticism of interwar Paris could make it easy to forget the humanity of *indigènes* and could make a few images of blackness appear to stand for all men of African descent.

She investigated the conflicts between the duties of colonialism and the pleasures of exoticism most explicitly in her last two books, both published in Paris in 1925: the aforementioned *Mes inconnus chez eux: Mon amie Fatou, Citadine* and *Mes inconnus chez eux: Mon ami Soumaré, Laptot* (My Strangers at Their Home: My Friend Soumaré, Docker). In these works she pursued the subjects of her first one, the Senegalese *tirailleurs*, onto their own territory. She offered respect for Africans as a starting point for any attempt at a civilizing mission, and lived up to her own standards by always residing with African families during her stay and learning how to dress like them. She was ruthless with Europeans, including herself, for example commenting multiple times on how ridiculous she felt being carried around West Africa (although she rarely got down and walked). She also noted that she had to overcome the suspicions that arose as soon as local Africans realized she was atypical for a colonialist. They questioned her agenda for she refused to wear the symbol of power that was the white colonial costume, and chose to sit in a second- instead of first-class train compartment. Eventually her interpreter and others exclaimed: "I saw you doing everything here just as you would in Paris: what good luck for a colony."[85] When in a position of power, for example when sitting in a first-class car with amenities and watching fourth-class passengers take bathroom breaks outdoors between train stops, she was distressed by other first-class passengers' finicky reactions. While in Koussoura, Nigeria, she tempered a comment she made about how locals should learn to speak French with a self-deprecating rebuttal: "I don't have much aptitude for emitting and remembering indigenous sounds. I really have trouble saying yes or no—after all, these are difficult words."[86]

Her response to the imbalances in power that she perceived and in which she herself was involved was by no means a straightforward political reaction. Instead, she suggested a form of reverse exoticism—albeit not quite in the manner put forth by anti-imperial men. Like them Cousturier saw exoticism, and in particular negrophilia, as a means for establishing superficial and then more profound contact between the races. For her, unlike with anti-imperialists, the entirety of the solution to the colonial dilemma lay in placing black men and women in contact with white metropolitan ones. African women, for example, could initiate exchanges in Paris: "It is easy to predict the success these darling stars would have in Paris, if one could transport them there without dimming their flame; they would allow even the most uninitiated public a comfortable and irresistible initiation to *l'art nègre*."[87] In this work published in the year (and thus written before) Baker first took Paris by storm, she noted that the enthrallment with the *tumulte noir* dismayed administrators and settlers who feared negrophilia might unbalance the colonial order of things: "This blasted black race pleases; it would please whites too much if they weren't careful! It disconcerts because of the originality, the lightness and the intensity in life of all its physical and intellectual forms."[88] Unlike reluctant colonizers, she reveled in this imbalance, suggesting "one should eat a little black, think a little black; one should need the industry, opinions, art, friendship, and social as well as sexual love of blacks."[89] Cousturier summed up her rejection of the settlers' denigration of Africans at the end of her last work when she advocated interracial contact even while recognizing a worker-boss divide that she believed made race and class interchangeable:

If between Whites and Blacks, despite the contract between vanquished and victor, worker and boss, there exists an attraction based on color and form, a sexual attraction, then the interracial griping loses all meaning. It would be as though lovers reproached one another for being different sexes. It would be the reproach of fools. But perhaps Whites are just that?[90]

By focusing upon the mutual attraction inherent in interracial relations she presented the advantages of pursuing the initial artistic attraction of exoticism ("color and form") to its logical, sexual conclusion. Thus she suggested that white colonial administrators who wished to ignore the sensuality of their connection to the black race should instead use it as the foundation of the civilizing mission, even while recognizing like colonial migrants themselves the irreverent power of interracial relationships.

Cousturier, even while not overtly engaging with precise political parties, nonetheless was uneasy enough with distinctions of power to recognize that "race in the language of the strong means class; everyone knows that," an extraordinary statement that with its apparently Marxist import echoed anti-imperialist ideas.[91] Cousturier recognized throughout her work that categories such as race, class, or sex were all used to limit access to privilege. For example, she did not hesitate to compare black colonial women cleaning her apartment in Siguiri, Guinea, to the men who cleaned the streets of Paris.[92] Indeed, alongside her gender and her artistically-motivated fascination with the *vogue nègre*, Cousturier gave a third reason for her grasp of the colonial situation: she considered herself to be "Parisian" and not merely French when overseas. One African man explained that he had come to speak with her entirely because of this attribute: "If it were only those from Paris here, all the blacks in the colony, they would no longer be miserable."[93] Being from a metropolis that invited interactions among so many different people interested in the cultural and political ramifications of colonialism influenced her (and other Parisians', she implied) even-handed reading of the colonial situation once overseas. Her insight was a variation on those of Fanon and the Nardal sisters' when they stated that Antilleans grasped the true meaning of their colonial and racial situation only after experiencing the metropole.

As a result, although she rarely shied from applying an exoticizing gaze to those around her, Cousturier was saluted by members of interracial and anti-imperialist organizations in Paris. René Maran was one of several black Parisians who admired and defended Cousturier's vision. After meeting Cousturier, Maran wrote an article for the African American newspaper *Opportunity* titled "The Harriet Beecher Stowe of France" comparing her to the abolitionist who wrote *Uncle Tom's Cabin*. He defended Cousturier against the charges of bolshevism that had sullied her image after the publication of her works, charges that reflected the extent to which her ideas and their presentation were considered provocative even as they replicated some of the voyeurism of negrophilia. He identified her instead as a pacifist who "believes in the internationalism of races and religions" (phrasing that foreshadowed the coming work of the Nardal sisters).[94] Maran was not alone in championing her, and indeed black organizations' steady admiration for Cousturier may account for the charges of bolshevism in the first place. Léon Werth, Maran's fellow journalist at *Les Continents*, wrote a gracious piece in which he noted that Cousturier was rewarded in her defense of blacks with the establishment of an astonishing osmosis between herself and the subjects of her studies.[95] Readers of *La Race Nègre* and members of the LDRN were aware of Cousturier as well, with articles announcing the second and third anniversaries of her 1925 death in 1927 and 1928. In 1927, unable to organize a pilgrimage to her grave in the famous Parisian Père-Lachaise cemetery, the LDRN still encouraged members to purchase her works, "scintillating with novel ideas, in which Lucie Cousturier's heart of gold overflows, streaming with generosity for us. There is no better way for *nègres* to celebrate the anniversary of her death than to read and reread her books, striving to understand her ideas; to absorb her courageous concepts on *nègre* and colonial issues; and most importantly trying to apply them to current realities."[96] In 1928 an LDRN delegation placed flowers on Cousturier's tomb on the anniversary of her death.[97] As late as 1935 Kouyaté asked the publisher, Jean-Richard Bloch of the Librairie Rieder, for a list of all Cousturier's works that he intended to print (perhaps in his new paper, *Africa*).[98] The Parisian Africans and Antilleans' fascination with Cousturier even crossed ideological lines, for *La Dépêche Africaine* also placed her in the canon of postwar colonial literature, alongside Gide and Maran.[99]

Denise Moran Savineau witnessed the full effect of the *vogue nègre* upon Parisian circles in a way that Cousturier never could. Writing in the 1930s Moran, who wrote under her maiden name, saw less hope in the phenomenon and painted a stark picture of the colors and forms of colonialism after she visited French West Africa as an official representative of colonialism. Born in Paris, Moran studied music before obtaining her *brevet supérieur*, a state-administered educational examination for women over eighteen. Almost immediately thereafter she started writing about social questions in an evolution resembling that of Netter and Martin. Moran's first articles, written rather incongruously for the right-leaning *Le Journal* and the politically involved left-leaning *Le Quotidien*, gave no indication of her future interest in the colonies, which sparked when she accompanied her husband Edmond Jean Savineau to French West Africa. After attending the Ecole Normale Supérieure also attended by leading black intellectuals like Aimé Césaire, Moran's husband became a teacher, a journalist, and a close friend of André Gide before working as secretary to the governor of Chad, Marcel de Coppet.[100] Denise Moran on her own initiative founded two schools for *indigènes* while in Africa and became their headmistress. Moran was also one of the first women employed by the colonial administration, working as a technical counselor for education for the French West African administration and writing a report. Her focus upon the conditions of black women and children came fifteen years after Cousturier's, and under the different circumstances of the Popular Front.

In 1936 Moran discovered that a commission of inquiry was being set up by the newly appointed governor general of West Africa, de Coppet. The commission was established in response to the concerns of the Section Française de l'Internationale Ouvrière party, which by then grouped socialists in opposition to communists, and the Ligue des Droits de l'Homme (League for the Rights of Man). By the mid-1930s the lobbying efforts of anti-imperialists and pacifists had finally resulted in an official, although minimal, response by the Popular Front government. It brought together a coalition of left-wing parties, but was also the first to grant women positions of governmental power, a natural decision since both the Communists in 1920 and the Radicals in 1924 had opened their doors to women. Thus Cécile Brunschvicg, whose interest in colonialism followed a similar arc to that of fellow reformist feminists, became the undersecretary of state for education. The Popular Front government also included a minister of the colonies, Marius Moutet, who along with the Prime Minister Léon Blum had previously called for independence, autonomy, and even self-government for the colonies. By 1936 the government was downplaying these ideals in favor of a stringent enforcement of the civilizing mission. However, a commission was nevertheless set up that included delegates from the Ligue des Droits de l'Homme and concentrated specifically upon the situation of colonized women in French West Africa. In March 1937 Moran asked to join the Commission, addressing correspondence to her and her husband's former administrative superior in Chad (French Equatorial Africa), de Coppet. She was appointed to lead an investigation on family life and educational facilities. Evading the constraints of her assignment, she studied the colonial justice system, visited penitentiaries and health facilities, inspected schools, visited agricultural businesses and local markets, and reported on forced labor and colonial taxation. Aside from the fact that a woman wrote a critical report with a sharp focus upon social injustices, perhaps just as surprising was de Coppet's response.[101] He forwarded the results to Minister Moutet in Paris, and used them to question the under-funding of elementary schools in the capital of the French Sudan, Bamako, the depressing interior of orphanages destined for *métis* children, and the level of teaching at schools run by nuns who allegedly discriminated against black students. While some governors of French West Africa denied the report's validity, others corroborated Moran's work, and de Coppet used it to confront the governors under his jurisdiction.

Moran's aptitude as a colonial critic on the administrative level was rare indeed, even if the Popular Front context lent new impetus to these questions. Her right to compile such a report was especially astonishing since she had previously written a critical work based upon her experiences overseas. Unlike Cousturier, Moran's first and only substantial work, *Tchad* (Chad), published by the major Paris-based press Librairie Gallimard in 1934, predated her official report and focused on a different part of Africa.[102] Written in memory of her husband "dead in Chad in the service of the *noirs*," her book was in the same series as other works criticizing worldwide injustice such as André Malraux's *La Condition humaine* (The Human Condition) and André Gide's *Voyage au Congo* (Journey to the Congo) and *Le Retour du Tchad* (Return from Chad). Moran recognized Gide as an activist forefather but believed that three years of colonial experience justified the publication of a new work based on observations she made while working as a primary school teacher. As she traveled throughout Chad, Moran also became a healer after noting that some nurses did not sterilize their needles and other equipment because they were treating Africans. Like other feminists, Moran focused upon education, the *métis*, prostitution, and interracial relationships, but she did so with far less humor and forgiveness for the French than even Cousturier. She was contemptuous of most fellow white colonial women, who warned her against traveling to Chad because she would not find boutiques or have a social life there. When she arrived in Fort-Lamy, Chad, she did so as an asexual being whose femininity had been erased by travel: "We were greeted with Hello Gentlemen. We were expecting a lady . . . I laugh, and the error is cleared up. But do Madames usually trot along toward Chad in casino-type finery? There are excuses, and much bustling about. Was I not seasick in a whaling boat? Isn't it just horrid, this trip, for a 'lady?'"[103] In her amused battle with stereotypes of femininity, Moran was true to the reputation established by fellow women writers that women were independent and intelligent critics of colonialism. On the other hand, with her mocking rebukes of dolled-up creatures she risked undoing any solidarity she might otherwise have created with white colonial women and their husbands.

Moran, who witnessed the peak of the Parisian negrophilia Cousturier hoped would solve racial tensions, did not share her optimism with respect to the impact that it might have. She observed race conflicts overshadowing those of class or sex within the colonies and spoke about that strife with her Parisian audience. To reach her potentially indifferent readers Moran used her schoolchildren, who drew the illustrations for the work. While reading in class they came across the word *égal* (equal), which the student Abakar defined "as: White is not equal to Black" just as he defined *libre* (free) as "before the Whites . . . the Blacks were free."[104] Of the *Liberté, Egalité, Fraternité* motto that theoretically guided France in her development of the civilizing mission, not much remained in Moran's Chad.

Yet like Cousturier, Moran saw some hope. One drunken man she met shouted in her direction "colonial life today is a pretty sight! One can't touch a *nègre* without those bloody * . . . * who call themselves the Ligue des Droits de l'Homme starting to bawl!"[105] After publishing *Tchad*, and before returning to French West Africa to write a report for the Ministry of Colonies, Moran traveled to the Soviet Union in 1935. Upon her return to Paris she became an active supporter of the

Ligue des Droits de l'Homme and of other organizations, including the League Against Imperialism, whose meetings she attended in 1935 when it began pooling resources with the UTN and the Comité Mondial des Femmes Contre la Guerre et le Fascisme (World Committee of Women Against War and Fascism, CMFGF), to promote freedom of speech and end violence within the French colonies and elsewhere.[106] Indeed, she presided over at least one of the Comité Mondial Contre la Guerre et le Fascisme's 1935 meetings at which the communist UTN member Stéphane Rosso spoke, and which would likely have been attended by Paulette Nardal.[107] Around this time period, a Grand Gala for the Fraternity of Races was organized featuring Antillean, Cambodian, Cameroonian, French, Moroccan, Jewish, and other performances. Tickets could be bought from the UTN, the CMFGF, the Ligue des Femmes pour la Paix (League of Women For Peace), and so forth, which meant that members of all these organizations found themselves at least occasionally in the same rooms.[108]

Moran's transition to an international, Paris-based anti-imperialism reflected the intensification of propaganda during the mid-1930s by organizations such as the CMFGF, one of the many associations grouped under the Union Française pour le Suffrage des Femmes (UFSF). Six hundred and seventy Frenchwomen had mandates for its 1934 Paris congress titled the Congrès Mondial des Femmes contre la Guerre et le Fascisme (World Congress of Women against War and Fascism). They were of different backgrounds from the leaders of the UFSF and CNFF, being an overwhelmingly communist group that also counted self-identified socialists, pacifists, or feminists.[109] The African American Scottsboro mother Ada Smith was one of the speakers and asked women to help free her sons. A colonial commission set up during the congress upheld many ideals promulgated during the 1931 Estates General of Feminism and in *La Française*, especially with regard to women and children, but went on to demand total independence for the colonies. Although the organizations did not see eye to eye, the CMFGF and other antifascist and anti-imperialist organizations established a link between radical associations such as the UTN and moderate feminist ones. The Martinican woman Amita Very, admired in *Le Cri des Nègres*, was a member of the CMFGF and of course Paulette Nardal was also active with the organization. In 1935, the CMFGF asked Cécile Brunschvicg to recognize that "today, blood is running in Ethiopia; women and children have found death because of bombardments; the number of military victims on both sides continues to grow."[110] They asked that all French feminist organizations gather to coordinate their ideas on pacifism and feminism. The collaboration, although limited, appealed to *La Française*, which had already published "A call from women of the black race" that focused upon Paulette Nardal's cause, the Italo-Ethiopian conflict, and begged Frenchwomen to join black ones in supporting the League of Nations.[111] Readers of *La Française* were only introduced to Paulette Nardal by name much later, in 1939, via her mother Louise, who was admired for her success in giving each of her (also highly regarded) girls a profession.[112] But in 1935 they were already well aware of one of her causes.

By 1937 feminists in France had goals in common other than suffrage. Pacifism, antifascism, and colonialism invited them to circumvent political affiliations and other differences. Thus the UFSF aligned itself with the ideas of the CMFGF and women of the African diaspora during a National Congress of the UFSF held in Paris on June 26 and 27, 1937. The congress voted to approve a text that decried "When [women] insist upon the recognition of our rights as humans, we are fighting the same battle as all those who suffer for their race, their beliefs, their class, or their opinions."[113] Gender and race had been compellingly labeled as one and the same categories for denying rights.

Amidst this growing political turmoil, Moran's harsh words were well received, for example with a very flattering review in *La Française*. The journalist Jane Catulle-Mendès granted Moran authority as she wrote: "She is a realist. She writes what she has seen, without using her imagination to invent things."[114] There is no indication that Moran's work produced any shockwaves nor that she was accused of bolshevism like Cousturier, perhaps because it was published soon after Gide's, but perhaps also because her ideals were in sync with the larger context of the Popular Front and growing cooperation amidst disparate political and social groups. Could it be that ultimately Cousturier's references to interracial sexuality were also more provocative than Moran's political commentary? In any event, Moran was read by Frenchwomen; and with the ensuing colonial report became one of very few women to directly challenge colonialism through its administrative system.

Women's Rights in the Colonies

The transition from Cousturier's hope to Moran's anger reflected the contrast between the optimism of the early *vogue nègre* and the concerns surrounding the worldwide turmoil of the mid-1930s. Feminists throughout France faced the continued withholding of suffrage, and both radicals and communists were disappointed with the Popular Front's inaction in this respect. Colonial causes gave feminist organizations and individual women a different path through which to explore their relationship to a state that was still structured to deny them suffrage. Some women interested in colonialism, such as Oulié, turned to writing mildly critical travelogues. Others, including Moran, indicted colonial officials. The greatest outrage for some, however, stemmed not from the well-documented colonial injustices, although these clearly elicited responses, but from the Projet Viollette. Moran was able to take advantage of the Popular Front's relative tolerance to write her report, but that same indulgence outraged others.

In 1931, as the Estates General gathered feminists from around France, Maurice Viollette, the future minister of state under Léon Blum's Popular Front and governor general of Algeria from 1925 to 1927, proposed what became known as the Projet Viollette. He wanted to grant French citizenship to educated and influential Algerians without making them abandon their *statut personnel* (personal status) as Muslims, a complex "privilege" that simultaneously protected local family law and marriage from French modifications and kept Muslims from becoming full French citizens. His project, renamed the Blum-Viollette Plan under the Popular Front, aimed to grant citizenship only to twenty-one thousand out of a potential five million Algerians in 1936.[115] Although the plan focused on Algeria, Frenchwomen's outraged reaction in *La Française* as early as 1931 gives some indication of the extent to which white women's engagement with colonialism was paradoxical. The 1931 Estates General ended with a resolution published in *La Française* that claimed the vote for Frenchwomen based upon their contribution to life in the colonies.[116] With this impetus, a writer for *La Française* argued that "France's policies are tending toward giving political rights to more and more categories of *indigènes*, thereby forcing women into a position of inferiority in the colonized milieus."[117] She revealed with "position of inferiority" the complex hierarchies of colonial society, and some Frenchwomen's desire to stay toward the top of those race and gender-based hierarchies. To them it made no sense to deny women rights based on their sex when these were being extended even to men of color. Here, "women" really meant white women.[118] In other words, their whiteness should guarantee the vote, rather than their sex, which was being unjustly used against them. Indeed some specifically argued that French/white women overseas be given the vote (even as those in the metropole continued to have it denied) in recognition of their pivotal role in maintaining the fabric of society in the colonies.[119]

Others took a more internationally humanistic stance on the Projet Viollette, even while defending the rights of Frenchwomen overseas. One journalist, for example, scrutinized the new proposal by arguing (in the vein of Cousturier): "It would mean substituting for the idea of 'race,' against which our inner sense of fundamental human equality rebels, that of 'sex,' just as ugly and just as dangerous. Indeed neither race nor sex mark the value of a human being, which is instead marked by noble-heartedness and spirit; and one's rights must be in proportion to the services rendered to the community to which one belongs."[120] Her definitions of identity, the dangers of categorization, and their relationship to citizenship reflected beliefs common to many women who were aware of France's imperial standing. Citizenship had to be earned, and whether in the colonies or in the metropole, a demonstration of humanity and the development of a social conscience should be one's best hope for obtaining it. As these reactions to the extension of civil rights and suffrage to African men indicate, the potential alliances between anti-imperialists and feminists were rife with complex pitfalls and tensions.

As mothers and pacifists, feminists believed they naturally excelled at the civilizing mission in a manner that men could not. Women who took their role as critics seriously and wrote about their sympathy for black, colonized men and women were stimulated by the belief that they were partners in the struggle for suffrage, independence, and active citizenship. Frenchwomen and people of African descent sought political power, representation, and equality with the men who dominated the republic. In the pages of *La Française* one white woman who spent a fair amount of time in Paris and overseas was even so bold and consequential as to argue that there was no reason to keep the vote from women of color, such as educated ones from the French West Indies, since often even those presumed to be "primitive" lived in matriarchal societies and were capable of governing themselves.[121]

Feminist writers in the colonial metropolis also governed themselves, using Paris-based associations and publishing houses to confront the exoticism of negrophilia and the Colonial Exposition with what they had learned through personal experiences in the capital and overseas. As the Popular Front's requests for reports on indigenous women suggest, feminist writers and organizations' growing interest in colonized women and children found administrative outlets. In the heyday of the 1920s jazz age, women such as Cousturier argued that the *vogue nègre* could transform, in the best of ways, the relationships between black and white, men and women. By the 1930s, Moran and others recognized the danger of allowing the escapism provided by exoticism to distract from the harsh realities of colonial injustices. The turning points for women in the colonial metropolis were similar to those of black Parisian groups: the lack of suffrage following World War I encouraged organized activism and alternative forms of political communication. The Colonial Exposition invited a specifically feminist gathering, the Estates General of Feminism, that, like the anti-exposition, showcased an unofficial, in this case feminine, vision of colonialism and, like the host city itself, forced women with very different colonial experiences into one room to consider its possibilities and repercussions. The Scottsboro Affair, the Italo-Ethiopian war, and the internationalism of antifascism and pacifism galvanized women from different backgrounds and feminist persuasions to take a harder look at the colonial project. Finally, the Popular Front both granted and spurred women to carve out a space in which to transform their interest in the colonial question into political action.

These writers went further and more regularly afield during the interwar period than most dwelling in the colonial metropolis. Tracing their travels from the Parisian to overseas spaces and back again reveals yet another dimension of the city as a colonial metropolis that repeatedly drew back into its fold both the physical bodies and the works of art of those explicitly describing and confronting colonialism. The many ties linking the metropolis and overseas territories contributed to anchoring the city securely within the empire and entwining the colonies firmly with the capital. Paris was a pivotal zone through which publications and their writers passed before being disseminated to an empire-wide audience. The fact that these women and their writings went through Paris before and after far-reaching travels reflects not only how they came to terms with colonialism, but also how their ideas resonated within and influenced a public sphere in which colonialism was increasingly contested by different interest groups during the interwar period. No matter how varied their backgrounds, feminisms, and responses to the questions provoked by colonialism, these writers agreed that prevailing definitions and assumptions of identity, whether through citizenship, race, or sex, were warped by the "minor transgressions" of dominant, white Frenchmen. In so doing they reached various levels of understanding and at times even empathy with Africans and people of African descent both in colonial spaces overseas and in Paris. Women both shared and shaped the colonial metropolis and its links to the colonial peripheries along with these African and Antillean men and women.

CONCLUSION

The 1927 letterhead of the Ligue de Défense de la Race Nègre (LDRN) included an image of a black woman who stands strong, tall, and bare-breasted upon a globe. One foot placed firmly on North and West Africa, and the other trampling portions of the United States, she raises her right arm aloft, bearing a torch. Europe appears miniscule on the map, almost hidden behind her leg and the striped cloth, or *pagne*, girding her waist. The address on the letterhead reads: "43, rue du Simplon, Paris 18ᵉ." The image is striking for several reasons. First, a woman draws the viewer in, although the organization she represents was overwhelmingly male and offered little room for black or white women. Second, her muscular shoulders and forearm suggest a defiant offensive against all those oppressing people with ties to Africa. Third, although the globe symbolizes the worldwide perspective of the offensive, Paris is its crucial site, since the organization's headquarters are located in this metropolis.

In 1932, as we have seen, the LDRN split. The more moderate contingent retained rights to the Ligue's name and trademark graphic. Thus the Union des Travailleurs Nègres (UTN), which thereafter represented the militant segment of Paris's black population, needed a new symbol for its letterhead and newspaper masthead. Muscles rippling, clothed only in a loincloth, a black man dominates the globe. Western Europe is all but hidden behind his left foot, which rests upon the continent of Africa. His right one has dug into North America. Three regions written out in boldface lettering draw the eye to Africa, the Caribbean, and America (the fourth geographic location, Florida, is identified with smaller characters). The reference to the

213

slave trade is unmistakable: the black man clutches in both hands a thickly wrought chain that surrounds the planet. His contracting biceps and triceps have just broken two of its links. Behind him, in the East, a star is rising. When contrasted with the image of the black woman, this one is all the more captivating. First, the LDRN's strong woman was replaced with the UTN's overpowering, masculinity-radiating figure. Second, the globe was redesigned and rotated to spell out the triangle of the slave trade at its center. Third, with a star in the backdrop symbolizing communism's support, this black man is retaliating against his oppressors. Was this communist star a thorny issue for ambivalent UTN members? Perhaps, for by its July-August 1933 issue, the UTN's newspaper, *Le Cri des Nègres*, had removed the entirety of this emblem from its masthead.[1]

For a while though, these two emblems coexisted. Taken together, they very much represent a particular moment in France's colonial history: the interwar years. The nuances of such images, and the interplay between them, are illustrative of the questions that shaped this book. What were the links between the *vogue nègre* and anti-imperial politics? Among other things: a city, its inhabitants, and the colonial framework. What does considering Paris as a colonial metropolis help us to understand about this city, the imperial nation-state that encased it, and the politics and social lives of those encapsulated by its many spaces? As black and white men and women moved through Paris, they changed its streetscapes. Connections in love, friendship, and even the briefest of exchanges on a street corner added a personal and political dimension to performance and spectatorship, becoming the points of departure for critiques of French culture, society, and politics.

Such contacts pushed inhabitants of the colonial metropolis to respond to France's Empire. Many of the black men who arrived in France during or immediately after World War I quickly organized into intellectual, political, and social groups that wanted equality or independence, subversively questioned France's colonial policy, and showed general disdain for the Parisian fascination with exoticism. Colonial workers sought strength in the broad sweep of the category *noir*, or black. They appeared to "colonize" the capital, leading even the police charged with their surveillance to dub them a black colony. In Paris they balanced politics and life, including relationships with politically engaged white women. When the *vogue nègre* and colonial policies threatened black men, they reestablished their sense of self in two ways. They manipulated the French fascination with blackness by carving a space for their views within the culture of exoticism. Simultaneously they expressed their frustrations and opinions in ways that brought to the fore their masculinity, as evidenced by their depiction of a black man dominating the globe.

Black and white women were also invested in rendering the imperial nation-state more permeable, even while carefully structuring their responses to the masculinity of the colonial world. The Nardal sisters, for example, developed a feminine race consciousness while situating themselves as links between metropole and colonies. As active participants in milieus both intellectual and working-class, they moved confidently amidst often male black and white intellectuals, workers, and revolutionaries. During the early and mid-1930s, much like black colonial men and women, white feminists' demands were convoluted and wide-ranging. Some argued for reform while others insisted upon a complete overhaul of the colonial system on the premise that in the colonies French men had reproduced social injustices, inequalities, and spurious definitions of citizenship reminiscent of the lack of women's rights in the metropole. The self-interested call for civil rights or suffrage was not far removed from their comments on colonialism. These women therefore allow us to further reflect upon the many ways in which the *vogue nègre* trickled into the public sphere, how and why colonial migrants came into contact with other Parisians, and how these women's resulting cognizance of the imperial setting made colonial concerns natural companions to social ones. Even in a metropolitan setting Empire hovered, inducing connections among Parisians in a range of manners and localities. The struggles for agency explored in this book were encased in an imperial setting that these men and women manipulated, and by which they were stimulated.[2]

The topics that frame this book—anti-imperialism, feminism, colonialism, and the role of Paris as the cosmopolitan locus for transnational encounters—are still relevant today. Of course, they have been transformed by the passing of time, republics, wars, and even colonialism, with France's overseas lands now either independent or incorporated as departments and territories. Yet as the 2005 riots in and around Paris (and throughout France), and the 2009 strikes, riots, and other expressions of discontent in Guadeloupe, Martinique, French Guiana, and La Réunion have shown, such questions have surfaced during the Fifth Republic (1958–present) in discussions of integration, exclusion, immigration, racism, and anti-globalization, among many other subjects. Investigating continuity within these ideas invites an entirely new project, as does an exploration of the possibility for other such colonial cities and spaces (Marseille jumps to mind), an in-depth study of the links between black and other colonial migrants, or the tracing of each of the individuals described here beyond the interwar period. At this point, it is worth drawing some of these women and men's stories through the war whose outbreak defines the close of this work.

When World War II broke out, Léopold Sédar Senghor was called up to serve in the colonial infantry in which he had done his military service. He was taken prisoner of war by the Germans and spent two years in a camp in France before being released. He went on to teach on the outskirts of Paris for the duration of the war (he had become an *agrégé*, or prestigious qualified teacher, in 1935). In these experiences he was luckier than Tiémoko Garan Kouyaté, who was arrested by the Gestapo in France in 1943, arrived at the concentration camp Mauthausen (in Austria) on September 18, 1943—classified as a political prisoner—and died in the camp under unknown circumstances described vaguely as "heart failure" on July 4, 1944.[3] Aimé Césaire returned to Martinique before the war started, after publishing negritude's call to battle in 1939: *Cahier d'un retour au pays natal* (Notebook of a Return to My Native Land).[4] In Martinique, he found himself during the early years of the war under the control of the Vichy government, which the Germans allowed to control southern France and certain colonies in exchange for collaboration with Nazi policies and acceptance of the German occupation of northern France (including Paris). Yet Césaire found a way to challenge Vichy: cultural rebellion. For four years Césaire, along with his wife Suzanne and other Martinican intellectuals, published the journal *Tropiques*. They eschewed open rebellion, instead using cannibalistic and surrealistic language to transmit messages of dissidence and resistance to Vichy and colonialism.[5] The apparent lapse of the severe Vichy censorship in the case of *Tropiques* demonstrates yet again how in times of duress, or while under surveillance, black culture could be used to dissimulate subversion.[6] In retrospect Césaire explained: "We produced a cultural review . . . But only because we could do nothing *else!* You had to be extremely careful; don't forget that we were subjected to censorship, the cultural might make it through, just barely, but only if you were *very* careful!"[7]

After the war, the anti-imperial activism first advocated by LDRN and UTN members made a stronger statement than the poetics of negritude. Yet at the same time, in the late 1940s and the 1950s negritude thinkers—not early anti-imperialists—became widely recognized for their early development of a race consciousness. In 1948 the politically committed French writer Jean-Paul Sartre celebrated negritude as a philosophy in which gaining control over the French language allowed black writers to assert their own culture.[8] Reactions to negritude were nonetheless ambivalent. Communists rejected the idea that culture should take precedence over the politics of a class struggle. The potentially racist idea that black men were fundamentally different from white ones, both on the surface and in their essence, bothered some observers. Finally, the elitism of a movement driven by highly educated men who wrote in French—and were thus fundamentally detached from many of the Africans for whom they wrote—disturbed other critics. Thus negritude's recognition as a cultural phenomenon celebrating blackness ironically coincided with the post–World War II period when the anti-imperial struggle had finally become widespread enough in its political activism that its dissimulation in culture was no longer necessary.

Thirty-three years after Jane Nardal's February 1928 article "Black Internationalism," Senghor argued that without the *vogue nègre*, the political poetics of blackness might never have existed. He specifically identified the black topography of Montmartre and the Left Bank: "It is in Paris that, following the ethnographers, we rediscovered *Négritude*, that is to say the cultural mores of the Negro-African Civilization; gift of emotion and gift of sympathy; gift of rhythm and gift of form; gift of image and gift of myth; communal and democratic spirit."[9] When placed in the context of texts written during the 1920s and 1930s by members of the LDRN, the UTN, Jane and Paulette Nardal, and Roberte Horth, we see that there was, in fact, a direct link between the *vogue nègre* and the politics of race.

Paulette Nardal, like Césaire, returned to Martinique just before the war broke out, in her case to do research for a project with which the current Minister of the Colonies, Georges Mandel, had entrusted her.[10] To complete her work, she tried to return to Paris in September 1939, after the war's onset. However her ship was torpedoed by the Germans, and as she scrambled to board the British destroyer sent to pick up survivors her leg was badly damaged, leaving her disabled for life. After a long convalescence in England, she returned to her homeland in 1940 only to find that it was now under the control of the Vichy government. Once back in Martinique, Nardal did her part to resist the fascism against which she had spoken out so often in Paris by teaching English to Martinicans who wanted to escape the island and join General Charles de Gaulle's Free French troops. After the Free French gained control of the island in 1943, Nardal founded the Martinican branch of the Catholic Union Féminine Civique et Sociale with which she and Jane had first affiliated themselves in Paris. She continued to think about sisterhood through this organization, known locally as the Rassemblement Féminin; her establishment of a local literary circle; and her founding of the publication to which she and Jane contributed thoughts regarding the place of overseas women in post–World War II France: *La Femme dans la Cité*.

As for the white feminists of the colonial metropolis—they were granted the vote in 1944. It was extended several months later to An-

tillean women and in 1945 to the women of French Guiana and Madagascar, among other colonies (Senegalese women were excluded for a
while longer).[11] However the metropolitan struggle for women's rights
was also far from over—in their own eyes—and would resurface regularly during the Fourth and Fifth Republics.[12] White women's wartime
experiences, like those of black men and women, varied considerably.
Yvonne Netter, for example, was a feminist but she was also Jewish
and supported Zionism. She argued that the rights granted to Jewish
women in Palestine during the interwar years made it a perfect space
for women of that faith who were being persecuted in other parts of
the Middle East and North Africa. She still lived in Paris when she
converted to Catholicism in December 1940, but her conversion did
her little good and in 1941 she was removed from the Bar. Then she
was arrested in 1942, but managed to escape and remained hidden in
the Pyrenees mountains on France's border with Spain until the end
of the war.[13]

In contrast to both Nardal and Netter, Josephine Baker spent World
War II openly performing in the metropole and Algeria. She also
volunteered for the Resistance, although her prominence as a performer made it difficult for her to remain clandestine. In recognition
of her services, the French awarded her the *Légion d'Honneur*, the
Croix de Guerre, and the *Médaille de la Résistance* after the war. She
remained in France until her death on April 12, 1975. Baker remains
emblematic in French culture today. In 2001, the Théâtre des Champs-
Elysées, where she had first performed in the *Revue Nègre*, organized
a retrospective exhibition to celebrate that performance. Periodically,
articles in prominent French newspapers such as *Le Monde*, *Libéra-
tion*, and *Le Figaro* commemorate her career, often with the help of
photographs showcasing her nudity and exoticism.[14] Strolling along
the Parisian banks of the river Seine today, browsing the bookstalls,
you will frequently come across reproductions of Paul Colin's Baker
posters alongside those of Banania ads using a stereotyped Senegalese *tirailleur* to represent the chocolatey drink.[15] You will discover a
Josephine Baker swimming pool laying on floats in the Seine River
on the edge of the thirteenth arrondissement. Baker also became an

unwitting star of the quirky French animated film *Les Triplettes de Belleville* (The Triplets of Belleville, 2003). In the opening sequence a Baker-like figure dances on a stage in a banana skirt. Suddenly, she is mobbed by the audience's tailcoat and top hat–sporting men who rush on stage while metamorphosing into monkeys, rip her bananas off even as she dances, and eat them. This eccentric representation of Baker illustrates the ongoing, although also parodied and criticized, role of the exotic in representations of French colonialism.[16]

Black Sun

Almost fifty years after the *vogue nègre* took Paris by storm, the Guadeloupean Daniel Maximin wrote the novel *Isolé soleil* (Lone Sun, 1981). In it, he tells the historically grounded story of a black Antillean woman in 1930s Paris. Siméa, the protagonist, is forced to abort the child of a white man. Still groggy from the drugs, she recounts her experience as a black woman in the metropolis. Her hallucinations of Paris spin from the origins of the negritude movement with Césaire to the nightclub *La Cabane Cubaine*, where she relaxed with other members of the black community while listening to jazz and dancing, to surrealist poetry intermingled with racial dialogue. Lonely, afraid, she pleads for help: "I need the hand of a woman, of a woman-sun, of a black sun, of a very *nègre* black, of a very *marron nègre* for my defense, my legitimate defense," with *marron* here a reference to an escaped slave.[17] In 1929 Paulette Nardal was also intrigued by the visceral links between black women and the sun in "Actions de Grâces" (Thanksgivings), a short article in *La Dépêche Africaine* that glorified spring as a revitalizing force for Antillean women. "It seems that now everything has become light, light: the mild air, blue sky, the perfumes wafting from the trees, and above all the sun, finally triumphing over the grayness of winter."[18] The sun was an adornment for a Parisian topography that otherwise suffered from being "too civilized, too finished, too artificial." Even masculine associations such as the LDRN, in a reflection of the intriguing and ambivalent complexity of interracial interwar encounters, at one point in time chose a proud, powerful black woman as the guiding light in their racial struggle. She held a light that, shining over the globe, was in their own words "a watchword for rallying: a torch," or a sun.[19] This sun epitomized the outward gaze of Parisians, black and white, who contended with the colonial nature of the metropolis even as they pursued their politics of feminism and anti-imperialism. They crafted Paris into a space in which to consider and shape colonialism, but also simply in which to live.

NOTES

Introduction

1. CAOM, SLOTFOM II/21, Agent Joé, May 5, 1931.

2. CAOM, SLOTFOM II/21, Agent Joé, May 28, 1931. Agent Joé's words, and his entire story, can be considered examples of what James Scott calls a hidden transcript, which "consists of those offstage speeches, gestures, and practices that confirm, contradict, or inflect what appears in the public transcript." James C. Scott, *Domination and the Arts of Resistance: Hidden Transcripts* (New Haven CT: Yale University Press, 1990), 4–5.

3. Along with Philippe Dewitte, James Spiegler and Martin Steins produced foundational works based on this particular archival series and black anti-imperialism in general. More recently Brent Hayes Edwards has used SLOTFOM sources to investigate anti-imperialism's roots across the Atlantic, Gary Wilder to argue that France was an imperial nation-state and to explore colonial humanism, and Christopher Miller to locate the roots of negritude in the racial awareness of 1920s workers. Philippe Dewitte, *Les Mouvements nègres en France 1919–1939* (Paris: L'Harmattan, 1985); Brent Hayes Edwards, *The Practice of Diaspora: Literature, Translation, and the Rise of Black Internationalism* (Cambridge MA: Harvard University Press, 2003); Christopher L. Miller, *Nationalists and Nomads: Essays on Francophone African Literature and Culture* (Chicago: The University of Chicago Press, 1998); James Spiegler, "Aspects of Nationalist Thought among French-Speaking West Africans, 1921–1939" (Oxford University, 1968), Martin Steins, "Les antécédents et la génèse de la Négritude senghorienne" (Université de Paris III-Sorbonne Nouvelle, 1980); Gary Wilder, *The French Imperial Nation-State: Negritude and Colonial Humanism between the Two World Wars* (Chicago: The University of Chicago Press, 2005).

4. Numerous works have shaped and guided this book in important

ways. Early on, the following ones inspired this gendered and racial reading of Paris as a colonial space: Mary Louise Roberts, *Civilization Without Sexes: Reconstructing Gender in Postwar France, 1917–1927*, Women in Culture and Society (Chicago: University of Chicago Press, 1994); Tyler Edward Stovall, *Paris Noir: African Americans in the City of Light* (New York: Houghton Mifflin, 1996). On Paris, see also Jean-Paul Brunet, *Saint-Denis la ville rouge: Socialisme et communisme en banlieue ouvrière 1890–1939* (Paris: Hachette, 1980); Annie Fourcaut, *Bobigny, banlieue rouge* (Paris: Les Editions Ouvrières et Presses de la Fondation Nationale des Sciences Politiques, 1986); Patrice Higonnet, *Paris: Capital of the World* (Cambridge MA: Belknap, 2002); Benjamin Stora, "Les Algériens dans le Paris de l'entre-deux-guerres," in *Le Paris des étrangers depuis un siècle*, ed. André Kaspi and Antoine Marès (Paris: Imprimerie nationale, 1989).

5. Scholars who have confronted police archives with literary works by black men and women include Edwards, *Practice of Diaspora*; Wilder, *Imperial Nation-State*.

6. On soldiers see Marc Michel, *Les Africains et la Grande Guerre: L'appel à l'Afrique (1914–1918)* (Paris: Karthala, 2003), 191–97. Colonial workers, who were mostly recruited in China and Indochina, ended up numbering approximately 300,000. The number of workers from French West Africa was quite small, but 4,546 Malagasies were mobilized as colonial workers. Tyler Edward Stovall, "The Color Line Behind the Lines: Racial Violence in France during the Great War," *The American Historical Review* 103, no. 3 (1998): 741–42.

7. The breakdown of soldiers and workers from various colonies reveals that substantial numbers of colonial men were brought to France during the war. Most of the 500,000 colonial soldiers (for eight million Frenchmen) ended up fighting in France. Between 1914 and 1918, the French mobilized 166,000 West Africans, 46,000 Malagasies, 50,000 Indochinese, 140,000 Algerians, 47,000 Tunisians, and 24,300 Moroccans. French West Africans provided more recruits than any other colony. Richard S. Fogarty, *Race and War in France: Colonial Subjects in the French Army, 1914–1918*, War/Society/Culture (Baltimore: Johns Hopkins University Press, 2008), 2, 26–27, 298n1. On France's colonial soldiers and workers during World War I see also Charles John Balesi, *From Adversaries to Comrades-in-Arms: West Africans and the French Military, 1885–1918* (Waltham MA: 1979); Myron Echenberg, *Colonial Conscripts: The Tirailleurs Sénégalais in French West Africa, 1857–1960* (Portsmouth NH: Heine-

mann, 1991); Mar Fall, *Les Africains noirs en France: des tirailleurs sénégalais aux . . . blacks* (Paris: L'Harmattan, 1986); Joe Lunn, *Memoirs of the Maelstrom: A Senegalese Oral History of the First World War* (Oxford: James Currey, 1999); Gregory Mann, *Native Sons: West African Veterans and France in the Twentieth Century* (Durham NC: Duke University Press, 2006); Jean Vidalenc, "La main d'œuvre étrangère en France et la Première Guerre Mondiale (1901–1926)," *Francia* 2 (1974).

8. See the introductory notes to the CAOM's SLOTFOM archives and CAOM, SLOTFOM I/4, September 13, 1924, and June 6, 1932. Numbers are difficult to determine in part because the French did not include race as a category on their censuses.

9. Dewitte, *Mouvements nègres*, 26; Georges Mauco, *Les étrangers en France: Leur rôle dans l'activité économique* (Paris: Librairie Armand Colin, 1932), 175.

10. Dewitte, *Mouvements nègres*, 25–26, 40; Philippe Dewitte, "Le Paris noir de l'entre-deux-guerres," in *Le Paris des étrangers depuis un siècle*, ed. André Kaspi and Antoine Marès (Paris: Imprimerie nationale, 1989), 159. On numbers see also Gregory Mann, "Immigrants and Arguments in France and West Africa," *Comparative Studies in Society and History* 45, no. 2 (2003): 368.

11. Roberts, *Civilization Without Sexes*; Jürgen Habermas, *The Structural Transformation of the Public Sphere: An Inquiry into a Category of Bourgeois Society*, trans. Thomas Burger, 10th ed. (Cambridge MA: MIT Press, 1999).

12. Cooper attributes this phrase to Jane Burbank. Frederick Cooper, *Colonialism in Question: Theory, Knowledge, History* (Berkeley and Los Angeles: University of California Press, 2005), 154.

13. Wilder, *Imperial Nation-State*, 19.

14. Wilder, *Imperial Nation-State*, 8.

15. Gérard Noiriel, *Le creuset français: histoire de l'immigration, XIX–XXe siècle* (1988; repr., Paris: Seuil, 1992).

16. See for example Edwards, *Practice of Diaspora*; Michel Fabre, *La Rive noire: les écrivains noirs américains à Paris, 1830–1995*, Collection La rive noire (Marseille: Dimanche éditeur, 1999); Paul Gilroy, *The Black Atlantic: Modernity and Double Consciousness* (Cambridge MA: Harvard University Press, 1993); T. Denean Sharpley-Whiting, *Negritude Women* (Minneapolis: University of Minnesota Press, 2002); Michelle Ann Stephens, *Black Empire: The Masculine Global Imaginary of Caribbean Intel-

lectuals in the United States, 1914–1962 (Durham: Duke University Press, 2005); Stovall, *Paris Noir.*

17. On the colonial unconscious see Elizabeth Ezra, *The Colonial Unconscious: Race and Culture in Interwar France* (Ithaca NY: Cornell University Press, 2000).

18. Several scholars have suggested that more attention needs to be paid to differences within colonial communities amongst various classes, and in particular amongst soldiers, intellectuals, and workers. Erica J. Peters, "Resistance, Rivalries, and Restaurants: Vietnamese Workers in Interwar France," *Journal of Vietnamese Studies* 2, no. 3 (2007); Miller, *Nationalists and Nomads*; Wilder, *Imperial Nation-State.*

19. On gender as a category for historical analysis, see Joan Wallach Scott, "Gender: A Useful Category of Historical Analysis," in *Feminism and History*, ed. Joan Wallach Scott (New York: Oxford University Press, 1996). On gender and imperialism, see for example Antoinette M. Burton, *Burdens of History: British Feminists, Indian Women, and Imperial Culture, 1865–1915* (Chapel Hill: University of North Carolina Press, 1994); Nupur Chaudhuri and Margaret Strobel, eds., *Western Women and Imperialism: Complicity and Resistance* (Bloomington: Indiana University Press, 1992); Clare Midgley, ed., *Gender and Imperialism* (Manchester: Manchester University Press, 1998); Lora Wildenthal, *German Women for Empire, 1884–1945* (Durham NC: Duke University Press, 2001).

20. Much work remains to be done on black masculinity and manhood in the pre–World War II metropolitan context, although there are some intriguing analyses of such phenomena as *la sape* for the post–World War II period. Dominic Thomas also argues for considering gender and race together in Paris. Justin-Daniel Gandoulou, *Au coeur de la Sape: Moeurs et aventures des Congolais à Paris* (Paris: L'Harmattan, 1989); Dominic Thomas, *Black France: Colonialism, Immigration, and Transnationalism* (Bloomington: Indiana University Press, 2007). On masculinity in French and European history, see Christopher E. Forth and Bertrand Taithe, eds., *French Masculinities: History, Culture and Politics* (Basingstoke, UK: Palgrave Macmillan, 2007); George L. Mosse, *The Image of Man: The Creation of Modern Masculinity* (New York: Oxford University Press, 1996); Robert A. Nye, *Masculinity and Male Codes of Honor in Modern France* (New York: Oxford University Press, 1993).

21. A number of scholars are currently working on the link between Frenchwomen and Empire, although many of these studies are still unfin-

ished. Certainly, no equivalent to Antoinette Burton's work exists, for the moment, in the French context. Elisa Camiscioli's recent book is a wonderful example of the sort of work that is being done now: Elisa Camiscioli, *Reproducing the French Race: Immigration, Intimacy, and Embodiment in the Early Twentieth Century* (Durham NC: Duke University Press, 2009). On Frenchwomen and colonialism see also Julia Clancy-Smith, "The 'Passionate Nomad' Reconsidered: A European Woman in *L'Algérie Française* (Isabelle Eberhardt, 1877–1904)," in *Western Women and Imperialism: Complicity and Resistance*, ed. Nupur Chaudhuri and Margaret Strobel (Bloomington: Indiana University Press, 1992); Julia Ann Clancy-Smith and Frances Gouda, *Domesticating the Empire: Race, Gender, and Family Life in French and Dutch Colonialism* (Charlottesville: University Press of Virginia, 1998); Alice Conklin, "Redefining 'Frenchness': Citizenship, Race Regeneration, and Imperial Motherhood in France and West Africa, 1914–40," in *Domesticating the Empire: Race, Gender, and Family Life in French and Dutch Colonialism*, ed. Julia Ann Clancy-Smith and Frances Gouda (Charlottesville: University Press of Virginia, 1998); Anne Hugon, ed., *Histoire des femmes en situation coloniale: Afrique et Asie, XXe siècle* (Paris: Karthala, 2004); Yvonne Knibiehler and Régine Goutalier, *La femme au temps des Colonies* (Paris: Stock, 1984); Patricia Lorcin, "Sex, Gender, and Race in the Colonial Novels of Elissa Rhaïs and Lucienne Favre," in *The Color of Liberty: Histories of Race in France*, ed. Sue Peabody and Tyler Stovall (Durham: Duke University Press, 2003); Sakina Messaadi, *Nos sœurs musulmanes ou le mythe féministe, civilisateur, évangélisateur du messianisme colonialiste dans l'Algérie colonisée* (Alger: Houma, 2002).

22. Frederick Cooper and Laura Ann Stoler, eds., *Tensions of Empire: Colonial Cultures in a Bourgeois World* (Berkeley and Los Angeles: University of California Press, 1997), 4. Mrinalini Sinha warns us, however, of the difficulties of recognizing "simultaneously the specificities of [the metropole and the colony's] separate imperial locations." Mrinalini Sinha, "Britishness, Clubbability, and the Colonial Public Sphere: The Genealogy of an Imperial Institution in Colonial India," *The Journal of British Studies* 40, no. 4 (October 2001): 491.

23. Gregory Mann, "Locating Colonial Histories: Between France and West Africa," *American Historical Review* 110, no. 2 (2005): 410.

24. Tyler Stovall, during a plenary session at the French Colonial Historical Society's annual conference, asked in the context of his talk how

the metropole might be transformed into a colonial space and also what happens when the center (metropole) and the periphery (empire) coincide in one space. Tyler Stovall, "Plenary Session: Trente ans d'histoire coloniale des deux côtés de l'Atlantique," *French Colonial Historical Society 30th Annual Conference* (Washington DC): May 6–8, 2004.

25. On these terms, see for example: Petrine Archer-Straw, *Negrophilia: Avant-Garde Paris and Black Culture in the 1920s* (New York: Thames & Hudson, 2000); Brett A. Berliner, *Ambivalent Desire: The Exotic Black Other in Jazz-Age France* (Amherst: University of Massachusetts Press, 2002); Jody Blake, *Le Tumulte Noir: Modernist Art and Popular Entertainment in Jazz-Age Paris, 1900–1930* (University Park: Pennsylvania State University Press, 1999); James Clifford, "1933 February: Negrophilia," in *A New History of French Literature*, ed. Denis Hollier (Cambridge MA: Harvard University Press, 1989). On perceptions of Africans, see also: William B. Cohen, *The French Encounter with Africans: White Response to Blacks, 1530–1880* (Bloomington: Indiana University Press, 1980); Sieglinde Lemke, *Primitivist Modernism: Black Culture and the Origins of Transatlantic Modernism* (New York: Oxford University Press, 1998).

26. Walter Benjamin, "Paris, Capital of the Nineteenth Century," in *Reflections: Essays, Aphorisms, Autobiographical Writing* (New York: Schocken Books, 1986), 152.

27. Benjamin, "Paris," 152.

28. Denis Hollier, *Absent Without Leave: French Literature Under the Threat of War*, trans. Catherine Porter (Cambridge MA: Harvard University Press, 1997), chapter 10.

29. While there are many possible definitions of *l'imaginaire social*, this one sums them up rather well. Sarah Maza, *The Myth of the French Bourgeoisie: An Essay on the Social Imaginary, 1750–1850* (Cambridge MA: Harvard University Press, 2003), 10. Archer-Straw, *Negrophilia*; Thomas G. August, *The Selling of the Empire: British and French Imperialist Propaganda, 1890–1940* (Westport CT: Greenwood, 1985); Leora Auslander and Thomas C. Holt, "Sambo in Paris: Race and Racism in the Iconography of the Everyday," in *The Color of Liberty: Histories of Race in France*, ed. Sue Peabody and Tyler Edward Stovall (Durham: Duke University Press, 2003); Berliner, *Ambivalent Desire*; Blake, *Tumulte Noir*; Pascal Blanchard, Eric Deroo, and Gilles Manceron, *Le Paris noir* (Paris: Hazan, 2001); Ezra, *Colonial Unconscious*; Mireille Rosello, *Declining the Stereotype: Ethnicity and Representation in French Cultures*, Contemporary French Culture and

Society (Hanover NH: University Press of New England, 1997); William H. Schneider, *An Empire for the Masses: The French Popular Image of Africa, 1870–1900* (Westport CT: Greenwood, 1982); T. Denean Sharpley-Whiting, *Black Venus: Sexualized Savages, Primal Fears, and Primitive Narratives in French* (Durham NC: Duke University Press, 1999).

30. These are not quite the contact zones of which Mary Louise Pratt speaks, although they certainly bear some resemblance to her extremely useful proposal that there exist "social spaces where disparate cultures meet, clash, and grapple with each other, often in highly asymmetrical relations of domination and subordination." Perhaps in part because this study focuses upon margins, highly uneven distinctions in power remain surprisingly absent in the sorts of interactions analyzed here. Mary Louise Pratt, *Imperial Eyes: Travel Writing and Transculturation* (London: Routledge, 1992), 4.

31. Wilder dubs them "participant observers" and Morlat confirms their investment. Patrice Morlat, *Les affaires politiques de l'Indochine, 1895–1923: les grands commis, du savoir au pouvoir* (Paris: Harmattan, 1995), 304; Wilder, *Imperial Nation-State*, 158.

32. Patrice Morlat, *La répression coloniale au Vietnam (1908–1940)* (Paris: L'Harmattan, 1990), 188.

33. Agent Thomas was Dang Dinh Tho, recruited in prison. Agent Jean was the 1st Sergeant Lâm. Agent Marcel was Corporal Pham-Van-Mach. Morlat, *La répression coloniale*, 189n13; Morlat, *Les affaires politiques*, 297–98.

34. Some spies were asked not only to spy upon but also to disrupt the colonial milieus, for example turning North Africans against Vietnamese. Morlat, *Les affaires politiques*, 305.

35. At first the CAI focused on Vietnamese workers and soldiers but quickly expanded to include Malagasy and West African soldiers, manual laborers, students, and others. CAOM, SLOTFOM I/4. For more on the police and surveillance of colonial migrants, see also Morlat, *La répression coloniale*; Peters, "Resistance, Rivalries"; Clifford Rosenberg, *Policing Paris: The Origins of Modern Immigration Control Between the Wars* (Ithaca: Cornell University Press, 2006). Also very useful are the following texts on the French surveillance and reception of migrants: Mary Dewhurst Lewis, *The Boundaries of the Republic: Migrant Rights and the Limits of Universalism in France, 1918–1940* (Stanford: Stanford University Press, 2007); Neil MacMaster, *Colonial Migrants and Racism: Algerians in France,*

1900–62 (London: MacMillan, 1997); Janine Ponty, *Polonais méconnus: Histoire des travailleurs immigrés en France dans l'entre-deux-guerres* (Paris: Publications de la Sorbonne, 1990); Todd Shepard, *The Invention of Decolonization: The Algerian War and the Remaking of France* (Ithaca: Cornell University Press, 2006); Maxim Silverman, *Deconstructing the Nation: Immigration, Racism, and Citizenship in Modern France* (London: Routledge, 1992); Paul A. Silverstein, *Algeria in France: Transpolitics, Race, and Nation* (Bloomington: Indiana University Press, 2004); Alexis Spire, *Etrangers à la carte: L'administration de l'immigration en France, 1945–1975* (Paris: Grasset, 2005).

36. Morlat, *La répression coloniale*, 189nn12–13.

37. Similar requests for raises—generally less threatening—suggest spies were paid between 600 and 800 francs. CAOM, SLOTFOM I/7, dossier "traitement du personnel," July 27, 1925. Throughout this dossier there are several references to salaries.

38. In December 1931, one agent discovered he had not received his salary. His complaints were brushed aside by superiors: he had not provided any information during the month. In fact, he was asked to take 300 generously proffered francs and return to French Indochina. CAOM, SLOTFOM II/9, December 2, 1931.

39. CAOM, SLOTFOM II/2, Agent Coco, Années 1937–1938, September 25, 1937.

40. CAOM, SLOTFOM III/111, rapport de Joé, May 10, 1931.

41. To protect their identities, it was not uncommon for agents to list their true names in the third person when covering an event. Thus it makes sense that Joé would have signed with his pseudonym even while listing his real name and complaints in the report. Morlat, *Les affaires politiques*, 298.

42. For Joé's note see CAOM, SLOTFOM II/21, dossier "Notes prises par l'Agent Joé 1929–1930," sous-dossier "Joé 1931," Agent Joé, May 5, 1931. Note: the date in question should be May 6, the opening day; he may have been thrown off by his arrest, or simply in a hurry, when writing the report. Ramananjato's name was mentioned in descriptions of the same event in CAOM, SLOTFOM III/111, sous-dossier "Comité Central," rapport de Joé, May 10, 1931; SLOTFOM III/111, sous-dossier "Comité Central," May 19, 1931 (no signature); and AN, F/7/13168, PROM, May 1931: 7.

43. According to Dewitte, Ramananjato was a relative newcomer to the political scene when he joined the LDRN in September 1929. Dewitte,

Mouvements nègres, 214. Moreover, one of Agent Joé's very first meetings with his contact at the CAI took place in August 1929. In his note on the meeting, Joé asserts that he is happy to be doing his part, as a French citizen, for his country. CAOM, SLOTFOM II/21, Agent Joé, August 13, 1929.

44. Morlat, *La répression coloniale*, 190n16.

45. CAOM, SLOTFOM II/21, dossier "Notes prises par l'Agent Joé 1929–1930," sous-dossier "Joé 1931," Agent Joé, May 5, 1931.

46. CAOM, SLOTFOM III/III, sous-dossier "Comité Central," rapport de Joé, May 25, 1931.

47. Morlat, *La répression coloniale*, 189.

1. Josephine Baker

1. Nancy Nenno, "Femininity, the Primitive, and Modern Urban Space: Josephine Baker in Berlin," in *Women in the Metropolis: Gender and Modernity in Weimar Culture*, ed. Katharina von Ankum (Berkeley and Los Angeles: University of California Press, 1997), 147–48.

2. Pierre de Régnier, "La Revue Nègre," *Candide*, no. 87, November 12, 1925.

3. Jules-Rosette recently completed a very thorough study of how Baker's performances both on and off stage helped to establish her status as a cultural symbol. Bennetta Jules-Rosette, *Josephine Baker in Art and Life: The Icon and the Image* (Urbana: University of Illinois Press, 2007). Other thought-provoking studies include: Michael Borshuk, "'Queen of the Colonial Exposition': Josephine Baker's Strategic Performance," in *Critical Voicings of Black Liberation: Resistance and Representation in the Americas*, ed. Hermine D. Pinson, Kimberly L. Phillips, Lorenzo Thomas, and Hanna Wallinger (Piscataway NJ: Transaction, 2003); Lemke, *Primitivist Modernism*; Sharpley-Whiting, *Black Venus*. Baker's biographies include Lynn Haney, *Naked at the Feast: A Biography of Josephine Baker* (New York: Dodd, Mead, 1981); Phyllis Rose, *Jazz Cleopatra: Josephine Baker in Her Time* (New York: Doubleday, 1989); Ean Wood, *The Josephine Baker Story* (London: Sanctuary, 2000).

4. In the rousing words of Edwards, *Practice of Diaspora*, 130.

5. Ezra, *Colonial Unconscious*, 152–53.

6. Elizabeth Ezra takes the distinctive approach of focusing entirely upon texts that were not explicitly colonial and that appeared to celebrate cultural mixity even while unconsciously promoting the will to dominate.

Most of the critics and texts discussed here are more direct in their discomfort with the mixing of cultures. Ezra, *Colonial Unconscious*, 6, 8.

7. Nenno, "Femininity." Sweeney also offers a subtle reading of the tension between Baker's American modernism and African "primitivism" in *La Revue Nègre* in Carole Sweeney, *From Fetish to Subject: Race, Modernism, and Primitivism, 1919–1935* (Westport CT: Praeger, 2004).

8. Rose, *Jazz Cleopatra*, 5.

9. Jacques Patin, *Le Figaro*, October 7, 1925.

10. Patin, *Le Figaro*, October 7, 1925.

11. René Bizet, "La Revue nègre," *Candide*, no. 82, October 8, 1925.

12. Roberts, *Civilization Without Sexes*, 13.

13. Roberts, *Civilization Without Sexes*, 14.

14. Her astuteness in shaping her body and dancing to resist the danger that might have otherwise been associated with them has been studied by Michael Borshuk, "An Intelligence of the Body: Disruptive Parody through Dance in the Early Performances of Josephine Baker," in *Embodying Liberation: The Black Body in American Dance*, ed. Dorothea Fischer-Hornung and Allison Goeller (Piscataway NJ: Transaction, 2001).

15. Conklin has written a seminal study on the French civilizing mission, including how it changed over time and the implications of World War I for its previously liberal tendencies. Alice L. Conklin, *A Mission to Civilize: The Republican Idea of Empire in France and West Africa, 1895–1930* (Stanford: Stanford University Press, 1997).

16. See Jean Fayard, *Candide*, October 2, 1930; Robert Brisacq, *La Volonté*, October 11, 1930; Georges Courseules, *L'Ordre*, January 5, 1931; and Colette in Pepito Abatino and Josephine Baker, *Pepito Abatino présente Josephine Baker vue par la presse française* (Paris: Isis, 1931).

17. Jean Sejournet, *Le Concours médical*, February 8, 1931. Translated by S. P. Boittin. A similar language was also used by Gustave Fréjaville, *Comoedia*, October 9, 1930: "through everything she learned from Old Europe," and Dominique Sorder, *Action Française*, November 7, 1930: "civilization has done its work," all in Abatino and Baker, *Pepito Abatino présente Josephine*.

18. Jacques Patin, "Casino de Paris," *Figaro*, October 9, 1930: "refined, whom Paris has transformed," in Abatino and Baker, *Pepito Abatino présente Josephine*.

19. Gérard Bauer, *Le Romantisme de Couleur*, Lecture of January 20, 1930, in Abatino and Baker, *Pepito Abatino présente Josephine*.

20. G. de Pawlowski, *Le Journal*, October 9, 1930, in Abatino and Baker, *Pepito Abatino présente Josephine*.

21. This lightening was part of how Baker sculpted her body. Jules-Rosette, *Josephine Baker in Art and Life*, 145.

22. See Nenno, "Femininity," 157–58.

23. Berliner, *Ambivalent Desire*, 148. Berliner has studied ethnographic images of black women, for example those who wore labrets, and analyzed the relationship between photographs and the eroticization of the other within a scientific context.

24. Marcel Sauvage, *Voyages et aventures de Joséphine Baker* (Paris: Marcel Seheur, 1931), 29.

25. Gérard d'Houville, *Figaro*, October 24, 1930, in Abatino and Baker, *Pepito Abatino présente Josephine*.

26. Bibliothèque de l'Arsenal (hereafter ARS), Collection Rondel (hereafter Ro.), 18.937, Program, "Paris Qui Remue."

27. Gérard d'Houville, *Figaro*, October 24, 1930, in Abatino and Baker, *Pepito Abatino présente Josephine*.

28. Several times, reviewers compared the two stars, often arguing that Baker had won the so-called battle between the women. G. de Pawlowski, in the program for "Paris Qui Remue," wrote, "we are witnessing here the same vigorous evolution that transformed, in a few years, thanks to dogged work, Mistinguett the *café-concert* singer into the great, dancing star of our music-halls." ARS, Ro. 18.937.

29. *L'Illustration*, in November 1930 wrote that she was "the frenetic and unbridled soul of jazz" who since then had disciplined her effervescent nature. ARS, Ro. 18.937. Gustave Fréjaville wrote in *Comoedia*, October 9, 1930, that she "was able to discipline her instinct, and acquire the measure of harmony." ARS, Ro. 18.937.

30. ARS, Ro. 18.937, no author, "Pointe sèche exécuté au Casino de Paris—Joséphine Baker," *Quotidien*, October 12, 1930.

31. ARS, Ro. 18.937, Clément Vautel, "Mon Film," *Journal*, October 14, 1930.

32. ARS, Ro. 18.937, Georges Pioch, "Merci pour la Négresse," *le Soir*, September 21, 1930.

33. ARS, Ro. 18.937, Marcel Sauvage, "Exotisme de music-hall" *l'Intransigeant*, September 1930.

34. ARS, Ro 18.937, G. de Pawlowski, "Paris qui remue," *le Journal*, October 9, 1930.

35. Jules-Rosette, *Josephine Baker in Art and Life*, 214. Gendron argues that the avant-garde was active in the commodification of all things black. Bernard Gendron, *Between Montmartre and the Mudd Club: Popular Music and the Avant-Garde* (Chicago: University of Chicago Press, 2002), 107.

36. Clifford, "1933," 901.

37. Andreas Huyssen, *After the Great Divide: Modernism, Mass Culture, Postmodernism* (Bloomington: Indiana University Press, 1986).

38. Bennetta Jules-Rosette, *Black Paris: The African Writers' Landscape* (Urbana IL: University of Illinois Press, 1998), 30.

39. Jules-Rosette has demonstrated how Baker reflects the utopian in Bennetta Jules-Rosette, "Josephine Baker and utopian visions of Black Paris," *Journal of Romance Studies* 5, no. 3 (2005).

40. Daniel-Henry Kahnweiler, "L'Art nègre et le cubisme," *Présence Africaine* 3 (1948): 367.

41. Clifford, "1933," 903.

42. Léopold Sédar Senghor cited in Frank Ténot's preface to André Schaeffner and André Coeuroy, *Le Jazz* (Paris: Jean-Michel Place, 1988), 4.

43. Max Horkheimer and Theodor W. Adorno, "The Culture Industry: Enlightenment as Mass Deception," in *Dialectic of Enlightenment: Philosophical Fragments*, ed. Gunzelin Schmid Noerr (Stanford CA: Stanford University Press, 2002), 117.

44. Jensen brings up another aspect of the diffusion Roberts discusses. While analyzing an earlier moment in the discourse of modernism, Jensen demonstrates how the modern had a veneer of individuality but was nonetheless commercial and often lacking in ideology. In Baker's case modernity was diffused through a similar process, with managers substituted for art dealers. Robert Jensen, *Marketing Modernism in Fin-de-Siècle Europe* (Princeton NJ: Princeton University Press, 1994); Roberts, *Civilization Without Sexes*, 16.

45. Horkheimer and Adorno, "Culture Industry," 124.

46. Sauvage was later replaced by the writer Georges Simenon, known for the Maigret detective novels, who briefly became Baker's lover as well as her secretary. Wood, *Josephine Baker Story*, 119.

47. Jules-Rosette argues that Baker was an author even when not listed as such. Jules-Rosette, *Josephine Baker in Art and Life*, 157.

48. Josephine Baker and Marcel Sauvage, *Les mémoires de Joséphine Baker*, 4th ed. (Paris: Kra, 1927), 28.

49. Baker and Sauvage, *Les mémoires de Joséphine*, 31.

50. Pierre K., "Ode à la danseuse noire," in Baker and Sauvage, *Les mémoires de Joséphine*, 185–87.

51. Josephine Baker and André Rivollet, *Une vie de toutes les couleurs: souvenirs recueillis par André Rivollet*, Collection "Arc-en-ciel" (Grenoble: B. Arthaud, 1935).

52. Sharpley-Whiting, *Black Venus*.

53. Rose, *Jazz Cleopatra*, 111.

54. Nenno, "Femininity," 157.

55. Rose, *Jazz Cleopatra*, 111.

56. Stovall, *Paris Noir*, 33.

57. Robert Brissacq, *Paris Soir*, December 1, 1930, in Abatino and Baker, *Pepito Abatino présente Josephine*.

58. Josephine Baker, preface to *Mon sang dans tes veines*, by De la Camara and Pepito Abatino (Paris: Isis, 1931), 4.

59. Baker, preface to *Mon sang*, by Camara and Abatino, 6.

60. Camara and Abatino, *Mon sang*, 12.

61. Camara and Abatino, *Mon sang*, 178.

62. Karen C. C. Dalton and Henry Louis Gates Jr., "Josephine Baker and Paul Colin: African American Dance Seen through Parisian Eyes," *Critical Inquiry* 24, no. 4 (1998): 918.

63. Claude Pétry, in *Paul Colin et les spectacles: Nancy, Musée des beaux-arts, 2 mai–31 juillet 1994* (Nancy: Musée des beaux-arts, 1994), 14.

64. Alain Weill, in *Paul Colin et les spectacles*, 20.

65. Alain Carrier, in *Paul Colin et les spectacles*, 21.

66. Paul Colin, *La Croûte: souvenirs* (Paris: Table Ronde, 1957), 81.

67. These celebrities are identified in *Paul Colin et les spectacles*, 28.

68. Baker in Paul Colin, Georges (Rip) Thénon, and Josephine Baker, *Le tumulte noir* (Paris: Editions d'Art Succès, 193?).

69. Colin gives readers a taste of his political engagement through the sketches in his memoirs. Colin, *La Croûte*.

70. Sharpley-Whiting clearly demonstrates this colonial positioning. Sharpley-Whiting, *Black Venus*, 4. The surrealist Buñuel thought very little of Baker when he visited the film's set. Luis Buñuel, *My Last Sigh*, trans. Abigail Israel (New York: Alfred A. Knopf, 1983), 90. On the colonial genre of film, see David Henry Slavin, *Colonial Cinema and Imperial France, 1919–1939: White Blind Spots, Male Fantasies, Settler Myths* (Baltimore: Johns Hopkins University Press, 2001).

71. Ezra deconstructs these Orientalist and Africanist signifiers. Ezra, *Colonial Unconscious*, 124.

72. Dudley Andrew, *Mists of Regret: Culture and Sensibility in Classic French Film* (Princeton NJ: Princeton University Press, 1995), 107.

73. Clotilde Chivas-Baron, *La femme française aux colonies*, Vies coloniales (Paris: Larose Editeurs, 1929), 188. Translated by S. P. Boittin.

74. Marthe Oulié, *Les Antilles, filles de France: Martinique, Guadeloupe, Haïti*, Voyageuses de lettres (Paris: Fasquelle Editeurs, 1935), 19. Translated by S. P. Boittin.

75. Odette Arnaud, *Mer Caraïbe* (Paris: Denoël et Steele, 1934), 165. Translated by S. P. Boittin.

76. "Au fil de l'heure," *La Dépêche Africaine* 1, no. 2 (February 1928).

77. P. Baye-Salzmann, "Maurice Hamel et Joséphine Baker," *La Dépêche Africaine* 1, no. 2 (February 1928): 4.

78. Charles Denys, "Le Péril Noir," *La Dépêche Africaine* 3, no. 31 (December 1930): 2.

79. Denys, "Le Péril Noir," 2.

80. Modris Eksteins, *Rites of Spring: The Great War and the Birth of the Modern Age* (New York: Anchor Books, 1990).

81. Andrée Nardal, "Etude sur la Biguine Créole," *La Revue du Monde Noir, The Review of the Black World, 1931–1932*, Collection Complète, no. 2 (repr., Paris: Jean-Michel Place, 1992): 51/121.

82. Several documents corroborate what may have been a one-time encounter. The fascination on the part of informants with such an improbable encounter, as well as a certain anxiety when faced with the possibility of ties existing between a prominent social figure in France and a communist worker, probably explain the insistence upon the event. CAOM, SLOTFOM II/16, "Rapports de Joé," Agent Joé, n.d., hand-written on A4 paper, "Fête nègre du 1er avril;" CAOM, SLOTFOM III/34, sous-dossier "Entr'aide Coloniale Féminine," Agent Paul, March 10, 1933, "Réunion des membres du bureau de l'Union des Travailleurs Nègres le jeudi 9 mars 1933 à 20h30;" CAOM, SLOTFOM III/53, sous-dossier "Union des Travailleurs Nègres," Agent Paul, March 10, 1933, and March 17, 1933; CAOM, SLOTFOM III/79, PROM, 1932–33, March 1933.

83. Claire Lemercier, "Le Club du Faubourg: Tribune libre de Paris, 1918–1939," (Paris: Institut d'études politiques de Paris, 1995).

84. CAOM, SLOTFOM III/37, sous-dossier: "Correspondance concernant

le Comité de Défense de la Race Nègre," Agent Joé, December 19, 1930, translated by S. P. Boittin.

85. CAOM, 2MiA/242, F. Merlin, "Réponse à Joséphine Baker," *Le Cri des Nègres* 5, no. 25 (February 1936): 4, translated by S. P. Boittin. Merlin was adjunct mayor of Epinay-sur-Seine. On Mussolini see Wood, *Josephine*, 186–87.

86. "Kouyaté, . . . a while ago left his job as a walk-on at the Casino de Paris." CAOM, SLOTFOM II/19, "notes de l'Agent Paul et Coco," rapport de Coco, June 8, 1929.

87. CAOM, 2MiA/242, "Vie des noirs à Paris," *Africa* 1, no. 4 (July–August 1936).

88. Ezra, *Colonial Unconscious*, 19.

89. Dana S. Hale, *Races on Display: French Representations of Colonized Peoples, 1886–1940* (Bloomington: Indiana University Press, 2008).

90. ARS, Ro. 18.937, Georges Pioch, "Merci pour la Négresse," *Le Soir*, September 21, 1930. Pioch called Baker "a remarkable businesswoman."

91. "Joséphine Baker, L'Idole de Bronze," *Jazz, A Flippant Magazine: La plus parisienne des Revues Anglo-Américaines* 3, no. 3 (February 20, 1927): 4–5.

92. ARS, Ro. 18.937, Fernand Divoire, "Danses au Casino de Paris," *Gringoire*, October 3, 1930. Another reviewer added: "an artist such that the spectacle in which she collaborates finds itself renewed, that it receives from her impulse and rhythm, a rhythm made of youth, playfulness, spontaneity, generous outpouring." Louis Léon-Martin, "Au Casino de Paris, Paris qui remue," *Paris-Midi*, October 8, 1930.

93. ARS, Ro. 18.937, Jean Fayard, *Candide*, October 2, 1930: "Because of the presence of Josephine Baker, they abundantly incorporated colonial themes."

2. Dancing Dissidents & Dissident Dancers

1. CAOM, SLOTFOM II/21, notes prises par l'agent Joé 1929–1930, September 21, 1929.

2. Alain Corbin undertook the formidable task of a history of the senses in France, tracing scapes of sight, sound, smell, taste, and touch for example in Alain Corbin, *Le miasme et la jonquille: l'odorat et l'imaginaire social XVIIIe–XIXe siècles*, Collection historique (Paris: Aubier Montaigne, 1982); Alain Corbin, *Les cloches de la terre: paysage sonore et culture sensible dans les campagnes au XIXe siècle*, L'Evolution de l'humanité (Pa-

ris: A. Michel, 1994). Simone Delattre studied Parisian nights in the nineteenth century, exploring how the absence of light, and therefore of sight, reshaped the city after dark. Adrian Rifkin created an archeology of city sounds and used it to present aspects of Parisian pleasure in the first half of the twentieth century. Peter Fritzsche built an urban topography. The titles alone of works such as Tyler Stovall's *Paris Noir* hint at the transformative influence of blacks' visual presence within the metropole. Blanchard, Deroo, and Manceron, *Le Paris noir;* Simone Delattre, *Les douze heures noires: la nuit à Paris au XIXe siècle*, Evolution de l'humanité (Paris: Albin Michel, 2000); Peter Fritzsche, *Reading Berlin 1900* (Cambridge MA: Harvard University Press, 1996); Adrian Rifkin, *Street Noises: Parisian Pleasure 1900–40* (New York: Manchester University Press, 1995); Stovall, *Paris Noir.*

3. Victor Sablé, *Mémoires d'un foyalais: Des îles d'Amérique aux bords de la Seine* (Paris: Maisonneuve et Larose, 1993), 63.

4. Charles Baudelaire, *Un peintre de la vie moderne, Constantin Guys* (Paris: Keiffer, 1923); Benjamin, "Paris"; Walter Benjamin and Rolf Tiedemann, *The Arcades Project* (Cambridge MA: Belknap, 1999), Graeme Gilloch and Walter Benjamin, *Myth and Metropolis: Walter Benjamin and the City* (Cambridge, UK: Polity Press, 1996).

5. Judith R. Walkowitz, *City of Dreadful Delight: Narratives of Sexual Danger in Late-Victorian London* (London: Virago Press, 1992).

6. On spectacles in an urban context, see for example Rhonda K. Garelick, *Rising Star: Dandyism, Gender, and Performance in the Fin de Siècle* (Princeton NJ: Princeton University Press, 1998); Vanessa R. Schwartz, *Spectacular Realities: Early Mass Culture in Fin-de-Siècle Paris* (Berkeley and Los Angeles: University of California Press, 1998).

7. On the *banlieue rouge* see also Brunet, *Saint-Denis;* Fourcaut, *Bobigny*; Tyler Edward Stovall, "From Red Belt to Black Belt: Race, Class, and Urban Marginality in Twentieth-Century Paris," in *The Color of Liberty: Histories of Race in France*, ed. Sue Peabody and Tyler Stovall (Durham: Duke University Press, 2003).

8. Christopher Miller analyzed the event "as a form of *state-sponsored hallucination.*" Miller, *Nationalists and Nomads*, 65. For a detailed description of the Colonial Exposition, see Catherine Hodeir and Michel Pierre, *L'exposition coloniale*, La Mémoire du siècle (Brussels: Complexe, 1991). See also Ezra, *Colonial Unconscious*; Herman Lebovics, *True France: Wars*

Over *Cultural Identity, 1900–1945* (Ithaca NY: Cornell University Press, 1992); Panivong Norindr, *Phantasmatic Indochina: French Colonial Ideology in Architecture, Film, and Literature* (Durham NC: Duke University Press, 1996). Useful background is also provided in Schneider, *Empire for the Masses.*

9. Catherine Coquery-Vidrovitch, "La colonisation française 1931–1939," in *Histoire de la France Coloniale 1914–1990*, ed. J. Thobie, et al. (Paris: Armand Colin, 1990), 218.

10. According to Christopher Miller, Socé has generally been viewed as a "minor" writer. Miller, *Nationalists and Nomads*, 59.

11. Ousmane Socé, *Mirages de Paris* (Paris: Nouvelles Editions Latines, 1937), 18.

12. Socé, *Mirages*, 40.

13. Socé, *Mirages*, 69.

14. Socé, *Mirages*, 26.

15. Socé, *Mirages*, 183.

16. Socé, *Mirages*, 233.

17. Géo Baysse, *En dansant la biguine, Souvenir de l'Exposition coloniale* (Paris: Senlis, 1931), 98.

18. Baysse, *En dansant la biguine*, 51.

19. Baysse, *En dansant la biguine*, 47, 56.

20. Baysse, *En dansant la biguine*, 103.

21. Jean Camp and André Corbier, *A Lyauteyville, Promenade Humoristique et Sentimentale à Travers l'Exposition Coloniale* (Paris: Editions N.E.A., 1931), 91.

22. Camp and Corbier, *Lyauteyville*, 115.

23. Paul Guillaume, "L'Art Nègre & L'Esprit de l'Epoque," *La Dépêche Africaine* 1, no. 1 (February 1928): 6.

24. For more on surrealists and ethnography, which during the 1920s and 1930s often manifested itself as a form of collection, see James Clifford, "On Ethnographic Surrealism," *The Predicament of Culture: Twentieth-Century Ethnography, Literature, and Art* (Cambridge MA: Harvard University Press, 1988). On the surrealists, including some of their links to negritude, see Archer-Straw, *Negrophilia*; Pierre Daix, *La vie quotidienne des surréalistes 1917–1932* (Paris: Hachette, 1993); Hollier, *Absent Without Leave*; Adriana Moro, *Négritude e Cultura Francese, Surrealismo chiave della Négritude?* (Alessandria, Italy: Edizioni dell'Orso, 1992).

25. Cunard specifically mentions that Aragon, Breton, Eluard, Sadoul, and Leiris fit her analysis. Nancy Cunard, *These Were the Hours: Memoirs of My Hours Press Réanville and Paris 1928–1931* (Carbondale: Southern Illinois University Press, 1969), 42.

26. Marcel Griaule, *Mission ethnographique et linguistique Dakar-Djibouti organisée par l'Institut d'ethnologie de l'Université de Paris et le Muséum national d'histoire naturelle* (1930).

27. Michel Leiris, *L'âge d'homme* (Paris: Gallimard, 1939), 159–60.

28. André Schaeffner and André Cœuroy, *Le Jazz*, (1926; repr., Paris: Jean-Michel Place: 1988): 116–17.

29. Gisèle Dubouillé, "Nouveaux Disques de Musique nègre," *La Revue du Monde Noir* 3 (1932): 55/187.

30. ARS, Ro. 585, André Cœuroy et André Schaeffner, *Paris-Midi*, June 1925.

31. Studies on jazz include: Chris Goddard, *Jazz Away From Home* (New York: Paddington, 1979); Ludovic Tournès, *New Orleans sur Seine: Histoire du jazz en France* (Paris: Librairie Arthème Fayard, 1999); Ron Welburn, "Jazz Magazines of the 1930s: An Overview of Their Provocative Journalism," *American Music* 5, no. 3 (1987). Studies that encompass the cultural diffusion of jazz and the multiple meanings with which it was associated include: Matthew F. Jordan, "Jazz Changes: A History of French Discourse on Jazz from Ragtime to Be-Bop" (PhD diss., Claremont Graduate School, 1998); Denis-Constant Martin and Olivier Roueff, *La France du jazz: Musique, modernité et identité dans la première moitié du XXe siècle* (Marseille: Parenthèses, 2002); Seth Matthew Schulman, "The Celebrity Culture of Modern Nightlife: Music-Hall, Dance, and Jazz in Interwar Paris, 1918–1930" (PhD diss., Brown University, 2000).

32. Jeffrey H. Jackson, *Making Jazz French: Music and Modern Life in Interwar Paris*, American encounters/global interactions (Durham: Duke University Press, 2003), 4–6. Jackson also devotes part of his work to the difficulty of understanding how jazz was defined during the interwar years.

33. Hughes Panassié, *Le Jazz Hot* (Paris: R.A. Corrêa, 1934), 98, 122. Panassié also wrote under the pseudonym Ache Pé, and in *Jazz-Tango* emphasized the importance of listening to jazz in Harlem, and of becoming familiar with great black musicians including Earl Hines, Don Redman, and Louis Armstrong. See amongst others: Hughes Panassié, *Revue*

Ja$\chi\chi$-Tango 3 and 4 (December 1930): 7; Ache Pé, *Ja$\chi\chi$-Tango* 5 (February 1, 1931): 17.

34. Archives de la Préfecture de Police de Paris (APP), DA742, Circulaires 201 à 400, Réglementation étrangers 1924–1927, JD/MS 23.10.30, Service de la Main d'œuvre Etrangère.

35. "Réflexions d'un profane," *Revue Ja$\chi\chi$-Tango* 2 (November 15, 1930): 10.

36. Stéphane Mougin, "Négromanie," *Revue Ja$\chi\chi$-Tango* 15 (December 15, 1931): 7. Such complaints were made through at least 1935: E. Lauret, "Un cri d'alarme," *Revue Ja$\chi\chi$-Tango-Dancing* 59 (September 1935): 7; E. Lauret, "Après le cri d'alarme," *Revue Ja$\chi\chi$-Tango-Dancing* 60 (November 1935). The scholar Philippe Gumplowicz mentions that musicians noted a "racket of *nègres*" which led people to be "astounded by blows on cymbals, because *nègres* are making them" ("ébahit devant des coups de cymbales, parce que ce sont des Nègres qui les donnent"). One man put it even more bluntly: "You have to be pigmented, or you're out" ("il faut que tu sois pigmenté, sinon, couic"). Philippe Gumplowicz, *Le roman du ja$\chi\chi$ première époque: 1893–1930* (Paris: Librairie Arthème Fayard, 1991), 329–30.

37. Jackson notes that "to many French performers throughout the interwar era, the problem of jazz as a foreign music had more to do with the players who came from abroad and took their jobs than it did with jazz's challenges to French civilization." Jackson, *Making Ja$\chi\chi$ French*, 143.

38. Cited in Goddard, *Ja$\chi\chi$ Away From Home*, 19.

39. Likewise anti-imperialist Tiémoko Garan Kouyaté worked at the Casino de Paris. Samuel Ralaimongo supplemented his income working with an insurance agency by working at the Folies Bergères at night. He was one of at least twelve blacks who worked there. CAOM, SLOTFOM II/4, Agent Désiré, January 8, 1926 and SLOTFOM II/12, Agent Désiré, June 16, 1929.

40. Goddard, *Ja$\chi\chi$ Away From Home*, 19. Romans' disguise, imposed by the owner as a condition for his hire, was uncovered by the owner's daughter, who ran her hand over his face only to find his blackness rub off on her fingers. Afterward, the owner kept him behind a plant for the duration of the gig.

41. Paulette Nardal, "Le Nouveau Bal Nègre de la Glacière," *La Dépêche Africaine* 14 (May 1929): 3. The theme came up again in: Paulette

Nardal, "Musique Nègre: Antilles et Aframérique," *La Dépêche Africaine* 25 (June 1930): 5.

42. Ernest Léardée et al., *La Biguine de l'Oncle Ben's: Ernest Léardée raconte* (Paris: Caribéennes, 1989), 171.

43. Léardée et al., *La Biguine*, 174.

44. Jacqueline exclaims upon entering the *Cabane Cubaine* "I see that there are two times as many whites as there are *noirs*." Socé, *Mirages*, 67.

45. Léardée et al., *La Biguine*, 174.

46. Socé, *Mirages*, 73–74.

47. Paulette Nardal, "Le Nouveau Bal Nègre de la Glacière," *La Dépêche Africaine* 14 (May 1929): 3.

48. Andrée Nardal, "Etude sur la Biguine Créole," *La Revue du Monde Noir* 2:51/121. Other Antilleans felt similarly defensive when it came to the beguine. Charles Saint-Cyr was another author who stigmatized the "merchandise for export" commonly known to Parisians as beguine. *L'Etudiant Martiniquais* 1, no. 1 (January 15, 1932): 7.

49. *Jazz-Tango* 25 (October 1932): 10.

50. "Bal Nègre," *La Française* (February 19, 1927).

51. Léardée et al., *La Biguine*, 194.

52. Socé, *Mirages*, 77.

53. Although no special dispensation was required to access these documents, in keeping with the French tradition of respecting the details of people's private lives, I am omitting last names in this section of the book.

54. CAOM, SLOTFOM II/11, Agent Désiré, November 26, 1931.

55. CAOM, SLOTFOM III/73, SRI, May 7, 1935. In this particular incident the race of the woman and the other man was not noted.

56. *Détective* is one of the primary sources, along with recordings of a variety of songs, that Rifkin uses in his analysis of the sights and sounds of Paris in a popular context. Rifkin, *Street Noises*.

57. Léardée et al., *La Biguine*, 151.

58. Berliner recounts the event of December 16, 1928. Berliner, *Ambivalent Desire*, 211–12.

59. Jane Nardal, "Pantins Exotiques," *La Dépêche Africaine* 1, no. 8 (October 15, 1928): 2.

60. Sablé, *Mémoires d'un foyalais*, 63. Note that while Sablé's descriptions are striking, his memories were not always accurate. He writes, for example, that *La Revue du Monde Noir* existed from 1932 to the outbreak of World War II, which is false. Sablé, *Mémoires d'un foyalais*, 69.

61. Brett Berliner argues metropolitans sought "to view and to participate in a sexual and racial drama of their own making." Berliner, *Ambivalent Desire*, 209.

62. Berliner, *Ambivalent Desire*; Yaël Simpson Fletcher, "Unsettling Settlers: Colonial migrants and racialised sexuality in interwar Marseilles," in *Gender, Sexuality and Colonial Modernities*, ed. Antoinette Burton (New York: Routledge, 1999); Matt K. Matsuda, *Empire of Love: Histories of France and the Pacific* (Oxford: Oxford University Press, 2005); Tyler Edward Stovall, "Love, Labor, and Race: Colonial Men and White Women in France during the Great War," in *French Civilization and Its Discontents: Nationalism, Colonialism, Race*, ed. Tyler Edward Stovall and Georges Van Den Abbeele, After the Empire: The Francophone World and Postcolonial France (Lanham MD: Lexington Books, 2003).

63. Stovall, "Love, Labor, and Race," 297.

64. BMD, DOS 396 FRA, Blanche Vogt, "Le problème de l'amour aux Antilles: Maternité de Couleur," *Minerva* (May 17, 1936).

65. Stovall, "Love, Labor, and Race," 312.

66. Rakoto may of course have been truly in love with this woman, but even the suggestion of scheming for citizenship helps us to understand the stigma surrounding some interracial relationships.

67. Sablé, *Mémoires d'un foyalais*, 36.

68. Sablé, *Mémoires d'un foyalais*, 36.

69. CAOM, SLOTFOM II/16, rapports de Joé, March 12, 1932.

70. CAOM, SLOTFOM III/36, "Sur les membres de la colonie camerounaise à Paris," Laurent Kingué and Henri Priso.

71. CAOM, SLOTFOM III/36, Agent Joé, November 26, 1930.

72. CAOM, SLOTFOM II/12, Agent Désiré, August 28, 1930.

73. CAOM, SLOTFOM II/21, Agent Joé, February 7, 1930.

74. Léardée et al., *La Biguine*, 175–77.

75. CAOM, SLOTFOM II/21, Agent Joé, September 7, 1931.

76. BMD, DOS FAU, Maxime Revon, "Courrier des Lettres—Blanche et Noir," *l'Ami du Peuple*, n.d.

77. BMD, DOS FAU, Louise Faure-Favier, "Le premier voyage aérien Paris-Londres-Paris," *l'Illustration*, June 17, 1922; Louise Faure-Favier, "Un reportage radiodiffusé du bord d'un avion survolant la nuit la capitale illuminée," *Le Journal*, November 30, 1932. Her publications include Lucien Bossoutrot, *La Belle aventure du Goliath de Paris à Dakar* (Paris: La

Renaissance du Livre, 1925); Louise Faure-Favier, *Guide des voyages aériens, Paris-Londres* (Paris: Ch. Bernard, 1921); Louise Faure-Favier, *Les Chevaliers de l'air* (Paris: la Renaissance du livre, 1922); Louise Faure-Favier, *Guide des voyages aériens, Paris-Lausanne* (Paris: Ch. Bernard, 1922); Louise Faure-Favier, *Guide des voyages aériens, Paris-Tunis, Paris-Lyon-Marseille-Ajaccio-Tunis, Tunis-Bône et Lyon-Genève* (Paris: Ch. Bernard, 1930).

78. Louise Faure-Favier, *Souvenirs sur Guillaume Apollinaire* (Paris: B. Grasset, 1945).

79. Perhaps as a result, Faure-Favier wrote several volumes of poetry, interestingly enough all devoted to Paris, later in life. Louise Faure-Favier, *Notre île Saint-Louis* (Paris: Montjoie, 1946); Louise Faure-Favier, *Visages de la Seine* (Paris: Points et Contrepoints, 1951); Louise Faure-Favier, *De mes fenêtres sur la Seine, poèmes* (Paris: Points et Contrepoints, 1953).

80. Berliner has worked on this novel. Berliner, *Ambivalent Desire*, 61–69.

81. See Théodore Joran, *Les Féministes avant le féminisme* (Paris: 1910).

82. Louise Faure-Favier, *Blanche et Noir* (Paris: Ferenczi et Fils, 1928), 88.

83. Faure-Favier, *Blanche et Noir*, 162.

84. Faure-Favier, *Blanche et Noir*, 166.

85. Faure-Favier, *Blanche et Noir*, 180.

86. Faure-Favier, *Blanche et Noir*, 212.

87. Faure-Favier, *Blanche et Noir*, 227.

88. Louise Faure-Favier, "Autour de 'Blanche et Noir,'" *La Dépêche Africaine* 1, no. 10 (December 1928): 1.

89. Faure-Favier, *Blanche et Noir*, 88.

90. Victor Margueritte, *La Garçonne* (Paris: E. Flammarion, 1922). Mary Louise Roberts discusses the implications of this text at some length in her work. Roberts, *Civilization Without Sexes*, chapter 2.

91. BMD, DOS FAU, Maxime Revon, "Courrier des Lettres—Blanche et Noir," *l'Ami du Peuple*, n.d.

92. Pierre Baye-Salzmann, "Blanche et Noir par Madame Louise Faure-Favier," *La Dépêche Africaine* 1, no. 7 (September 1928): 6.

93. Louise Faure-Favier, "Autour de 'Blanche et Noir,'" *La Dépêche Africaine* 1, no. 10 (December 1928): 1.

3. A Black Colony?

1. CAOM, SLOTFOM III/79, PROM, December 1932.

2. Edwards considers that "arguably more than anywhere else in the world" Paris fulfills this function. Edwards, *Practice of Diaspora*, 25.

3. Note that the "dette de sang" also worked in the other direction: for the privilege of living under French rule, imperial subjects and citizens should be prepared to fight for France. Fogarty, *Race and War*, 15–16. On the "dette de sang" see also Dewitte, *Mouvements nègres*.

4. Mann, *Native Sons*, 5.

5. Rosenberg, *Policing Paris*, 133–38.

6. As we saw in chapter 2, the majority of those belonging to organizations such as the CDRN, LDRN, and UTN were manual laborers, or workers. Note that police archives were generated by the state, not the city.

7. David H. Slavin, "The French Left and the Rif War, 1924–25: Racism and the Limits of Internationalism," *Journal of Contemporary History* 26, no. 1 (1991).

8. Dewitte, *Mouvements nègres*, 109; Claude Liauzu, *Aux origines des tiers-mondismes: colonisés et anticolonialistes en France 1919–1939* (Paris: L'Harmattan, 1982), 129–30.

9. J. Ayo Langley, "Pan-Africanism in Paris, 1924–36," *The Journal of Modern African Studies* 7, no. 1 (1969): 75.

10. CAOM, SLOTFOM III/24, "Ligue de défense de la Race Nègre, rapports d'Agents," untitled, July 1926.

11. Alice Conklin, "Who Speaks for Africa? The René Maran-Blaise Diagne Trial in 1920s Paris," in *The Color of Liberty: Histories of Race in France*, ed. Sue Peabody and Tyler Edward Stovall (Durham: Duke University Press, 2003).

12. Lamine Senghor should not be confused with the more well known Léopold Sédar Senghor, who went on to become Senegal's first president. For more on Lamine Senghor see Mann, "Locating Colonial Histories."

13. Lamine Senghor was personally affected by this situation since he claimed that he was born in Dakar (which made him a French citizen), but his Four Commune status was challenged by colonial authorities who subsequently reduced his pension. Miller, *Nationalists and Nomads*, 23–24. Miller bases his statement upon Iba Der Thiam, "L'Evolution politique et syndicale du Sénégal colonial de 1840–1936" (Ph.D. dissertation, Université de Paris I, 1982–1983), 7: 2916–18. The "fraud" was discovered in 1925.

Senghor pleaded his innocence while other members of the black community were outraged at the attempt to lessen his soldier's pension as a result of his changed status.

14. AN, F/7/13166, PROM, March 1927: 11.

15. On Senghor's time away from Paris see for example CAOM, SLOTFOM III/37, Agent Désiré, October 16, 1926; AN, F/7/13166, PROM, March 1927: 16. On Kouyaté taking control see AN, F/7/13166, PROM, September 1927: 5–6.

16. CAOM, SLOTFOM III/24, Agent Désiré, November 26, 1927; AN, F/7/13166, PROM, November 1927: 5.

17. CAOM, SLOTFOM III/24, Agent Désiré, December 3, 1927; AN, F/7/13166, PROM, December 1927: 15.

18. AN, F/7/13168, PROM, April 1932: 8–9 and F/7/13168, PROM, May 1932: 9.

19. CAOM, SLOTFOM III/24, Agent Victor, March 29, 1932.

20. Dewitte, *Mouvements nègres*, 29–33.

21. AN, F/7/13168, PROM, June 1932: 7.

22. AN, F/7/13168, PROM, June 1932: 7.

23. AN, F/7/13168, PROM, September 1932: 14.

24. CAOM, SLOTFOM III/68, PROM, October 1933.

25. Langley demonstrates in detail how Africans and Antilleans formulated increasingly radicalized demands for liberation. Langley, "Pan-Africanism in Paris."

26. AN, F/7/13170, "Propagande communiste aux colonies," Brussels, "rapport pour Son Excellence sur l'attitude au Congrès anticolonial des Français ou sujets français qui y ont participé," February 15, 1927.

27. CAOM, SLOTFOM III/34, sous-dossier Entr'aide Coloniale Féminine, May 25, 1934. On Kouyaté see also Dewitte, *Mouvements nègres*; Edwards, *Practice of Diaspora*, 250.

28. CAOM, SLOTFOM III/111, Ligue de Défense de la Race Nègre, Rapport de Victor, January 11, 1932.

29. CAOM, SLOTFOM III/24, Agent Désiré, March 1, 1927. The reasons for such hostility were probably personal as well as political. Several documents mention a feud, although without details, between the attacker—Gothon-Lunion—and Senghor. On a different occasion someone threw a rock at Senghor's head, allegedly on indirect orders from the Ministry of Colonies. CAOM, SLOTFOM III/24, Agent Désiré, November 13, 1926.

30. AN, F/7/13166, PROM, March 1927: 16–17.

31. Dewitte, *Mouvements nègres*, 196.

32. CAOM, SLOTFOM III/24, Agent Désiré, January 29, 1931; SLOTFOM III/111, January 25, 1931.

33. AN, F/7/13168, PROM, January 1931: 9; CAOM, SLOTFOM II/3, Agent Victor, February 17, 1932.

34. CAOM, SLOTFOM III/111, Agent Joé, July 14, 1930.

35. On the linguistic origins and evolutions of *métis* and *mulâtres* see: Robert Chaudenson, "Mulâtres, métis, créoles . . ." in *Métissages Tome II: Linguistique et anthropologie*, ed. Jean-Luc Alber, Claudine Bavoux, and Michel Watin (Paris: L'Harmattan, 1992). For an excellent description of the 19th-century history of the term *métis*, including its biological and social implications, see: Owen White, *Children of the French Empire: Miscegenation and Colonial Society in French West Africa, 1895–1960* (Oxford: Oxford University Press, 1999). Also see: Jean Benoist, "Le métissage: biologie d'un fait social, sociologie d'un fait biologique," in *Métissages Tome II: Linguistique et anthropologie*, ed. Jean-Luc Alber, Claudine Bavoux, and Michel Watin (Paris: L'Harmattan, 1992).

36. Miller reminds us *nègre* had a number of connotations, including ghostwriter. Christopher L. Miller, *Blank Darkness: Africanist Discourse in French* (Chicago: University of Chicago Press, 1985).

37. CAOM, SLOTFOM III/24, Agent Désiré, February 1, 1927.

38. AN, F/7/13166, PROM, October 1927: 7. On the language of race see also Jennifer Anne Boittin, "Black in France: The Language and Politics of Race during the Late Third Republic," *French Politics, Culture & Society* 27, no. 2 (Summer 2009).

39. Frantz Fanon, *Peau noir, masques blancs* (Paris: Editions du Seuil, 1952), 182.

40. Frantz Fanon, *Toward the African Revolution (Political Essays)*, trans. Haakon Chevalier (New York: Grove, 1969), 17, 21.

41. CAOM, SLOTFOM III/73, Agent Paul, November 11, 1932.

42. CAOM, SLOTFOM III/89, PROM, July 1926; AN, F/7/13166, PROM, January 1927: 8.

43. *La Race Nègre* first appeared just as the CDRN began to crumble (and apparently to counter the rival newspaper of the divided organization, *La Dépêche Africaine*). CAOM, 2MiA/242, Le Comité, "Le Mot 'nègre,'" *La Voix des Nègres* 1, no. 1 (January 1927): 1. Miller suggests that this article marks "a *rehabilitation of blackness through language*—a project

that generations since have attributed only to the Negritude of Léopold Sédar Senghor and Césaire." Miller, *Nationalists and Nomads*, 33.

44. The tradition of using hierarchies of race and mixedness to define legal status in the AOF in all likelihood added to the implications of race-based name-calling. For more on this question as well as Diagne's politics and the West African struggle for rights, see Wesley G. Johnson Jr., *The Emergence of Black Politics in Senegal: The Struggle for Power in the Four Communes, 1900–1920* (Stanford: Stanford University Press, 1971).

45. This was the case, for example, in Porto Novo. Michel, *Les Africains et la Grande Guerre*, 23.

46. For more on citizenship and suffrage overseas, see Catherine Co-query-Vidrovitch, "Nationalité et citoyenneté en Afrique occidentale française: Originaires et citoyens dans le Sénégal colonial," *Journal of African History* 42, no. 2 (2001): 285–305.

47. Dewitte suggests that the switch to communism was both abrupt and complete in 1927, but for members, accepting communist influences was far more complex. Dewitte, *Mouvements nègres*, 154.

48. CAOM, SLOTFOM III/24, Agent Désiré, February 2, 1929, and March 9, 1929.

49. AN, F/7/13167, PROM, December 1928: 12–13.

50. AN, F/7/13167, PROM, February 1929: 18.

51. CAOM, SLOTFOM III/53, January 26, 1935.

52. CAOM, SLOTFOM III/91, "Note sur la situation de fait actuelle de nos diverses possessions au point de vue de la propagande révolutionnaire," April 29, 1925.

53. CAOM, SLOTFOM III/91, Note pour le Ministre du Ministère des Colonies, December 11, 1924.

54. CAOM, SLOTFOM III/91, Note pour le Ministre du Ministère des Colonies, December 11, 1924.

55. CAOM, SLOTFOM III/111, Bingerville, Dakar, February 8, 1928.

56. The International Red Aid, a charity organization, was another Moscow-based association often in direct communication with colonial migrants. AN, F/7/13167, PROM, April 1930: 5–7. On blacks and the Communist Party see also Kate A. Baldwin, *Beyond the Color Line and the Iron Curtain: Reading Encounters between Black and Red, 1922–1963* (Durham: Duke University Press, 2002); Abiola Irele, "Pan-Africanism and African Nationalism," *Odu* 6 (1971); Langley, "Pan-Africanism in Paris"; Jakob Moneta, *La politique du Parti communiste français dans la question colo-*

niale, 1920–1963 (Paris: Maspero, 1971); Manuela Semidei, "Les socialistes français et le problème colonial entre les deux guerres (1919–1939)," *Revue française de sciences politiques* XVIII, no. 6 (1968).

57. CAOM, SLOTFOM III/47, Comité Syndical International des Ouvriers Nègres, *Sous le Joug de l'Impérialisme: Les orgies impérialistes en Afrique.*

58. AN, F/7/13167, PROM, September 1930: 23–24.

59. AN, F/7/13167, PROM, January 1929: 28–29.

60. John D. Hargreaves, "The Comintern and Anti-Colonialism: New Research Opportunities," *African Affairs* 92, no. 367 (1993): 261.

61. Ezra explores the changing relationship between communists and anti-imperialists when she compares the official reaction of *l'Humanité* to the 1931 Colonial Exposition and the 1937 Popular Front's World Fair. The PCF overwhelmingly supported the 1937 World Fair, even though it showcased imperialism. Ezra, *Colonial Unconscious,* 29. Furthermore Slavin argues that in response to the Rif War in 1924–25 the PCF also came short of its stated goals of anti-imperialism. Indeed, it resisted orders from Moscow demanding a stance against colonialism. Part of the problem was ongoing prejudice in the PCF's ranks. Slavin, "French Left and Rif War," 7.

62. Pierre Lacan, "Aux côtés des travailleurs immigrés," seventeen articles in *L'Humanité* from December 12, 1934, to January 16, 1935; Maurice Lebrun, "La vie misérable des travailleurs étrangers," four articles in *L'Humanité* from November 25 to December 3, 1931. On newspapers and immigrants see Ralph Schor, *L'immigration en France 1919–1939: Sources imprimées en langue française et filmographie* (Nice: Centre de la Méditerranée Moderne et Contemporaine, 1986).

63. Georges Altman, "Prolétaires de tous les pays," seventeen articles in *L'Humanité* from August 15 to September 26, 1926.

64. Liauzu, *Aux origines des tiers-mondismes,* 135, chapters 4 and 5.

65. Woodford McClellan, "Africans and Black Americans in the Comintern Schools, 1925–1934," *The International Journal of African Historical Studies* 26, no. 2 (1993).

66. Hargreaves, "Comintern and Anti-Colonialism," 259.

67. AN, F/7/13167, PROM, August 1929: 11–17.

68. Much has been written about the Scottsboro Affair and its repercussions. See for example Dan T. Carter, *Scottsboro: A Tragedy of the American South* (Baton Rouge: Louisiana State University Press, 1969); James E. Goodman, *Stories of Scottsboro,* 1st Vintage Books ed. (New York: Vintage Books, 1994).

69. J. A. Miller, Susan D. Pennybacker, and Eve Rosenhaft, "Mother Ada Wright and the International Campaign to Free the Scottsboro Boys, 1931–1934," *The American Historical Review* 106, no. 2 (2001).

70. Miller, Pennybacker, and Rosenhaft, "Mother Ada Wright," 416.

71. CAOM, SLOTFOM III/24, Agent Paul, November 3, 1929.

72. AN, F/7/13167, PROM, November 1929: 6.

73. Kouyaté, among others, makes this argument. CAOM, SLOTFOM III/24, Agent Joé, December 31, 1930.

74. CAOM, SLOTFOM III/24, Agent Paul, March 2, 1931.

75. André Breton et al., "Ne Visitez pas l'Exposition Coloniale," May 1931, in *Tracts Surréalistes et Déclarations Collectives*, ed. José Pierre (Paris: Eric Losfeld, 1980).

76. AN, F/7/13168, PROM, September 1931: 4–6.

77. Cited in David Caute, *The Fellow-Travellers: Intellectual Friends of Communism*, Rev. ed. (New York: Yale University Press, 1988), 165. Anson Rabinbach adds his own thoughts on antifascism, explaining it "was the binary of binaries, the geopolitical and cultural bifurcation between spirit and power [*Geist* and *Macht*], humanism and terror, reason and un-reason, past and future, that framed the first half of this century." Anson Rabinbach, "Introduction: Legacies of Antifascism," *New German Critique*, no. 67 (Winter, 1996): 5.

78. CAOM, SLOTFOM II/19, Agent Paul, June 23, 1933.

79. In an interview with his biographer Janet Vaillant, Senghor stated that he had never heard of "Garan Kouyaté, Tovalou Houénou, [and] Emile Faure." Later Léopold Sédar Senghor rectified part of his statement: "from René Maran to the *demoiselles* Nardal, and through Lamine Senghor and Thiémokho Garang Kouyaté [sic]. We were little influenced by these Negroes, although somewhat more influenced by those participating in *La Revue du Monde noir*, by Paulette Nardal and the Doctor Price-Mars, without omitting the Negro-Americans." Janet G. Vaillant, *Black, French, and African: A Life of Léopold Sédar Senghor* (Cambridge MA: Harvard University Press, 1990), 359n41. Senghor's rebuttal was part of his response to Martin Steins's thesis. Léopold Sédar Senghor, "Thèse de Martin Steins," [typescript, 1981], 17–18. Miller, *Nationalists and Nomads*, 37–38n67.

80. On the Stavisky Affair see David Clay Large, *Between Two Fires: Europe's Path in the 1930s*, 1st ed. (New York: Norton, 1990).

81. Adolphe Mathurin, interview with J. S. Spiegler, *Aspects of Na-*

tionalist Thought among French-Speaking West Africans, 1921–1939 (Ph.D. diss., Oxford University, 1968), 209n4, cited in Edwards, *Practice of Diaspora*, 274. Mathurin's anticommunist stance makes his presence on the streets of Paris in an essentially leftist movement all the more interesting. The black community truly drew together when faced with more pressing problems than their precise brand of radical activism.

82. CAOM, SLOTFOM III/77, PROM, July 1934.

83. CAOM, SLOTFOM III/77, PROM, July 1934.

84. *L'Humanité*, May 1, 1934, cited in CAOM, SLOTFOM III/77, PROM, July 1934.

85. CAOM, SLOTFOM III/47, Note on the "Ligue Internationale contre l'Oppression Coloniale et l'Impérialisme."

86. Archives Nationales, Dakar, Sénégal (hereafter ANS), 2G29/13, Rapport politique annuel 1929: 7.

87. ANS, 2G27/21, Rapport politique annuel 1927: 16.

88. ANS, 2G34/12. See for example Rapport politique annuel 1934: 17–18, 27.

89. ANS: 2G27/12, Rapport politique AOF 1927: 9–10, 16–17; 2G29/13, Rapport politique d'ensemble 1929; 2G30/6, rapport politique AOF 1930: 21–22; 2G34/12, Rapport politique annuel 1934: 24–26; 11D1/23, circulaire no. 257, May 8, 1928; 11D1/151, most of sous-dossier affaires politiques 1932–36 including February 13, 1932, no. 281, March 16, 1934, no. 93, January 28, 1935, no. 410, March 11, 1935, May 19, 1936, and no. 2278/DS, October 29, 1938; 11D1/0152, for example no. 2393/SU, November 24, 1939 and no. 530/SU, April 5, 1940; 11D1/0313, no. 269 B/P, May 4, 1931; 11D1/337, Rapport politique AOF 1931.

90. On anti-imperial politics in Africa see Solofo Randrianja, *Société et luttes anticoloniales à Madagascar* (Paris: Karthala, 2001); Ibrahima Thioub, "Savoirs interdits en contexte colonial: La politique culturelle de la France en Afrique de l'Ouest," in *"Mama Africa": Hommage à Catherine Coquery-Vidrovitch*, ed. Chantal Chanson-Jabeur and Odile Goerg (Paris: L'Harmattan, 2005).

4. Reverse Exoticism & Masculinity

1. AN, F/7/13168, PROM, November 1932: 12.

2. Morlat, *Les affaires politiques*, 297.

3. CAOM, SLOTFOM III/79, PROM, December 1932.

4. CAOM, SLOTFOM III/79, PROM, June 1933.

5. CAOM, SLOTFOM III/79, PROM, June 1933.

6. Black masculinity as well as the presence of women in anti-imperial circles remains understudied in the francophone context. However the interwar and postwar Anglophone contexts provide useful analytical frameworks. Consider for example Martin Summers, who looks "at the ways in which African American and African Caribbean immigrant men constructed a gendered self through rhetoric, organizational activities, literature, and daily public rituals of performance" in the United States. Martin Summers, *Manliness and Its Discontents: The Black Middle Class and the Transformation of Masculinity, 1900–1930* (Chapel Hill: University of North Carolina Press, 2004), 4. See also: Gail Bederman, *Manliness & Civilization: A Cultural History of Gender and Race in the United States, 1880–1917* (Chicago: University of Chicago Press, 1995); Hazel V. Carby, *Race Men* (Cambridge MA: Harvard University Press, 1998); Tim Edwards, *Cultures of Masculinity* (New York: Routledge, 2006); Mrinalini Sinha, *Colonial Masculinity: The 'Manly Englishman' and the 'Effeminate Bengali' in the Late Nineteenth Century* (Manchester: Manchester University Press, 1995); Richard Smith, *Jamaican volunteers in the First World War: Race, masculinity and the development of national consciousness* (Manchester: Manchester University Press, 2004); Stephens, *Black Empire*.

7. CAOM, SLOTFOM III/79, PROM, May 1933.

8. Negrophilia belongs in the literary and intellectual tradition of exoticism, which Brett Berliner defines as the exaltation or denigration of the other. Berliner, *Ambivalent Desire*, 4. Exoticism further presupposes, according to Roger Célestin, "a relation between a (Western) Self and a (exotic) Other that is *fluctuatingly tenuous or strong*." Roger Célestin, *From Cannibals to Radicals: Figures and Limits of Exoticism* (Minneapolis: University of Minnesota Press, 1996), 7.

9. Michelle Stephens has argued, "blackness, then, as much as any other racialized consciousness during this period, was an imaginary burdened by the national." Stephens, *Black Empire*, 5.

10. James Scott suggests that scholars should look at not just extraordinary but also ordinary modes of resistance, including cultural resistance. Thus "the symbols, the norms, the ideological forms they create constitute the indispensable background to their behavior." While reverse exoticism in its overtly political form might still fall under the category of explicit, self-conscious resistance, masculinity and intermarriage are both forms of everyday resistance. James C. Scott, *Weapons of the Weak: Ev-*

eryday Forms of Peasant Resistance (New Haven: Yale University Press, 1985), 38.

11. Studies of divergences between the Left's revolutionary calls for political change, and its conservative resistance to popular culture across Europe (and not only during the interwar period) include Richard Bodek, "The Not-So-Golden Twenties: Everyday Life and Communist Agitprop in Weimar-Era Berlin," *Journal of Social History* 30, no. 1 (1996); Anne E. Gorsuch, "Soviet Youth and the Politics of Popular Culture during NEP," *Social History* 17, no. 2 (1992); Uta G. Poiger, *Jazz, Rock, and Rebels: Cold War Politics and American Culture in a Divided Germany* (Berkeley and Los Angeles: University of California Press, 2000); S. Frederick Starr, *Red and Hot: The Fate of Jazz in the Soviet Union, 1917–1991*, 2nd ed. (New York: Limelight Editions, 1994). For a perspective on how the Left embraced popular culture, see Eric Hobsbawm, *Uncommon People: Resistance, Rebellion and Jazz* (New York: New Press, 1998).

12. CAOM, SLOTFOM III/78, "Union des Travailleurs Nègres organise une grande fête," Agent Joé, December 5, 1932 ; Agent Paul, December 4, 1932.

13. CAOM, SLOTFOM III/79, PROM, December 1932.

14. CAOM, SLOTFOM II/16, Agent Joé, December 5, 1932.

15. CAOM, SLOTFOM II/16, Agent Joé, March 24, 1933.

16. CAOM, SLOTFOM III/53, Agent Paul, March 5, 1933.

17. CAOM, SLOTFOM II/16, Agent Joé, April 3, 1933.

18. CAOM, SLOTFOM III/53, Agent Paul, April 2, 1933.

19. CAOM, SLOTFOM III/24, Agent Désiré, July 4, 1927.

20. AN, F/7/13168, PROM, November 1932: 9.

21. CAOM, SLOTFOM II/16, Agent Joé, November 25, 1932; Agent Joé, December 9, 1932.

22. CAOM, SLOTFOM II/2, Agent Coco, February 15, 1938; March 13, 1938.

23. CAOM, SLOTFOM II/16, Agent Joé, April 3, 1933.

24. For the March 1934 monthly assembly of the UTN, Joé listed a number of newcomers who had recently joined the Union—he was unable to name them all. CAOM, SLOTFOM II/16, March 19, 1934.

25. AN, 200MI/3025 (21G27), Agent Désiré, July 6, 1926.

26. CAOM, SLOTFOM III/79, PROM, December 1932.

27. The police believed most blacks lived in the fifteenth and twentieth arrondissements. CAOM, SLOTFOM III/53, March 19, 1935.

28. CAOM, SLOTFOM III/27, excerpt from Léon Sazie, *La Dépêche Coloniale*, Saturday, June 2, 1928.

29. Bederman, *Manliness & Civilization*, 7.

30. Judith Surkis argues that "while masculinity was tautologically conferred on men by male citizenship, its meaning remained unstable." In partial contrast, Robert Nye argues "in a society governed by honor, masculinity is always in the course of construction but always fixed, a *telos* that men experience as a necessary but permanently unattainable goal." Judith Surkis, *Sexing the Citizen: Morality and Masculinity in France, 1870–1920* (Ithaca NY: Cornell University Press, 2006), 8; Nye, *Masculinity and Male Codes*, 13.

31. Stephens argues that "the inescapable hybridity of imperial history is revealed in black global stories and world histories that embody black political desires in specifically gendered and sexualized constructions of the race." Stephens, *Black Empire*, 8. The workers of interwar Berlin developed a far more ardent culture of masculinity. Eve Rosenhaft, "Organising the 'Lumpenproletariat': Cliques and Communists in Berlin during the Weimar Republic," *The German Working Class 1888–1933*, ed. Richard J. Evans (Totowa NJ: Barnes & Noble Books, 1982).

32. CAOM, SLOTFOM III/24, LDRN, rapports d'agents, Note de l'Agent Désiré, July 6, 1926.

33. CAOM, SLOTFOM III/24, LDRN, rapports d'agents, Note de l'Agent Désiré, May 24, 1927. On Agent Désiré see Morlat, *Les affaires politiques*, 304.

34. CAOM, SLOTFOM III/24, LDRN, rapports d'agents, Note de l'Agent Désiré, May 24, 1927.

35. APP, BA1714, "Sur les journaux étrangers, souvent interdits, à Paris," Dossier 2100–5, January 1929.

36. One example of such a situation occurred in April 1930. AN, F/7/13167, PROM, April 1930: 7.

37. CAOM, SLOTFOM II/12, Agent Désiré, December 16, 1929.

38. CAOM, SLOTFOM III/24, Agent Paul, December 4, 1930.

39. AN, F/7/13168, PROM, December 1930: 8. Mme Kodo-Kossoul's report stated amongst other things that blacks in Paris were not interested in the LDRN, which, financially, had entered troubled waters.

40. According to Nye, "honor is a masculine concept. It has traditionally regulated relations among men, summed up the prevailing ideals of manliness, and marked the boundaries of masculine comportment."

When applied to cultures far removed from the nineteenth-century French upper classes, such a definition still appears to hold true. Nye, *Masculinity and Male Codes*, vii.

41. Edward Berenson, *The Trial of Madame Caillaux* (Berkeley: University of California Press, 1993), 170.

42. CAOM, SLOTFOM III/53, Agent Joé, August 29, 1932. It appears that only once did a white man and his black wife participate in an UTN meeting, and both remained nameless, so an in-depth discussion of this particular inversion of the Parisian norm is difficult, if not impossible. CAOM, SLOTFOM II/16, Agent Joé, March 19, 1934.

43. AN, F/7/13168, PROM, September 1932: 14.

44. CAOM, SLOTFOM II/2, Agent Joé, October 12 and December 24, 1937.

45. Frantz Fanon, *Black Skin, White Masks*, trans. Charles Lam Markmann (New York: Grove, 1967), 63.

46. René Maran, *Un homme pareil aux autres* (Paris: Albin Michel, 1947).

47. Fanon, *Black Skin*, 69.

48. Fanon, *Black Skin*, 71.

49. Gwen Bergner, "Who Is That Masked Woman? Or, the Role of Gender in Fanon's *Black Skin, White Masks*," PMLA 110, no. 1 (1995): 80.

50. Fanon, *Black Skin*, 156.

51. Fanon, *Black Skin*, 151, 156, 158, 171.

52. Mary Ann Doane, *Femmes Fatales: Feminism, Film Theory, Psychoanalysis* (New York: Routledge, 1991), 218.

53. Claude McKay, *A Long Way From Home* (London: Pluto, 1985), 278–81.

54. Yaël Fletcher suggests that "this gendering of racial oppression made women as a group, whether black or white, a central force for (or against) the anticolonial nationalist project." Fletcher, "Unsettling Settlers," 89.

55. Mark Naison, *Communists in Harlem during the Depression* (Urbana: University of Illinois Press, 1983), 136–37.

56. Claude McKay, *Banjo* (London: X Press, 2000), 175.

57. McKay, *Banjo*, 178.

58. CAOM, SLOTFOM III/53, Agent Joé, September 5, 1932.

59. CAOM, SLOTFOM II/2, Agent Joé, Années 1937–1938, April 12, 1938.

60. On honor and family ties during the Third Republic, see Berenson, *Trial of Madame Caillaux*.

61. CAOM, SLOTFOM III/68, PROM, July 1933. Dewitte notes in passing that at one point Ramananjato had a French partner. This may or may not be the future Mme Ramananjato continually referred to in police reports. Dewitte, *Mouvements nègres*, 214.

62. CAOM, SLOTFOM III/77, PROM, August and September 1934.

63. CAOM, SLOTFOM II/2, Agent Joé, Années 1937–1938, January 30, 1938.

5. In Black & White

1. A similar role was fulfilled by black women in the Jim Crow South. After African American men were disenfranchised, African American women created links to the white community. Glenda Elizabeth Gilmore, *Gender and Jim Crow: Women and the Politics of White Supremacy in North Carolina, 1896–1920* (Chapel Hill: University of North Carolina Press, 1996).

2. *La Dépêche Africaine* also briefly reappeared in January 1938.

3. On *La Dépêche Africaine*'s circulation see CAOM, SLOTFOM III/24, LDRN, rapports d'agents, January 1929. Similar figures were repeated in the police archives: APP, BA1714, "Sur les journaux étrangers, souvent interdits, à Paris," Dossier 2100–5, January 1929. On *La Race Nègre* and *Le Cri des Nègre*'s circulation see CAOM, SLOTFOM III/24, LDRN, rapports d'agents, January 1929; CAOM, SLOTFOM III/24, LDRN, rapport de Paul, December 16, 1930; CAOM, SLOTFOM III/24, LDRN, rapport de Paul, September 19, 1933.

4. CAOM, SLOTFOM III/71, PROM, August 1928: 6.

5. CAOM, SLOTFOM III/88, PROM, May 1928: 5; June 1928: 15; July 1928: 9.

6. APP, BA 1714, "Sur les journaux étrangers," Dossier 2100–5, January 1929.

7. APP, BA 1714, "Sur les journaux étrangers," Dossier 2100–5, January 1929.

8. For example, a picture of bodies hanging from trees in the Congo, where revolt was punished with violent repression. *La Race Nègre* 2, no. 1 (March 1929): 3. See also photos presented during the anti-Exposition in 1931, showing bodies hanging from trees, heads without bodies, and so forth. *Le Cri des Nègres* 1, no. 2 (September 1931): 1.

9. "The Comité de Défense de la Race Nègre is currently inactive.

Only 'la Dépêche Africaine' ensures the liaison among its members and they participate in its editing and writing as much as they like." APP, BA1714, "Sur les journaux étrangers," Dossier 2100–5, January 1929.

10. At 75 centimes, *La Dépêche Africaine* was 25 centimes more expensive than *Le Cri des Nègres*.

11. CAOM, 2MiA/242, "Informations," *La Race Nègre* 4, no. 1 (July 1930): 4.

12. CAOM, SLOTFOM III/24, LDRN, rapports d'agents, January 1929.

13. CAOM, 2MiA/242, "To be or not to be," *La Race Nègre* 5, no. 1 (February 1932): 3.

14. Obscene publications that were censored for "affront to decency" included: *Beauté Magazine*; *Pour Lire à Deux*; *Paris-Magazine*; *Sex-Appeal*; *Pages Folles*; *Paris Plaisirs*; *L'Humour*; *Sans Gêne*; *La Madelon*; and *Frou-Frou*. APP, BA2244, "Livres et publications interdits."

15. Many newspapers regularly banned for political reasons were affiliated with organizations linked to the PCF such as: Fédération des Jeunesses Communistes; Union des Etudiants Communistes de France; Association Républicaine des Anciens Combattants (ARAC); Secours Populaire de France et des Colonies; Mouvement Populaire "Paix et Liberté"; Union des Comités de Femmes de l'Ile de France; Confédération Générale des Paysans Travailleurs. APP, BA1714, "Liste des publications (autre que les publications licencieuses) et journaux politiques dont l'Exposition ou la Vente sont interdites par M le Préfet de Police."

16. For example the North African, independence-seeking and/or PCF-affiliated newspapers *L'Ikdam de Paris*, February 1, 1927; *Al Alam Al Ahmar*, August 23, 1926; *Al Raïat Al Hamra*, June 29, 1927; and *Al Chab Al Ibriki*, January 24, 1926; as well as the French Indochinese independence-seeking *Viet Nam*, September 24, 1927 and *Viet-Nam-Hon*, August 23, 1926. APP, BA1714, "Journaux Coloniaux Interdits."

17. APP, BA1714, "Sur les journaux étrangers," January 1929.

18. CAOM, 2MiA/242, Raymond Brière de l'Isle, "De l'utilité d'un Comité de Défense de la Race Nègre en France," *La Voix des Nègres* 1, no. 1 (January 1927): 2.

19. CAOM, 2MiA/242, Luscap-Norbert "Les propos d'Alexandre," *La Race Nègre* 4, no. 5 (August 1931): 1.

20. CAOM, SLOTFOM II/19, Notes de l'Agent Paul et Coco 1929–1934, Paul, January 7, 1934.

21. CAOM, 2MiA/242, "Les femmes dans la bataille," *Le Cri des Nègres* Nouvelle Série 3, no. 6 (June 1934): 3.

22. CAOM, 2MiA/242, "Appel à nos sœurs les femmes des peuples opprimés," *Le Cri des Nègres*, Nouvelle Série 3, no. 7 (July 1934): 3.

23. CAOM, 2MiA/242, "Réalités coloniales: la femme noire en Afrique," *Le Cri des Nègres*, Nouvelle Série 4, no. 15 (March-April 1935): 1; "Un cadeau de la colonisation: la prostitution," no. 16 (May 1935): 4.

24. Spivak explains that "both as object of colonialist historiography and as subject of insurgency, the ideological construction of gender keeps the male dominant. If, in the context of colonial production, the subaltern has no history and cannot speak, the subaltern as female is even more deeply in shadow." Gayatri Chakravorty Spivak, "Can the Subaltern Speak?" *Marxism and the Interpretation of Culture*, ed. Cary Nelson and Lawrence Grossbert (Urbana: University of Illinois Press, 1988), 287.

25. One of the earliest scholars to study this genesis of the negritude movement was Lilyan Kesteloot, "Les Ecrivains noirs de langue française: Naissance d'une littérature" (Doctoral, Université Libre de Bruxelles, Institut de Sociologie, 1963). Several scholars have since responded to clarify assumptions that she made without full access to primary sources. They include Edward O. Ako, "L'Etudiant Noir and the Myth of the Genesis of the Negritude Movement," *Research in African Literatures* 15, no. 3 (1984); Langley, "Pan-Africanism in Paris"; Jean Pandolfi, "De Légitime Défense à Tropiques: Invitation à la Découverte," *Europe: Revue Littéraire Mensuelle*, 1980; Noureini Tidjani-Serpos, "Histoire de Trois Revues Pionnières," *L'Afrique Littéraire et Artistique* 45 (1977). More recently, scholars have addressed the more openly communist and controversial men whose 1920s ideas on anti-imperialism set the tone for the negritude movement. Edwards, *Practice of Diaspora*; Gilroy, *Black Atlantic*; Miller, *Nationalists and Nomads*. On negritude, see also Fall, *Africains noirs en France*, Jacques Louis Hymans, *Léopold Sédar Senghor: An Intellectual Bibliography by Jacques Louis Hymans* (Edinburgh: Edinburgh University Press, 1971); Irele, "Pan-Africanism."

26. In particular, Sharpley-Whiting, *Negritude Women*. Also timely were the very intriguing analyses presented by Edwards, *Practice of Diaspora*; Robert P. Smith Jr., "Black Like That: Paulette Nardal and the Negritude Salon," *CLA Journal* 45, no. 1 (2001); Carole Sweeney, "Resisting the Primitive: The Nardal Sisters, *La Revue du Monde Noir* and *La Dépêche Africaine*," *Nottingham French Studies* 43, no. 2 (Summer 2004). In

its breadth, the most thorough study of the Nardal sisters is Musil's dissertation. Emily Kirkland McTighe Musil, "*La Marianne Noire*: How Gender & Race in the Twentieth Century Atlantic World Reshaped the Debate about Human Rights" (PhD diss., UCLA, 2007).

27. Edwards, *Practice of Diaspora*, 120.

28. See in particular the exchange surrounding Brent Hayes Edwards's *The Practice of Diaspora*: Brent Hayes Edwards, "Pebbles of Consonance: A Reply to Critics," *Small Axe* 9, no. 17 (March 2005); T. Denean Sharpley-Whiting, "Erasures and the Practice of Diaspora Feminism," *Small Axe* 9, no. 17 (March 2005); Michelle Ann Stephens, "Disarticulating Black Internationalisms: West Indian Radicals and *The Practice of Diaspora*," *Small Axe* 9, no. 17 (March 2005).

29. On black feminism, see for example Patricia Hill Collins, *Black Feminist Thought: Knowledge, Consciousness, and the Politics of Empowerment*, 2nd ed. (New York: Routledge, 2000); Beverly Guy-Sheftall, ed., *Words of Fire: An Anthology of African-American Feminist Thought* (New York: New Press, 1995).

30. One thing that Edwards and Sharpley-Whiting agree upon was that this feminism was still "nascent." Edwards, *Practice of Diaspora*, 122; Sharpley-Whiting, "Erasures," 132. Both Evelyn Brooks Higginbotham and Rosalyn Terborg-Penn underscore the importance of taking individual women's situations into account within studies based upon overarching theories such as black feminism or African feminism. Hazel V. Carby, in analyzing language, hierarchies, and power, also warns against positing absolute forms of identity and explains that the "struggle within and over language reveals the nature of the structure of social relations and the hierarchy of power, not the nature of one particular group." Hazel V. Carby, *Reconstructing Womanhood: The Emergence of the Afro-American Woman Novelist* (New York: Oxford University Press, 1987), 17; Evelyn Brooks Higginbotham, "African-American Women's History and the Metalanguage of Race," *Signs* 17, no. 2 (Winter 1992); Rosalyn Terborg-Penn, "African Feminism: A Theoretical Approach to the History of Women in the African Diaspora," in *Women in Africa and the African Diaspora*, ed. Rosalyn Terborg-Penn and Andrea Benton Rushing (Washington DC: Howard University Press, 1996), 30.

31. These appellations have been suggested respectively by Edwards, *Practice of Diaspora*; Musil, "*La Marianne Noire*", 217. On African feminism see Terborg-Penn, "African Feminism," 25.

32. Sharpley-Whiting argues that Nardal's lack of attention to African American women (and focus instead upon African American men) precludes her from the designation "black feminist internationalist," and suggests instead the term "nascent *masculinist*, diasporic feminist." Edwards replies that African American women did not pay particular attention to their francophone counterparts and that a definition of "nascent *masculinist*, diasporic feminist" might be useful. In *Negritude Women*, Sharpley-Whiting argues that "feminist" and *féministe* do not mean the same thing, and in the end does not appear to use either term to describe Nardal. Edwards, "Pebbles of Consonance," 137; Sharpley-Whiting, *Negritude Women*, 21–22; Sharpley-Whiting, "Erasures," 131–32.

33. Evelyn Brooks Higginbotham, *Righteous Discontent: The Women's Movement in the Black Baptist Church, 1880–1920* (Cambridge MA: Harvard University Press, 1993).

34. Musil, *"La Marianne Noire"*, 23; Smith, "Black Like That," 54.

35. CAOM, SLOTFOM III/24, LDRN, Maurice Satineau, Comité de défense des intérêts de la race noire.

36. CAOM, SLOTFOM III/24, LDRN, Maurice Satineau, Comité de défense des intérêts de la race noire.

37. "Notre but, notre programme," *La Dépêche Africaine* 1, no. 1 (February 1928): 1.

38. Marguerite Martin, *Les Droits de la Femme* (Paris: Rivière, 1912); Marguerite Martin, *Féminisme et Coéducation* (Paris: Rivière, 1914), Marguerite Martin, "Le Rôle des Femmes dans la Paix" (paper presented at the Ordre Maçonnique Mixte International le Droit humain, Fédération Française, Salle des Fêtes du Grand Orient de France, Paris 13e, Thursday, February 25, 1926).

39. Marguerite Martin, "A Mes Soeurs," *La Dépêche Africaine* 1, no. 1 (February 1928): 1.

40. Sharpley-Whiting, *Negritude Women*, chapter 2.

41. Jane Nardal, "L'Internationalisme Noir," *La Dépêche Africaine* 1, no. 1 (February 1928): 5.

42. AN, 200MI/3025 (21G27), 1926.

43. Paulette Nardal, "Le nègre et l'art dramatique," *La Dépêche Africaine* 1, no. 3 (May 1928): 4.

44. Paulette Nardal, "Une femme sculpteur noire," *La Dépêche Africaine* 3, nos. 27 and 28 (August and September 1930): 5.

45. Paulette Nardal, "Le concert du 6 octobre à la Salle Hoche," *La Dépêche Africaine* 1, no. 9 (November 1928): 6.

46. Paulette Nardal, "l'Exil," *La Dépêche Africaine* 2, no. 19 (December 1929): 6.

47. Musil, *"La Marianne Noire"*, 173–74.

48. Paulette Nardal, "Histoire martiniquaise," *La Dépêche Africaine* 2, no. 15 (August 1929): 3 and "Pour les sinistrés de la Martinique," *La Dépêche Africaine* 2, no. 19 (December 1929): 1.

49. Carly Boussard, "Aparté," *La Dépêche Africaine* 1 no. 2 (February 1928): 4.

50. Carly Boussard, "Aparté," *La Dépêche Africaine* 1, no. 3 (May 1928): 4.

51. Carly Boussard, "l'Opinion de M. Henry Bordeaux sur la jeunesse contemporaine," *La Dépêche Africaine* 1, no. 5 (July 1928): 6.

52. Marguerite Martin, "Promenade Dominicale: Impressions sur le village nègre," *La Dépêche Africaine* 1, no. 2 (February 1928): 4.

53. APP, BA1714, "Sur les journaux étrangers," Dossier 2100–5, January 1929.

54. Marcelle Besson, "La femme et l'action coloniale," *La Dépêche Africaine* 1, no. 6 (August 1928): 7.

55. Marcelle Besson, "Vers une Meilleure Politique Coloniale: La collaboration franco-indigène," *La Dépêche Africaine* 1, no. 7 (September 1928): 1.

56. Marcelle Besson, "Le problème du logement," *La Dépêche Africaine* 2, no. 14 (May 1929): 2. Also see her follow-up articles: Marcelle Besson, "Les assurances sociales pour tous," *La Dépêche Africaine* 2, no. 16 (September 1929): 2; Marcelle Besson, "L'accès à la petite propriété," *La Dépêche Africaine* 2, no. 19 (December 1929); and Marcelle Besson, "La maison pour tous," *La Dépêche Africaine* 3, no. 25 (June 1930): 4.

57. On the *cercle d'amis* see Edwards, *Practice of Diaspora*, 152; Musil, *"La Marianne Noire,"* 66.

58. Louis Achille, "Préface," *La Revue du Monde Noir* no. 1 (1932; repr., Paris: Jean-Michel Place, 1992): xv.

59. Smith, "Black Like That," 61.

60. Louis Achille, "Préface," *La Revue du Monde Noir* no. 1 (1932; repr., Paris: Jean-Michel Place, 1992): xv.

61. Edwards explains "what is especially important and particularly

unique about the circle around the Nardal sisters is that it cleared space for a kind of feminist practice that otherwise was not possible in the midst of the *vogue nègre* in Paris." Edwards, *Practice of Diaspora*, 158.

62. "Ce que nous voulons faire," *La Revue du Monde Noir*, no. 1 (1932; repr., Paris: Jean-Michel Place, 1992): 1/3.

63. Sharpley-Whiting, *Negritude Women*, 57.

64. CAOM, SLOTFOM II/11, Agent Désiré, September 10, 1931.

65. Sharpley-Whiting, *Negritude Women*, 59.

66. Gender aside, Tidjani-Serpos has argued that another important political dimension to the paper was sustained anti-Americanism. Tidjani-Serpos, "Histoire de Trois Revues," 56.

67. Paulette Nardal, "Eveil de la Conscience de Race/Awakening of Race Consciousness," *La Revue du Monde Noir* no. 6 (1932; repr., Paris: Jean-Michel Place, 1992): 26/344.

68. Nardal, "Eveil de la Conscience de Race," 29/347.

69. Paulette Nardal to J. L. Hymans, letter of November 17, 1963, cited in Hymans, *Léopold Sédar Senghor*, 36.

70. Musil, *"La Marianne Noire"*, 49.

71. Roberte Horth, "Histoire sans importance/A thing of no importance," *La Revue du Monde Noir*, no. 2 (1932; repr., Paris: Jean-Michel Place, 1992): 49/119.

72. Paulette Nardal, "Eveil de la Conscience de Race," 29/347.

73. Kesteloot's work provoked debate in part because she devoted a third of it to a discussion of *L'Etudiant Noir* as foundational for negritude, although she had never seen the paper. Thus some challenge the extent to which it should be viewed as the moment of cultural awakening for black students in Paris. In addition to those scholars listed previously, see Olivier Dubuis, *L'Afrique reconnue: Panorama de la littérature négro-africaine* (Kinshasa, Zaire: Leco, 1969), 30; Irene Dobbs Jackson, "La Négritude: marche d'un phénomène," in *Littératures ultramarines de langue française: genèse et jeunesse*, ed. Thomas H. Geno and Roy Julow (Sherbrooke QC: Naaman, 1974), 24.

74. At least two issues of the paper have been found, but there were also at least two copies of its predecessor, titled *L'Etudiant Martiniquais*, that showed some continuity with *L'Etudiant Noir*. See: André Midas, "A Propos de l'Association," *L'Etudiant Noir* 1, no. 1 (March 1935): 2 ; J. Sauphanor, "Réflexions sur une réunion d'Etudiants Martiniquais," *L'Etudiant*

Noir 1, no. 1 (March 1935): 3; Gilbert Gratiant, "Mulâtres . . . pour le bien et le mal," *L'Etudiant Noir* 1, no. 1 (March 1935): 5.

75. Gary Wilder argues that "like the Nardal circle, these students sought to formulate a modern Afro-French cultural identity." Wilder, *Imperial Nation-State*, 185–86.

76. Aimé Césaire, "Nègreries: Jeunesse noire et Assimilation," *L'Etudiant Noir* 1, no. 1 (March 1935): 3.

77. Léopold Sédar Senghor, "L'Humanisme et nous: René Maran," *L'Etudiant Noir* 1, no. 1 (March 1935): 4.

78. Gilbert Gratiant, "Mulâtres . . . pour le bien et le mal," *L'Etudiant Noir* 1, no. 1 (March 1935): 5.

79. Paulette Nardal, "Guignol Ouolof," *L'Etudiant Noir* 1, no. 1 (March 1935): 4.

80. Etienne Léro was another person who sometimes breached class. He was an active member of the UTN in 1932 and 1933, regularly attending and sometimes even presiding over meetings. CAOM, SLOTFOM V/23, dossier *Le Cri des Nègres*, Agent Joé, August 22, 1933; SLOTFOM III/53, dossier UTN, Agent Joé, March 6, 1933, Agent Joé, June 27, 1932, and no author, December 12, 1933.

81. CAOM, 2MiA/242, "On nous prie d'insérer," *Le Cri des Nègres*, Nouvelle Série 4, no. 17 (June 1935): 1.

82. CAOM, SLOTFOM III/73, sous-dossier Comité International pour la Défense du Peuple Ethiopien, September 4, 1935.

83. CAOM, SLOTFOM III/73, dossier SRI, sous-dossier Ligue Anti-Impérialiste, October 11, 1935.

84. Her presence was mentioned a few times including in connection to a series of complications, the nature of which were never discussed, which placed her in opposition to certain members of the UTN. CAOM, SLOTFOM III/73, sous-dossier SRI, September 17, 1935, and September n.d., 1935.

85. CAOM, SLOTFOM III/73, "AG de l'UTN," October 5, 1935.

86. CAOM, SLOTFOM III/73, dossier SRI, sous-dossier Comité international pour la défense du peuple éthiopien, October 25, 1935; Ministry of the Interior to the Minister of the Colonies, "Note relative à une réunion organisée le 22 courant, par le comité International pour la Défense du Peuple éthiopien," October 28, 1935.

87. BNF, Paulette Nardal, "'Levée des races,' extrait de *Métromer*," *Le Périscope Africain* 7, no. 318 (October 19, 1935).

88. "Grand rassemblement des Femmes Belges pour la défense de la

paix," *Les Femmes dans l'Action Mondial,* no. 15 (December 1935–January 1936).

89. CAOM, 2MiA/242, "Une Antillaise ovationnée dans un meeting contre la guerre à Bruxelles," *Le Cri des Nègres,* Nouvelle Série 4, no. 23 (December 1935): 1.

90. CAOM, 2MiA/242, "Lettre," *La Race Nègre* 1, no. 4 (November and December 1927): 1; "Adresse du Président J.-B. Danquah," *La Race Nègre* 2, no. 1 (March 1929): 4. The other publications by a woman were excerpts of an article and a poem written by Jeanne Marquès. CAOM, 2MiA/242, "Le Nègre à travers la presse," *La Race Nègre* 1, no. 4 (November and December 1927): 5; "A ma pauvre négresse," 1, no. 5 (May 1928): 5.

91. CAOM, 2MiA/242, Jeanne Kodo-Kossoul, "Les noirs n'aiment pas l'injustice," *Le Cri des Nègres,* Nouvelle Série 5, no. 25 (February 1936): 2.

92. CAOM, 2MiA/242, Jeanne Kodo-Kossoul, "Tergiversations néfastes," *Le Cri des Nègres,* Nouvelle Série 5, no. 26 (March 1936): 2.

93. BNF, Paulette Nardal, "Les colonies françaises," *La Femme dans la Vie Sociale* 12, no. 117 (February 1939): 1.

94. BNF, "Vrai mariage en Afrique noire," *La Femme dans la Vie Sociale* 12, no. 112 (July–August 1939): 1.

95. BNF, Jane Zamia-Nardal, "Une figure qui disparaît: La Lavandière noire," *La Femme dans la Vie Sociale* 11, no. 107 (February 1938): 2.

96. Musil also describes her as patriotic and cosmopolitan. Musil, *"La Marianne Noire",* 5. Joan Wallach Scott, *Only Paradoxes to Offer: French Feminists and the Rights of Man* (Cambridge MA: Harvard University Press, 1996).

97. CAOM, SLOTFOM II/2, Agent Coco, Conférence donnée par ROSSO, Saturday, April 9, 1938. Other interactions with the UTN included SLOT-FOM II/2, Agent Joé, April 12, 1938; Agent Coco, May 26, 1938.

98. Musil has found evidence that corroborates such a voyage, but dating it to 1937. Perhaps this was a second planned voyage. Musil, *"La Marianne Noire",* 162.

6. *"These Men's Minor Transgressions"*

1. Mme Winter Frappier de Montbenoit, "Les femmes de couleur devant la colonisation," *La Dépêche Africaine* 3, no. 23 (April 15, 1930): 2. It seems likely that la Française Créole was closely related to the UFSF and the CNFF from its inception. BHVP, Groupes et associations suffragistes, Boîte 3, "Articles dans *La Française,* sur la Section Créole." Note that

Winter-Frappié's name was also repeatedly spelled as Winter-Frappier, and Winter-Frapié—the spelling I am using in the text is that most consistently present throughout the years and articles. In notes I replicate the spelling in the article byline.

2. Mme Winter Frappier de Montbenoit, "Les métis des colonies," *La Dépêche Africaine* 3, no. 25 (June 1930): 4.

3. There was a previously established tradition of Frenchwomen engaging in questions of race, colonialism, and slavery, for example during and after the French Revolution of 1789. They included Olympe de Gouges, who was guillotined during the Terror, Germaine de Staël, Sophie Doin, and Claire de Duras, whose novella *Ourika* gives the perspective of a black slave woman. Gregory S. Brown, *A Field of Honor: Writers, Court Culture and Public Theater in French Literary Life from Racine to the Revolution* (New York: Columbia University Press, 2002); Doris Y. Kadish and Françoise Massardier-Kenney, eds., *Translating Slavery: Gender and Race in Frenchwomen's Writing, 1783–1823* (Kent OH: The Kent State University Press, 1994).

4. These new colonies included Algeria, French West and Equatorial Africa, Madagascar, and French Indochina. During the early Third Republic one feminist who immersed herself in this mediation was Hubertine Auclert, a republican who lived in Algeria from 1888 to 1892. Steven Hause, *Hubertine Auclert: The French Suffragette* (New Haven CT: Yale University Press, 1987), chapter 7; Carolyn J. Eichner, "*La citoyenne* in the World: Hubertine Auclert and Feminist Imperialism," *French Historical Studies* 32, no. 1 (Winter 2009): 63–84.

5. Janet R. Horne, "In Pursuit of Greater France: Visions of Empire among Musée Social Reformers, 1894–1931," in *Domesticating the Empire: Race, Gender and Family Life in French and Dutch Colonialism*, ed. Julia Ann Clancy-Smith and Frances Gouda (Charlottesville: University Press of Virginia, 1998), 36.

6. Conklin, "Redefining 'Frenchness,'" 287n11. Knibiehler and Goutalier explain that historians lack the sources that would allow us to gather statistics on women's presence in the colonies. Knibiehler and Goutalier, *La femme au temps des Colonies*, 19–20.

7. Conklin explores the transition to an administrative frame of mind which made a female presence in the colonies desirable in Conklin, "Redefining 'Frenchness.'" Natalism, the fear that France was being threat-

ened with a depopulation crisis, is discussed at length by Camiscioli, *Reproducing the French Race*, and Roberts, *Civilization Without Sexes*.

8. Sara L. Kimble, "Emancipation Through Secularization: French Feminist Views of Muslim Women's Condition in Interwar Algeria," *French Colonial History* 7 (2006): 109.

9. There are some fascinating correlations between French feminists' approaches to imperialism during the interwar years and those of British feminists at the turn of the century. Burton writes that "arguments for recognition as imperial citizens were predicated on the imagery of Indian women, whom British feminist writers depicted as helpless victims awaiting the representation of their plight and the redress of their condition." Whereas British feminists before World War I focused on Indian women to justify their own emancipation, French feminists after World War I responded differently to indigenous women in different parts of the world, distinguishing between African, Muslim, and Antillean women, and pausing to admire cultures that were more matriarchal than their own. Burton, *Burdens of History*, 7. See also Kathleen M. Blee, *Feminism and Antiracism: International Struggles for Justice* (New York: New York University Press, 2001); Wildenthal, *German Women for Empire*.

10. Camiscioli, *Reproducing the French Race*, chapter 5.

11. Christine Bard, *Les femmes dans la société française au 20e siècle* (Paris: Armand Colin, 2001), 92.

12. Martin, *Les Droits de la Femme*; Martin, *Féminisme et Coéducation*. At the BMD only two documents appear to mention her (091 MAR and 370 MAR).

13. Christine Bard, "Les féminismes en France. Vers l'intégration des femmes dans la Cité 1914–1940. Thèse de doctorat sous la direction de Michelle Perrot. Volume 4." (Université de Paris VII, 1993), 946.

14. Martin, *Les Droits de la Femme*, 30–31.

15. Martin, "Le Rôle des Femmes dans la Paix," 4.

16. BMD DOS NET, C. Nicault, "Yvonne Netter, avocate, militante, féministe et sioniste," *Archives Juives, Revue d'histoire des Juifs de France* 30, no. 1 (1er semestre 1997): 116–21 in sous-dossier "Articles sur Yvonne Netter (postérieurs à 1945)," 117.

17. BMD DOS NET, "Articles sur Yvonne Netter," Boîte No. 4, sous-dossier "Coupures Critiques des livres d'Yvonne Netter" and sous-dossier "Coupures de presse sur Yvonne Netter (entre-deux-guerres)." Her works included Yvonne Netter, *Le Code de la femme* (Paris: Editions du

Progrès Civique, 1926); Yvonne Netter, *Code pratique de la femme et de l'enfant* (Paris: Librairie Hachette, 1930); Yvonne Netter, *Plaidoyer pour la femme française* (Paris: Gallimard, 1936).

18. Netter, *Plaidoyer pour la femme française*, 23.

19. Conklin, "Who Speaks for Africa?," 307.

20. Works that trace the lives of Frenchwomen during World War I include: Margaret H. Darrow, *French Women and the First World War: War Stories of the Home Front* (Oxford: Berg, 2000); Laura Lee Downs, *Manufacturing Inequality: Gender Division in the French and British Metalworking Industries, 1914–1939* (Ithaca NY: Cornell University Press, 1995); Susan R. Grayzel, *Women's Identities at War: Gender, Motherhood, and Politics in Britain and France during the First World War* (Chapel Hill NC: University of North Carolina Press, 1999).

21. Conklin, "Redefining 'Frenchness,'" 67.

22. Hause and Kenney argue that suffrage was an established movement. Bard maintains that it was far more dynamic during the interwar years than many people assume. Steven Hause and Anne R. Kenney, *Women's Suffrage and Social Politics in the French Third Republic* (Princeton NJ: Princeton University Press, 1984); Bard, *Les femmes dans la société*. For more on suffrage in the French Third Republic see for example: Karen Offen, "Defining Feminism: A Comparative Historical Approach," *Signs* 14, no. 1 (Autumn, 1988); Karen Offen, "Depopulation, Nationalism, and Feminism in Fin-de-Siecle France," *The American Historical Review* 89, no. 3 (1984); Felicia Gordon and Máire Cross, *Early French Feminisms, 1830–1940: A Passion for Liberty* (Brookfield, VT: Elgar, 1996); Paul Smith, *Feminism and the Third Republic: Women's Political and Civil Rights in France, 1918–1945*, Oxford Historical Monographs (Oxford: Oxford University Press, 1996).

23. Bard, *Les femmes dans la société*, 90.

24. Hause and Kenney, *Women's Suffrage and Social Politics*, 36–37, 87.

25. Hause and Kenney, *Women's Suffrage*, 250.

26. Hause and Kenney, *Women's Suffrage*, 138, 250.

27. Even this moderation did not allow the UFSF to escape charges of leftist political activism. A March 8, 1933, letter written by Jean Vicat of the *Jeunesses Patriotes* charged: "An intense propaganda is currently being pushed all over France by l'UFSF" and "one must note that the 'Union' systematically conceals the names of its true leaders, too well known as members of the Radical-Socialist Party [sic], the Ligue des Droits de

l'Homme, and other left-wing organizations." Even moderate feminists could generate fear amongst certain cross-sections of the right-wing population. CAF, Fonds Brunschvicg, IAF197, Relations avec d'autres organismes.

28. Hause and Kenney, *Women's Suffrage and Social Politics*, 254.

29. Bard, *Les femmes dans la société*, chapter 4.

30. Mme Winter Frappier de Montbenoit, "L'Evolution de la femme indigène," *La Dépêche Africaine* 3, no. 24 (May 1930): 4.

31. Winter Frappier de Montbenoit, "L'Evolution," 4.

32. Mme Winter Frappier de Montbenoit, "Les femmes de couleur devant la colonisation," *La Dépêche Africaine* 3, no. 23 (15 April 1930): 2.

33. *Békés*, the white descendants of the first colonizers, form a ruling class in the old colonies and tend to have an extremely rigid understanding of race relations and hierarchies.

34. "Lois Malgaches—Le Mariage," La Femme aux Colonies, *La Française* (January 15, 1927).

35. On the Musée Social and its visions of Empire see Horne, "In Pursuit of Greater France." Winter-Frappié lectured at the Musée Social for example on December 27, 1929, on the topic of Malagasy women. "La Femme aux colonies," *La Française* (December 21 and 28, 1929).

36. Winter-Frappié, "Femmes Noires," La Femme dans les Colonies, *La Française* (March 26, 1927).

37. Soeur Marie-André du Sacré-Cœur, *La femme noire en Afrique occidentale* (Paris: Payot, 1939).

38. Sister Marie-André du Sacré-Cœur, excerpt from an article originally published in *L'Union*, "Revue de la Presse: La condition juridique de la femme noire," *La Française* (April 9, 1938).

39. "Afrique: Les Femmes de Kibiro," *La Française* (April 17, 1937).

40. Horne, "In Pursuit of Greater France," 39.

41. "Etats Généraux du Féminisme—La Femme dans la France Coloniale" and "Les Facilités du Déplacement" in *La Française* (May 9, 1931).

42. Cécile Brunschvicg, "Etats Généraux du Féminisme: Les Femmes dans la France Coloniale," *La Française* (May 2, 1931).

43. CAF, Fonds Cécile Brunschvicg, IAF253, Etats Généraux du Féminisme Session de 1931, préparation 1930–1931. The letter accompanying this questionnaire was originally written in December 1930 and signed by the president of the CNFF (at the time Mme Avril de Sainte-Croix) and the

Secretary General Mme Pichon-Landry. Women were asked to return the questionnaire by March 1, 1930, to Pichon-Landry.

44. R. Dogimont, "Les Femmes Missionnaires aux Colonies," *La Française* (July 11 and July 18, 1931). The articles reproduced her report to the Etats Généraux in its entirety.

45. Mme Marius Leblond, "Situation Légale et Morale de la Femme Indigène en Afrique Occidentale Française, Equatoriale, à Madagascar, dans les Vieilles Colonies," May 30–31, 1931, in CAF, Fonds Cécile Brunschvicg, 1AF253, Etats Généraux du Féminisme Session de 1931, préparation 1930–1931.

46. R. Dogimont, "Les Femmes Missionnaires aux Colonies," *La Française* (July 11, 1931).

47. Mme Letellier, "Les Carrières Médico-Sociales aux Colonies," May 30–31, 1931, in CAF, Fonds Cécile Brunschvicg, 1AF253, Etats Généraux du Féminisme Session de 1931, préparation 1930–1931.

48. CAF, Fonds CNFF, 2AF21, Etats Généraux du Féminisme 1931.

49. A notorious precursor to the women travelers explored here was Isabelle Eberhardt. Clancy-Smith, "'Passionate Nomad.'"

50. Jennifer E. Milligan, *The Forgotten Generation: French Women Writers of the Inter-War Period*, Berg French Studies (Oxford: Berg, 1996), 145. On women writers during this period, see also Susan Rubin Suleiman, *Subversive Intent: Gender, Politics, and the Avant-Garde* (Cambridge MA: Harvard University Press, 1990).

51. Anne Sauvy, "La littérature et les femmes," *Histoire de l'édition française*, ed. Henri Jean Martin, Roger Chartier, and Jean-Pierre Vivet (Paris: Promodis, 1982), 250. Patricia Lorcin notes two strains of colonial literature into which most white women writers fit: exoticism, illustrated during the Third Republic by Pierre Loti or Jules Verne, and "new" colonial realism. Lorcin, "Sex, Gender, and Race," 109.

52. Marthe Oulié, "Les animaux dans la peinture de la Créte préhellénique" (Université Paris IV, 1926).

53. BMD DOS OUL, newspaper clippings.

54. Travel novels produced by Oulié included Marthe Oulié, *Le prince de Ligne: un grand seigneur cosmopolite au XVIIIe siècle*, *Figures du passé* (Paris: Hachette, 1926); Marthe Oulié, *Jean Charcot* (Paris: Gallimard, 1938); Marthe Oulié, *Finlande, terre du courage* (Paris: Flammarion, 1940); Marthe Oulié, *Quand j'étais matelot*, la Route (Paris: Rédier, 1930); Marthe Oulié, *Bidon 5: En Rallye à travers le Sahara* (Bar-le-Duc: Ernest

Flammarion, 1931); Marthe Oulié and Hermine de Saussure, *Croisière de "Perlette," 1700 milles dans la mer Egée* (Paris: Hachette, 1926).

55. BMD DOS OUL, *La Française* (December 8, 1934) and (November 9, 1936).

56. Marthe Oulié, "Martiniquaises d'aujourd'hui," *La Française* 28, no. 1172 (December 14, 1935). Here *La Française* excerpted an article initially printed in *le Journal*.

57. Oulié, "Martiniquaises d'aujourd'hui."

58. Oulié, *Les Antilles Filles*, 36.

59. Oulié, *Les Antilles Filles*, 33.

60. Oulié, *Les Antilles Filles*, 128, 131.

61. Oulié, *Les Antilles Filles*, 186.

62. Oulié, *Les Antilles Filles*, 40.

63. Marthe Oulié, "La Femme dans la France coloniale," *La Française* (September 5, 1931). Original article in *L'Intransigeant*, n.d.

64. BMD, *Bulletin de l'Union des Femmes Coloniales* 14, no. 75 (January 1937).

65. Marthe Oulié, "Mlle Suzanne Sylvain érudite haïtienne," *La Française* 29, no. 1203 (October 10, 1936).

66. APP, BA2272, Mouvements féministes, sous-dossier Union Féminine française, "Lettre d'une Martiniquaise," Fort-de-France July 2, 1918, in *l'Evolution féminine* 1, no. 7 (July 7, 1918): 7. This excerpt was used by the anonymous author to disprove the stereotypes forced upon the Creole woman. The term Creole is ambivalent: although referring to white individuals from the colonies, the term denotes a racial difference between French Creoles and the metropolitan French. Miller, *Blank Darkness*, 93–107.

67. Thus did M. le recteur Hardy, in a November 1938 conference in Lille, describe the typical colonial woman. "La Femme coloniale," *La Française* (January 7 and 14, 1939).

68. Henriette d'Alexis, "Lettre d'Afrique," *La Française* (October 31, 1931).

69. Huguette Champy, "La Femme aux Colonies," *La Française* (February 16, 1935).

70. Ida R. Sée, "Infirmières coloniales," *La Française*, no. 1160 (September 21, 1935).

71. "It is not superfluous to point out to antifeminists, some of whom are notorious colonials, the important role of Frenchwomen in [spreading]

the civilization that France brings to African lands," wrote Mme Valentine Leblond in an article originally published in *La Vie* and reproduced as "Les Femmes Françaises au Togo," *La Française* (November 25, 1933).

72. BMD, DOS OUL, newspaper clippings.

73. Oulié tells the story of an old black man who was being congratulated on the marriage of his son, a *tirailleur*, to a white Parisian. The man's response was: "It's not possible. She wouldn't have wanted my son. She is perhaps very light, but she must not be a White woman [une Blanche] in the end!" Oulié, *Les Antilles Filles*, 185.

74. Sue Peabody and Tyler Edward Stovall, eds., *The Color of Liberty: Histories of Race in France* (Durham: Duke University Press, 2003), 3.

75. André Gide, *Voyage au Congo: carnets de route* (Paris: Gallimard, 1927); André Gide, *Le retour du Tchad: suite du Voyage au Congo, carnets de route* (Paris: Gallimard, 1928). Note that Cousturier's maiden name appears to have been Brû according to the BN-OPALE PLUS catalogue.

76. Susan Jean Brubaker-Cole, "Decentering Imperial Culture: Colonial Influences on French National Culture in the Literary Works of Cousturier, Soupault, Leblond and A. H. Bâ" (PhD diss., Yale University, 2000), 39.

77. CAOM, SLOTFOM V/6, *Les Continents* 1, no. 11 (October 15, 1924).

78. Lucie Cousturier, *Des inconnus chez moi*, 2nd ed. (Paris: Editions de la Sirène, 1920), 104.

79. Cousturier, *Inconnus chez moi*, 105.

80. Cousturier, *Inconnus chez moi*, 17.

81. Cousturier, *Inconnus chez moi*, 229.

82. Lucie Cousturier, *Mes inconnus chez eux: Mon amie Fatou, citadine*, 2 vols., vol. 1 (Paris: Rieder, 1925), 196–97.

83. Cousturier, *Inconnus chez moi*, 287.

84. Lucie Cousturier, *La Forêt du Haut-Niger*, ed. George Besson (Bruges, Belgium: les Cahiers d'aujourd'hui, 1923), 15. She returned to this theme in Lucie Cousturier, *Mes inconnus chez eux: Mon ami Soumaré, Laptot*, 2 vols., vol. 2 (Paris: Rieder, 1925), 106.

85. Cousturier, *Mon amie Fatou*, 42.

86. Cousturier, *Mon amie Fatou*, 161.

87. Cousturier, *Mon amie Fatou*, 218.

88. Cousturier, *Mon amie Fatou*, 245.

89. Cousturier, *Mon amie Fatou*, 173.

90. Cousturier, *Mon ami Soumaré*, 263.

91. Cousturier, *Mon ami Soumaré*, 262.

92. Cousturier, *Mon amie Fatou*, 205.

93. Cousturier, *Mon amie Fatou*, 94.

94. Roger Little, "René Maran on Lucie Cousturier, a Champion of Racial Understanding," *Research in African Literatures* 34, no. 1 (2003): 130.

95. CAOM, SLOTFOM V/6, Léon Werth, *Les Continents* 1, nos. 13 and 14 (November 15, 1924).

96. CAOM, 2MiA/242, *La Race Nègre* 1, no.1 (June 1, 1927): 2.

97. CAOM, SLOTFOM III/24, Ligue de défense de la Race Nègre, rapports d'Agents, June 12, 1928. The commemoration was also announced in CAOM, 2MiA/242, *La Race Nègre* 1, no.3 (May 5, 1928): 2.

98. CAOM, SLOTFOM III/78, Lettres de la Ligue à des particuliers, "Lettre de Kouyaté à Jean-Richard Bloch," May 17, 1935.

99. Pierre Baye-Salzmann, "Blanche et Noir par Madame Louise Faure-Favier," *La Dépêche Africaine* 1, no. 7 (September 1928): 6.

100. BMD DOS MOR. Very little information exists at the BMD. Moran's name is misspelled, and information about her husband is also sparse. Since Moran worked for the office of then Governor of Chad and future Governor-General of French West Africa Marcel de Coppet, it seems likely that her husband did too.

101. Ghislaine Lydon, "Women, Children and the Popular Front's Missions of Inquiry in French West Africa," in *French Colonial Empire and the Popular Front: Hope and Disillusion*, ed. Tony Chafer and Amanda Sackur (Basingstoke, UK: Palgrave Macmillan, 1999), 181. See also Ghislaine Lydon, "The Unraveling of a Neglected Source: A Report on Women in Francophone West Africa in the 1930s," *Cahiers d'Etudes Africaines* 37, no. 3 (1997). The report has recently been published as Denise Savineau, *La famille en AOF: Condition de la femme, rapport inédit, présentation et étude de Claire H. Griffiths* (Paris: L'Harmattan, 2007).

102. Moran also exposed French children to questions of race: Denise Moran, "Noirs et Blancs," *Les Livrets de Mon Camarade*, no. 14 (December 1, 1936).

103. Denise Moran, *Tchad*, Colonies et Colonisation (Paris: Gallimard, 1934), 15.

104. Moran, *Tchad*, 174.

105. Moran, *Tchad*, 261.

106. Her presence at meetings was documented by informants: CAOM, SLOTFOM III/73, sous-dossier "Ligue anti-impérialiste," May 1935.

107. Bibliothèque de documentation internationale contemporaine (BDIC), Fonds Ligue des droits de l'homme (LDH), F DELTA RES 798/68, dossier 6, February 16, 1935.

108. CAOM, SLOTFOM III/78, "Grand Gala pour la Fraternité des Races," March 18 (193?).

109. BHVP, Fonds Bouglé, Associations Pacifistes Boîte 1, Comité Mondial des Femmes, ed., *Rassemblement Mondial des Femmes!* (N.p.: Mondiales, n.d.).

110. CAF, IAF525, Fonds Brunschvicg, Relations avec les membres, sous-dossier "Comité National des Femmes contre la guerre et le fascisme," November 4, 1935.

111. "Un appel des femmes de race noire," *La Française* (September 21, 1935): 1.

112. "L'Exemple d'une Martiniquaise," *La Française* (May 20 and 27, 1939).

113. CAF, Fonds Brunschvicg, IAF30, "Congrès national de l'UFSF tenu à Paris les 26 et 27 juin 1937," original manifest written in October 1936.

114. Jane Catulle-Mendès, "Les Livres," *La Française* (June 30, 1934), in CAF, IAF323, Fonds Brunschvicg.

115. France Totsain, "The Popular Front and the Blum-Viollette Plan," in *French Colonial Empire and the Popular Front: Hope and Disillusion*, ed. Tony Chafer and Amanda Sackur (Basingstoke, UK: Palgrave Macmillan, 1999), 222.

116. CAF, Fonds CNFF, IAF21, Etats Généraux du Féminisme 1931.

117. "Le Vote des femmes et l'influence française aux colonies," *La Française* (June 25, 1932).

118. For an enlightening analysis of black versus white feminism, see Higginbotham, "African-American Women's History." On whiteness see also Tyler Edward Stovall, "National Identity and Shifting Imperial Frontiers: Whiteness and the Exclusion of Colonial Labor after World War I," *Representations*, no. 84 (2003).

119. See for example an article reprinted from *La Dépêche Coloniale* in *La Française*: Clotilde Chivas-Baron, "Le vote des femmes coloniales françaises," *La Française* (November 30, 1935). See also "Le Vote des femmes et l'influence française aux colonies," *La Française* (June 25, 1932).

120. G. Vallé-Genairon, "Le Vote des indigènes et les femmes françaises," *La Française* (January 30, 1937).

121. Clotilde Chivas-Baron, "Le vote des femmes coloniales françaises," *La Française* (November 30, 1935).

Conclusion

1. This image of a black man appeared on the masthead starting in August 1931. It faded in and out and after early 1933 was rarely seen.

2. Felix Driver and David Gilbert, eds., *Imperial cities: Landscape, Display and Identity* (Manchester: Manchester University Press, 1999).

3. Thanks to Eve Rosenhaft for sharing this information, which she found through the Red Cross International Tracing Service. On the Mauthausen camp records see Marin Wetzlmaier and Sugyu Özkan, "In ihren Augen waren wir Tiere," *Salzburger Nachrichten* (May 27, 2009).

4. Aimé Césaire, *Cahier d'un retour au pays natal*, with a preface by André Breton (Paris: Bordas, 1947).

5. Aimé Césaire was amongst those who suggested that colonial practices led to a progressive "savaging" of the European continent, making colonial practices akin in some ways to fascism. Bernadette Cailler, "De Simone Weil à Aimé Césaire: Hitlérisme et entreprise coloniale," *L'Esprit Créateur*, no. 32 (1992): 101. On Vichy's impact overseas see Eric Thomas Jennings, *Vichy in the Tropics: Pétain's National Revolution in Madagascar, Guadeloupe, and Indochina, 1940–1944* (Stanford CA: Stanford University Press, 2001); Dennis McEnnerney, "Frantz Fanon, The Resistance, and the Emergence of Identity Politics," *The Color of Liberty: Histories of Race in France*, ed. Sue Peabody and Tyler Stovall (Durham NC: Duke University Press, 2003).

6. "Pour une lecture critique de 'Tropiques,'" Aimé Césaire and René Ménil, "Tropiques," (Paris: Jean-Michel Place, 1978), xxv. Also see René Ménil, "Sous l'Amiral Robert: *Tropiques* Témoin de la Vie Culturelle," *La Martinique sous l'Amiral Robert, Les Cahiers du CERAG*, no. 37 (1979).

7. "Entretien avec Aimé Césaire par Jacqueline Leiner," Césaire and Ménil, "Tropiques," viii.

8. Léopold Sédar Senghor, ed., *Anthologie de la nouvelle poésie nègre et malgache de langue française, précédée de Orphée Noir par Jean-Paul Sartre* (Paris: Presses universitaires de France, 1948).

9. Léopold Sédar Senghor, "Comment nous sommes devenus ce que nous sommes," *Afrique Action* (January 30, 1961): 17.

10. Musil, "*La Marianne Noire*", 179–80.

11. Musil, "*La Marianne Noire*", 188–89.

12. Claire Duchen, *Women's Rights and Women's Lives in France 1944–1968* (New York: Routledge, 1994); Joan Wallach Scott, *Parité!: Sexual Equality and the Crisis of French Universalism* (Chicago: University of Chicago Press, 2005).

13. BMD, DOS NET, Boîte numéro 4, Sous-dossier "Articles sur Yvonne Netter (postérieurs à 1945)," C. Nicault, "Yvonne Netter, avocate, militante féministe et sioniste," *Archives Juives* 30, no. 1 (1997): 116–21.

14. The BMD keeps an open dossier for articles on Baker. BMD DOS BAK.

15. The ongoing reproduction of racial images has been analyzed by a number of scholars, including Auslander and Holt, "Sambo in Paris"; Rosello, *Declining the Stereotype*.

16. For discussions of race, exclusion, and identity in the second half of the twentieth century, see for example Herrick Chapman and Laura Frader, eds., *Race in France: Interdisciplinary Perspectives on the Politics of Difference* (New York: Berghahn Books, 2004); Herman Lebovics, *Bringing the Empire Back Home: France in the Global Age* (Durham NC: Duke University Press, 2004); Benjamin Stora and Emile Temime, eds., *Immigrances: L'immigration en France au XXe siècle* (Paris: Hachette, 2007).

17. Daniel Maximin, *L'Isolé soleil* (Paris: Éditions du Seuil, 1981), 128.

18. Paulette Nardal, "Actions de Grâces,"*La Dépêche Africaine* 2, no. 14 (May 1929): 3.

19. CAOM, 2MiA/242, *La Voix des Nègres*, "Le Mot Nègre" 1, no. 1 (January 1927): 1.

BIBLIOGRAPHY

Archival Sources

Archives de la Préfecture de Police de Paris (APP). Séries BA, DA, GA.

Archives Nationales, Section contemporaine (AN). Séries F7 and F21.

Archives Nationales, Dakar, Sénégal (ANS). Séries 2G and 11D.

Bibliothèque de l'Arsenal des Arts et du Spectacle (ARS). Collection Rondel.

Bibliothèque de Documentation Internationale Contemporaine (BDIC). Fonds Ligue des Droits de l'Homme (LDH).

Bibliothèque Historique de la Ville de Paris (BHVP). Fonds Bouglé.

Bibliothèque Marguerite Durand (BMD).

Centre des Archives du Féminisme (CAF). Fonds Brunschvicg and Fonds CNFF (includes *La Française*).

Centre des Archives d'Outre-Mer (CAOM). Série Service de Liaison avec les Originaires des Territoires Français d'Outre-Mer (SLOTFOM); 2MiA242 (newspapers).

Colin, Paul, Georges Thénon (Rip), and Josephine Baker. *Le Tumulte Noir*. Paris: Editions d'Art Succès, 193?

Congrès Générale du Travail Unitaire (Section française de l'International Syndicale Rouge). "Congrès National Ordinaire, 6ème Congrès de la C.G.T.U." Paris, November 8–14, 1931. Conférence Nationale Féminine, Conférence des Jeunes Travailleurs.

Conseil National des Femmes Françaises. *Etats Généraux du Féminisme*. 1931.

Institut de la Mémoire de l'Edition Contemporaine (IMEC). Fonds Flammarion.

Numéro spécial du Droit des Femmes, "La Femme Indigène" 27. Paris: Edition de La Ligue Française pour le Droit des Femmes, September 1931.

Published Works

Abatino, Pepito, and Josephine Baker. *Pepito Abatino présente Josephine Baker vue par la presse française*. Paris: Editions Isis, 1931.

Ako, Edward O. "L'Etudiant Noir and the Myth of the Genesis of the Negritude Movement." *Research in African Literatures* 15, no. 3 (1984): 341–53.

Alber, Jean-Luc, Claudine Bavoux, and Michel Watin, eds. *Métissages Tome II: Linguistique et anthropologie*. Paris: L'Harmattan, 1992.

Allegret, Marc. *Zou Zou*. 1934; New York: Kino, 1989.

Amselle, Jean-Loup, ed. *Les migrations africaines: réseaux et processus migratoires*. Paris: Librairie François Maspero, 1976.

Andrew, Dudley. *Mists of Regret: Culture and Sensibility in Classic French Film*. Princeton NJ: Princeton University Press, 1995.

Archer-Straw, Petrine. *Negrophilia: Avant-Garde Paris and Black Culture in the 1920s*. New York: Thames & Hudson, 2000.

Asante, S. K. B. *Pan-African Protest: West Africa and the Italo-Ethiopian Crisis, 1934–1941*. London: Longman, 1977.

Au Temps du Boeuf sur le Toit 1918–1928. Paris: Artcurial, 1981.

August, Thomas G. *The Selling of the Empire: British and French Imperialist Propaganda, 1890–1940*. Westport CT: Greenwood, 1985.

Auslander, Leora, and Thomas C. Holt. "Sambo in Paris: Race and Racism in the Iconography of the Everyday." In *The Color of Liberty: Histories of Race in France*, edited by Sue Peabody and Tyler Edward Stovall, 147–84. Durham NC: Duke University Press, 2003.

Baker, Jean Claude, and Chris Chase. *Joséphine: Une vie mise à nue*. Translated by Marie-France Pavillet. Paris: Editions A Contrario, 1995.

Baker, Josephine, Jo Bouillon, and Jacqueline Cartier. *Joséphine*. Collection Vécu. Paris: R. Laffont, 1976.

Baker, Josephine, and André Rivollet. *Une vie de toutes les couleurs: souvenirs recuellis par André Rivollet*. Collection "Arc-en-ciel." Grenoble: B. Arthaud, 1935.

Baker, Josephine, and Marcel Sauvage. *Les mémoires de Joséphine Baker*. 4th ed. Paris: Kra, 1927.

Baldwin, Kate A. *Beyond the Color Line and the Iron Curtain: Reading Encounters between Black and Red, 1922–1963*. Durham NC: Duke University Press, 2002.

Balesi, Charles John. *From Adversaries to Comrades-in-Arms: West Africans and the French Military, 1885–1918.* Waltham MA: African Studies Association, 1979.

Balibar, Etienne. "Le racisme de classe." In *Race, nation, classe: Les identités ambiguës,* edited by Etienne Balibar and Immanuel Wallerstein, 272–88. Paris: Découverte & Syros, 1997.

Bard, Christine. "Les féminismes en France. Vers l'intégration des femmes dans la Cité 1914–1940. Thèse de doctorat sous la direction de Michelle Perrot. Volume 4." Université de Paris VII, 1993.

————. *Les femmes dans la société française au 20e siècle.* Paris: Armand Colin, 2001.

Barou, Jacques. *Travailleurs africains en France: Rôle des cultures d'origine.* Grenoble: Presses Universitaires de Grenoble, 1978.

Baudelaire, Charles. *Un peintre de la vie moderne, Constantin Guys.* Paris: Keiffer, 1923.

Baysse, Géo. *En dansant la biguine, Souvenir de l'Exposition coloniale.* Paris: Senlis, 1931.

Becker, Lucille Frackman. *Twentieth-Century French Women Novelists.* Boston MA: G. K. Hall, 1989.

Bederman, Gail. *Manliness & Civilization: A Cultural History of Gender and Race in the United States, 1880–1917.* Chicago: University of Chicago Press, 1995.

Benjamin, Walter. "Paris, Capital of the Nineteenth Century." In *Reflections: Essays, Aphorisms, Autobiographical Writing,* 146–62. New York: Schocken, 1986.

Benjamin, Walter, and Rolf Tiedemann. *The Arcades Project.* Cambridge MA: Belknap, 1999.

Benoist, Jean. "Le métissage: biologie d'un fait social, sociologie d'un fait biologique." In *Métissages Tome II: Linguistique et anthropologie,* edited by Jean-Luc Alber, Claudine Bavoux, and Michel Watin, 13–22. Paris: L'Harmattan, 1992.

Berenson, Edward. *The Trial of Madame Caillaux.* Berkeley: University of California Press, 1993.

Bergner, Gwen. "Who Is that Masked Woman? Or, the Role of Gender in Fanon's *Black Skin, White Masks.*" PMLA 110, no. 1 (1995): 75–88.

Berlière, Jean-Marc. *La police des moeurs sous la IIIe République.* Paris: Seuil, 1992.

————. "A Republican Political Police? Political Policing in France under the Third Republic, 1875–1940." In *The Policing of Politics in the*

Twentieth Century: Historical Perspectives, edited by Mark Mazower, 27–55. Providence RI: Berghahn, 1997.

Berliner, Brett A. *Ambivalent Desire: The Exotic Black Other in Jazz-Age France*. Amherst: University of Massachusetts Press, 2002.

Bernard-Duquenet, Nicole. "Les débuts du syndicalisme au Sénégal au temps du Front populaire." *Le Mouvement social*, no. 101 (1977): 37–59.

Blake, Jody. *Le Tumulte Noir: Modernist Art and Popular Entertainment in Jazz-Age Paris, 1900–1930*. University Park: Pennsylvania State University Press, 1999.

Blanc-Chaléard, Marie-Claude, Caroline Douki, Nicole Dyonet, and Vincent Milliot, eds. *Police et migrants: France 1667–1939*. Rennes: Presses Universitaires de Rennes, 2001.

Blanchard, Pascal, Eric Deroo, and Gilles Manceron. *Le Paris noir*. Paris: Hazan, 2001.

Blanche, Jacques-Emile. *Propos de peintre, de Gauguin à la Revue Nègre*. Paris: Emile-Paul Frères, 1928.

Blee, Kathleen M. *Feminism and Antiracism: International Struggles for Justice*. New York: New York University Press, 2001.

Bodek, Richard. "The Not-So-Golden Twenties: Everyday Life and Communist Agitprop in Weimar-Era Berlin." *Journal of Social History* 30, no. 1 (1996): 55–78.

Boittin, Jennifer Anne. "Black in France: The Language and Politics of Race during the Late Third Republic." *French Politics, Culture & Society* 27, no. 2 (Summer 2009): 23–46.

———. "In Black and White: Gender, Race Relations, and the Nardal Sisters in Interwar Paris." *French Colonial History* 6 (2005): 119–35.

Bonnet, Jean-Charles. *Les Pouvoirs publics français et l'immigration dans l'entre-deux-guerres*. Lyon: Centre d'histoire économique et sociale de la région lyonnaise, 1976.

Bonvoisin, Samra-Martine, and Michèle Maignien. *La presse féminine*. Paris: Presses Universitaires de France, 1986.

Borshuk, Michael. "An Intelligence of the Body: Disruptive Parody through Dance in the Early Performances of Josephine Baker." In *Embodying Liberation: The Black Body in American Dance*, edited by Dorothea Fischer-Hornung and Allison Goeller, 41–57. Piscataway NJ: Transaction, 2001.

———. "'Queen of the Colonial Exposition': Josephine Baker's Strategic Performance." In *Critical Voicings of Black Liberation: Resistance and*

Representation in the Americas, edited by Hermine D. Pinson, Kimberly L. Phillips, Lorenzo Thomas, and Hanna Wallinger, 47–66. Piscataway NJ: Transaction, 2003.

Bossoutrot, Lucien. *La Belle aventure du Goliath de Paris à Dakar.* Paris: La Renaissance du Livre, 1925.

Breton, André, Paul Eluard, et al. "Ne Visitez pas l'Exposition Coloniale." May 1931. In *Tracts Surréalistes et Déclarations Collectives*, edited by José Pierre, 194–95. Paris: Eric Losfeld, 1980.

Bricktop, and James Haskins. *Bricktop.* New York: Atheneum, 1983.

Brown, Gregory S. *A Field of Honor: Writers, Court Culture and Public Theater in French Literary Life from Racine to the Revolution.* New York: Columbia University Press, 2002.

Brubaker-Cole, Susan Jean. "Decentering Imperial Culture: Colonial Influences on French National Culture in the Literary Works of Cousturier, Soupault, Leblond and A. H. Bâ." PhD diss., Yale University, 2000.

Brunet, Jean-Paul. *La police de l'ombre: Indicateurs et provocateurs dans la France contemporaine.* Paris: Seuil, 1990.

————. *Saint-Denis la ville rouge: Socialisme et communisme en banlieue ouvrière 1890–1939.* Paris: Hachette, 1980.

Buñuel, Luis. *My Last Sigh.* Translated by Abigail Israel. New York: Knopf, 1983.

Burton, Antoinette M. *Burdens of History: British Feminists, Indian Women, and Imperial Culture, 1865–1915.* Chapel Hill: University of North Carolina Press, 1994.

————. *Dwelling in the Archive: Women Writing House, Home, and History in Late Colonial India.* New York: Oxford University Press, 2003.

Cailler, Bernadette. "De Simone Weil à Aimé Césaire: Hitlérisme et entreprise coloniale." *L'Esprit Créateur*, no. 32 (1992): 97–107.

Camara, De la, and Pepito Abatino. *Mon sang dans tes veines.* Paris: Isis, 1931.

Camiscioli, Elisa. *Reproducing the French Race: Immigration, Intimacy, and Embodiment in the Early Twentieth Century.* Durham NC: Duke University Press, 2009.

Camp, Jean, and André Corbier. *A Lyauteyville, Promenade humoristique et sentimentale à travers l'Exposition Coloniale.* Paris: N.E.A., 1931.

Carby, Hazel V. *Race Men.* Cambridge MA: Harvard University Press, 1998.

—————. *Reconstructing Womanhood: The Emergence of the Afro-American Woman Novelist.* New York: Oxford University Press, 1987.

Carter, Dan T. *Scottsboro: A Tragedy of the American South.* Baton Rouge: Louisiana State University Press, 1969.

Caute, David. *The Fellow-Travellers: Intellectual Friends of Communism.* Rev. ed. New York: Yale University Press, 1988.

Célestin, Roger. *From Cannibals to Radicals: Figures and Limits of Exoticism.* Minneapolis: University of Minnesota Press, 1996.

Césaire, Aimé. *Cahier d'un retour au pays natal.* With a preface by André Breton. Paris: Bordas, 1947.

Césaire, Aimé, and Alioune Diop. "Lettre à Maurice Thorez." Paris: Présence Africaine, 1956.

Césaire, Aimé, and René Ménil. "Tropiques." Paris: Jean-Michel Place, 1978.

Chafer, Tony, and Amanda Sackur. *French Colonial Empire and the Popular Front: Hope and Disillusion.* Basingstoke, UK: Palgrave Macmillan, 1999.

Chanson-Jabeur, Chantal, and Odile Goerg, eds. *"Mama Africa": Hommage à Catherine Coquery-Vidrovitch.* Paris: L'Harmattan, 2005.

Chapman, Herrick, and Laura Frader, eds. *Race in France: Interdisciplinary Perspectives on the Politics of Difference.* New York: Berghahn, 2004.

Chaudenson, Robert. "Mulâtres, métis, créoles . . ." In *Métissages Tome II: Linguistique et anthropologie,* edited by Jean-Luc Alber, Claudine Bavoux, and Michel Watin, 23–37. Paris: L'Harmattan, 1992.

Chaudhuri, Nupur, and Margaret Strobel, eds. *Western Women and Imperialism: Complicity and Resistance.* Bloomington: Indiana University Press, 1992.

Chevalier, Louis. *Classes laborieuses et classes dangereures à Paris pendant la première moitié du XIXe siècle.* Paris: rééd. Le Livre de poche Pluriel, 1984.

—————. *La formation de la population parisienne au XIXe siècle.* Paris: Presses Universitaires de France, 1950.

Chivas-Baron, Clotilde. "De la préparation de la femme à la vie coloniale." In *La Vie aux Colonies: préparation de la femme à la vie coloniale,* edited by Fédération Française de l'Enseignement Ménager. Paris: Larose, 1938.

—————. *La femme française aux colonies.* Vies coloniales 2. Paris: Larose, 1929.

————. "Le milieu colonial." In *La Vie aux Colonies: préparation de la femme à la vie coloniale*, edited by Fédération Française de l'Enseignement Ménager. Paris: Larose, 1938.

Clancy-Smith, Julia. "The 'Passionate Nomad' Reconsidered: A European Woman in *L'Algérie Française* (Isabelle Eberhardt, 1877–1904)." In *Western Women and Imperialism: Complicity and Resistance*, edited by Nupur Chaudhuri and Margaret Strobel, 61–78. Bloomington: Indiana University Press, 1992.

Clancy-Smith, Julia Ann, and Frances Gouda. *Domesticating the Empire: Race, Gender, and Family Life in French and Dutch Colonialism*. Charlottesville: University Press of Virginia, 1998.

Clifford, James. "1933 February: Negrophilia." In *A New History of French Literature*, edited by Denis Hollier, 901. Cambridge MA: Harvard University Press, 1989.

————. "On Ethnographic Surrealism." In *The Predicament of Culture: Twentieth-Century Ethnography, Literature, and Art*, 117–51. Cambridge MA: Harvard University Press, 1988.

Cohen, William B. *The French Encounter with Africans: White Response to Blacks, 1530–1880*. Bloomington: Indiana University Press, 1980.

Colin, Paul. *La Croûte: souvenirs*. Paris: Table Ronde, 1957.

————. *Paul Colin et les spectacles: Nancy, Musée des beaux-arts, 2 mai–31 juillet 1994*. Nancy: Musée des beaux-arts, 1994.

Collins, Patricia Hill. *Black Feminist Thought: Knowledge, Consciousness, and the Politics of Empowerment*. 2nd ed. New York: Routledge, 2000.

Comité Mondial des Femmes, ed. *Rassemblement Mondial des Femmes!* N.p.: Mondiales, n.d.

Condemi, Concetta. *Les Cafés-Concerts, histoire d'un divertissement*. Paris: Quai Voltaire, 1992.

Conklin, Alice. "Redefining 'Frenchness': Citizenship, Race Regeneration, and Imperial Motherhood in France and West Africa, 1914–40." In *Domesticating the Empire: Race, Gender, and Family Life in French and Dutch Colonialism*, edited by Julia Ann Clancy-Smith and Frances Gouda, 65–83. Charlottesville: University Press of Virginia, 1998.

————. "Who Speaks for Africa? The René Maran-Blaise Diagne Trial in 1920s Paris." In *The Color of Liberty: Histories of Race in France*, edited by Sue Peabody and Tyler Edward Stovall, 302–37. Durham NC: Duke University Press, 2003.

Conklin, Alice L. *A Mission to Civilize: The Republican Idea of Empire in*

France and West Africa, 1895–1930. Stanford CA: Stanford University Press, 1997.

Cooper, Frederick. *Colonialism in Question: Theory, Knowledge, History*. Berkeley and Los Angeles: University of California Press, 2005.

———. "Decolonizing Situations: The Rise, Fall, and Rise of Colonial Studies, 1951–2001." *French Politics, Culture, & Society* 20, no. 2 (2002): 47–76.

Cooper, Frederick, and Laura Ann Stoler, eds. *Tensions of Empire: Colonial Cultures in a Bourgeois World*. Berkeley and Los Angeles: University of California Press, 1997.

Coquery-Vidrovitch, Catherine. "Colonisation ou impérialisme: la politique africaine de la France entre les deux guerres." *Mouvement Social* 107 (1979): 51–76.

———. "La colonisation française 1931–1939." In *Histoire de la France Coloniale 1914–1990*, edited by J. Thobie, G. Meynier, C. Coquery-Vidrovitch and C.-R. Ageron. Paris: Armand Colin, 1990.

———. "Nationalité et citoyenneté en Afrique occidentale français: Originaires et citoyens dans le Sénégal colonial." *Journal of African History* 42, no. 2 (2001): 285–305.

Corbin, Alain. *Le miasme et la jonquille: l'odorat et l'imaginaire social XVIIIe–XIXe siècles*. Collection historique. Paris: Aubier Montaigne, 1982.

———. *Le territoire du vide: l'Occident et le désir du rivage, 1750–1840*. Collection historique. Paris: Aubier, 1988.

———. *Le village des cannibales*. Collection historique. Paris: Aubier, 1990.

———. *Les cloches de la terre: paysage sonore et culture sensible dans les campagnes au XIXe siècle*. L'Evolution de l'humanité. Paris: A. Michel, 1994.

———. *Les filles de noce: misère sexuelle et prostitution, 19e et 20e siècles*. Collection historique. Paris: Aubier Montaigne, 1978.

———. "Les paysans de Paris: Histoire des Limousins du bâtiment au XIXe siècle." *Ethnologie française* 10 (1980): 169–76.

Cousturier, Lucie. *Des inconnus chez moi*. 2nd ed. Paris: Sirène, 1920.

———. *La Forêt du Haut-Niger*. Edited by George Besson. Bruges, Belgium: Les Cahiers d'aujourd'hui, 1923.

———. *Mes inconnus chez eux*. Vol. 2, *Mon ami Soumaré, Laptot*. Paris: Rieder, 1925.

————. *Mes inconnus chez eux*. Vol. 1, *Mon amie Fatou, citadine*. Paris: Rieder, 1925.

Cunard, Nancy. *Black Man and White Ladyship: An Anniversary*. Toulon: A. Bordato, 1931.

————. *These Were the Hours: Memoirs of My Hours Press Réanville and Paris 1928–1931*. Carbondale: Southern Illinois University Press, 1969.

————, ed. *Negro: anthology*. London: Wishart, 1934.

Daix, Pierre. *La vie quotidienne des surréalistes 1917–1932*. Paris: Hachette, 1993.

Dalton, Karen C. C., and Henry Louis Gates Jr. "Josephine Baker and Paul Colin: African American Dance Seen through Parisian Eyes." *Critical Inquiry* 24, no. 4 (1998): 903–34.

Damas, Léon, and Robert Desnos. *Pigments*. Paris: GLM, 1937.

Darrow, Margaret H. *French Women and the First World War: War Stories of the Home Front*. Oxford: Berg, 2000.

Daum, Christophe. *Les associations de Maliens en France: Migrations, développement et citoyenneté*. Paris: Karthala, 1998.

Delattre, Simone. *Les douze heures noires: la nuit à Paris au XIXe siècle*. Evolution de l'humanité. Paris: Albin Michel, 2000.

Demartini, Anne-Emmanuelle and Dominique Kalifa, ed. *Imaginaire et sensibilités au XIXe siècle: études pour Alain Corbin*. Paris: Créaphis, 2005.

Desanti, Dominique. *La femme au temps des années folles*. Paris: Stock / L. Pernoud, 1984.

Deschamps, Hubert. "France in Black Africa and Madagascar between 1920 and 1945." In *Colonialism in Africa 1870–1960*, vol. 2, edited by L. H. Gann and P. Duignan, 226–50. Cambridge: Cambridge University Press, 1970.

Dewitte, Philippe. "Le Paris noir de l'entre-deux-guerres." In *Le Paris des étrangers depuis un siècle*, edited by André Kaspi and Antoine Marès, 156–69. Paris: Imprimerie nationale, 1989.

————. *Les Mouvements nègres en France 1919–1939*. Paris: L'Harmattan, 1985.

Doane, Mary Ann. *Femmes Fatales: Feminism, Film Theory, Psychoanalysis*. New York: Routledge, 1991.

Downs, Laura Lee. *Manufacturing Inequality: Gender Division in the French and British Metalworking Industries, 1914–1939*. Ithaca NY: Cornell University Press, 1995.

Driver, Felix, and David Gilbert, eds. *Imperial Cities: Landscape, Display, and Identity*. Manchester: Manchester University Press, 1999.

Dubuis, Olivier. *L'Afrique reconnue: Panorama de la littérature négro-africaine*. Kinshasa, Zaire: Editions Leco, 1969.

Duchen, Claire. *Women's Rights and Women's Lives in France 1944–1968*. New York: Routledge, 1994.

Dufoix, Patrick Weil and Stéphane, ed. *L'esclavage, la colonisation, et après* . . . Paris: Presses Universitaires de France, 2005.

Echenberg, Myron. *Colonial Conscripts: The Tirailleurs Sénégalais in French West Africa, 1857–1960*. Portsmouth NH: Heinemann, 1991.

Edwards, Brent Hayes. "Pebbles of Consonance: A Reply to Critics." *Small Axe* 9, no. 17 (March 2005): 134–49.

———. *The Practice of Diaspora: Literature, Translation, and the Rise of Black Internationalism*. Cambridge MA: Harvard University Press, 2003.

Edwards, Tim. *Cultures of Masculinity*. New York: Routledge, 2006.

Eichner, Carolyn J. "*La citoyenne* in the World: Hubertine Auclert and Feminist Imperialism." *French Historical Studies* 32, no. 1 (Winter 2009): 63–84.

Eksteins, Modris. *Rites of Spring: The Great War and the Birth of the Modern Age*. New York: Anchor, 1990.

Evans, Martha Noel. *Masks of Tradition: Women and the Politics of Writing in Twentieth-Century France*. New York: Cornell University Press, 1987.

Ezra, Elizabeth. *The Colonial Unconscious: Race and Culture in Interwar France*. Ithaca NY: Cornell University Press, 2000.

Fabre, Michel. *La Rive noire: les écrivains noirs américains à Paris, 1830–1995*. Collection La rive noire. Marseille: Dimanche éditeur, 1999.

Fall, Mar. *Les Africains noirs en France: des tirailleurs sénégalais aux . . . blacks*. Paris: L'Harmattan, 1986.

Fanon, Frantz. *Black Skin, White Masks*. Translated by Charles Lam Markmann. New York: Grove, 1967.

———. *Peau noir, masques blancs*. Paris: Seuil, 1952.

———. *Toward the African Revolution (Political Essays)*. Translated by Haakon Chevalier. New York: Grove, 1969.

Faure-Favier, Louise. *Blanche et Noir*. Paris: Ferenczi et Fils, 1928.

———. *Ces choses qui seront vieilles*. Paris: La Renaissance du livre, 1919.

———. *De mes fenêtres sur la Seine, poèmes*. Paris: Points et Contrepoints, 1953.

——. *Guide des voyages aériens, Paris-Lausanne*. Paris: Bernard, 1922.

——. *Guide des voyages aériens, Paris-Londres*. Paris: Bernard, 1921.

——. *Guide des voyages aériens, Paris-Tunis, Paris-Lyon-Marseille-Ajaccio-Tunis, Tunis-Bône et Lyon-Genève*. Paris: Bernard, 1930.

——. *Les Chevaliers de l'air*. Paris: La Renaissance du livre, 1922.

——. *Notre île Saint-Louis*. Paris: Montjoie, 1946.

——. *Six contes et deux rêves*. Paris: Figuière, 1918.

——. *Souvenirs sur Guillaume Apollinaire*. Paris: Grasset, 1945.

——. *Visages de la Seine*. Paris: Points et Contrepoints, 1951.

Fédération Française de l'Enseignement Ménager, ed. *La Vie aux Colonies: préparation de la femme à la vie coloniale*. Paris: Larose, 1938.

Fletcher, Yaël Simpson. "'Capital of the Colonies': Real and Imagined Boundaries between Metropole and Empire in 1920s Marseilles." In *Imperial Cities: Landscape, Display, and Identity*, edited by Felix Driver and David Gilbert, 136–54. Manchester: Manchester University Press, 1999.

——. "Unsettling Settlers: Colonial Migrants and Racialized Sexuality in Interwar Marseilles." In *Gender, Sexuality, and Colonial Modernities*, edited by Antoinette Burton. New York: Routledge, 1999.

Fogarty, Richard S. *Race and War in France: Colonial Subjects in the French Army, 1914–1918*. War/Society/Culture. Baltimore: Johns Hopkins University Press, 2008.

Forbes, Jack D. *Africans and Native Americans: The Language of Race and the Evolution of Red-Black Peoples*. 2nd ed. Urbana: University of Illinois Press, 1993.

Forth, Christopher E., and Bertrand Taithe, eds. *French Masculinities: History, Culture and Politics*. Basingstoke, UK: Palgrave Macmillan, 2007.

Fourcaut, Annie. *Bobigny, banlieue rouge*. Paris: Les Editions Ouvrières et Presses de la Fondation Nationale des Sciences Politiques, 1986.

Fritzsche, Peter. *Reading Berlin 1900*. Cambridge MA: Harvard University Press, 1996.

Gandoulou, Justin-Daniel. *Au coeur de la Sape: Moeurs et aventures des Congolais à Paris*. Paris: L'Harmattan, 1989.

Garelick, Rhonda K. *Rising Star: Dandyism, Gender, and Performance in the Fin de Siècle*. Princeton NJ: Princeton University Press, 1998.

Garrioch, David. *Neighbourhood and Community in Paris, 1740–1790*. Cambridge Studies in Early Modern History. Cambridge: Cambridge University Press, 1986.

Gendron, Bernard. *Between Montmartre and the Mudd Club: Popular Music and the Avant-Garde*. Chicago: University of Chicago Press, 2002.

Gide, André. *Le retour du Tchad: suite du Voyage au Congo, carnets de route*. Paris: Gallimard, 1928.

————. *Voyage au Congo: carnets de route*. Paris: Gallimard, 1927.

Gilloch, Graeme, and Walter Benjamin. *Myth and Metropolis: Walter Benjamin and the City*. Cambridge, UK: Polity, 1996.

Gilmore, Glenda Elizabeth. *Gender and Jim Crow: Women and the Politics of White Supremacy in North Carolina, 1896–1920*. Chapel Hill: University of North Carolina Press, 1996.

Gilroy, Paul. *The Black Atlantic: Modernity and Double Consciousness*. Cambridge MA: Harvard University Press, 1993.

Ginio, Ruth. *French Colonialism Unmasked: The Vichy Years in French West Africa*. Lincoln: University of Nebraska Press, 2006.

Girardet, Raoul. *L'idée coloniale en France*. Paris: Table Ronde, 1972.

Glaes, Gillian Beth. "The Mirage of Fortune: West African Immigration to Paris and the Development of a Post-Colonial Immigrant Community, 1960–1981." PhD diss., University of Wisconsin–Madison, 2007.

Goddard, Chris. *Jazz Away From Home*. New York: Paddington, 1979.

Goodman, James E. *Stories of Scottsboro*. New York: Vintage Books, 1994.

Gordon, Felicia, and Máire Cross. *Early French Feminisms, 1830–1940: A Passion for Liberty*. Brookfield VT: Elgar, 1996.

Gorsuch, Anne E. "Soviet Youth and the Politics of Popular Culture during NEP." *Social History* 17, no. 2 (1992): 189–201.

Grayzel, Susan R. *Women's Identities at War: Gender, Motherhood, and Politics in Britain and France during the First World War*. Chapel Hill: University of North Carolina Press, 1999.

Green, Nancy L. *Repenser les migrations*. Le noeud gordien. Paris: Presses Universitaires de France, 2002.

Gréville, Edmond. *Princesse Tam Tam*. 1935; New York: Kino, 2005.

Griaule, Marcel. *Mission ethnographique et linguistique Dakar-Djibouti organisée par l'Institut d'ethnologie de l'Université de Paris et le Muséum national d'histoire naturelle*, 1930.

Gruber, Helmut and Pamela Graves, eds. *Women and Socialism/Socialism and Women: Europe between the Two World Wars*. New York: Berghahn, 1998.

Gumplowicz, Philippe. *Le roman du jazz première époque: 1893–1930.* Paris: Librairie Arthème Fayard, 1991.

Guy-Sheftall, Beverly, ed. *Words of Fire: An Anthology of African-American Feminist Thought.* New York: New Press, 1995.

Habermas, Jürgen. *The Structural Transformation of the Public Sphere: An Inquiry into a Category of Bourgeois Society.* Translated by Thomas Burger. 10th ed. Cambridge MA: MIT Press, 1999.

Haggerty, Michael, and Michel Leiris. "L'Autre qui apparaît chez vous." *Jazz Magazine* 325 (1984): 34–36.

Haine, W. Scott. *World of the Paris Cafe: Sociability Among the French Working Class, 1789–1914.* Baltimore: Johns Hopkins University Press, 1996.

Hale, Dana S. "French Images of Race on Product Trademarks during the Third Republic." In *The Color of Liberty: Histories of Race in France,* edited by Sue Peabody and Tyler Edward Stovall, 131–46. Durham NC: Duke University Press, 2003.

———. *Races on Display: French Representations of Colonized Peoples, 1886–1940.* Bloomington: Indiana University Press, 2008.

Hall, Catherine. *Civilizing Subjects: Metropole and Colony in the English Imagination, 1830–1867.* Chicago: University of Chicago Press, 2002.

Haney, Lynn. *Naked at the Feast: A Biography of Josephine Baker.* New York: Dodd, Mead, 1981.

Hargreaves, J.D. "The Comintern and Anti-Colonialism: New Research Opportunities." *African Affairs* 92, no. 357 (1993): 255–61.

Hause, Steven. *Hubertine Auclert: The French Suffragette.* New Haven CT: Yale University Press, 1987.

Hause, Steven, and Anne R. Kenney. "The Limits of Suffragist Behavior: Legalism and Militancy in France, 1876–1922." *American Historical Review* 86, no. 4 (1981): 781–806.

———. *Women's Suffrage and Social Politics in the French Third Republic.* Princeton NJ: Princeton University Press, 1984.

Hélenon, Véronique. "Races, statut juridique et colonisation: Antillais et Africains dans les cadres administratifs des colonies françaises d'Afrique." In *L'esclavage, la colonisation et après . . . France, Etats-Unis, Grande-Bretagne,* edited by Patrick Weil and Stéphane Dufoix, 229–43. Paris: Presses Universitaires de France, 2005.

Hemery, D. "Du patriotisme au marxisme: l'immigration vietnamienne en France de 1926 à 1930." *Le Mouvement social* 90 (1975): 3–54.

Higginbotham, Evelyn Brooks. "African-American Women's History and the Metalanguage of Race." *Signs* 17, no. 2 (Winter 1992): 251–74.

———. *Righteous Discontent: The Women's Movement in the Black Baptist Church, 1880–1920.* Cambridge MA: Harvard University Press, 1993.

Higonnet, Patrice. *Paris: Capital of the World.* Cambridge MA: Belknap, 2002.

Hobsbawm, Eric. *Uncommon People: Resistance, Rebellion and Jazz.* New York: New Press, 1998.

Hodeir, Catherine, and Michel Pierre. *L'exposition coloniale.* La Mémoire du siècle. Brussels: Complexe, 1991.

Hollier, Denis. *Absent without Leave: French Literature under the Threat of War.* Translated by Catherine Porter. Cambridge MA: Harvard University Press, 1997.

Horkheimer, Max, and Theodor W. Adorno. "The Culture Industry: Enlightenment as Mass Deception." In *Dialectic of Enlightenment: Philosophical Fragments*, edited by Gunzelin Schmid Noerr, 94–136. Stanford CA: Stanford University Press, 2002.

Horne, Janet R. "In Pursuit of Greater France: Visions of Empire among Musée Social Reformers, 1894–1931." In *Domesticating the Empire: Race, Gender, and Family Life in French and Dutch Colonialism*, edited by Julia Ann Clancy-Smith and Frances Gouda, 21–42. Charlottesville: University Press of Virginia, 1998.

Horne, John. "Immigrant Workers in France During World War I." *French Historical Studies* 14, no. 1 (Spring 1985): 57–88.

Hugon, Anne, ed. *Histoire des femmes en situation coloniale: Afrique et Asie, XXe siècle.* Paris: Karthala, 2004.

Huyssen, Andreas. *After the Great Divide: Modernism, Mass Culture, Postmodernism.* Bloomington: Indiana University Press, 1986.

Hymans, Jacques Louis. *Léopold Sédar Senghor: An Intellectual Bibliography.* Edinburgh: Edinburgh University Press, 1971.

Institut national de la statistique et des études économiques. *Les Etrangers en France.* Paris: INSEE, 1994.

Irele, Abiola. "Pan-Africanism and African Nationalism." *Odu* 6 (1971): 111–19.

Jackson, Irene Dobbs. "La Négritude: marche d'un phénomène." In *Littératures ultramarines de langue française: genèse et jeunesse*, edited by Thomas H. Geno and Roy Julow, 21–31. Sherbrooke QC: Naaman, 1974.

Jackson, Jeffrey H. *Making Jazz French: Music and Modern Life in Interwar Paris*, American Encounters/Global Interactions. Durham NC: Duke University Press, 2003.

Jennings, Eric Thomas. *Vichy in the Tropics: Pétain's National Revolution in Madagascar, Guadeloupe, and Indochina, 1940–1944.* Stanford CA: Stanford University Press, 2001.

Jensen, Robert. *Marketing Modernism in Fin-de-Siècle Europe.* Princeton NJ: Princeton University Press, 1994.

Johnson, Wesley G., Jr. *The Emergence of Black Politics in Senegal: The Struggle for Power in the Four Communes, 1900–1920.* Stanford CA: Stanford University Press, 1971.

Joran, Théodore. *Les Féministes avant le féminisme.* Paris, 1910.

Jordan, Matthew F. "Jazz Changes: A History of French Discourse on Jazz from Ragtime to Be-Bop." PhD diss., Claremont Graduate School, 1998.

Jules-Rosette, Bennetta. *Black Paris: The African Writers' Landscape.* Urbana: University of Illinois Press, 1998.

———. "Identity Discourses and Diasporic Aesthetics in Black Paris: Community Formation and the Translation of Culture." *Diaspora: A Journal of Transnational Studies* 9, no. 1 (2000): 39–58.

———. "Josephine Baker and Utopian Visions of Black Paris." *Journal of Romance Studies* 5, no. 3 (2005): 33–50.

———. *Josephine Baker in Art and Life: The Icon and the Image.* Urbana: University of Illinois Press, 2007.

———. "Two Loves: Josephine Baker as Icon and Image." *Emergences* 10, no. 1 (2000): 55–77.

Kadish, Doris Y., and Françoise Massardier-Kenney, eds. *Translating Slavery: Gender and Race in French Women's Writing, 1783–1823.* Kent OH: Kent State University Press, 1994.

Kahnweiler, Daniel-Henry. "L'Art nègre et le cubisme." *Présence Africaine* 3 (1948): 367–77.

Kalifa, Dominique. *Crime et culture au XIXe siècle.* Paris: Perrin, 2005.

Kaspi, André, and Antoine Marès, eds. *Le Paris des étrangers depuis un siècle.* Paris: Imprimerie Nationale, 1989.

Kater, Michael H. "Forbidden Fruit? Jazz in the Third Reich." *American Historical Review* 94, no. 1 (1989): 11–43.

Kesteloot, Lilyan. "Les Ecrivains noirs de langue française: Naissance d'une littérature." Doctoral, Université Libre de Bruxelles, Institut de Sociologie, 1963.

Kimble, Sara L. "Emancipation through Secularization: French Feminist Views of Muslim Women's Condition in Interwar Algeria." *French Colonial History* 7 (2006): 109–28.

King, Adele. *French Women Novelists: Defining a Female Style.* Basingstoke, UK: Macmillan, 1989.

Knibiehler, Yvonne, and Régine Goutalier. *La femme au temps des Colonies.* Paris: Stock, 1984.

Lahs-Gonzales, Olivia, ed. *Josephine Baker: Image and Icon.* St. Louis MO: Reedy, 2006.

Lambert, Raphaël. "The Construction of the Other and the Self in André Gide's *Travels in the Congo* and Frantz Fanon's *Black Skin, White Masks.*" *Studies in Twentieth Century Literature* 27, no. 2 (2003): 291–310.

Langley, J. Ayo. "Pan-Africanism in Paris, 1924–36." *Journal of Modern African Studies* 7, no. 1 (1969): 69–94.

Large, David Clay. *Between Two Fires: Europe's Path in the 1930s.* New York: Norton, 1990.

Léardée, Ernest, Jean Pierre Meunier, Brigitte Léardée, and Gaston Monnerville. *La Biguine de l'Oncle Ben's: Ernest Léardée raconte.* Paris: Caribéennes, 1989.

Lebovics, Herman. *Bringing the Empire Back Home: France in the Global Age.* Durham NC: Duke University Press, 2004.

———. *Imperialism and the Corruption of Democracies.* Durham NC: Duke University Press, 2006.

———. *True France: Wars Over Cultural Identity, 1900–1945.* Ithaca NY: Cornell University Press, 1992.

Légitime Défense. Paris: Jean-Michel Place, 1979.

Leiris, Michel. *L'âge d'homme.* Paris: Editions Gallimard, 1939.

Lemercier, Claire. "Le Club du Faubourg: Tribune libre de Paris, 1918–1939." Master's thesis, Institut d'études politiques de Paris, 1995.

Lemke, Sieglinde. *Primitivist Modernism: Black Culture and the Origins of Transatlantic Modernism.* New York: Oxford University Press, 1998.

"Léon Damas: Interviewed Feb. 18, 1977." *Journal of Caribbean Studies* 1, no. 1 (Winter 1980): 63–73.

Lewis, Mary Dewhurst. *The Boundaries of the Republic: Migrant Rights and the Limits of Universalism in France, 1918–1940.* Stanford CA: Stanford University Press, 2007.

————. "The Company of Strangers: Policing Migration and Nation in Marseille." *French Politics, Culture, & Society* 20, no. 3 (Fall 2002): 65–96.

————. "The Strangeness of Foreigners: Policing Migration and Nation in Interwar Marseille." In *Race in France: Interdisciplinary Perspectives on the Politics of Difference*, edited by Herrick Chapman and Laura Frader, 77–107. New York: Berghahn, 2004.

Liauzu, Claude. *Aux origines des tiers-mondismes: colonisés et anticolonialistes en France 1919–1939.* Paris: L'Harmattan, 1982.

Little, Roger. "Blanche et Noir: Louise Faure-Favier and the Liberated Woman." *Australian Journal of French Studies* 36, no. 2 (1999): 214–28.

————. "René Maran on Lucie Cousturier, a Champion of Racial Understanding." *Research in African Literatures* 34, no. 1 (2003): 126–36.

Lorcin, Patricia. "Sex, Gender, and Race in the Colonial Novels of Elissa Rhaïs and Lucienne Favre." In *The Color of Liberty: Histories of Race in France*, edited by Sue Peabody and Tyler Stovall, 108–30. Durham NC: Duke University Press, 2003.

Lunn, Joe. *Memoirs of the Maelstrom: A Senegalese Oral History of the First World War.* Oxford: James Currey, 1999.

Lüsebrink, Hans-Jürgen. "Métissage culturel et société coloniale: émergence et enjeux d'un débat, de la presse coloniale aux premiers écrivains africains (1935–1947)." In *Métissages Tome I: Littérature-histoire*, edited by Jean-Claude Carpanin Marimoutou and Jean-Michel Racault, 109–18. Paris: L'Harmattan, 1992.

Lydon, Ghislaine. "The Unraveling of a Neglected Source: A Report on Women in Francophone West Africa in the 1930s." *Cahiers d'Etudes Africaines* 37, no. 3 (1997): 555–84.

————. "Women, Children and the Popular Front's Missions of Inquiry in French West Africa." In *French Colonial Empire and the Popular Front: Hope and Disillusion*, edited by Tony Chafer and Amanda Sackur, 170–87. Basingstoke, UK: Palgrave Macmillan, 1999.

MacMaster, Neil. *Colonial Migrants and Racism: Algerians in France, 1900–62.* London: MacMillan, 1997.

Marimoutou, Jean-Claude Carpanin, and Jean-Michel Racault, eds. *Métissage Tome I: Littérature-histoire.* Paris: L'Harmattan, 1992.

Manchuelle, François. "Background to Black African Emigration to France: The Labor Migrations of the Soninke, 1848–1987." PhD diss., University of California Santa Barbara, 1987.

——. *Willing Migrants: Soninke Labor Diasporas, 1848–1960.* Athens: Ohio University Press, 1997.

Mann, Gregory. "Immigrants and Arguments in France and West Africa." *Comparative Studies in Society and History* 45, no. 2 (2003): 362–85.

——. "Locating Colonial Histories: Between France and West Africa." *American Historical Review* 110, no. 2 (2005): 409–34.

——. *Native Sons: West African Veterans and France in the Twentieth Century.* Durham NC: Duke University Press, 2006.

Maran, René. *Batouala: Véritable roman nègre.* Paris: Albin Michel, 1938.

——. *Un homme pareil aux autres.* Paris: Albin Michel, 1947.

Margueritte, Victor. *La Garçonne.* Paris: Flammarion, 1922.

Markovitz, Irving Leonard. *Léopold Sédar Senghor and the politics of Negritude.* New York: Atheneum, 1969.

Martin, Denis-Constant, and Olivier Roueff. *La France du jazz: Musique, modernité et identité dans la première moitié du XXe siècle.* Marseille: Parenthèses, 2002.

Martin, Marguerite. *Féminisme et coéducation.* Paris: Rivière, 1914.

——. "Le Rôle des femmes dans la paix." Paper presented at the Ordre Maçonnique Mixte International le Droit humain, Fédération Française, Salle des Fêtes du Grand Orient de France, Paris 13e, Thursday, February 25, 1926.

——. *Les Droits de la femme.* Paris: Rivière, 1912.

Martinkus-Zemp, Ada. *Le Blanc et le Noir: essai d'une description de la vision du Noir par le Blanc dans la littérature française de l'entre-deux-guerres.* Paris: Nizet, 1975.

Matsuda, Matt K. *Empire of Love: Histories of France and the Pacific.* Oxford: Oxford University Press, 2005.

Mauco, Georges. *Les étrangers en France et le problème du racisme.* Paris: La pensée universelle, 1984.

——. *Les étrangers en France: Leur rôle dans l'activité économique.* Paris: Armand Colin, 1932.

Maximin, Daniel. *L'Isolé soleil.* Paris: Seuil, 1981.

Maza, Sarah. *The Myth of the French Bourgeoisie: An Essay on the Social Imaginary, 1750–1850.* Cambridge MA: Harvard University Press, 2003.

Mazower, Mark, ed. *The Policing of Politics in the Twentieth Century: Historical Perspectives.* Providence RI: Berghahn, 1997.

McClellan, Woodford. "Africans and Black Americans in the Comintern Schools, 1925–1934." *International Journal of African Historical Studies* 26, no. 2 (1993): 371–90.

McEnnerney, Dennis. "Frantz Fanon, The Resistance, and the Emergence of Identity Politics." In *The Color of Liberty: Histories of Race in France*, edited by Sue Peabody and Tyler Stovall, 95–107. Durham NC: Duke University Press, 2003.

McKay, Claude. *Banjo*. London: X Press, 2000.

———. *A Long Way from Home*. London: Pluto, 1985.

McMillan, James F. *Housewife or Harlot: The Place of Women in French Society, 1870–1940*. New York: St. Martin's, 1981.

Ménil, René. "Sous l'Amiral Robert: *Tropiques* Témoin de la Vie Culturelle." *La Martinique sous l'Amiral Robert, Les Cahiers du* CERAG, no. 37 (1979): 144–53.

Merriman, John M. *The Margins of City Life: Explorations on the French Urban Frontier, 1815–1851*. New York: Oxford University Press, 1991.

Messaadi, Sakina. *Nos sœurs musulmanes ou le mythe féministe, civilisateur, évangélisateur du messianisme colonialiste dans l'Algérie colonisée*. Alger: Houma, 2002.

Michel, Marc. *Les Africains et la Grande Guerre: L'appel à l'Afrique (1914–1918)*. Paris: Karthala, 2003.

Midgley, Clare, ed. *Gender and Imperialism*. Manchester: Manchester University Press, 1998.

Miller, Christopher L. *Blank Darkness: Africanist Discourse in French*. Chicago: University of Chicago Press, 1985.

———. "Hallucinations of France and Africa in the Colonial Exhibition of 1931 and Ousmane Socé's Mirages de Paris." *Paragraph: A Journal of Modern Critical Theory* 18, no. 1 (1995): 39–63.

———. *Nationalists and Nomads: Essays on Francophone African Literature and Culture*. Chicago: University of Chicago Press, 1998.

Miller, J. A., Susan D. Pennybacker, and Eve Rosenhaft. "Mother Ada Wright and the International Campaign to Free the Scottsboro Boys, 1931–1934." *American Historical Review* 106, no. 2 (2001): 387–430.

Milligan, Jennifer E. *The Forgotten Generation: French Women Writers of the Inter-War Period*. Oxford: Berg, 1996.

Milza, Pierre. "Le fascisme italien à Paris." *Revue d'histoire moderne et contemporaine* 30 (July–September 1983): 420–52.

———, ed. *Les Italiens en France de 1914 à 1940*. Rome: Ecole française de Rome, 1986.

Mitchell, Timothy. *Colonising Egypt*. Berkeley: University of California Press, 1991.

Moneta, Jakob. *La politique du Parti communiste français dans la question coloniale, 1920–1963.* Paris: Maspero, 1971.

Moody, Bill. *The Jazz Exiles: American Musicians Abroad.* Reno: University of Nevada Press, 1993.

Moran, Denise. *Cette sacrée gamine.* Paris: La Bibliothèque Française, 1945.

———. *Le meurtre d'André Aliker.* Paris: Défense-éditions, 1936.

———. "Noirs et Blancs." *Les Livrets de Mon Camarade,* no. 14 (December 1, 1936).

———. *Ta douce moitié.* Paris: la Bibliothèque Française, 1946.

———. *Tchad.* Colonies et Colonisation. Paris: Gallimard, 1934.

Morlat, Patrice. *La répression coloniale au Vietnam (1908–1940).* Paris: L'Harmattan, 1990.

———. *Les affaires politiques de l'Indochine, 1895–1923: les grands commis, du savoir au pouvoir.* Paris: Harmattan, 1995.

Moro, Adriana. *Négritude e Cultura Francese, Surrealismo chiave della Négritude?* Alessandria, Italy: Orso, 1992.

Mosse, George L. *The Image of Man: The Creation of Modern Masculinity.* New York: Oxford University Press, 1996.

Müller, Ernst Wilhelm. "L'Etudiant Noir, négritude et racisme: Critique d'une critique." *Anthropos: International Review of Anthropology and Linguistics* 91, no. 1–3 (1996): 5–18.

Musil, Emily Kirkland McTighe. *"La Marianne Noire:* How Gender & Race in the Twentieth Century Atlantic World Reshaped the Debate about Human Rights." PhD diss., UCLA, 2007.

Naison, Mark. *Communists in Harlem during the Depression.* Urbana: University of Illinois Press, 1983.

Nardal, Paulette. "Martinique" and "Guadeloupe." In *Guides des Colonies Françaises, Martinique, Guadeloupe, Guyane et St. Pierre-Miquelon.* Paris: Société d'Editions Géographiques, Maritimes et Coloniales, 1931.

Nenno, Nancy. "Femininity, the Primitive, and Modern Urban Space: Josephine Baker in Berlin." In *Women in the Metropolis: Gender and Modernity in Weimar Culture,* edited by Katharina von Ankum, 145–61. Berkeley and Los Angeles: University of California Press, 1997.

Netter, Yvonne. *Code pratique de la femme et de l'enfant.* Paris: Hachette, 1930.

———. *Le Code de la femme.* Paris: Progrès Civique, 1926.

———. *Plaidoyer pour la femme française.* Paris: Gallimard, 1936.

Noiriel, Gérard. *Le creuset français: histoire de l'immigration, XIX–XXe siècle.* 1988. Reprint, Paris: Seuil, 1992.

Noiriel, Gérard, and Dominique Borne. *Population, immigration et identité nationale en France: XIXe–XXe siècle.* Paris: Hachette, 1992.

Norindr, Panivong. *Phantasmatic Indochina: French Colonial Ideology in Architecture, Film, and Literature.* Durham NC: Duke University Press, 1996.

Nye, Robert A. *Masculinity and Male Codes of Honor in Modern France.* New York: Oxford University Press, 1993.

Offen, Karen. "Defining Feminism: A Comparative Historical Approach." *Signs* 14, no. 1 (Autumn 1988): 119–57.

——. "Depopulation, Nationalism, and Feminism in Fin-de-Siecle France." *American Historical Review* 89, no. 3 (1984): 648–76.

Onana, Charles. *Joséphine Baker contre Hitler: La star noire de la France Libre.* Paris: Duboiris, 2006.

Orwell, George. *Down and Out in Paris and London.* London: Penguin, 2001.

Ory, Pascal. "L'histoire culturelle de la France contemporaine: question et questionnement." *Vingtième Siècle* 16 (Oct.–Dec. 1987): 67–82.

Oulié, Marthe. *Bidon 5: En Rallye à travers le Sahara.* Bar-le-Duc, France: Flammarion, 1931.

——. *Charcot of the Antarctic.* New York: Dutton, 1939.

——. *Décoration égéenne.* Paris: Calavas, 1926.

——. *Finlande, terre du courage.* Paris: Flammarion, 1940.

——. *Jean Charcot.* Paris: Gallimard, 1938.

——. *Le cosmopolitisme du prince de Ligne: 1735–1814.* Paris: Hachette, 1926.

——. *Le prince de Ligne; un grand seigneur cosmopolite au XVIIIe siècle.* Figures du passé. Paris: Hachette, 1926.

——. "Les animaux dans la peinture de la Créte préhellénique." Université Paris IV, 1926.

——. *Les Antilles, filles de France: Martinique, Guadeloupe, Haïti.* Voyageuses de lettres. Paris: Fasquelle, 1935.

——. *Quand j'étais matelot.* La Route. Paris: Rédier, 1930.

Oulié, Marthe, and Hermine de Saussure. *Croisière de "Perlette," 1700 milles dans la mer Egée.* Paris: Hachette, 1926.

Ourgaut, Ch. *La surveillance des étrangers en France: thèse pour le doctorat présentée et soutenue publiquement en Décembre 1937 par Ch. Ourgaut.*

Université de Toulouse. *Faculté de Droit.* Toulouse: Imprimerie du Sud-Ouest, 1937.

Ousmane, Sembène. *Le docker noir.* Paris: Présence Africaine, 1973.

Paligot, Carole Reynaud. *Races, racisme et antiracisme.* Paris: Presses Universitaires de France, 2007.

Panassié, Hughes. *Le Jazz Hot.* Paris: R. A. Corrêa, 1934.

Pandolfi, Jean. "De Légitime Défense à Tropiques: Invitation à la Découverte." *Europe: Revue Littéraire Mensuelle* (1980): 97–107.

Peabody, Sue, and Tyler Edward Stovall, eds. *The Color of Liberty: Histories of Race in France.* Durham NC: Duke University Press, 2003.

Perrot, Michelle. "Les rapports entre ouvriers français et étrangers, 1871–1893." *Bulletin de la Société d'histoire moderne* 12, no. 1 (1960): 4–9.

Person, Yves. "Le Front populaire au Sénégal (mai 1936–octobre 1938)." *Le Mouvement social* 107 (1979): 77–101.

Peters, Erica J. "Resistance, Rivalries, and Restaurants: Vietnamese Workers in Interwar France." *Journal of Vietnamese Studies* 2, no. 3 (2007): 109–43.

Pierre, José, ed. *Collectives Tome 1, 1922–1939.* Paris: Losfeld, 1980.

Poiger, Uta G. *Jazz, Rock, and Rebels: Cold War Politics and American Culture in a Divided Germany.* Berkeley and Los Angeles: University of California Press, 2000.

Ponty, Janine. *Polonais méconnus: Histoire des travailleurs immigrés en France dans l'entre-deux-guerres.* Paris: Publications de la Sorbonne, 1990.

Pratt, Mary Louise. *Imperial Eyes: Travel Writing and Transculturation.* London: Routledge, 1992.

Putnam, Walter. "Writing the Wrongs of French Colonial Africa: *Voyage au Congo* and *Le Retour du Tchad.*" In *André Gide's Politics: Rebellion and Ambivalence,* edited by Tom Conner, 89–110. New York: Palgrave, 2000.

Quiminal, Catherine. *Gens d'ici, Gens d'ailleurs: Migrations Soninké et transformations villageoises.* Paris: Bourgois, 1991.

Rabinbach, Anson. "Introduction: Legacies of Antifascism." *New German Critique,* no. 67 (Winter 1996): 3–17.

Randrianja, Solofo. *Société et luttes anticoloniales à Madagascar.* Paris: Karthala, 2001.

Regester, Charlene. "The Construction of an Image and the Deconstruction of a Star: Josephine Baker Racialized, Sexualized, and Politicized in the African American Press, the Mainstream Press, and FBI Files." *Popular Music and Society* 24, no. 1 (2000): 31–84.

Rey, René. *La police des étrangers en France: thèse pour le doctorat présentée et soutenue le 15 mai 1937 à 14 heures par René Rey*. Université de Paris. Faculté de Droit. Paris: Presses Modernes, 1937.

Rifkin, Adrian. *Street Noises: Parisian Pleasure 1900–40*. New York: Manchester University Press, 1995.

Roberts, Mary Louise. *Civilization without Sexes: Reconstructing Gender in Postwar France, 1917–1927*. Women in Culture and Society. Chicago: University of Chicago Press, 1994.

Rochefort, Florence. "La citoyenneté interdite ou les Enjeux du suffragisme." *Vingtième Siècle*, no. 42 (1994): 41–51.

Rose, Phyllis. *Jazz Cleopatra: Josephine Baker in Her Time*. New York: Doubleday, 1989.

Rosello, Mireille. *Declining the Stereotype: Ethnicity and Representation in French Cultures*. Contemporary French Culture and Society. Hanover NH: University Press of New England, 1997.

Rosenberg, Clifford. *Policing Paris: The Origins of Modern Immigration Control Between the Wars*. Ithaca NY: Cornell University Press, 2006.

Rosenhaft, Eve. "Organizing the 'Lumpenproletariat': Cliques and Communists in Berlin during the Weimar Republic." In *The German Working Class 1888–1933*, edited by Richard J. Evans, 174–219. Totowa NJ: Barnes & Noble, 1982.

Saada, Emmanuelle. *Les enfants de la colonie: Les métis de l'Empire français entre sujétion et citoyenneté*. Paris: Découverte, 2007.

———. "Race and Sociological Reason in the Republic: Inquiries on the Métis in the French Empire (1908–37)." *International Sociology* 17, no. 3 (2002): 361–91.

———. "Une nationalité par degré: Civilité et citoyenneté en situation coloniale." In *L'esclavage, la colonisation, et après . . .*, edited by Patrick Weil and Stéphane Dufoix, 193–227. Paris: Presses Universitaires de France, 2005.

Sablé, Victor. *Mémoires d'un foyalais: Des îles d'Amérique aux bords de la Seine*. Paris: Maisonneuve et Larose, 1993.

Sachs, Maurice. *Au temps du Boeuf sur le Toit*. Paris: Nouvelle Revue Critique, 1939.

Sacré-Cœur, Soeur Marie-André du. *La femme noire en Afrique occidentale*. Paris: Payot, 1939.

Sauvage, Marcel. *Les secrets de l'Afrique Noir: sous le feu de l'équateur*. 1937. Reprint, Paris: Grasset, 1981.

—. *Voyages et aventures de Joséphine Baker*. Paris: Marcel Seheur, 1931.

Sauvy, Anne. "La littérature et les femmes." In *Histoire de l'édition française*, vol. 4, edited by Henri Jean Martin, Roger Chartier, and Jean-Pierre Vivet, 243–55. Paris: Promodis, 1982.

Savineau, Denise. *La famille en AOF: Condition de la femme, rapport inédit*, edited by Claire H. Griffiths. Paris: L'Harmattan, 2007.

Schaeffner, André, and André Coeuroy. *Le Jazz*. 1926. Reprint, Paris: Jean-Michel Place, 1988.

Schneider, William H. *An Empire for the Masses: The French Popular Image of Africa, 1870–1900*. Westport CT: Greenwood, 1982.

Schor, Ralph. *L'immigration en France 1919–1939: Sources imprimées en langue française et filmographie*. Nice: Centre de la Méditerranée Moderne et Contemporaine, 1986.

Schulman, Seth Matthew. "The Celebrity Culture of Modern Nightlife: Music-Hall, Dance, and Jazz in Interwar Paris, 1918–1930." PhD diss., Brown University, 2000.

Schwartz, Vanessa R. *Spectacular Realities: Early Mass Culture in Fin-de-Siècle Paris*. Berkeley and Los Angeles: University of California Press, 1998.

Scott, James C. *Domination and the Arts of Resistance: Hidden Transcripts*. New Haven CT: Yale University Press, 1990.

—. *Weapons of the Weak: Everyday Forms of Peasant Resistance*. New Haven CT: Yale University Press, 1985.

Scott, Joan Wallach. "Gender: A Useful Category of Historical Analysis." In *Feminism and History*, edited by Joan Wallach Scott, 152–80. New York: Oxford University Press, 1996.

—. *Only Paradoxes to Offer: French Feminists and the Rights of Man*. Cambridge MA: Harvard University Press, 1996.

—. *Parité!: Sexual Equality and the Crisis of French Universalism*. Chicago: University of Chicago Press, 2005.

Semidei, Manuela. "Les socialistes français et le problème colonial entre les deux guerres (1919–1939)." *Revue française de sciences politiques* XVIII, no. 6 (1968): 1117–53.

Senghor, Léopold Sédar, ed. *Anthologie de la nouvelle poésie nègre et mal-gache de langue française, précédée de Orphée Noir par Jean-Paul Sartre.* Paris: Presses universitaires de France, 1948.

————. *The Collected Poetry.* Translated by Melvin Dixon. CARAF Books. Charlottesville: University Press of Virginia, 1991.

————. "Comment nous sommes devenus ce que nous sommes." *Afrique Action* (January 30, 1961): 16–18.

————. "Pierre Teilhard de Chardin et la Politique Africaine." In *Cahiers Pierre Teilhard de Chardin.* Paris: Seuil, 1962.

Sharpe, Jenny. *Allegories of Empire: The Figure of Woman in the Colonial Text.* Minneapolis: University of Minnesota Press, 1993.

Sharpley-Whiting, T. Denean. *Black Venus: Sexualized Savages, Primal Fears, and Primitive Narratives in French.* Durham NC: Duke University Press, 1999.

————. "Erasures and the Practice of Diaspora Feminism." *Small Axe 9,* no. 17 (March 2005): 129–33.

————. *Negritude Women.* Minneapolis: University of Minnesota Press, 2002.

Shepard, Todd. *The Invention of Decolonization: The Algerian War and the Remaking of France.* Ithaca NY: Cornell University Press, 2006.

Silverman, Maxim. *Deconstructing the Nation: Immigration, Racism, and Citizenship in Modern France.* London: Routledge, 1992.

Silverstein, Paul A. *Algeria in France: Transpolitics, Race, and Nation.* Bloomington: Indiana University Press, 2004.

Sinha, Mrinalini. "Britishness, Clubbability, and the Colonial Public Sphere: The Genealogy of an Imperial Institution in Colonial India." *Journal of British Studies 40,* no. 4 (October 2001): 489–521.

————. *Colonial Masculinity: The "Manly Englishman" and the "Effeminate Bengali" in the Late Nineteenth Century.* Manchester: Manchester University Press, 1995.

Slavin, David. *Colonial Cinema and Imperial France, 1919–1939: White Blind Spots, Male Fantasies, Settler Myths.* Baltimore: Johns Hopkins University Press, 2001.

————. "The French Left and the Rif War, 1924–25: Racism and the Limits of Internationalism." *Journal of Contemporary History 26,* no. 1 (1991): 5–32.

Smith, Paul. *Feminism and the Third Republic: Women's Political and Civil Rights in France, 1918–1945.* Oxford: Oxford University Press, 1996.

Smith, Richard. *Jamaican Volunteers in the First World War: Race, Masculinity and the Development of National Consciousness.* Manchester, UK: Manchester University Press, 2004.

Smith, Robert P., Jr. "Black Like That: Paulette Nardal and the Negritude Salon." *CLA Journal* 45, no. 1 (2001): 53–68.

Socé, Ousmane. *Mirages de Paris.* Paris: Latines, 1937.

Spiegler, James. "Aspects of Nationalist Thought among French-Speaking West Africans, 1921–1939." PhD thesis, Oxford University, 1968.

Spire, Alexis. *Etrangers à la carte: L'administration de l'immigration en France, 1945–1975.* Paris: Grasset, 2005.

Spivak, Gayatri Chakravorty. "Can the Subaltern Speak?" In *Marxism and the Interpretation of Culture,* edited by Cary Nelson and Lawrence Grossbert, 271–313. Urbana: University of Illinois Press, 1988.

Starr, S. Frederick. *Red and Hot: The Fate of Jazz in the Soviet Union, 1917–1991.* 2nd ed. New York: Limelight, 1994.

Steins, Martin. "Les antécédents et la génèse de la Négritude senghorienne." PhD thesis, Université de Paris III–Sorbonne Nouvelle, 1980.

Stephens, Michelle Ann. *Black Empire: The Masculine Global Imaginary of Caribbean Intellectuals in the United States, 1914–1962.* Durham NC: Duke University Press, 2005.

———. "Disarticulating Black Internationalisms: West Indian Radicals and *The Practice of Diaspora.*" *Small Axe* 9, no. 17 (March 2005): 100–11.

Stora, Benjamin. "Les Algériens dans le Paris de l'entre-deux-guerres." In *Le Paris des étrangers depuis un siècle,* edited by André Kaspi and Antoine Marès, 140–55. Paris: Imprimerie nationale, 1989.

Stora, Benjamin, and Emile Temime, eds. *Immigrances: L'immigration en France au XXe siècle.* Paris: Hachette, 2007.

Stovall, Tyler Edward. "The Color Line behind the Lines: Racial Violence in France during the Great War." *American Historical Review* 103, no. 3 (1998): 737–69.

———. "From Red Belt to Black Belt: Race, Class, and Urban Marginality in Twentieth-Century Paris." In *The Color of Liberty: Histories of Race in France,* edited by Sue Peabody and Tyler Stovall, 351–69. Durham NC: Duke University Press, 2003.

———. "Love, Labor, and Race: Colonial Men and White Women in France during the Great War." In *French Civilization and Its Discontents: Nationalism, Colonialism, Race,* edited by Tyler Edward Stovall and Georges Van Den Abbeele, 297–31. Lanham MD: Lexington, 2003.

―――. "National Identity and Shifting Imperial Frontiers: Whiteness and the Exclusion of Colonial Labor after World War I." *Representations*, no. 84 (2003): 52–72.

―――. *Paris Noir: African Americans in the City of Light*. New York: Houghton Mifflin, 1996.

Stovall, Tyler Edward, and Georges Van Den Abbeele, eds. *French Civilization and Its Discontents: Nationalism, Colonialism, Race*. After the Empire: The Francophone World and Postcolonial France. Lanham MD: Lexington, 2003.

Suleiman, Susan Rubin. *Subversive Intent: Gender, Politics, and the Avant-Garde*. Cambridge MA: Harvard University Press, 1990.

Summers, Martin. *Manliness and Its Discontents: The Black Middle Class and the Transformation of Masculinity, 1900–1930*. Chapel Hill: University of North Carolina Press, 2004.

Surkis, Judith. *Sexing the Citizen: Morality and Masculinity in France, 1870–1920*. Ithaca NY: Cornell University Press, 2006.

Le Surréalisme au service de la Révolution: Collection complète. Paris: Jean-Michel Place, 1976.

Sweeney, Carole. *From Fetish to Subject: Race, Modernism, and Primitivism, 1919–1935*. Westport CT: Praeger, 2004.

―――. "Resisting the Primitive: The Nardal Sisters, *La Revue du Monde Noir* and *La Dépêche Africaine*." *Nottingham French Studies* 43, no. 2 (Summer 2004): 45–55.

Taguieff, Pierre-André. *La force du préjugé: Essai sur le racisme et ses doubles*. Saint-Amand: Découverte, 1992.

Terborg-Penn, Rosalyn. "African Feminism: A Theoretical Approach to the History of Women in the African Diaspora." In *Women in Africa and the African Diaspora*, edited by Rosalyn Terborg-Penn and Andrea Benton Rushing, 23–41. Washington DC: Howard University Press, 1996.

Thioub, Ibrahima. "Savoirs interdits en contexte colonial: La politique culturelle de la France en Afrique de l'Ouest." In *"Mama Africa": Hommage à Catherine Coquery-Vidrovitch*, edited by Chantal Chanson-Jabeur and Odile Goerg, 75–97. Paris: L'Harmattan, 2005.

Thomas, Dominic. *Black France: Colonialism, Immigration, and Transnationalism*. Bloomington: Indiana University Press, 2007.

Tidjani-Serpos, Noureini. "Histoire de Trois Revues Pionnières." *L'Afrique Littéraire et Artistique* 45 (1977): 54–68.

Totsain, France. "The Popular Front and the Blum-Viollette Plan." In *French Colonial Empire and the Popular Front: Hope and Disillusion*, edited by Tony Chafer and Amanda Sackur. Basingstoke, UK: Palgrave Macmillan, 1999.

Tournès, Ludovic. *New Orleans sur Seine: Histoire du jazz en France*. Paris: Arthème Fayard, 1999.

Vaillant, Janet G. *Black, French, and African: A Life of Léopold Sédar Senghor*. Cambridge MA: Harvard University Press, 1990.

Vidalenc, Jean. "La main d'oeuvre étrangère en France et la Première Guerre Mondiale (1901–1926)." *Francia* 2 (1974): 524–50.

Visel, Robin. "A Half-Colonization: The Problem of the White Colonial Woman Writer." *Kunapipi* 10, no. 3 (1988): 39–45.

Von Eschen, Penny M. *Race Against Empire: Black Americans and Anticolonialism 1937–1957*. Ithaca NY: Cornell University Press, 1997.

Walkowitz, Judith R. *City of Dreadful Delight: Narratives of Sexual Danger in Late-Victorian London*. London: Virago Press, 1992.

Weil, Patrick. *Qu'est-ce qu'un Français?: histoire de la nationalité française depuis la Révolution*. Paris: Grasset, 2002.

Weill, Alain, and Jack Rennert, eds. *Paul Colin, Affichiste*. Paris: Denoël, 1989.

Welburn, Ron. "Jazz Magazines of the 1930s: An Overview of Their Provocative Journalism." *American Music* 5, no. 3 (1987): 255–70.

White, Owen. *Children of the French Empire: Miscegenation and Colonial Society in French West Africa, 1895–1960*. Oxford: Oxford University Press, 1999.

———. "Networking: Freemasons and the Colonial State in French West Africa, 1895–1914." *French History* 19, no. 1 (2005): 91–111.

Wildenthal, Lora. *German Women for Empire, 1884–1945*. Durham NC: Duke University Press, 2001.

Wilder, Gary. *The French Imperial Nation-State: Negritude and Colonial Humanism between the Two World Wars*. Chicago: University of Chicago Press, 2005.

Wood, Ean. *The Josephine Baker Story*. London: Sanctuary, 2000.

Yee, Jennifer. *Clichés de la femme exotique: un regard sur la littérature coloniale française entre 1871 et 1914*. Paris: L'Harmattan, 2000.

INDEX

In the France Overseas series

CPSIA information can be obtained
at www.ICGtesting.com
Printed in the USA
LVHW030359071219
639752LV00003B/70/P